THE MUSICAL WORLDS OF LERNER & LOEWE

GENE LEES

Robson Books

First published in Great Britain in 1991 by
Robson Books Ltd, Bolsover House, 5–6
Clipstone Street, London W1P 7EB

**British Library Cataloguing in Publica-
tion Data**
Lees, Gene
   The musical worlds of Lerner
   and Loewe.
   1. United States. Popular music
   I. Title
   782.421640922

   ISBN 0 86051 740 3

Printed in Great Britain by St. Edmunds-
bury Press, Bury St. Edmunds, Suffolk

Contents

Preface

There are two dubious sources of history: printed matter and memory. Alas we are dependent on them. Newspapers and magazines make mistakes, though for the most part journalists are conscientious, and disinterested, and so their reports are often more reliable than the recollections of participants in events. Any researcher becomes aware that personal testimony is not necessarily dependable. With the greatest sincerity, different witnesses will give differing, even contradictory, versions of an incident. The longer the time since an event, the greater the chance that its witnesses will be mistaken about it.

A great many of the people associated with Lerner and Loewe have written memoirs. These books have been helpful in the writing of this one. But I have treated them with caution, finding discrepancies in versions of events. In addition, there are biographies of Kurt Weill, Julie Andrews, Rex Harrison, and, as of 1989, five of Richard Burton. A list of these sources will be found in the bibliography at the back of this volume.

Alan Jay Lerner's autobiographical monograph, *The Street Where I Live,* was useful, but he could be careless with facts, and a number of things he states firmly in that book are not so.

Wherever I was unable to resolve discrepancies between sources, I have given the variant testimonies, leaving it to the reader to select the one he or she likes best.

I thank Dr. Roderick Bladel and Bob Taylor of the Performing Arts Division of the New York Public Library at Lincoln Center for their patient help in researching printed sources. So too the staff of Toronto's Metropolitan Reference Library. Luis Ferrer of the *New York Times* morgue staff was my gracious guide through the 1920s issues of the paper. Miles Kreuger, director of the Institute of the American Musical, was enormously helpful, as were Mario Mercado and others on the staff of the Kurt Weill Foundation for Music. My nephew, Justin Suttle, helped with the preliminary newspaper research.

I thank Jane Dystel for suggesting the book in the first place.

A great many people were generous with recollections when I interviewed them, among them Maurice Abravanel, Franz Allers, Marion Bell Charlesworth, Don Chastain, Alexander H. Cohen, Gloria Greer, David Grossberg, Mary Jolliffe, Miles Kreuger, Burton Lane, Karen Gundersen Lerner, André Previn, Dan Sischer, John Springer, Charles Strouse, Ruth Boyd Talbott, Jonathan Tunick, Hugh Walker, Benjamin Welles, and Stone (Bud) Widney. A number of these persons accorded me the further kindness of reading the manuscript in whole or in part in the search for accuracy. Gene Kelly read it with particular reference to the making of *An American in Paris,* and I thank him.

Nancy Olson Livingston declined to be interviewed, explaining to me on the telephone that she was writing her own memoirs. I made notes of our conversation and to that limited extent I did interview her. But she gave many newspaper interviews during her marriage to Alan Lerner, and so consistent is the tone of her voice as captured in these articles that I felt the reporters had done a good job and I have drawn on their work extensively.

I am grateful to a number of journalist colleagues for leads, suggestions, and entrees: Tom Tomizawa of NBC News, David Binder of the *New York Times,* and Richard Harwood of the *Washington Post,* all of them friends from our days in the city room of the *Louisville Times,* alas now defunct; Harry Allen, a friend from days at the *Toronto Telegram,* also alas now defunct; Harold C. Schoenberg of the *New York Times;* and Henry Pleasants of the *International Herald-Tribune.*

Among the most valuable resources made available to me were two long interviews with Lerner and Loewe (the former taped during the filming of *Paint Your Wagon*) done by broadcaster and film historian Tony Thomas. I am grateful to Tony for the gift of those tapes. Thanks also to Kurt Thometz for leads and for finding some of the books I needed. And for unflagging moral support, Wanda Vallillee, Harold and Evelyn Gaylor, and Ida and James Lincoln Collier.

I was asked why I have been so meticulous about citing dates and newspaper sources. It is because I prefer to make sources clear in the text rather than scatter it with footnotes. As John Barrymore put it, footnotes when you are reading come like a knock on a downstairs door when you are upstairs making love. I think I have managed to make clear to the reader the sources whose comments were made in interviews with me. Comments made to Tony Thomas are always attributed, sometimes directly and at others with the designation (TT).

Although I didn't interview him specifically for this book, I had many long conversations about musical theater with the late Joshua Logan when we worked on a show together, and if (as is evident in the book) I thought Josh was out of his element in movies, he was a great stage director, and a generous teacher to me, and I remember him with affection and respect. I had many such conversations with my dear friend Johnny Mercer. I learned only after finishing the book that Alan Lerner considered Johnny the greatest American lyricist of the twentieth century. So do I, though Lerner was the better theater lyricist. Johnny and I talked endlessly of shows and the lyricist's craft, and he respected Lerner's work as much as I do. I had similar, though only a few, conversations with Harold Arlen, Yip Harburg, and Arthur Schwartz, all of whom contributed subtly to this book.

There is much more in this book about Alan Lerner than about Fritz Loewe. Loewe wrote music for only six stage musicals, five of them with Lerner, and two films, and retired early. Lerner wrote book and lyrics for thirteen stage musicals and the scripts for six movies, two of which he produced, and he published two books. He did far more work away from Loewe than he did with him, collaborating with some of the best-known names in film and theater music, including John Barry, Leonard Bernstein, Burton Lane, André Previn, Richard Rodgers, Charles Strouse, and Kurt Weill. Loewe kept his private life very private indeed, whereas Alan's was flamboyant, making incessant headlines. Fritz avoided publicity; Alan relished it. Fritz dropped out of show business almost entirely, occasionally turning up now and then to offer comment on Alan's life, rather like a Greek chorus, then leaving the stage again. It was inevitable that Lerner would dominate this book.

If Alan Lerner were alive to consult with me, and I were to raise the point of a dedication, I think I know the name we would in the end agree upon. And so it is.

This book is dedicated to the memory of Larry Hart.

one

THE MODES OF MUSIC

n 1703, in an essay on government, the Scottish patriot Andrew Fletcher wrote, "Let me make the songs of a nation and I care not who makes its laws."

The import is clear: song shapes the thinking of a people, who then determine its laws. Rock singers in the mid-1960s urged the use and legalization of drugs. Twenty-five years later, drug use in America had so overwhelmed the legal system that the possibility of legalization was under serious public consideration.

The Ancient Greeks believed that the modes of music affected the emotions and behavior in specific ways. Modes are scale forms; in recent centuries we have tended to use mostly the major and minor modes, but there are others. A story attributed to Pythagoras tells of a boy whose passions were so aroused by the Phrygian mode that he almost assaulted a woman, only to be calmed in the nick of time by the sound of the Hypophrygian mode. The Greeks thought that the modes in general use could affect even the laws of the state, and they urged caution with modes thought on the one hand to induce weakness of character and, on the other, to induce warlike or anti-social feelings. This has not been proved; neither has it been disproved. There isn't a neurologist alive, not even neurologists who are also musicians, who can tell you how and why music affects the emotions, though some of them, in arcane treatises, have tried. They know only that it does. An experiment in Japan showed that music we would call soothing increased lactation in nursing mothers. Martial music is written and performed because it arouses feelings of bravery and patriotism and imagined glory. Irving Berlin recognized the phenomenon in the lyrics to *Alexander's Ragtime Band,* when he wrote that the protagonist of the song can play a bugle call that is so natural that it makes you want to go to war. That music can cause antisocial behavior has been obvious in thirty years of rock music, with its attendant riots and occasional killings and with the rock groups themselves demolishing hotel rooms and even recording studios and casually ordering that the costs be put on the bill.

Shelley said that "poets are the unacknowledged legislators of the world." When words are wedded to music, the persuasive effect is inestimable. The people of the record industry have generally denied that this is so. On the contrary, music sets up moods that make the listener curiously susceptible to the words that go over it or with it. Vast numbers of people can be induced to buy a product by the artful fusion of words, music, and visual image.

The entertainment industry, including the movies, record manufacturers, and broadcasting companies, has for years denied that entertainment, and in particular music, has the power to influence society. This is risible, of course. Even as they are so protesting, TV and radio time salesmen solicit business on the ground that these media can and do alter public behavior. Advertising by cigarette companies, which always entailed music, was long ago barred from television and then radio. It is difficult to argue that you can induce the public to use tobacco through the use of words and music but you cannot by the same means induce it to use, say, marijuana.

Of all the forms of music, the most obviously persuasive is the song, that blending of melody and verbal images that is the way most people experience the art. Instrumental music, which requires a certain amount of experience in what is essentially an abstract language, is for a selective, dedicated minority. Song is for everybody.

Song has always had a hypnotically persuasive effect, as witness

The Battle Hymn of the Republic, Dixie, The Internationale, and *La Marseillaise.* Music may, as Congreve said, have charms to soothe a savage breast; it also has the capacity to inflame. Peter Yarrow of Peter, Paul and Mary once said that they had the power to swing a federal election. That group alone perhaps did not, but collectively the rock and folk singers did have such power. Lyndon Johnson left the White House never understanding that he had been ejected not so much by Eugene McCarthy and Bobby Kennedy as by Bob Dylan and Pete Seeger and friends. Seeger's *Where Have All the Flowers Gone?* was Johnson's dirge, and nothing in his post–White House writings and interviews indicated that he had even a remote grasp of the forces that had driven him from power. But then, few other people had either.

In the 1920s Richard Rodgers and Lorenz Hart became increasingly concerned with the strength of the story in the shows for which they wrote songs. Through the 1920s and '30s and '40s, the integration of songs and book grew more and more sophisticated, until in Rodgers and Hammerstein's *Oklahoma!* it reached a pinnacle.

During that period, the popular music of the United States attained an unprecedented level of quality. It was a time when much popular music was good and much good music was popular.

It is hard for people under, say, forty-five—particularly those just now discovering what a treasury of great song was amassed in America in the twentieth century's first six decades—to realize that this was the music you heard daily on the radio. The melodies were intelligent, the lyrics often exquisitely literate. To be sure, there were in the 1930s and '40s *The Hut-Sut Song, A-Tisket A-Tasket, The Beer Barrel Polka, Three Little Fishes, Mairzy Doats,* and other silly songs, but nobody wrote sober analyses of them and acclaimed them timeless poetry. They were known as novelties, something like cartoons in song, and they did not predominate. The fascination of young people of that time with this literate music can be seen in the fact that every candy store near a high school carried a magazine that contained all the current lyrics. It existed for one reason: kids bought it. They memorized its contents: the language of Hart, Harburg, Hammerstein, Fields, Porter, Mercer, and, yes, Maxwell Anderson and Ogden Nash. Their sense of the English language was shaped by those writers of songs far more than by any high school courses on Tennyson, Shakespeare, Dickens, Conrad, and Hawthorn. If you wonder why young people now, including those old enough to have grown up on the Rolling

Stones, so often are limited to a rudimentary English, listen to the songs that shaped their thinking.

The emphasis of the songs of that earlier period, and of the movies as well, not to mention mass-magazine fiction, was on romantic love. Except in the work of the time of the trouveres and troubadours of eleventh- to fourteenth-century Provence, there has never been such a preoccupation with romantic love: the exaltation of finding it, the consolation of possessing it, the devastation of losing it. And song had been given an enormous new power through two technical innovations: radio and recording.

These innovations made possible a dissemination and constant repetition of music unlike anything the world had ever known. In time music came to be heard everywhere, even in elevators and shoestores and diners and dentists' offices, on airplanes and in trucks and cars. It became utterly, inescapably ubiquitous, not necessarily to the benefit of the human nervous condition and certainly not to the improvement of the general public taste.

Love was everything; the Gershwins got it right when they wrote *Love Is Sweeping the Country.* In the depths of the Depression, and then amid the horrors of World War II, the dream of love, the hope of love, gave succor. The dream had this advantage: like the radio from which people absorbed it, it was free. The songs did not teach the reality that marriage is not necessarily an easy business. Indeed, love was supposed to be the solution to any and every problem. The movies told us so. The songs told us so. American songwriters may have expressed a naïve vision of life, but they expressed it well. Alan Jay Lerner and Frederick Loewe were not in at the start of that era of romanticism, which produced some of the loveliest love songs in history. Lerner and Loewe came at the end of the tradition.

Lerner grew up in the 1920s and '30s on Rodgers and Hart, Rodgers and Hammerstein, Cole Porter, Dietz and Schwartz, Jerome Kern, Vincent Youmans, Harold Arlen, Yip Harburg, Hoagy Carmichael, Johnny Mercer, Irving Berlin, Vernon Duke, Harry Warren, Dorothy Fields, and their peers. These people got to Broadway a generation before Lerner and Fritz Loewe did. Loewe, on the other hand, grew up on Viennese operetta, the tradition of Lehar and Oscar Straus and of course Johann Strauss the Younger.

Thus Lerner and Loewe combined in their work two important musical strains. Fritz Loewe never became an American composer in the way Kurt Weill did. He was Viennese to the day he died.

Broadly speaking, American musical theater begins in the work of Irving Berlin and his departure from the tradition of Viennese operetta. It climbs steadily in craftsmanship in the works of the songwriters just mentioned. The transition from trivial stories begins in the collaboration of Guy Bolton, P. G. Wodehouse, and Jerome Kern, proceeds with Rodgers and Hart, and evolves through *Show Boat* by Jerome Kern and Oscar Hammerstein II, *Porgy and Bess* by the Gershwins and Dubose Hayward, and Frank Loesser's *The Most Happy Fella.* The songs are more carefully crafted to advance the story or reveal the characters. In due course, the musical theater came to be dominated by Rodgers and Hammerstein. But it reaches its apogee in *My Fair Lady.* After that it begins its long descent to its present darkness, lightened occasionally by sparks from Stephen Sondheim.

The first successful Lerner and Loewe musical, *Brigadoon,* arrived on Broadway March 13, 1947, giving us *The Heather on the Hill, Almost Like Being in Love,* and *There But for You Go I.*

It is hard to believe that within eight years that era of literate popular music would be moribund, doomed by the avarice of the record industry and the dismantling of the radio networks, which for a short time had raised the aesthetic standards of the entire North American continent. Alec Wilder's book *The American Song: The Great Innovators 1900–1955* (New York, Oxford University Press, 1972) is the best study of the rise and fall of great American song. "After that the amateurs took over," said Mr. Wilder, with whom in his later years I often discussed the subject.

Alan Lerner said that lyric-writing was a minor art lying somewhere between carpentry and photography. He is not to be taken too seriously on this point. Boris Vian, the French novelist and lyricist, used to say that he was prouder of his lyrics than his books. Lyric-writing is unique in that, to an extent that occurs in no other form of writing, people voluntarily, even eagerly, commit your words to memory. Your thoughts become part of their thoughts. This is why popular music has an almost unimaginable influence, for either good or ill.

At a technical level, lyric-writing is the most exacting of all literary crafts, as Lerner knew perfectly well. It is far harder to write lyrics than "poetry," which, in our time, consists largely of a kind of euphonious (though not always) prose cut arbitrarily into lines of uneven lengths. Poetry was harder to write when it was metric, and rhymed; it is still harder to write when it must be fitted to music, with the speech inflections matching the contours of a melody and the mood reflecting the content of the harmony. Lerner did it brilliantly; and Fritz Loewe equally brilliantly was able to capture speech inflections of the English language—which was not his own—in his music. Johnny Mercer once said to me, "I think writing music takes more talent, but writing lyrics takes more courage." He was right.

Excepting in an early work with Earle T. Crooker, Fritz Loewe had only one collaborator, Alan Jay Lerner, as he had only one wife, from whom he was divorced; Lerner, on the other hand, had many: Loewe, Kurt Weill, Burton Lane, Leonard Bernstein, André Previn, John Barry, Charles Strouse, and experimentally at the end, Andrew Lloyd Webber. This brings the total to eight. Lerner also had eight wives.

Lerner died at sixty-seven. Fritz Loewe, despite two heart attacks, made it to eighty-six, having expended his latter years in travel and gambling and haute cuisine and the very young women whom he collected like toys and kept on his yacht off Cannes or in his apartment in Manhattan or the house in Palm Springs, California. The bed there was on a turntable in a room walled mostly in glass, and at the push of a button could be rotated to give him another view of the surrounding desert and mountains. His first twenty years of trying to make it in the world of big-time show biz were spent in various depths of poverty, and he scraped out a living, he said, as a cowboy in Montana and a boxer in Brooklyn.

In the early 1940s, Lerner and Loewe wrote two musicals now more or less forgotten, but their third, *The Day Before Spring,* ran 165 performances and garnered them $250,000 for the movie rights, a substantial sum at the time. Then they gave the world *Brigadoon* in 1947, which ran 581 performances in New York; *Paint Your Wagon* (1951), which ran 289 performances; *My Fair Lady* (1956), 2,717 performances during its original run on Broadway, and in London, at Drury Lane, where it opened in 1958, 2,281; and their last important stage work together, *Camelot,* which in its first incarnation went 873 performances on Broadway. Lerner's collaborations with other composers were, like seven of his marriages, failures, with the possible exception of *Coco,* which he wrote with André Previn, a special case in that it survived on the strength of Katharine Hepburn's performance in the title role more than on the score.

The writers of a musical often make their biggest money after it closes on Broadway, since it then goes into summer stock and amateur theatricals, which pay a percentage of the box office receipts to the librettist, lyricist, and composer. Lerner was the librettist *and* lyricist of his major shows. In addition, there are London productions of successful shows, and, finally, translations. *My Fair Lady* gave Columbia Records the biggest-selling album in the history of the company up to that time; *Camelot* for a long while ran it second. And a composer and lyricist are paid for all the performances of their work on radio and television.

It is impossible to determine how much money Alan Jay Lerner acquired in his lifetime, both inherited and earned. A newspaper report in 1981 said that he was believed to have made $30 million from his shows. This is probably a conservative estimate. So it is almost inconceivable that he could die comparatively broke, but he managed to accomplish this feat through his dispersal of alimony to former wives, his own wanton spending, and bad business management.

The American lyricist and the Austrian composer had several things in common. Both were small. Lerner used to say of Loewe that he wore lifts in his shoes so high that his ears popped when he took them off at night. Lerner said his own height was five-six-and-a-half, but there is evidence that he was only five-five. Both did some boxing in their youth. Both were habituated Don Juans. After one divorce, however, Loewe remained steadfast in his devotion to his young playmates. Why did Lerner marry eight times when, with his money, he could—and did—have all the affairs he wanted?

"I've often asked myself that question," said Benjamin Welles, his longtime friend. "I often asked *him* the question. And I never got a straight answer. He would laugh about his multiple marriages. I think Alan was a tremendous romantic. He always had a vision of a girl in a belted raincoat meeting him in an airport somewhere and flying off to Morocco or some other exotic spot. He was always chasing that romantic dream."

When Lerner was on his game, he was probably the best theatrical lyricist in American history. There are remarkable felicities in his work, and no musical up to that time had the sustained brilliant virtuosity of lyric-writing that Lerner achieved in *My Fair Lady*. He would never give Broadway a show that good again. But nobody else would either.

Lerner was not universally liked. Indeed, Fritz Loewe and he were often at loggerheads. Composer Burton Lane, his collaborator in writing *On a Clear Day You Can See Forever,* is one of the associates who say he was extremely self-destructive. Actress Nancy Olson, his wife when he was writing *My Fair Lady*—it is dedicated to her—said, "Alan was a poet. I don't think his ego would let him face up to the fact that he was not really a book writer."

Startled, I cited the example of *My Fair Lady.* "But that's Shaw," she said, referring to the play *Pygmalion* from which it was adapted.

"Yes," I said, "but I have made a page-by-page comparison of the play and *My Fair Lady,* and there's much in there that is not in Shaw." As I realized later, Lerner based his work more on the 1938 film than on Shaw's original play.

"But he had Shaw's subtext," Olson said.

And he had Moss Hart. How much *My Fair Lady*'s structure owes to the intercession of Hart, its director, we may never know, although it is a subject we shall have to address in due course. If *Camelot*'s problems were never really solved, it may be because they were not soluble. But those of *My Fair Lady* were, and it is a more satisfying work than *Pygmalion.*

"Alan was always trying to top *My Fair Lady* and couldn't," Karen Gundersen Lerner, his fifth wife, said, "It drove him crazy. We were lying in bed one night, watching the eleven o'clock news. There was a report that Neil Simon had his tenth or eleventh hit. Alan cried."

two

FRITZ:
THE EARLY
YEARS

n 1966, Fritz Loewe told Cecil Smith of the *Los Angeles Times* that the American musical is the only great contribution the United States had made to the art of the world. Admirers of jazz, of course, would take umbrage at that statement, as they do whenever some denizen of Broadway makes it. They insist that jazz is America's only original art form, and, on balance, it would seem that jazz has the better claim. Neither form, however, is without precedents and antecedents, and each form takes its particular coloration out of a fusion of elements. In the case of American musical theater, what distinguishes it from Viennese operetta is a particular rhythmic character that it gets from jazz. Without American musical theater, there would still be jazz; without jazz, there would be no distinctively American musical theater. Both, it should be noted, have debts to the minstrel shows of the late nineteenth century.

Alan Jay Lerner was aware that American musical theater had some sort of debt to jazz. His last important piece of writing was not a musical but a prose work, a book titled *The Musical Theatre: A Celebration,* completed only weeks before his death on June 13, 1986. It is an excellent piece of work, on its own terrain, which is theater. But in it, Lerner reveals that his understanding of jazz was tenuous at best, though he ascribes importance to it. First of all, he accepts the theory of a simple New Orleans genesis of jazz, which has been called increasingly into question by modern scholarship. Every bordello, he writes, "had either a jazz soloist or a jazz combo. The music was sometimes called ragtime, but its generic title was Dixieland." It was not called ragtime—ragtime is a specialized form—and the term "Dixieland" was a later coinage, derived from the Original Dixieland Jazz Band, a white group that began recording in 1918.

"Out of Storyville," Lerner writes, "came such classics as *Basin Street Blues,* and, of course, the most famous of all, *When the Saints Go Marching In.* That particular song started as a funeral march when a beloved lady or performer had passed on to green pastures. The coffin was held high and paraded around Storyville, surrounded by trumpet and trombone sending the deceased to heaven on a Dixie beat." *Basin Street Blues* did not come out of Storyville and was never performed in New Orleans funeral services; it was published in 1929, a composition by Spencer Williams, a university-trained pianist who by then was in Paris, writing for Josephine Baker. Coffins were not held high: they were taken in dignity to the cemetery, accompanied by music of appropriate gravity. It was on the way *back* from the grave that the band broke into its celebrated and celebratory shouting.

"What distinguished black music from all other until that time," Lerner says, "and what is fundamentally the definition of jazz, is the afterbeat. When you clap your hands or tap your feet on the second and fourth beat of the bar, that is jazz." That is not so. Jazz is much more complex than that, a music of sophisticated collective instrumental improvisation—even that of New Orleans was highly sophisticated—that may at times put the pulse on one and three, though it does usually emphasize the afterbeat. But so does rock and roll, and that assuredly isn't jazz.

Though Lerner lacked insight into jazz, he did apparently understand that it had not touched Fritz Loewe. Recognizing this, Lerner told Mark Steyn, who quoted him in the *Independent* (London), "Fritz was the greatest melodist since Jerome Kern. There was wistful tenderness to his melody, plus a soaring quality. Fundamentally, he didn't have rhythm, but he did have tempo, so, although his music doesn't have the afterbeat of jazz, he often swings without realizing it. For example, *Almost Like Being in Love* can swing, but it also has a great melody."

In an obituary printed in the *London Daily Telegraph,* an anonymous author wrote: "The folklore element and the lilting melodies in Loewe's characteristic musical style were what gave his songs and scores their universal appeal. Anyone familiar with the idiom of Central European music could easily identify the source of many of Loewe's tunes. Thus the song *I Could Have Danced All Night,* in *My Fair Lady,* began as a standard in the cabarets of Weimar Berlin nightclubs; while the syncopation of Eliza Doolittle's other main number, *Wouldn't It Be Loverly,* has its roots in the rhythms of the Hungarian csardas."

"Without the presence of the black race in America," Lerner wrote, "there never would have been the popular music or the popular musical theater that we know today."

But Fritz Loewe's musical sensibilities—unlike those of Gershwin, Kern, Arlen, Loesser, Schwartz, or Youmanns—were untouched by black music; they were entirely European. He did not emigrate to the United States until he was twenty-three, by which time his musical character was formed. Irving Berlin, considered the founder of an American idiom in popular music, was also born abroad, in Russia, but his parents brought him to America when he was four, and he grew up on the streets of New York.

Loewe was aware of his strengths and limitations. In an interview with the noted film historian Tony Thomas, taped at Loewe's home in Palm Springs for the Canadian Broadcasting Corporation, the composer asserted: "I never was really a songwriter. I always considered myself a dramatic composer. A dramatic composer is someone that can illustrate in music any emotion."

And Loewe did it well, in his own way and in his natural idiom, which was that of Viennese operetta. So rooted was he in Vienna that many of his obituaries gave that city as his birthplace. Others gave it as Berlin. The latter were correct, on the authority of Loewe himself. On the Tony Thomas tape, he says, in his soft Viennese accent—he never did get the hang of the letter *w;* it came out as *v,* and his *r*'s are very Viennese—"I was born in Berlin of Viennese parents. My father was a famous musical star and a very fine actor."

"You are known," Thomas says, "as having been a child prodigy. Is it true?"

"Yes. At the age of thirteen I played with symphony orchestras all over Europe as a soloist, and I gave piano recitals all over Europe."

"When you look back on it, does it seem like an unnatural thing to have done for a child?"

"No. I played piano beautifully when I was five. Long before I had lessons. Playing the piano, music, is to me like breathing in and breathing out. Nothing unusual. It was always my life, and I've never had to study with it, except to acquire the technique."

"Of course, you grew up in difficult times. You were a teenager during the First World War. How did the end of that war leave you and your family?"

"Very hungry. I hadn't eaten for four years. No meat, no butter, no sugar, no fat, no anything. I have never forgotten it, and that is one of the reasons that I enjoy life as much as I do."

The wellspring of the American musical is to be found in the *opera-bouffe* of Jacques Offenbach, a German Jew by birth though he lived and worked in Paris and his shows were in French. Offenbach's *Orfée aux enfers* is, in French, deliciously sarcastic and mocking. "In the musical theater," Lerner wrote, "[Offenbach] was indeed the father of us all."

The next major figures in the line of descent is the team of William S. Gilbert and Arthur Sullivan. "We all come from Gilbert," Johnny Mercer used to say. Lerner wrote, "P. G. Wodehouse, Lorenz Hart, Cole Porter, Ira Gershwin, Oscar Hammerstein and their contemporaries and descendants, all owe their lyrical, genetic beginning to W. S. Gilbert." The Gilbert and Sullivan musicals are not particularly melodic, since Sullivan's compositional talents were made subservient to Gilbert's literate wit—a fact Sullivan resented, for all the success of their work. The music has a *recitativo* quality that sets it apart from American musical theater, for which the music has usually been written first.

For melody in the late nineteenth and early twentieth centuries, one must look to Vienna and the works of Johann Strauss, including his eleven operettas, which reached their apogee in the magnificent *Die Fledermaus*. The next master is Franz Lehar, a Hungarian by birth, whose *The Merry Widow* opened in Vienna in 1905, six years after the death of Strauss. When it opened in Berlin, the role of Prince Danilo was played by Edmund Loewe. Many brief biographies of Frederick Loewe say that his father created the role of Danilo. He didn't. According to the reliable 1947 book on Viennese operetta *Die Wiener Operette,* the first tenor to sing the part was Louis Treumann, who performed it when the show premiered at the Theater an der Wien on December 30, 1905. Edmund Loewe apparently took over the role for the Berlin opening. Fritz told Franz Allers that his father also did the first American tour.

Like Offenbach, Oscar Straus—no relation to Johann—was Jewish and born in Germany. And he was the last of the great composers of romantic Viennese operettas. His most famous work was *The Chocolate Soldier,* which was based on George Bernard Shaw's comedy *Arms and the Man.* It was Shaw's practice to present his plays in Germany in German, where they were invariably lauded, before the English originals were offered up to the mercies of the London critics. He did not realize that, because they wrote the dialogue for the operetta, the adapters of his play would by German law receive *all* the royalties. This seems to have had some bearing on his opposition to any further musical adaptations of his work. The lead in *The Chocolate Soldier* was Edmund Loewe.

Frederick Loewe was born June 10, 1901. His mother, Rosa, was the daughter of a Viennese *baumeister* (builder). She was a sometime actress who wore lipstick and smoked cigarettes back in that perfumed age of waltzes and mazurkas, which Frederick heard an aunt playing on the family baby grand. His mother also appears to have had a lively imagination. In his later years Loewe kept an album of family pictures by his bedside. Gloria Greer, a friend of this period of his life, examined that book. She said that his mother was a very pretty girl in her youth, with a small turned-up nose and a Gibson Girl figure. A later photo, published in *Time* magazine, shows her to have grown plump. She managed to convince a few people that she had been the mistress of the Archduke Ferdinand, heir to the throne of the Austro-Hungarian Empire whose assassination at Sarajevo was the proximate cause of World War I, but nobody knows whether this was the truth.

Fritz invariably told interviewers that at the age of five he wrote his first tune and at nine another song that was interpolated into a sketch with which his father toured Europe.

According to Benjamin Welles, a friend through most of the lyricist's life, Lerner said Fritz Loewe's mother was of an old military family. There appears then to have been some sort of conflict between the father, who wanted the boy to have a musical education, and the mother, who wanted him to go to military school.

Welles said, "Fritz's mother finally won the battle and sent him to military academy." Long afterward Loewe remembered the wrought-iron gates of the school, in Berlin, closing behind him as his mother, smiling, blew him a kiss and said, "Good-bye, my love, be happy."

"Because of his antecedents," Benjamin Welles said, "he was brutalized by the German children, treated as an outcast because he was half Jewish. The young German military caste, the children of that caste, were very anti-Semitic. He had a very unhappy time at school, and that's one of the reasons, I think, that despite his wonderful talent, he was very insecure in later life. Only when his talent was recognized in terms that really mattered to him, and that is financially, did he start to have some security."

No other source I found indicates that Loewe was half Jewish. Fritz told Gloria Greer that he was enrolled at the academy when he was very young, eight years old or so. He was thus the smallest child in the school, and it was for this reason he was tormented by older and larger boys. Out of the need to defend himself, he developed into a scrappy little fighter. But for whatever reason, he seems to have been mistreated at the school and he hated it.

The circumstances in which Loewe got out of the military academy are unclear, but he was soon enrolled in Stern's Conservatory, where he prepared for a career as a concert pianist. In 1916, at fifteen, he said, he wrote a song called *Katrina* about "the girl with the best legs in Berlin" that sold 2 million copies of sheet music. It is worth remembering that figure; we shall have occasion to wonder what happened to the royalties from it.

Show business people have always had a reputation for being sexually profligate, and Rosa's boast of having been the mistress of the Archduke suggests that the Loewe family was no exception. Frederick's taste for the ladies seems to have manifested itself early. He claimed that he had his first sexual experience when he was two and a half and his first affair at nine—with his governess. "I thought I was abnormally precocious until I read Kinsey," he said years later. By the time he was in his late teens, he was a chronic partygoer, earning his welcome at the piano, playing a full repertoire, Liszt, Beethoven, Lehar. He was blond, slim, and good-looking, with a head rather too large for his body, and he was, by his own testimony, cocky and sure of himself. A friend from his conservatory days described him as "a sexual democrat." When he ran out of credit at a favorite bordello, he said, he paid up his bill by entertaining fellow clients on the madam's piano. But he was studying, too. The standard brief biographies handed out by his publicists, and Loewe's own stories to interviewers, said that his piano teachers in Berlin included Ferrucio Busoni and Eugene d'Albert, and that he studied composition and orchestration with Emil Nikolaus von Reznicek. At the age of thirteen, he said, he was the youngest piano soloist to appear with the Berlin Symphony Orchestra. He turned thirteen in 1914.

But a puzzle arises. If he studied with Busoni, when?

Feruccio Busoni was born close to Florence; his father's mother was German, but Busoni was always proud of his Italian nationality. He was a prodigy pianist in his childhood and later was recognized as one of the great pianists in history. He held that career in some contempt, however, aspiring to be recognized as a composer, an ambition that would never be completely fulfilled. He is known chiefly today for his transcriptions of Bach music.

Fritz Loewe was nine years old in 1910. In 1910–11, Busoni was touring in recitals in the United States. In 1913, he was in Italy, director of the Lido Musicale of Bologna. With the outbreak of World War I, he left Germany to make another U.S. concert tour and settled in the fall of 1915 in Zurich, where, in common with many artists repelled by the slaughter, he remained for the duration. Thus it is highly unlikely that young Loewe could have studied with him in Berlin before the war; and in any case Busoni wasn't in Berlin for much of that time.

And it is virtually impossible that he studied with Busoni after the war. Busoni did not return to Berlin until the fall of 1920, when he was asked to become a teacher of composition at that State Academy of Arts and Sciences. His health was by now failing, and he taught only six months of the year, master classes in composition. These were held in his apartment in the Charlottenburg district of Berlin. Further, he accepted only five students that first year, three of whom came with him from Zurich and only one of whom was born in Germany: Kurt Weill. Later, in Rockland County, New York, Kurt Weill and Fritz Loewe were friends and poker-playing companions. Yet Ronald Sanders, author of a well-researched biography of Weill (*The Days Grow Short*, Holt Rinehart and Winston, New York, 1980) does not suggest that Weill knew Loewe in Germany. It will be found that students of teachers of such eminence as Busoni always form a loose union. The students of Nadia Boulanger, for example, more or less know about each other, and usually know personally those members of their own generation among that group. Weill, thirteen months Loewe's senior, continued his studies with Busoni until 1923, receiving his diploma from the Academy of Arts and Sciences in December of that year. Every biography of Busoni mentions Kurt Weill, usually several times, and Busoni himself refers to him in one of his letters. Nowhere in all this writing is there a single reference to Frederick Loewe. Busoni died July 27, 1924. Ronald Sanders refers to Weill as "the young man who was to become the most famous of his pupils." Since Fritz Loewe was a more famous composer than Weill, at least with audiences of the English-speaking world, this raises the possibility that Frederick Loewe was never a pupil of Busoni's. And if this is so, it must be said, in fairness, that he would not be the first or last man to arrive in America trailing credentials he did not actually have. In those days before computers and casual trans-Atlantic telephone calls, it was not as easy as it is now to check on an immigrant's background.

By now inflation was wasting Germany and Austria, like a hideous disease. Before the war, the rate of exchange was four marks to the American dollar. At the end of 1920 it was seventy-five to the dollar, and Kurt Weill was teaching for payment in such real goods as butter. In January 1923, the mark had fallen to 48,000 to the dollar; by November to 400 million, and soon—about the time Adolf Hitler tried his beer hall putsch in Munich—to an incredible four trillion.

The hardship of those years, when the bank accounts of even the very wealthy simply evaporated, may have had something to do with Edmund Loewe's attitude to America. Fritz said, "My father loved America and he had been here twice before and he wanted to take me out of Europe, into the new world. There are people that want to go and have adventures, and he was one of them, obviously." Loewe told Miles Kreuger, now the director of the Institute of the American Musical, that his father first visited America in 1894, and returned in 1904: "I came with him then. I was three years old. He played in a Viennese operetta in the Irving Place Opera House, a first-rate theater." He also told Kreuger that he emigrated to America in 1923. But the date he gave Tony Thomas was 1924. He said:

"About two days after I arrived in America in 1924, I played Town Hall. I got at that time $150 for it, and never bothered to look at a newspaper. And I never went to the agency again. They didn't know how to reach me. I suppose this is how it happened. I couldn't speak English."

He also said, on other occasions, that he played a week at the Rivoli theater.

But the story is hard to believe. How did he get an engagement, only two days after he arrived in New York, at Town Hall, whose facilities must be booked far in advance? Had the engagement been set before he left Austria? Which agency booked him there? How is it that it did not know how to reach him? When no calls came, why was he not curious enough to call the agency? Did Loewe mean that he got rave reviews that he failed to read, and, unaware of a success in his Town Hall concert, abandoned any hope of a concert career? Or did he get bad reviews?

How well did Frederick Loewe play piano? One man whose opinion on the subject is valuable is Harold C. Shonberg, the esteemed music critic of the *Times* for many years, now semiretired. Shonberg, who is himself a pianist, once heard Loewe play privately at home. The technique of any instrumentalist who turns to full-time composition as a profession inevitably deteriorates, sometimes drastically. But Loewe played well; not superlatively, to be sure, but well. And, Shonberg added, "You could tell that at one time he had had excellent training and had been a fine pianist."

Time magazine, in a story published when Lerner and Loewe were working on *Camelot*, said:

"In 1924, accompanying his father on a tour of what Loewe Sr called 'the only country left on the globe,' Fritz landed in the U.S. He apparently failed to persuade the critics—or himself—that the piano was the only career for Fritz Loewe. But a concert life, he told himself, was just so much acrobatics, while a steady job in an orchestra was 'like being in a union'; he pawned his career for seven years of wildly miscellaneous jobs."

Loewe several times told interviewers that in 1923 he won the Hollander medal in Berlin, indicating a certain amount of stature in the concert field. Then why, if he failed in a Town Hall concert, did he not return to Europe, where, he said, he had played with many of the major symphony orchestras, to pursue his profession, instead of endangering his hands in the boxing ring? And what became of the royalties from *Katrina?* Of course it is possible that the money evaporated in the postwar inflation.

According to Lerner, Edmund Loewe made his last trip to America in 1923 on the invitation of the writer and theatrical impresario David Belasco. He was accompanied by his wife and Fritz, who was then twenty-two. While the show in which he was to appear for

Belasco was in rehearsal, the elder Loewe died, leaving Fritz and his mother stranded in New York without money. Lerner wrote that Edmund Loewe had been "an inveterate gambler, a trait inherited by his son, thus proving the Lysenkian theory that an acquired instinct can be inherited." It proves no such thing, of course, though it does prove Lerner's susceptibility to dubious theories.

In the legend that Fritz erected around himself, a Rockaway Beach fight promoter started him on a boxing career. The story bothers me. It apparently also bothers the well-informed British writer Benny Green. Green is the editor of an excellent collection of Lerner's lyrics titled *A Hymn to Him* (London, Pavilion Books, 1987), which I strongly commend to you. In an obituary published in the *London Guardian* on February 16, 1988, he wrote: "Exactly how the master of romantic melody ended up in a prize ring has never quite been explained but Alan Jay Lerner once described to. me what happened: 'Fritz had a strategy for the Canzoneri fight, to box on the retreat and keep out of Canzoneri's reach. He was convinced he could have danced all night. Canzoneri's reach turned out to be just a little longer than Fritz had figured. Fritz was stopped in the first.' "

Fritz told an Associated Press writer, "I was quite a dandy, very agile, quick on my feet and very deft with a slap-like jab. I'd won eight fights in a row in the 120-pound class, and then I ran into an up and coming fighter named Tony Canzoneri.

"He took me out with one punch in the first round. Other fellows who'd been knocked out used to tell me they actually heard birdies singing. I guess that's where my musical background came in. I heard a whole symphony.

"When I came to in the dressing room, the string section was just going by. Playing very beautifully too, I might add. No, it wasn't a lullaby. It was something triumphant."

Fritz told Tony Thomas that the fight took place in 1924, in a Brooklyn armory. He said that six months later Canzoneri won his first world championship.

Composer Burton Lane, himself a pianist, noted that most pianists just won't do anything that might injure their hands.

"Then," Fritz said, "I was for a time a horseback-riding teacher in New Hampshire—I was very good on a horse. For $60 a month, with room and board, seemed very good to me. I hate to think what some composers must have done at times."

"You became a vagabond," Thomas said.

"Something of the kind."

Loewe always said he went to Montana, where he became a cowboy. Where he became an expert rider is nowhere revealed, though it is possible that he learned to ride in military academy. "You know, I once had a job carrying the mail to a gold mine 11,700 feet high in the mountains of Montana," he told a *New York Times* writer in 1964.

Tony Thomas asked him, "How did you finally get back into music?"

"Well, gradually it happened," Loewe replied. "I got me a piano and played . . . and somewhere they said, 'My God, where have you been?' At that time, you mustn't forget, this was before radio, not to mention television of course, and in little towns in the west, in Montana, nobody ever had heard piano-playing like that. Like, I gave a recital once, in Livingston, Montana, and it was advertised for one day, and sold out in the only cinema theater of the town, and I played the piano there, in a regular recital, and they never left their seats. They stayed during intermission with wide-open mouths. They never heard anything like that." That too is bothersome. How did he keep his technique up? Where did he practice? Does he wish us to believe that after seven years of not playing, he was able simply to sit down in a little Montana theater and dash off a dazzling recital?

Nor did Loewe ever explain how and why he returned to New York. In interviews over the years he said that he played piano in dives in Greenwich Village, Third Avenue bars, and restaurants in Yorkville (which, essentially, is East 86th Street), Manhattan's German quarter. Learning to play the organ, he worked at Keith's Albee in Brooklyn, and even, in that Prohibition era, played piano on a cruise ship that commuted between Miami and Havana for the edification of people with enough money to sail ninety miles to get a legal drink. "I was a bad sailor," he said, "and had to throw up after every chorus."

This mythic tale is based entirely on the testimony of Loewe himself. Nowhere in all the news and magazine stories about him does one find a corroborating witness to his first years in America. The story seemed as improbable to Ira Gershwin as it did to Benny Green. In a 1960 tribute to Loewe, Gershwin wrote:

"I first met Fritz about seven years ago. My wife and I found the stocky, blue-eyed composer fascinating. A few reminiscences of his early life in Vienna and Berlin . . . so intrigued us that we urged him to tell us more and more of his experiences and exploits. After a while the regaling began to make us feel a bit skeptical. We were listening to a man who sounded as though he were at once the reincarnation of Ignace Jan Paderewski, Casanova de Seingalt, Tom Mix, Brillat-Savarinn, Bet-a-Million Gates, and Terry McGovern. Not to mention Baron Munchausen.

"But it all turned out to be true."

Perhaps. Benny Green wrote in the Introduction to *A Hymn to Him* that the story has been "the source of incredulous astonishment to a great many people" because Tony Canzoneri was in his weight division "what someone like Vincent Youmans or Arthur Schwartz would be to the art of composing melodies."

Let us examine a little the career of Canzoneri to see why the story of an encounter between him and Fritz Loewe so bothers Benny Green and me.

Tony Canzoneri, born in Slidell, Louisiana, and raised in Brooklyn, was considered one of the great fighters in a golden age of boxing, the time of Dempsey, Firpo, Tunney. By 1920, when he was thirteen (and Fritz was nineteen), he had won seventeen amateur fights. He fought his first professional match when he was sixteen, the year Fritz arrived in America. Fritz said he fought Canzoneri in 1924 six months before the latter won the featherweight championship of the world. But Canzoneri didn't win that title until February 10, 1928. The *New York Times* didn't cover him at all in 1926, but from then on his frequent fights were closely monitored. Eight fights were reported by the *Times* in 1926, eleven in 1927. That is an arduous schedule for any boxer, and it is difficult to imagine that Canzoneri slipped another fight or two into it. If Fritz was merely wrong about the date and fought Canzoneri in 1927, rather than 1924, the *Times* almost certainly would have covered the event. And Canzoneri did not, as Lerner suggested, have a long reach. He was very tiny; a boxing writer noted that his girlfriend had bigger hands than he did.

So Fritz's story on the Canzoneri fight is hard to believe. On the other hand, John Springer, who was a publicist for Alan and Fritz at the time of *Camelot,* says, "I could imagine Alan embroidering a story, making up a beautiful, exciting publicity kind of story. Fritz didn't seemingly care enough about publicity. *Time* magazine was doing a story? He didn't care. Alan cared. Alan cared desperately. I think many of the conflicts between Alan and Fritz were because Alan was so hyper and Fritz was so laid back. Alan was always frenzied and frantic and hyper."

As for Fritz's statement that he didn't consult the newspapers after the putative Town Hall recital because he couldn't read English, that too is difficult indeed to credit. Surely he would not go to the trouble of giving a recital and then rest indifferent to the results. Somebody who spoke German doubtless would have told him how to get to Town Hall and what time to start the performance. For that matter, any waiter in Yorkville could have translated the reviews for him. And what reviews were there? The *New York Times* has always been conscientious about covering the concerts of young artists, particularly those who have achieved sufficient stature to play Town Hall. For example, on January 4, 1926, it reviewed a recital by a young pianist named Arthur Loesser. Loesser later became a distinguished academic, head of the piano department at the Cleveland Institute of Music. (And his brother Frank wrote, among other things, the musical *Guys and Dolls.*) But the *Times* does not mention Frederick Loewe in 1924; or in the decade after that.

The first eyewitness testimony to Loewe's career is the singer and actress Kitty Carlisle, who described meeting him to a *New York Post* writer: "That was about 1934, and Fritz played piano in the pit in my first Broadway show, *Champagne, Sec.* He'd come to my dressing room every evening and stand behind my chair while I was making up, and he'd say, 'Someday I'm going to write the best musical of Broadway.'"

Another memoir of Loewe in his years of obscurity comes from the playwright and director Edward Chodorov. In an article for the January 1977 issue of *Playbill,* Chodorov said:

"My first meeting with him came about because I needed incidental music for a play and a mutual friend suggested that a chap called Frederick Loewe could do it. I telephoned him and made a date to discuss my problem that evening at his flat on West 48th Street. It was, he warned me apologetically, a long hike up to the top floor.

"As I began to climb I heard someone playing a piece I recognized as Beethoven's Piano Sonata in C minor, and playing it beautifully. As I climbed it got louder. I had no doubt as to where the music was coming from; when I had puffed up to the top floor it was really crashing.

" 'What power! What sensitivity!' I thought as I stood enchanted outside the door listening and waiting for the break before the final movement.

"When I knocked, Fritz's voice, which I had only heard on the phone, called, 'Come in.'

"As I opened the door a wave of whisky smell hit me. A completely naked girl was seated with her back to me at the piano, her hands poised on the keyboard as she gazed up at her stark naked conductor facing her from the top of the piano, where he sat tailor-fashion, his legs tucked under him.

"He put a finger to his lips and beckoned me to a chair; then he swept down a hand and led the nude pianist into the last movement of Beethoven's C minor, perhaps the most spiritual music ever written for the piano.

"Since then I have had innumerable adventures with Fritz in various parts of the world, but none, to my mind, as surprising as my first."

Chodorov did not mention the date of this encounter, and so we have no way of knowing whether Loewe was yet married. It seems likely that he was: he met his wife-to-be three years before the encounter with Kitty Carlisle. If he arrived in America in 1924 and spent seven years in "wildly miscellaneous jobs," as Lerner put it, then he returned to New York from Montana in 1931.

In that year, Fritz went to a Fifth Avenue beauty parlor to meet one of his many girlfriends. As he waited for her, another of his girlfriends stepped out of a booth with a third girl, who was introduced to him as Ernestine—or Tina—Zwerleine. As he discovered immediately, she was Viennese.

"I was all finished," Tina told an interviewer years later. She was referring to her shampoo and wave.

"Completely," Fritz said with a smile, "and so was I."

Tina was in her teens when she came to New York with her parents.

"I loved everything that was American," she recalled, "and, above all, I wanted to be active and do things, like American girls."

Tina's father, like Fritz's, was famous in Vienna, so much so that the street on which the family lived was named after him. He was an architect who had designed many important buildings, including the Vienna city hall.

Fritz vowed to give up his girls and they were married. According to *Time*, they struggled through those Depression years in one room on Lexington Avenue. Fritz practiced, he said later, on a "very sad" upright piano rented for twelve dollars a month. Finally there came a time when he could not make the payment. Three husky men appeared to take the piano away. He sat down to play the piano one last time—Victor Herbert, then Liszt and Beethoven. He said, "Finally I was covered with sweat and I looked around. It was dark out. The three men were sitting on the floor. One called the others aside, and they talked for a few minutes. Then each man took out two dollars and gave it to me. This could only happen in America."

The fact that three times two makes six, not twelve, apparently didn't bother Fritz in telling the story, nor the *Time* writer quoting it. Perhaps he had six dollars of his own to add to the kitty. In any case, when he told the story to a *New York Post* reporter, there were two husky movers, not three, and he said he repaid them two years later.

In spite of a great shyness, Tina got a job as a John Frederics millinery model. She moved up in the company, becoming an executive, then joined Hattie Carnegie as an executive about 1942, and helped develop the wholesale hat department, which, in time, she came to head.

Fritz was determined to crash Broadway. In 1935, a year after he swore to Kitty Carlisle that he would someday write the greatest of all Broadway musicals, he succeeded in placing a song in a show. At the Lambs Club he met actor and singer Dennis King, who admired a melody Fritz had written. At that time, it was still customary to buy songs from outside sources for interpolation in scores. With a lyric by Irene Alexander and titled *Love Tiptoed Through My Heart,* King sang it in a show titled *Petticoat Fever.*

A year later, Fritz wrote a song called *A Waltz Was Born in Vienna* in collaboration with Boston-born writer Earle T. Crooker, whose credits included a Ph.D. from the University of Pennsylvania, Hollywood film scripts, and material for Beatrice Lillie as well as for reviews, including *Walk a Little Faster.* The song was first interpolated in a review called *The Illustrators' Show,* which lasted five performances. They resurrected the song for a show they wrote called *Salute to Spring,* produced by the St. Louis Municipal Opera in 1937. It became one of the hits of the summer, thereby attracting the attention of producer Dwight Deere Wiman, heir to the John Deere farm equipment fortune. He commissioned Crooker and Loewe to write an operetta score titled *Great Lady,* which had a muddled book set in two countries and two eras: France at the time of the Revolution and contemporary America.

Wiman tried to enlist the young Joshua Logan to direct it. Logan, however, had other commitments. In his autobiography, he noted: "Nevertheless, I read *Great Lady* and listened to the music which was by a wonderfully gifted young man named Fritz Loewe. I remember that Loewe's mouth fell wide apart when I said I couldn't do it because I didn't like the book."

Fritz said, "This Logan's a great man. He knows this show is lousy before we do." It opened in December 1938 and justified Logan's judgment. Despite the presence in its cast of Dorothy Kirsten, and choreography by Jerome Robbins, it died in twenty performances.

For the next four years, Fritz Loewe's writing was limited more or less to songs and special material for the annual Lambs Club *Gambols* show.

Discouraged by all his years of failure as a composer, Loewe decided to have another try at a concert career. In 1942, by which time he was forty-one, he tried a second New York recital, this time at Carnegie Hall, but the critical indifference to his playing dashed his hopes.

It was at this point that another producer, Henry Duffy, approached him at the Lambs Club with an offer to write some songs for *The Patsy*, a farce by Barry Connor that had already been adapted as a musical. It had been produced with a certain amount of success the previous year. Duffy wanted to replace its songs with most of those Crooker and Loewe had written for *Salute to Spring*, providing they could be adapted and updated. But with World War II now well under way Earle Crooker was in the navy, serving on the U.S.S. *Bataan*.

The accidental meeting of Lerner and Loewe at the Lambs Club has taken on the quality of legend in theater circles. And, as all legends, it occurs in various forms in the retelling. Fritz himself dispensed variant versions of it.

According to the most common, Fritz, preoccupied with the problem of finding another lyricist, took a wrong turn on his way to the men's room at the Lambs Club. He recalled, to a *Time* interviewer, "I always went through the main hall, but just that time, for no reason, I turned left in the grill room." En route, he passed the table of Alan Jay Lerner, a slim young man with spectacles. Lerner had written sketches for the *Gambols*. "You write good lyrics," said Loewe. "Would you like to do a musical with me?"

"Yes," replied Alan Jay Lerner, "I happen to have two weeks off."

In his autobiographical monograph *On the Street Where I Live*, Lerner wrote:

"Once a year I . . . wrote lyrics for the Lambs *Gambols*, the annual show. One day late in August of 1942, I was having lunch in the grill when a short, well-built, tightly strung man with a

large head and hands and immensely dark circles under his eyes
strode to a few feet from my table and stopped short. His destina-
tion was the men's room and he had gone the wrong way. He turned
to get back on the right road and suddenly he saw me. His name
was Frederick Loewe, Fritz to the membership, a Viennese . . .
ex–concert pianist and a talented, struggling composer. He came
to my table and sat down.

" 'You're Lerner, aren't you?' he asked.

"I could not deny it.

" 'You write lyrics, don't you?' he continued.

" 'I try,' I replied.

" 'Well,' he said, 'would you like to write with me?'

"I immediately said, 'Yes.' And we went to work."

three

ALAN: THE EARLY YEARS

*T*ime after time, journalists writing about Alan Jay Lerner have remarked that he was born wealthy, as if he were some exotic aberration in the history of American musical theater. Cole Porter inherited millions and married millions more. Richard Rodgers was the son of a physician father and a rich mother. Lorenz Hart, who grew up in a house with servants, was educated in private schools: Weingart's Institute and then the Columbia Grammar School, which Alan Jay Lerner later attended. In 1913, after a summer vacation in Europe, Hart entered Columbia College, where he met Richard Rodgers. Arthur Schwartz, the son of a lawyer, graduated Phi Beta Kappa from New York University, where he took a B.A. and LL.D., after which he earned a master's at Columbia and became a lawyer. Howard Dietz graduated from the Columbia College school of journalism. Jerome Kern was the son of a businessman who held a contract to water the streets of New York City, and he was educated at the New York College of Music and in Germany at the Heidelberg Conservatory.

Oscar Hammerstein II was the scion of a wealthy theatrical family. Vernon Duke was born Vladimir Dukelsky in northern Russia, a direct descendant of the kings of Georgia. He was educated at the Naval Academy in Kiev and then at the Kiev Conservatory. Lyricist John La Touche was educated at the Richmond Academy of Arts and Sciences and Columbia College. Lyricist and composer Harold Rome attended Trinity College in Hartford, Connecticut, took a Bachelor of Arts degree from Yale, then was graduated from the Yale school of architecture. Vincent Youmans' father was a famous, fashionable, and well-to-do hatter, with stores on upper and lower Broadway. Youmans grew up in Westchester, and was educated at private schools, Trinity in Mamaroneck and Heathcotte Hall in Rye, then at the Sheffield Scientific School at Yale University. Hoagy Carmichael held a law degree from Indiana University. Johnny Mercer was born wealthy, though his father lost his money in the 1929 crash. Burton Lane's father was a successful New York real estate operator. Lyricist Harold Adamson attended the University of Kansas and Harvard. Harold Arlen was an exception: he was the son of a cantor, and went to work as a musician at fifteen. The only true example of the Broadway composer risen from dire poverty is Irving Berlin. Possibly E. Y. "Yip" Harburg also could lay claim to a poor childhood. Harburg once told me that even the Gershwins were not poor. "At least the family could afford a piano," he said. "I remember the day they hauled it up the face of their building."

So the Broadway musical theater, despite notable exceptions in Berlin, Arlen, Harburg, and perhaps a few more, has almost from the beginning been the plaything of rich boys, and one rich girl: Dorothy Fields, the daughter of Lew Fields of the vaudeville team of Weber and Fields, who like Oscar Hammerstein II had all the doors open for her. No matter its usual designation as "popular" or "vernacular" music, the music of Broadway is music of the rich, by the rich, and for the rich.

And, let us note, for all Fritz Loewe would remark on his lean and hungry years, they occurred when he was an adult. As the child of an operetta star, he was exposed early to travel and culture, watched over by a governess, and given an excellent Berlin education. He was born to privilege.

So Alan Jay Lerner, far from being an exception in musical theater, was in accordance with the norm. "My Pappy was rich and my Ma was good-lookin'," he wrote, paraphrasing a lyric of Ira Gershwin's. His father, Joseph Lerner, native of Philadelphia, started his professional life as a dentist in Atlantic City. He abandoned dentistry to go into business when he was in his twenties. Some time before World War I he, with his brothers, converted a small blouse-making firm into the Lerner chain of women's stores, built it to national eminence, and ran it as chairman of the board. Though no member of the family has had any connection with the company for more than thirty-five years, the name "Lerner" is still written large on Main Streets and malls across America.

Alan Jay Lerner's secretary and assistant for fourteen years was a woman named Doris Shapiro, née Warshaw, who early in 1990 published a book about her association with Lerner titled *We Danced All Night* (William Morrow and Company, New York). Shapiro wrote: "I . . . spent my eighteenth year, after high school, working behind a counter selling $3.98 blouses and sweaters in one of his father's many Lerner shops. These shops operated on the principles of terror and slavery. There was always someone above watching you. When the executives paid a surprise visit, it was the tyrannical manager's turn to cringe. Even I got to watch someone: the stock clerk." Shapiro, who was paid $18 a week, certainly knew about the Lerner shops: her father was for years a production manager for the company, and even knew Alan's Uncle Michael, a famous sports fisherman.

Alan was born in New York City August 31, 1918, which made him Fritz Loewe's junior by a little more than seventeen years. Alan was the second of Joseph Lerner's three sons. Richard was his elder brother, Robert—always referred to by Alan as Bobby—the younger. "I was my father's favorite," Lerner wrote in *The Street Where I Live*, "and I adored him." But this conspicuous partiality made matters difficult for Alan at home. Lerner doesn't specify in what way, but it seems likely that his two brothers would resent it. At least once a week his father would phone home from his office, then send his car and chauffeur for Alan and take him to dinner and on the town, sometimes to the fights at Madison Square Garden. This early exposure is the source of Alan's later ambition to box. His father also had a deep love of musical theater, and from the time Alan was five there was scarcely a musical on Broadway that the father and son did not attend together.

Since Lerner reached five in 1924, the year that Paul Whiteman presented George Gershwin's *Rhapsody in Blue* at Aeolian Hall, this means he watched the unfolding of post-operetta American musical theater: the works of Rodgers and Hart, Kern and Hammerstein, Cole Porter, Vincent Youmans, and Dietz and Schwartz.

It would be difficult to exaggerate the value of this firsthand observation of the evolution of the art he would eventually practice. It tuned his ear for language, and his father helped in that, too: Lerner notes that all through his early years, he never sent his father a letter that did not come back with suggestions for improvement. His father was to some extent a Henry Higgins to the boy, and having lived with such a man surely is one of the reasons Lerner was able to solve the problems of turning George Bernard Shaw's play *Pygmalion* into a musical when others had failed.

But this was by no means the full extent of the father's influence on Alan's eventual writing.

The elder Lerner had only disdain for organized religion and gave his sons no religious training. "He claimed," Alan wrote, "to have faith in God but I doubt if he trusted him. He substituted resolve for prayer and accepted his aloneness as he accepted being a Jew with neither defiance, self-pity, pride, or resentment."

According to his friend Benjamin Welles, Alan would sometimes say in jest, "Remember, I'm only half Jewish." This would suggest that his mother was not Jewish. Three of Lerner's wives, Ruth Boyd, Marion Bell, and Karen Gundersen, who knew Lerner's mother, told me that she was. "His father was Russian Jewish, his mother German Jewish," Ruth Boyd said. "And in those days the Germans distinctly looked down on the Russian Jews." Doris Shapiro wrote that Alan "hated to be reminded he was Jewish."

Some time before Alan's tenth birthday, he asked his father where we go after we die. Joseph Lerner immediately replied, "Nowhere. And if anyone ever tells you differently, he's lying to you. You go to sleep, and never wake up."

Alan remembered that conversation all his life. The boy was horrified and for weeks afterward did not sleep well. He wrote that he was afraid to close his eyes and sought in the skies some sign that his father was wrong about death.

There is no trace of religion in any of the writings of Alan Jay Lerner, but there is an immense amount of fantasy, a fascination with superstition and the occult that is surprising in a man of his background. When he was twelve and at the Bedales School in England, which required its students to read the London Sunday *Times,* he noted in that journal that Sir Arthur Conan Doyle was going to deliver a paper on the nature and existence of God before the British Society for Psychic Research. Alan waited eagerly for the report on the address, but then read that Sir Arthur had died. He wrote to the society, seeking a copy of the speech. A reply advised him that no one had seen a copy and asked if he would like to join the society. He did, and began to receive its literature, most of which, he said, he did not understand.

Later he wrote: "They say the difference between the Oriental and the Occidental is that the Occidental is afraid of the mystery and the Oriental glories in it." This underlies a line Lerner wrote for the psychiatrist in *On a Clear Day You Can See Forever*: "The answers make us wise, but the questions make us human." Lerner said that from that time in the school library in England when he read of the Arthur Conan Doyle lecture, "nothing, outside of the theater, has intrigued me and sustained my unflagging interest more than the occult, extrasensory perception, reincarnation and all that is called metaphysical (until it is understood and becomes physical)."

Lerner consulted an astrologer to set the opening date for *Camelot*, saying, "Everybody has a favorite lunacy. This is mine." He had a fixation on the number thirteen; he considered it lucky. That belief in part led him into the most disastrous relationship of his lifetime.

A yearning to believe that there is something beyond death infuses his work. *The Day Before Spring* erases time barriers, with some of the characters coming from past eras. *Brigadoon* is about a town that returns to life every hundred years. *On a Clear Day You Can See Forever* deals with reincarnation. The lives of the protagonists of *Love Life* cover more than a century and a half. *Camelot* is drawn from a tale about early and half-pagan Christianity, filled with magic and a promise that this idealized kingdom will come again. It is worth noting that in the Jewish religion there is not the emphasis on life after death that one encounters in Christianity. Lerner in his writing constantly alludes to Christian ideas. Only one of his eight wives, Nina Bushkin, was Jewish. The symbology of Alan Jay Lerner's thought—absorbed from the culture around him and abetted by the attitudes of his father—is essentially Christian.

Alan was raised in a seventeen-room Park Avenue apartment with a paneled library and furnished with antiques, always aware of the tension between his parents. He told an interviewer in 1960 that his mother once slapped his face, saying, "You look too much like your father." Alan said, "My mother didn't start to love me until *Brigadoon*."

That Lerner, like most writers, drew on his own experience is obvious in his quatrain from *Love Life* in which one of the characters sings that his father was constantly absent from and indifferent to his home and his mother slapped him twice a day for resembling him. As we shall see later, Lerner, too, often lived apart from his wives.

His mother, Edith, a big woman, was born to wealth. She had studied voice in her youth, with Richard Rodgers' mother as her accompanist. She took Alan to concerts and museums and cathedrals. "But directly or indirectly, it was my father who created the child who became the father of the man," Lerner wrote.

"His influence on me was indelible and my love for him as alive as it was the day he died in 1954, but there were many issues where we parted company. Principally they were politics and women. He was a dedicated Republican, as had been his father before him, and was permanently but silently irritated when he discovered I was a liberal Democrat.

"As far as his attitude toward women was concerned, he never fully emerged from the Victorian era and regarded women as inferior to men. He believed . . . that the hallmark of maturity was the absence of a committed, romantic passion."

But Lerner's liberalism seems to have been largely symbolical and intellectual. Leonard Lyons, in a 1959 column in the *New York Post*, reported an incident that he could have known about only from Lerner himself. Lerner once told a cab driver to go up Park Avenue. The driver turned up Madison with that perversity that makes brothers of the cabbies of Paris and New York, stating the principle elaborated in the first line of the Declaration of Independence: "I'm as good as you," he said.

And Lerner replied, "No, you're not. I'm younger, more talented, more successful, fulfilling greater responsibilities. Go up Park."

It should also be noted that most of Lerner's wives came from wealthy and very social backgrounds, and for one who didn't—Marion Bell, his second wife, daughter of a railwayman—the relationship with him was a tragedy.

Lerner retained far more of his father's attitude to women than he apparently ever realized. It has been said that there is no more autobiographical work than *Gulliver's Travels.* Whereas we should view with caution the notion, derived from nineteenth century Romanticism, that the purpose of art is self-expression, it is safe to say that anything a man writes, what he *chooses* to write, inevitably manifests inner attitudes and beliefs. Even in the material he adapts—as in the cases of *My Fair Lady* and *Camelot*—from other media, he reveals his hidden interests. *My Fair Lady* is about a linguistic purist who raises a girl from the gutter to a level he can respect and then (at least in Lerner's version, if not Shaw's) falls in love with her. The same plot occurs in disguise in *On A Clear Day You Can See Forever. Camelot* is about King Arthur's relationship with weak and fallible Guinevere.

Lerner remembered his parents as perpetually fighting, separating, and reuniting. This continued for years. Lerner used to retell with apparent amusement the story of their final parting. Usually, on Friday nights, Joseph Lerner attended the prizefights in Madison Square Garden, for which he had a season ticket. One Saturday morning, as he was dressing to go to his office, his wife woke up and asked, "Who won the fight?" She had never done this before. Lerner had not gone to the fight—he'd spent it in someone's bed. He had to guess who'd won, the odds on a correct answer being even. As he read the sports page of the *New York Times* in the dining room, he realized he had given the wrong answer. Accepting with equanimity the futility of trying to explain, he finished breakfast, went to his office, telephoned the apartment, spoke to the maid who was in charge of his clothes, and told her to pack them. He sent his chauffeur for them and moved to the Waldorf, telling Alan that it seemed the only sensible thing to do. That was the end of the marriage.

Edith Lerner remarried, becoming Mrs. Edith A. Lloyd, and continued to live on Park Avenue.

On Sunday afternoons young Alan attended dancing classes, as children of his class commonly did, wearing white gloves. He always remembered an incident that occurred when he was ten years old. "The prettiest girl was, of course, the most popular," he recalled, "but I was too shy to make my presence felt. She lived on Fifth Avenue, so every Saturday I would place myself on a bench outside Central Park opposite her house, hoping I would see her come in or out and be able to dash across the street and speak to her without the competition of all the other white-gloved little brats." It is one of the loveliest locations in New York City. The city was beautifully clean in those days, and then as now the trees of the park overhung the Fifth Avenue sidewalk, paved with dark gray hexagonal blocks. The benches are against the low stone wall that demarks the park's boundary, and anyone sitting there can look up at the palisade of great and elegant apartment buildings whose high windows overlook the park's greenery. Lerner said that the girl never came by, and he learned afterward that he had a wrong address for her. Years later the bud of that memory blossomed into *On the Street Where You Live.*

Alan received his elementary education at Columbia Grammar
School in New York City. He had played the piano from the age of
five, and by the age of twelve, his exposure to musical theater had
kindled an ambition to write for it. He began writing songs in his
early teens. "To all of that," he wrote, "my father paid no attention.
He was not one of those who believed in encouraging children, nor
may I add, many years later when he saw I was serious, did he ever
discourage me. Fundamentally, I suppose, he simply hoped I
would not embarrass him." No matter the adulation Lerner held for
his father, even after Joseph Lerner's death, the relationship
doesn't sound very loving.

The father apparently partook of that Anglophilia that the possession of money so often engenders in Americans. He sent all
three of his sons to schools in England so that they might learn
the English language. Alan was enrolled at the Bedales School in
Petersfield, Hampshire, and later, when he returned to the United
States, at Choate, in Wallingford, Connecticut, whose headmaster,
George St. John, had modeled it on Eton. Alan wrote the school's
football song ("Gold and Blue, victorious ever, knows the way to
play") and was co-editor with John F. Kennedy of the school yearbook, *The Brief*. Alan's older brother, Richard, said of those prep
school years, "He was the only one I've ever known who could play
sixty minutes of gutsy football on a muddy field and not get his
uniform dirty."

Before and during the years at Choate, Lerner and his brother
Bobby spent summers with their mother in Europe. They traveled
through England, France, Austria, Hungary, and Italy, and eventually settled at the Lido in Venice. They would return to America
in time for Alan and Bobby to go back to school in the fall. It was
on one of their trans-Atlantic crossings that Lerner became friends
with Dan Sischer. Sischer, who was born in the same wealthy East
Side neighborhood as Alan, later was his classmate at Choate.
Sischer said it took heavy money to get into Choate, which always
had more applicants than it could accept. His own grandmother
was a Bloomingdale.

"I hated Choate," said Sischer, a retired real estate broker, in
1989. "There were only five Jews in the school, and then it became
seven, out of an enrollment of about five hundred. If you were a very
good athlete, you did just fine. I didn't have a problem, except that
I felt it, and I am not any more sensitive to being Jewish than
anyone else. It never seemed to bother Alan. It bothered me inside,

but I tried not to let it show, which isn't easy to do or not do when you're that age. But I got by.

"We all used to ogle some of the masters' wives, because some of them were very good-looking. Within the second day of the new school year, Jack Kennedy knew everybody's name, and if you had known what you know now, you'd have said, 'Boy, that guy's going to be a politician.' He had a gift for names, for knowing people; he was a perfectly delightful, pleasant extrovert.

"Alan used to do something wonderful for us. There was a piano in the Mellon Library at Choate, and every Sunday afternoon, Alan would be in there playing Porter, Kern, Gershwin, Rodgers and Hart, Berlin, all the great writers of the day. It was always a great moment for me and others at the school. This was the music that was at our eartips, because this is what we heard all day long on the radio. Those were the days when you'd listen to bands on the radio late at night. You'd hear, 'We now bring you the music of Isham Jones from the Rooftop Room of the Astor Hotel.' This was the kind of music we all loved, long before rock and roll.

"We thought Alan was marvelous, at twelve or thirteen. He was a very small guy and he couldn't have had very big hands. He had dirty blond hair. He was very affable. We knew he played the piano well, and I guess we knew he was a good student, because you always knew who wasn't. Alan was never under any constraints that I can recall. I have nothing but the nicest memories of the guy. In later years I used to see him in the street, oh, once a month. He was always most cordial. He'd discuss what he was doing for a minute or two and we'd go our separate ways."

His father simply ignored Alan's ambition to be a writer, ordaining that after Choate, the boy would go to the Sorbonne for French, then to some university in Spain for Spanish, after which he would attend the foreign service school at Georgetown and then enter the diplomatic service. But Alan was caught smoking at Choate. One version of the story says that it was in his room and that he was reported by a snitch.

Dan Sischer said, "We had a big woods behind the gym and the hockey rink where guys would go to smoke." Alan wrote in *The Street Where I Live* that he was caught smoking on a golf course. Wherever it was, we may note that he had already acquired the addiction to cigarettes. He was expelled. His angry father abandoned any idea of his pursuing a diplomatic career and sent him to an American rather than a foreign university, which Alan likened to punishing a prisoner by expelling him from jail.

In September 1936 Alan entered Harvard to major in French and Italian literature. During the two summer vacations of 1936 and '37, he studied music at the Juilliard School in New York. He noted in his book that Cambridge, Massachusetts, where Harvard is located, was 2,800 miles closer than the Sorbonne to Times Square. It was even closer to Boston, and Lerner was able to slip into town to see the new musicals. He said that he saw every show that was headed for Broadway via Boston, so he probably saw *I'd Rather Be Right, The Boys from Syracuse,* and *Too Many Girls,* by Rodgers and Hart, and *You Never Know, Leave It to Me,* and *Dubarry Was a Lady* by Cole Porter, all of which played there during that time.

One of his schoolmates, Stanley Miller, long afterward described him as he was in those days: a "youthful-looking guy" with a "very warm personality" who "never went with the crowd." He noted that Lerner lived in what was known as a "doghouse"—more elaborate undergraduate lodgings than the usual college dormitories—and had a piano in his room. Miller noted too that Lerner by now had a steady girlfriend, a pretty society girl named Ruth O'Day Boyd.

Ruth Boyd was the daughter of newspaper publisher William Boyd. After his death, her mother married Victor Ridder of the Knight-Ridder newspapers. Thus Ruth's background was entirely in newspaper publishing. She was educated at Todhunter, a progressive New York City school run by Eleanor Roosevelt. She met Alan not in New York but in Venice, where she had gone with her sister on vacation.

Edith Lerner took Bobby and Alan to Europe, as usual, in 1937, when the stirrings in Germany were altering the atmosphere. Alan remembered those summer excursions as marvelous experiences, but each year he was more anxious to return home. He said that when he got off the boat in New York in 1937, he never wanted to travel again. He would not return to Europe for nearly twenty years.

That summer of 1937, Alan turned nineteen. It was about this time that his father gave him a dark piece of advice. Joseph Lerner said to him, "Let me tell you something about women, son. You will have your troubles with them. We all do. There will be arguments; a marriage may not work; there may be times when you get into bed and not be able to function. But *always* remember this. No matter what happens, it's her fault. The proof of it is that you will go to bed with one woman on Monday and it will be a failure and another on Tuesday and it will be successful. You are the same person. Only the woman has changed. Therefore, whose fault is it? Hers."

It was a strangely warped piece of reasoning. Lerner said that he stared at his father in incredulity, but that he remembered the statement so vividly is the proof of its power. We can leave it to psychiatrists to speculate on how much it contributed to Alan's life of sequential polygamy.

John F. Kennedy had, like Alan, come up to Harvard from Choate, though there is no indication that they were chums. Not so Benjamin Welles, the son of Sumner Welles, Undersecretary of State under Franklin D. Roosevelt, whom Lerner considered his closest lifetime friend. "I know he called us best friends," Welles said long afterward, when he had retired from a distinguished career as a *New York Times* correspondent and was writing a biography of his father. "We were *very* close friends."

Cleveland Amory, Harvard class of '40, left a picture of Lerner in a column he wrote in 1960.

"The first time I met Alan Jay Lerner," Amory said, "he was a mere Harvard sophomore, only a cut—crew, of course—above a freshman, and I was a junior. Besides this, I was president-elect of the Harvard *Crimson*—a job so exalted that though you believed that life afterwards would probably go on from there, nothing else, on earth at least, would really matter very much. You had done all there was to do.

"We were not only examples of the famed Harvard 'indifference'—we were even indifferent to the indifference.

"Nonetheless, there was, in a corner of Harvard's Yard far removed from the inner sancta of the *Crimson,* a strange place which was—well, different. It was called the Hasty Pudding Club, and though it was, in the Boston-Harvard vernacular, a 'perfectly good' club—it had been founded in 1770—still it insisted on putting on each spring, for the edification of Boston debutantes and their beaux (as well as a few errant New Yorkers), a musical comedy.

"This particular show, in the spring of 1938, was entitled *So Proudly We Hail,* a satirical salute to Hitler, Mussolini, et al. Remarkable as it was as a show, it was even more remarkable for the fact that all three of its co-authors were not only sons of distinguished men but also the sons of men who were extreme individualists. One was Nathaniel Benchley, son of humorist Robert Benchley, another was Benjamin Welles, son of Undersecretary Sumner Welles, and the third was Alan Jay Lerner . . . The fact that all three such silver spoon second generation boys should go on from there to outstanding careers of their own would have seemed, at that time, an extraordinary defiance of the immutable laws of Harvard heredity.

"At the time I met Lerner he was a thin, wiry, dynamic young man with a large smile and a large pair of spectacles."

Ben Welles remembered him this way:

"He was short. He was what the French call *'costeau.'* He was husky and broad-shouldered.

"He was a very good dancer, very light on his feet and very agile, very quick, brimming with energy. Tremendous verve.

"I remember meeting him in Venice in the summer of 1937. I was in my junior summer before I became a senior. I was traveling with a couple of other guys from college, sort of dozing on the beach at the Lido. I heard the sound of feet running over the sand. Somebody accosted me, woke me up.

"Alan said, 'You're Ben Welles. You're mixed up with the Hasty Pudding.'

"I said, 'Yeah.'

"He said, 'I'd love to get into the Pudding.' He was then a freshman, going into his sophomore year. He was two years behind me. He was eligible to go in the Pudding in his sophomore year.

"So I said, very grandly, 'Well, young man, come and see me when we get back to college.' Sort of kidding him. He did. He looked me up. I liked him and we saw something of each other. I told some of the other Pudding guys about him. We could take in ten people a year. I said, 'I think this guy's a ringer, and we ought to get him in.' And we did. And that was the beginning of his fantastic career."

Cleveland Amory noted that for the Hasty Pudding show of 1938, *So Proudly We Hail,* and that of 1939, *Fair Enough,* Lerner wrote songs titled *Living the Life, By Chance to Dream,* and *Man About Town.* In 1938, Lerner, with Stanley Miller, also wrote an intimate review, called *The Little Dog Laughed.* Like Benjamin Welles, Miller would remain a friend.

During this time Lerner was taking flying lessons so that in the event of war with Germany, he would be able to enter the Army Air Corps. He was also on the Harvard boxing team. A boxing mishap assured that he would never fly and almost cost him his eyesight.

His boxing partner landed a left hook on the side of Alan's head, knocking him senseless. For the next two weeks, Alan's vision grew constantly dimmer, and at last an examination revealed that he had lost the retina of his left eye and was in danger of losing the vision of the right. He returned to New York and underwent several surgical operations, then spent a long period with his eyes blindfolded. When the blindfold at last was removed, he was forbidden to take part in any athletic activities whatever for at least five years, and warned that even bending over or sneezing could cost him the sight of his good eye. "It was one of the turning points in his life," Ben Welles said.

He returned to school and graduated in 1939, just in time to see his two brothers and many of his classmates go into military service and then to war. He was, he said later, anguished and ashamed that he was not with them. He made a personal appeal to the Surgeon General of the United States but still was unable to join the military. (In England at this time, an actor named Rex Harrison, also blind in one eye, was similarly trying to get into service.)

In the time immediately after graduation, Lerner was constantly in the company of Ben Welles and Stanley Miller. Welles said, "Stanley graduated with me in 1938. He went to work at NBC as a sort of elevator operator, the lowest rung on the ladder, I was a copy boy at the *New York Times,* Alan went to work as an advertising copy writer for Lord and Thomas, and the three of us would meet. We'd very often lunch together, and Miller would always go to the phone when the bill came. We laughed like hell about Miller. We were very fond of him.

"Miller and Alan would try to write songs together. They would go up to the Brill Building and go around trying to peddle their songs to all these hard-hearted professionals." The Brill Building, on Broadway, is so populated by music publishers that it has become a symbol of music-business cynicism. "Stanley had a great comic gift," Welles said. "He would imitate these people, talking out of the side of his mouth, as if he had a cigar in it. He said all these guys were called Manny. Everything was 'Manny this and Manny that. Hey, Manny, you want to come in and hear these two kids?' We got in the habit of calling each other Manny. When Lerner would call up long distance from around the world, he would say, 'Manny? How are you, old cock?'

"Alan and Stanley Miller and I became a sort of a great triumvirate. And I saw Alan progress and develop."

Alan still was going with Ruth O'Day Boyd, who like him had grown up in New York. Welles said: "Ruth Boyd was a girl of the same sort of background as Alan. She was very much the clean-cut young New York debutante. Ruthie Boyd and Alan were a wonderful little couple. They used to dance at the Stork Club, and they were like two little marionettes. They were beautiful dancers. She was a society girl. She was a childhood sweetheart. I always had some girl, but he was always with Ruth."

In 1940, Ruth Boyd and Lerner, then twenty-one, were married in New York City in a service conducted by a Roman Catholic monsignor. A daughter, Susan, was born three years later. "Although our marriage was not a happy one," he wrote, "it never occurred to me that it would end in divorce. When it did, at her request, it was under the friendliest of circumstances." Ruth denies this. She said, "I know Alan wrote that, but the divorce was *not* at my request."

And, after the divorce, she said, "We were always friends, all through the years."

"I went overseas in the army in 1942," Benjamin Welles said. "Stanley Miller went into the army, in radio, and he was in the North African landings." Depressed that his poor vision kept him out of the armed forces, Alan changed his associations completely, moving, as he put it, from the East Seventies to West Forty-fourth Street: he joined the Lambs Club and took residence there. It was at the Lambs that he met the man who did most to make him believe that he had the talent to make a life as a lyricist.

The man was a short, cigar-smoking, balding, lonely figure, tortured by his sexual ambivalence. He was also an alcoholic, and he was also Lorenz Hart, and on the subject of lyrics, his opinion was to be taken seriously.

Larry Hart was forty-four years old, and in the last phase of his life and career. He had been the partner of Richard Rodgers since they wrote Varsity shows during their student days at Columbia University. He had begun his professional career translating German plays for the Shubert brothers. Lerner estimated Hart's height at about four feet ten. "Because of his size," Lerner wrote in his autobiography, "the opposite sex was denied him and he was forced to find relief in the only other sex left." This is a curious remark. In Lerner's prose writings there are occasional flashes of hostility toward homosexuals. For example, in a footnote in *The Street Where I Live,* he tells us that on completing a lyric, he goes through it to remove the letter *s* wherever he can. This is a common fetish among lyricists; Ira Gershwin makes fun of it by deliberately using the letter repeatedly in *S'Wonderful.* Lerner writes, "*S* is a dangerous consonant. Too many can sound like a tea kettle, and with the growing shortage of male hormones it is even more precarious." Yet there were a good many homosexuals among his friends and professional associates, including Hart.

Lerner and Hart became good friends not, he said, because Hart found him interesting but because he was "so terrifyingly lonely." Lerner met him whenever Hart wished to play gin rummy, which Lerner played badly, he said, because he wasn't interested, and Hart played badly because he was usually drunk.

Joshua Logan, who also suffered pain from sexual ambivalence and went through periods of heavy drinking, had a somewhat different version of Hart's card playing. He describes it in his autobiography, *My Up and Down, In and Out Life,* an account of his own mental problems. Josh met Larry Hart when Rodgers and Hart were writing *I Married an Angel.* Rodgers wanted Logan to direct the show, and asked him to leave immediately for Atlantic City, where Hart was writing the second act. Rodgers warned him of Hart's eccentricities, saying "He disappears. A will o' the wisp. Just put your foot on his tail and get him to write that second act."

Josh once described to me his first encounter with Hart, including a few details that aren't in any of the books. In awe of his idol, he arrived at the Traymore Hotel in Atlantic City and went up to Hart's room. He found Hart smoking one of the long cigars for which he was known. When Josh tried to discuss the show, Hart cut him off, saying "Sit down. The first thing I'm going to do is teach you to play Cocksucker's Poker." And he explained that the only rule of the game was that it had no rules; you could cheat in any way, put cards up your sleeve, divert your adversary's attention and steal his cards, deal from the bottom of the deck. "He had," Josh wrote in his autobiography, "a dazzling number of ways to cheat and a childish delight in all of them."

Logan wrote, "He was always referred to as lovable—so diminutive, so antic—something to play with, like a frisky pup. Yet in truth he was a colossus. . . . He was the biggest little man I ever knew." Lerner described him as "kind, endearing, sad, infuriating, and funny, but at the time that I knew him, in a devastating state of emotional disarray." Lerner said, "I worshipped him."

There is a piece of evidence that Lerner also received early encouragement from Oscar Hammerstein. In later years, he told songwriter and music teacher Maury Yeston, who reported the conversation in the *Yale Review,* "When I was young, Oscar Hammerstein told me to come to his place from time to time to show him my work, and for him to give me some friendly advice." No printed corroboration of that relationship exists, but there is no reason to doubt Yeston. Hammerstein did the same thing for Stephen Sondheim; and Lerner did it for Yeston.

Having come under the patronage of Larry Hart, Lerner continued for a time to live at the Lambs Club, then moved to the Royalton hotel, down Forty-fourth Street from the Lambs, and after a year and a half there, to the Algonquin hotel on the same street, famous as the gathering place and sometime residence of Dorothy Parker, Franklin P. Adams, George Jean Nathan, Oscar Levant, H. L. Mencken, and other wits and intellectuals.

Lerner was now working as a radio writer. He said that he learned from this experience never to be afraid of deadlines, no matter how heavy the work load. He somewhat contradicted himself to Cleveland Amory, whom he told, "I wrote five hundred scripts in two years." When Amory asked if anything of the experience was now useful, Lerner said, "No—except the training and getting rid of the artistic illusion."

Lerner was writing five daytime shows a week, comedy material for a weekly show called *The Raleigh Room,* a one-hour Sunday program called *The Philco Hall of Fame, The Chamber Music Society of Lower Basin Street,* which starred Paul Lavalle and Dinah Shore, and daily sketches for Celeste Holm and Alfred Drake. He turned out scripts for *Cavalcade of America* and *Your Hit Parade* and material for Hildegarde and Victor Borge. He often said that he was on "a schedule so tight that it would only work if I didn't sleep on Monday nights." He told Tony Thomas that during that period he was writing stage plays at night, none of which was ever produced.

It was about then that the first meeting with Fritz Loewe took place. In 1956, Benny Gross of the *New York Daily News* did an interview with both men, recording still another version of how Lerner and Loewe met. He quoted Loewe as saying, "After I had bumped into Alan Jay at the Lambs, we struck up a conversation and I remarked to him I heard he wrote good lyrics. You see, he had written some for one of the shows staged at the club."

(Then it would seem likely, wouldn't it, that Loewe had heard some of them, not merely heard about them?)

Loewe continued: "Then I told him I had been commissioned to do a musical show based on the play *The Patsy,* and that although not a line had been written or even one tune composed so far, it was scheduled to go into rehearsal two weeks from the following Monday. (This was on Friday.) Alan answered that he was busy, but on

Sunday I phoned him that I had a $500 advance. Alan's reply was: 'I'll be right over!' And he was.''

Lerner gave yet another version of their meeting to Tony Thomas. In this one, it was he, not Fritz, who was on his way to the men's room. "I suppose the stars were looking down on us that day," he said. "I was on my way to wash my hands, actually. Fritz Loewe, who was sitting at a table in the restaurant, stopped me and he said, 'Say, you write lyrics, don't you?' And I said, 'Yes, I did, two years ago at college.'' He does not mention working on Lambs Club shows.

Lerner continued, "Fritz said, 'I don't have a lyricist. Do you want to write with me?' Well, I didn't even know who he was. I just said, 'Yes!' probably because I thought anybody who was a member of the Lambs Club must be a genius. Well, I didn't realize he was. So we started working together, just like that. We met that afternoon and started to work. We were together eighteen years, which is quite a hunk out of anybody's life.''

Whatever the details, they met at the Lambs. They were destined to make theatrical history.

four

ON TO BRIGADOON

Lerner and Loewe left immediately by train for Detroit. They revised the Loewe and Crooker songs and added new ones to *The Patsy*, now entitled *Life of the Party*. They completed the score, consisting of fourteen songs, in twelve days. The show, which opened in October 1942, ran nine weeks. As Lerner put it, "Had you been away for the weekend, you would have missed it." It was a phrase he liked, and would use repeatedly.

He and Fritz had discovered that they worked well together. "We could feel the movement in the structure of our work, and it wasn't termites," the composer said later. The following year the conductor and producer Mark Warnow asked them to write the songs for a musical titled *What's Up?* It had a book by Lerner and Arthur Pierson and a slight plot about an eastern potentate whose plane is forced to land at a girls' school. The cast included Jimmy Savo; George Balanchine was its co-director. It limped through sixty-three performances at the National Theater and died of its own deficiencies. Lerner described it as "ill-advised." Fritz Loewe said of it, *"What's Up?* Obviously, nothing was. It was awful."

In 1945, as World War II ended, Lerner's friends began returning, Ben Welles among them. "When I came back I caught up with Alan again," Welles said. "I had just gotten married. And then the *Times* sent me to China. Alan came down to Grand Central Station and saw us off on the train across the country to catch a boat.

"All our lives we saw a lot of each other. Stanley Miller was always with us. He went to Washington and worked at the Voice of America. He was a very sweet nebbish, who died of a heart attack."

That year of war's end, the next Lerner and Loewe collaboration made its way to Broadway. It was a show called *The Day Before Spring.*

Lerner was aware of the work of the conductor Maurice Abravanel. Abravanel, a French-speaking Sephardic Jew born January 6, 1903, in Salonika under Turkish rule and raised in Lausanne, Switzerland, had studied counterpoint and harmony in Berlin with Kurt Weill during Weill's own studies with Busoni. He had come to New York in 1936 to conduct at the Metropolitan Opera, and did not consider Broadway his specialty.

Just before his eighty-seventh birthday, Abravanel told me:

"An agent called me that Lerner wanted to interest me in their show. At that time I had only conducted Kurt Weill, outside of the Metropolitan Opera and all that. They dined me, they wined me, and we went to Fritz's studio which was at that time on Seventh Avenue at Fifty-eighth Street. There was a big building with a courtyard. His wife was *directrice* of Hattie Carnegie.

"Lerner told the story of the show, Fritz sat at the piano, Lerner sang it a little. I found an *enormous* talent in those two, especially in Lerner.

"Kurt Weill all his life looked for very distinctive libretti, and very good literary collaborators, Bertolt Brecht and Maxwell Anderson and so on. After that meeting I told Kurt how good Lerner was. I went one time to Lerner's apartment at the Algonquin, and he had a complete collection of Molière in French. I was very impressed that Alan had the combination of American spontaneity and freshness with French and European tradition to a great degree. It was unique.

"I agreed to conduct *The Day Before Spring.* There came the question of who would orchestrate. Outside of Kurt Weill, no one orchestrated his own shows on Broadway. I suggested and convinced Fritz to have an orchestrator named Hans Bernstein. He had no work. Absolutely nothing. Bruno Walter let him conduct backstage in the second symphony of Mahler. He told me one day, 'Look,

Maurice, I can't make it in this country with the name Hans Bernstein. I'm changing it to Harold Byrnes.' That was before Lennie Bernstein made it. The difference was that Hans Bernstein was from Hanover, and Lennie was from Boston.

"Harold Byrnes made a fantastic orchestration for the show. He was, by the way, a very good conductor, and a very good composer—a close friend to Alma Maria Mahler. He would do little things like coming one thirty-second before the downbeat. I had, I think, twenty-four men. When Rodzinski came, he said to me, 'What an orchestra. How many do you have? Forty, forty-five?' "

One of the marks of great orchestration is that it makes an orchestra sound much bigger than it is.

"But," Abravanel continued, "the musicians in New Haven couldn't play it when we opened. The producer wanted to change the orchestration, but I stuck to my guns. It was better in Boston and very good in New York, and it went very well.

"Those two kids, Alan and Fritz, loved me. But they were very vulnerable, when the show did not go well. The score is good, good Fritz Loewe. It was not very well cast. The text was in part surrealistic. A picture of Freud came to life. It was very interesting. But it was badly cast.

"I conducted it at first. Then I had to go to Australia. I put in Franz Allers. I had a slight problem with my foot. Franz conducted *The Day Before Spring* for me one night. Instead of everybody saying, 'Who is he?' he came in as a savior, and they all admired him."

Franz Allers told me, "October, if I am correct, the show opened on Thanksgiving Day, 1945. My improvised 'debut' happened a few days later." When Abravanel left the show, Allers replaced him full time. Thus began a very close friendship between Allers and Loewe.

Wolcott Gibbs wrote in the December 1, 1945, issue of *The New Yorker*, "*The Day Before Spring*, a new musical by Alan Jay Lerner, who wrote the book and lyrics, and Frederick Loewe, who contributed the music, is my kind of show. . . . It is generally literate, considerably above the average musically, very pretty to look at, and acted by a company who seem as if they might be a nice bunch to know. To keep this tribute from sounding as if I were related to the producer, a Mr. John C. Wilson, I'd better add that there are quite a few things the matter with it, including a good many stretches of dialogue that might have been scissored out of an old copy of *College Humor;* a first-act ballet, one of those numbers in which a couple of dancers interpret the love life of the principals, that just made me laugh rather nervously; and a comedy sketch, involving the shades of Plato, Voltaire, and Freud, that didn't make me laugh at all."

Gibbs said that "Mr. Lerner's rhymes are neat and witty . . . and the performers are kind enough to sing them audibly."

Maurice Abravanel said, "I liked Fritz and Alan both as human beings. But they were strange human beings. Alan's first wife, Ruth, was a lovely, lovely girl. I sat with her after the premiere of *The Day Before Spring*, because Alan didn't pay any attention to her. She told me she was alone. Alan didn't live with her. Alan would call her maybe once every two or three weeks. He and Fritz totally neglected their wives. They both lived at the Algonquin. I couldn't help feeling sorry for the two women, and I told them, 'That's not the way to treat your wives.' "

Long after, Ruth somewhat reluctantly confirmed to me that Alan had neglected her, saying almost in apology for him, "Everybody in show business leaves their wives alone, like people in politics.

"I thought Alan and Fritz were the two most wonderful people, and wonderful talents. Fritz was just a super guy, and a great musician."

The Day Before Spring survived through 167 performances and five months, which was not a successful run. Abravanel said, "When it did not go well, both simply broke down and went to bed. Lerner told Fritz, 'The thing to do is have new sheets, even in the middle of the day, so you can sleep.' "

Much later, Fritz said, *"The Day Before Spring* is the show that people always want to revive most urgently. Everybody said it was ten years ahead of its time and I'm just afraid that if they all of a sudden did it, they'd find out that no it wasn't, really, it belonged there."

Whatever its quality, it was the show that opened the door to Hollywood: while it was still in rehearsal, Alan took the script to Lillie Messinger, a literary consultant in the New York office of Metro-Goldwyn-Mayer, who became a lifelong friend and informal troubleshooter for Lerner. She loved it and recommended it to Louis B. Mayer, head of the studio. Mayer authorized its purchase for $250,000, a good sum at that time. Though it was never turned into a film, it added considerably to the bank account of Lerner, who didn't desperately need it, and Fritz Loewe, who did.

As Fritz put it, in the years between his arrival in the United States and the sale of that show to MGM, he'd had not ups and downs but only downs. "For twenty-one years I didn't eat properly," he said. "But then I began to eat very properly and very regularly." He remained conscious of the change, and twenty years later, in 1964, told a *New York Times* reporter: "The first time I ate properly was in 1944 when Alan Jay Lerner and I got $250,000 for the movie rights to *The Day Before Spring.*"

Lerner's penchant for fantasy and the yearning to erase time and death are already manifest in *The Day Before Spring.* These would come to flower in their next show, *Brigadoon,* on which Lerner started work almost immediately.

"The year was 1946," Lerner wrote in an article for the *New York Times* in October 1980, when *Brigadoon* was revived. "It was the third year of the golden era of musicals that had begun with *Oklahoma!* The brash, breezy, satirical musicals of the '30s had disappeared overnight with the beginning of World War II. The hunger for sentiment, joy and, if you will, escape had not only been captured by *Oklahoma!* but Rodgers and Hammerstein and the genius of Agnes de Mille had added a new dimension to musicals that became known as lyric theater."

Fritz discussed the question of a conductor with Maurice Abravanel. Abravanel could not take the job; he had been appointed director of the Utah Symphony in Salt Lake City, an orchestra formed the previous year that he would shape and develop and with which he would be associated for much of the rest of his life. Abravanel recalled: "I said it would be best for Fritz to have Franz Allers. Later Fritz told me that was the greatest thing I did for him, to give him Franz Allers." Allers would conduct every Lerner and Loewe show from that point on.

Already running on Broadway when *Brigadoon* opened was a substantial hit titled *Finian's Rainbow,* with songs by E. Y. (Yip) Harburg, considered one of the master lyricists in the history of the American musical, and Burton Lane, a composer who, like Fritz Loewe, had been trained as a concert pianist and published his first songs before he was out of his teens. He and Lerner knew each other slightly. "I met him either going into or out of an elevator," Lane remembered years later. "Alan was very superstitious. He was into astrology. Numerology—how many letters you had in your name. Everything. All the quack things. He was drawn to this kind of nonsense."

Finian's Rainbow too was a fantasy. It concerns an Irishman who steals a leprechaun's pot of gold and buries it in the American South. It combined elements of fairy tale with satire on racism in America.

"Brigadoon opened in the same year as *Finian's Rainbow,"* Burton Lane said. "We opened first. Four months later came *Brigadoon.* There was always a comparison. People got them confused."

Lerner always claimed that *Brigadoon* was an original tale that grew out of his admiration for the books of James M. Barrie, particularly those such as *Auld Licht Idylls* and *A Window in Thrums* set in the writer's native Scotland. He said the germ of the plot came to him from a muttered remark by Fritz Loewe to the effect that "faith moves mountains." Lerner said, "For a while, I had a play about faith moving mountains. From here we went to all sorts of miracles occurring through faith, and, eventually, faith moved a town."

Finally Lerner arrived at a plot about two Americans who stumble on a Scottish village they learn comes back to life one day in every hundred years. One of the Americans is an embodiment of jaded cynicism, the other an idealist. Their debate echoed Lerner's relationship with his father, a dispute that was perhaps still going on in himself.

Lerner noted that every producer on Broadway had turned *Brigadoon* down. He wrote, "The usual complaint was that it was not commercial, whatever that means. Since then I have come to believe that the best way to be commercial is by not being commercial." They had presented the show to the Theater Guild, whose executives professed interest if Lerner and Loewe would set their story not in Scotland but in the United States. The only major producer who had not heard the score was Cheryl Crawford. He and Fritz played the score for her.

Lerner wrote, "The angels looked down and smiled, she liked it and *Brigadoon* at last had a producer.

"It was a reasonably lavish show and the budget was fixed at $175,000! As laughable as that figure may seem today, it was not easy to come by. Fritz and I gave fifty-eight 'performances' for backers—meaning reading, singing and playing the entire play—before that exalted sum was finally corralled. Sometimes we would give three performances in one day and we were one week into rehearsal when we went through our act for the last time."

The show opened March 13, 1947, at the Ziegfeld Theater and received almost unanimously glowing reviews for such exquisite songs as *Almost Like Being in Love, There But for You Go I, The*

Heather on the Hill, I'll Go Home with Bonnie Jean, and *Come to Me, Bend to Me.* When it won the Critics' Circle award as the best musical of 1947, the citation read, "To *Brigadoon,* by Alan Jay Lerner and Frederick Loewe . . . because its taste, discretion and thoughtful beauty mark a high note in any season, and because it finds the lyric theater at its best." Burns Mantle listed it among the "Ten Best Plays of 1946–47" as representing "the emergence of the American musical play of quality."

It was at this time that the critic George Jean Nathan, who generally praised *Brigadoon* in the *New York Times,* attacked Lerner for "barefaced plagiarism." He said the plot was based on a German story, *Germelshausen,* by Friedrich Wilhelm Gerstacker. Nathan listed several sources whence Lerner might have derived the story.

Lerner was stung by the accusation, so much so that in 1978 in *The Street Where I Live* he took up the cudgel to bash Nathan, long since dead, for it:

"Nathan developed a high-school crush on the leading lady (of *Brigadoon*), invited her frequently to supper, and sent her all his books, each inscribed with an adolescent expression of endearment. One weekend he called to ask her out and discovered she was visiting me in the country, not for artistic reasons. This so enraged him that he devoted his entire next week's column to how I had stolen the plot of *Brigadoon* and *The Day Before Spring.* . . . His attacks continued for three weeks with such venom that the *New York Times* called me and offered me space to answer him, which I did, labeling the whole accusation as rubbish and documenting the developing of each play into the final product. Nathan took my article, deleted a sentence here and word there until it seemed as if I had confessed to plagiarism, and then published it in his annual yearbook of the theater."

This denunciation of Nathan, published thirty-one years after the event, is almost as petty and bitchy as Nathan's original charge. Nathan's accusation seems massively irrelevant, a little like charging Shakespeare with not having invented the plot of *Romeo and Juliet.* In turn Lerner's comment that the leading lady was visiting him in the country "not for artistic reasons" smacks of that sexual boasting that most men find extremely distasteful in the comparatively few men who indulge in it.

If Nathan wrote such letters, Lerner might well have had access to them. The girl in question was Marion Bell, whom Lerner met when she auditioned for the role of Fiona MacLaren in *Brigadoon.*

His paragraph on the incident tells us that he promptly set about conquering her, and later that year he divorced his wife, Ruth Boyd, for her.

Long afterward Marion Bell, who had read Lerner's book, denied the whole story. She told me: "Alan and I were living together. We lived in an apartment on Sixty-seventh Street. George Jean Nathan invited me to lunch. And that was to present me with an award. That's the only time I ever met the man. That's all I know about George Jean Nathan."

What about the love letters Lerner said Nathan wrote her? She replied, "If he did, I never saw them." And she added: "Alan and I were happiest when we were living together, and if that's what Alan wanted to remember, that's all right with me."

Everyone who knew her found Marion Bell striking, with hair usually described as raven-colored. Her photos show a fiery, flamboyant beauty. Ben Welles said, "Marion Bell was exactly the opposite" of Ruth Boyd. "She was *opulenta,* as the Spanish say—big-bosomed and sexy."

She was born in St. Louis, the daughter of a freight agent on the Wabash railroad. While she was appearing in *Brigadoon,* the *World-Telegram* ran a series on new talents in the New York theater, one of whom was Bell. "A railroader's family," she said in the interview, "moves a lot. But at fifteen, I was pretty well set in Los Angeles attending Hammond Hall."

Aspiring to an opera career, she went to Rome for a year and studied with Mario Marafioti, who had taught Grace Moore, among others. She returned to America as war threatened and studied with Nina Koshetz, then was signed by the San Francisco Opera Company for a series of leading roles. During one of these appearances, she was noticed by a Hollywood talent scout and signed to a film contract. She appeared in *The Ziegfeld Follies,* singing a duet from *La Traviata* with James Melton. She also appeared with the St. Louis Opera Company and the Opera Nacional in Mexico City.

She was appearing in summer stock when she was advised that Lerner and Loewe were casting for a romantic lead in a show called *Brigadoon.* She couldn't sleep the night before the audition, but got the role—and an invitation from Alan.

Marion told me she had little recollection of the audition. She said: "My memories are all very vague, because I don't live with them all the time. I remember going to New York—it must have been around September. The first day I was in New York, the Lyons Agency got in touch with me, and invited me over. I went over and Alan was there. He had been working toward a deadline and he was unshaven and he looked so strange. He said that he wanted to see me home. So would I wait until he got shaved? I said, All right. He got shaved and we went home in a taxi. I was staying at the Waldorf-Astoria. He gave me an audition with Fritz Loewe, and I sang *Solveg's Lied* from Grieg's *Peer Gynt Suite.* I don't remember what theater it was, but it was in a theater, and the stage light was on. And they hired me."

When the show reached the Boston tryouts phase, she told the *World-Telegram,* "I was jittery. Things were just generally snafu. I had on gray hose (to match the silver-buckled, black peasant shoes) instead of green. There was a flurry in the wings. Technicians hopped around like mad. Something happened to the backdrops! Then someone gasped. The tree roots were sticking up in the air!"

But the Boston reviews were good. Then came New York. "It was a breathless evening," she said. "The audience seemed enthusiastic. Our duet (with David Brooks) went smoothly . . . and here I am."

Throughout the *World-Telegram* piece, one can feel that she considers Broadway beneath her, despite the deceptive sense of stardom *Brigadoon* gave her. The writer said, "Marion would rather hum Puccini's *Butterfly* than don the pleated Scotch plaid of the MacLaren clan." And at the end of the piece, she is quoted as saying, "I love good music. The experience of appearing at the Metropolitan must be heavenly."

If the Broadway musical theater—and for that matter, much of its "straight" theater—has been the plaything of the rich, Marion Bell revealed a condescension for American musical art and the awed respect for that of Europe so common in Americans. That admiration also seems to hint at her social aspirations. Lerner, with his background, must have dazzled her.

In the course of her time in *Brigadoon,* she did something dangerous, something that undoubtedly caused her great pain and Lerner embarrassment. She gave a recital at Town Hall, singing the kind of music she respected: Handel, Bach, Mozart, de Falla. The next day a *New York Times* reviewer, identified only as N.S., wrote a review that must have been all the more painful to her in that it was tolerant. In essence it was a pat-on-the-shoulder, back-to-the-showers-kid review that said she might be good enough for Broadway but not for the world of oratorio, opera, and lieder.

We can imagine how she felt as she read it. And we can imagine too how Lerner, with all his highly social friends, felt about it.

Marion Bell was his new wife.

After a year in *Brigadoon,* Bell suffered what she later said was a recurrence of hepatitis but her mother said was a nervous breakdown. She had a history of mental problems. She told a reporter in 1960 that she had been analyzed nine times, and hospitalized in isolation during part of her year in *Brigadoon.*

She said, "Alan wanted me to be analyzed—he's always wanting people to be analyzed—and my first analyst was his analyst."

She said that Alan would go from one project to another, and when he was not engrossed in one of them, he liked evenings of poker or conversation with his friends, including artists and writers and intellectuals, many of whom he had known since his Harvard days. She said he prided himself on keeping in fit physical condition, spending much of his spare time swimming and playing tennis. This left little time for her. "When *Brigadoon* was playing," she said, "he was enthused about it and about me. But when it was over he became interested in the next play, and I wasn't part of it anymore. I was shy, so as soon as I discovered I might be in his way, I just withdrew."

Brigadoon was a substantial critical success, a modest commercial success. It ran 581 performances. Bell lasted a year in the show; the show lasted a year and a half; Lerner left her some six months after it closed. Her Broadway career ended, she sank from sight. She turned up briefly in 1960 in an unpublished *Time* magazine background report.

This is what Bell told me: "I went to Texas during the war, entertaining for special services. I entertained in the Waco hospital. They had too many patients, from Normandy and the African campaign. I caught infectious hepatitis. Six thousand men died of it. When I came down with it, the doctor said I should be in bed for two years. I didn't do that. I went home and went on working. It caught up with me later. That's what caused the mental breakdown. I was hospitalized six years. Then I came home to my parents in California in 1960."

Brigadoon established Lerner and Loewe as a major Broadway writing team. Yet for a time it seemed they would never write together again.

Fritz told Tony Thomas:

"I finally hit the right story with Lerner. The show before, *The*

Day Before Spring, was a charming musical, which was rather successful. Although it lost the money, it got the critical acclaim. The story didn't quite jell. So, *Brigadoon* was the first time that the story jelled. I would say that our work on *The Day Before Spring* was quite good. It was not any less good than it was in *Brigadoon.* It was cast right, it was right. You can miscast a hit show later on and get away with it. But when you start a musical show for the first time, the casting better be good. Because if you miscast it then, nobody will realize that it is a very good show but completely miscast."

And Alan told Tony:

"*Brigadoon* was the first realized effort that we had.

"I think the reason we were fortunate enough to receive some recognition was that it was a thing unto its own and it didn't try to sort of cash in on anything. And when you're desperate, sometimes, you say, 'Well, I might as well please myself,' and that's what you should have been doing in the first place."

"The most remarkable thing about *Brigadoon,*" Tony said to Lerner, "is its authentic Scottish flavor, the music and the lyrics and the story. Neither you nor Mr. Loewe are Scots."

"No. I'd never been to Scotland, though I'd been to school in England when I was a boy, and I had a Scottish roommate and that was about as close as I ever got to it. But I was a great James Barrie fan and I'd read everything of Barrie's until it was coming out of my ears. And, actually, as far as music is concerned, there is a great similarity that starts in the Middle East and runs right up through Hungary and France to Scotland where those melodies are very much the same, very much the same feeling.

"I said to Fritz one day, 'Isn't there any real Scottish music other than *Loch Lomond?*' And he said, 'Well, the most Scottish composer I know is Edvard Grieg.' So one day over at the library I looked it up and I discovered that Grieg's family name was McGregor. Either his grandfather or great-grandfather had come to Norway from Scotland. You find that open fifth running all through Grieg. It was very characteristic of Grieg's music and it's characteristic of Scottish music, and it can be seen in Hungarian and Czech and German music too."

Lerner's voice on the tape is elegant, softly resonant, quiet, and beautifully articulated. The letter *r* is so soft that it is almost missing from his speech, as it is with Boston people, southerners, and for that matter a good many English people. He says "fihst" for "first," for example. It is not, however, a regional accent. It is essentially an artificial accent, quite cultivated, and no doubt echoing the schools he had attended. Arthur Schwartz spoke somewhat like that, and André Previn does, too.

Immediately after *Brigadoon,* the newspapers began writing about them, though more about Lerner than Loewe, who seems from the start to have avoided publicity.

A *New York Post* article noted that Fritz and Tina called each other "Mutzi" and "Poodle" respectively, and that they were in Bermuda now for a few weeks. On April 5, 1947, twenty-three days after the opening of *Brigadoon,* the *New York Post*'s weekend magazine section ran a full-page article with pictures on Fritz and his wife. The article, a chronicle of trivia by Mary Braggiotti, has that curiously gooey tone common in women journalists writing about celebrities. She described a taffy-colored cocker spaniel that bounced around the room, then jumped up on a sofa between Fritz and Tina and licked Loewe's face.

"Taffy is a Broadway dog," Loewe said. "He was always very polite to me, but Tina was number one with him. He adored her. And what do you think? The day the reviews of *Brigadoon* came out he started chasing me around. He's been mine ever since." We recognize immediately that pleasantly bantering, send-up tone Loewe so often adopted when talking to reporters. You never know whether what he says is to be taken seriously or not.

The reporter noted that Loewe was the composer of the music for Broadway's newest hit show, and that Tina, as head of Hattie Carnegie's wholesale hat business, was one of the highest paid women in the fashion industry.

"Despite an unmusical haircut," Braggiotti wrote, without telling us what a musical haircut is, "Fritz looks more like a composer—or some sort of artist—than anything else. It's probably his large gray dreamy eyes. Tina, on the other hand, is a luscious little pink-and-white, blue-eyed blonde—about as far a cry from the executive type as you could find."

Tina said: "I like to work with hats. I think it is color in hats that interests me most."

Fritz said: "Music and color are the same thing. I will demonstrate." And he went to the grand piano at the end of the large living room and sat down, saying, "Let us think pink." Braggiotti wrote that after looking ceilingward for a second, he played "a few bars that are indisputably pink music."

"No, I have never played a hat," Fritz said.

"That's because he doesn't notice women's hats," Tina said. "He loves women's hair."

"I am not clothes-conscious at all," he said.

"In fact," Tina said, laughing, "he likes to compose in swimming trunks."

"I couldn't write a note with clothes on," Fritz said. "That is why I usually work in the morning before I'm dressed."

The story said that as soon as Fritz finished a tune, he played it for Tina, if necessary calling her at her office and performing it over the phone. "I'm always so flattered," she said.

The story said that when the Loewes were in New York they avoided nightclubs, read everything from Dostoevsky to *The Lost Weekend,* played gin rummy, had a martini before dinner, and always spoke English to each other.

Fritz said, "I think that the reason most people get divorced is that they weren't in love in the first place.

"Tina had faith in me. That's what made it possible for me to have a career."

Tina said, "Fritz is always courteous to me—always thoughtful and sweet. I think he must have a wonderful soul."

Fritz said, "Love . . . Love is all that counts."

Not long after this idyllic portrait was painted, the Loewes parted. On November 6, 1956, the *New York Times* reported:

Los Angeles, Nov. 5—A suit for separate maintenance brought against Frederick Loewe, Hollywood and Broadway composer, by his long-estranged wife was dismissed today with the explanation that she had settled for $150,000 in cash and $25,000 a year for life.

Mrs. Ernestine Loewe, once general manager for the Hattie Carnegie fashion enterprises, filed the Superior Court complaint here Sept. 17 on the ground of nonsupport.

She said her husband had agreed seven years ago to give her 20 per cent of his gross income, with minimum payments set at $5,200 a year. Mrs. Loewe complained he had failed to make any payments since June 30, 1956, although he had been earning $450,000 a year, chiefly from royalties, including those from his score for My Fair Lady.

Mrs. Loewe's attorneys said she would establish residence in Las Vegas, Nev., and would sue for divorce. The Loewes were married in 1931.

Fritz Loewe never said—publicly, at least—why they parted. After the separation, he went back to his young girls, if indeed he had ever really given them up.

One of the friends of his later years, writer and television broadcaster Gloria Greer, said she thought that, down deep, Fritz didn't really like women. He apparently didn't like his mother, something else he had in common with Lerner. Fritz always acknowledged, Greer said, that Tina sustained him during his lean years, thereby making his later success. Maurice Abravanel had long disapproved of the way Fritz treated Tina. He said in 1989: "Fritz let his wife down the moment he was in the chips."

Lerner would marry many—not all—of his later enamoratas. Fritz would not. After *Brigadoon,* Alan and Fritz went through the first of their many breakups.

Marion Bell characterized Lerner as intense in his work habits, suffering while he wrote, and leaning heavily on Fritz Loewe's advice. She said Lerner was unusually modest for one with so much talent, and she thought this very hesitancy drew him to Loewe's more mature and critical judgment.

This view is at variance with that of Benjamin Welles. "Alan once told me," he said, "that Fritz was a schizophrenic because his father was Austrian Jewish, his mother was gentile. That's why he was difficult. Very moody. He had these great waves. He always liked much younger girls. He always had a girl of seventeen or eighteen dangling around somewhere. He was a great swordsman. Alan was a great swordsman. The two of them had a great deal in common. They called each other 'my boy' and 'dear boy.'

"Alan told me that Fritz had such paranoia over nearly starving, being penniless for years, that finally when he got a check for two million from Metro-Goldywn-Mayer, he had it framed and put it up on the wall next to his piano at his home in Palm Springs. That was probably in the 1950s.

"Alan handled Fritz beautifully. He said that Fritz was a real pro. Now matter how late he was out the night before, if they were going to work at nine o'clock, he was on the job at nine o'clock. Alan said that when they started a new show, it took a while to get Fritz down to the grind, though once he got going he was fine. So, Alan said, 'I made a habit of throwing out the first two songs he wrote, no matter how good they were. I said they weren't good enough.' That was a technique Alan used to get Fritz down. Alan never worked with anyone else the way he worked with Fritz."

But Marion Bell insisted to me—more than forty years after she appeared in *Brigadoon*—that Fritz was the strong force in the relationship.

For whatever reason, it seemed at the time that the relationship had ended with *Brigadoon*. Lerner's next Broadway musical was written not with Fritz but with another composer born in Berlin: Kurt Weill.

Weill was one of a large group of artists who had emigrated to the United States to escape the rising sea of Hitler's horrors. He had been highly successful as a composer in his native country, producing an acerbic theater music that embodied the decadence of 1920s Berlin. The most successful of his European works, of course, was the *Three-Penny Opera*, a collaboration with poet and playwright Bertolt Brecht based on John Gay's bitterly sardonic *Beggar's Opera*.

In America, Weill had a series of collaborators. On arriving he had become involved with people in the Group Theater, including Cheryl Crawford, eventually to be a major producer of musicals. His first project in the new country had been *Johnny Johnson*, a sort of American *Good Soldier Schweik* written with playwright Paul Green.

Weill collaborated with Maxwell Anderson on *Knickerbocker Holiday*, set in the Dutch period of American history and starring Walter Huston as Peter Stuyvesant. The score produced *September Song*, which was to earn royalties for Weill and Anderson for years to come, though the show was only a modest success. Weill and his wife, Lotte Lenya, had rented a farmhouse on a wooded piece of property in Suffern, New York, so that they could be near Anderson, who had a home in New City, which is about thirty miles north of Manhattan. It is now a city of supermarkets and fast-food chains, of stoplights and sighing freeways, but in 1939, when the Weills moved there, it was bucolic. In his biography of Weill, Ronald Sanders wrote, "Anderson, a large bearlike figure of a man"— Anderson was six-foot-three— "whose personal presence was as commanding as his role in American drama, was the central figure in a sort of backwoods Greenwich Village that had grown up in Rockland County, where the painter Henry Varnum Poor and the actor Burgess Meredith, among other gifted friends of Anderson, were living in close proximity to him and to one another. The Weills were being drawn into this orbit." Others in that orbit included Milton Caniff, the cartoonist-author of the comic strip *Terry and the Pirates*, and his wife, Bunny, cartoonist Bill Mauldin, author Marion Hargrove, and Alan Jay Lerner. Weill met the brilliant playwright and director Moss Hart at a party given by Walter Huston in November 1939. Hart was then best known for the series of witty plays he had written in collaboration with George

S. Kaufman, including *The Man Who Came to Dinner,* which was running at that time. But he had also written, on his own, the libretti of musicals. After a number of conversations, Weill and Hart decided to do a musical involving psychoanalysis. Ira Gershwin agreed to do the lyrics. This was *Lady in the Dark,* which starred Gertrude Lawrence.

Then came *One Touch of Venus,* based on a novella by Thomas Anstey Guthrie drawn from the Pygmalion legend. Cheryl Crawford was its producer, the book was by Bella Spewack, and the lyrics were by Ogden Nash, known then only for his humorous light verse. The couturier Mainbocher designed fourteen costumes for Mary Martin for the show, which opened October 7, 1943, and ran 566 performances. (Mainbocher was a friend of hers and her husband, Richard Halliday. He turns up later in our story.) The hit from the show was *Speak Low,* another song that continued to make money for Weill. In 1947 came *Street Scene,* based on Elmer Rice's 1927 Pulitzer Prize play, a near-opera with music by Weill and lyrics by Langston Hughes. It ran on Broadway simultaneously with the Burton Lane–Yip Harburg *Finian's Rainbow* and Lerner and Loewe's *Brigadoon.* Weill was looking for another project.

Biographer Ronald Sanders wrote, "There had been a bit of a falling out between . . . Alan Jay Lerner and . . . Frederick Loewe, and [Cheryl Crawford] proposed that Lerner and Weill get together and do a show. There was no problem, since they already were neighbors in New City and both part of Anderson's circle there. They were agreeable to the idea, and the project with Lerner became Weill's next one."

Many people have attested to the rupture between Lerner and Loewe after *Brigadoon,* including Marion Bell. She said, "Right after *Brigadoon,* Fritz Loewe had a disagreement with Alan and they broke up. Fritz Loewe went to Hawaii. We didn't see Fritz for a year. Then he called us. Maybe by then he'd cooled down a bit. He was a good influence on Alan because he told Alan what to do and how to do it. But they had disagreements. I never knew what caused it." Neither does anyone else I have been able to find. But the schism assuredly happened.

Maurice Abravanel said he was the first to suggest a Weill-Lerner collaboration. "One day after *Brigadoon,* Fritz and I had luncheon," he told me. "I was worried about Kurt Weill not getting the right librettist. Obviously Kurt could not work with the Hammerstein type—AABA, AAAAA, repeat repeat. Ogden Nash on the other hand had gone a little far. Two thirds of the audience could not understand the incredible wonderful wit of his lyrics when sung. Fritz said to me about Alan, 'Oh, that son of a bitch! I will never work with him again.'

"I told Fritz, 'You are crazy. He writes you beautiful lyrics, good books. He's really the best on Broadway.' If Fritz told me what the problem was between them, I don't remember now. But he said, 'That son of a bitch, if I never write another note, I will not write with him again.'

"I am always straight from the shoulder, and I said, 'Now, Fritz, if you're serious, I'm going to tell Kurt, because I think they could hit it well together.' So I told Kurt, and he came to see *Brigadoon.*

"Kurt was a marvelous guy, but he had that funny superiority on his face. Afterward he said about Alan, 'Oh Maurice, that's not really up to my level.' But then later he worked with Alan on *Love Life.*"

Archivist Miles Kreuger said, *"Love Life* came about because Cheryl Crawford had produced Kurt Weill's *One Touch of Venus* in 1943 and Lerner and Loewe's *Brigadoon* in 1947 and felt that Alan with his brilliant mind and Kurt Weill with his brilliant mind must work together.

"Alan told me about it. Alan went up to South Mountain Road in New City, which is a remarkable little country road that later Bill Mauldin lived on, and Mary Mowbray Clarke, the famous landscape architect. Alan said he was walking up South Mountain Road, and suddenly the contrast between the vernal beauty of the countryside in New City compared with the urban quality of New York came to mind, and that drifted into an idea for a work about the industrial revolution and the effect that it has had on people's love life—and how simple and how natural love used to be. He created the characters of Samuel Cooper and his wife, in the early nineteenth century, who move with their children to a new town."

In a joint newspaper interview with the two writers, Weill said, "The only trouble with Alan is getting him to give me his lyrics." This complaint would be entered by other composers in the years ahead. Lerner said in turn, "And I can't give them up." Weill was then forty-eight, Lerner thirty. And the two men gave the usual mutual admiration comments that would mark all such interviews between Lerner and his collaborators in the future.

Kurt Weill, at five-three-and-a-half, was even smaller than Lerner. He had thinning dark hair, wore thick dark glasses, and smoked a pipe. Ronald Sanders notes that he had "psoriasis, a painful skin disease from which he had suffered all his life and which usually struck in periods of anxiety. This, indeed, was the way his body paid its price from time to time for the ironic calm he usually maintained during even the most frantic moments of assembling a production."

The book, an original by Lerner, reflected his inherent yearning to overcome time. The story follows a couple, Sam and Susan, through 157 years of married life, though they do not age in the course of the show. They pass through the Industrial Revolution, the suffragette movement, Prohibition, and the Great Depression. In the opening scene a magician saws Susan in half. She discovers that she is half homemaker and mother and half provider. Lerner's lyrics for the most part were acerbic, because, as he wrote at the time, "The subject, briefly, is the decline of American home life in the past century or so and the resultant unhappiness and confusion of the average family."

Miles Kreuger said, "They have a lovely life. As the decades go by they don't change, they don't become older, but the world around them changes. Soon there is a factory in the distance. Instead of working at home as a cooper, a person who makes barrels, Sam goes off to work every day in this factory that's now polluting the air. Eventually he goes to work for the railroads. By the end of Act One, nearly a century has gone by. It's the 1920s, and he has become a traveling salesman who will prostitute his feelings to suit the client, no matter what the client wants. Contrasted with the scenes of the Cooper family are vaudeville sketches, mordant parodies which comment on the activities onstage. It's Greek chorus as vaudeville. At the end it all falls apart, it becomes madness."

Lerner described the work as "an experiment with form." He said, "We tried to employ practically every form of dramatic storytelling. For example, one scene is written in the American ballad style; another is like a little musical play; another is in sketch form; another is in musical comedy form, and still another is straight dramatic form."

Love Life was produced by Cheryl Crawford, directed by Elia Kazan, choreographed by Michael Kidd, had settings by Boris Aronson and costumes by Lucinda Ballard, and starred Nanette Fabray and Ray Middleton. It opened on the evening of Thursday, October 7, 1948, at the 46th Street Theater. Despite so distinguished a company, it got mixed reviews. Brooks Atkinson described it as "a general gripe masquerading as entertainment." George Jean Nathan, perhaps still stung by Lerner's response to his charge that *Brigadoon* was plagiarized, pouted that the chorus girls were "so deficient of physical charm" that they could be in *Tortilla Flat*—surely a peculiar complaint about a serious show. But John Chapman called it "superb," Ward Morehouse praised its "gaiety, spontaneity, and originality," and George Freedley called it "the most intelligent and adult musical yet offered on the American stage."

"There were," Ronald Sanders wrote, "many clever ideas in the script, but they certainly were marred throughout by a peculiar kind of special pleading, as well as by an unwarranted intellectual pretentiousness. At that time and in years to come, Lerner had an occasional propensity for playing fantastic historical games with often questionable result. Cheryl Crawford, who concedes that the *Love Life* script had major shortcomings, notes also how it affected Weill's work. 'Because Kurt's score served the style of the writing,' she observes, 'it didn't have the warmth of his best ballads.' "

Maurice Abravanel said, "*Love Life* is to me the least successful of Alan's books. And not the best of Kurt's music, either."

Miles Kreuger is among the show's defenders. He said, "It was a brilliant work. I think, and so did Alan, that it was the best thing he had done for the stage. I think *Love Life*'s script is far and away the best thing Alan Jay Lerner ever wrote for the stage. It is totally original, and it has a remarkable vision of how to use musical theater as dramaturgy to make a philosophic point. Unfortunately, in 1948 when it opened, it was not the philosophic point American audiences wanted to hear. It was a harsh criticism of American values. We had just won the Second World War and we were very self-satisfied."

The show produced one hit song, *Here I'll Stay with You,* and another of modest charm, *Green-Up Time.* "*Green-Up Time* always made me laugh," Lerner said. "There was a minor strain in everything Kurt wrote. So I said, 'Let's write a really happy song about spring.' And he came back and played that, and there was a minor in it again. But I suppose in every joy there is a little sadness, so he may be right." (TT)

Love Life struggled along for seven months, finally closing after 252 performances.

I find the show, both the script and the score, very peculiar. There is some ungainly writing in it, both libretto and lyrics. *Here I'll Stay with You* could have been produced by any journeyman Tin Pan Alley lyricist. Another song includes the grammatical anomaly "He'll be part of me, I'll be part of he." Nothing justifies this solecism; if Lerner meant this and other lines to be sardonic, the humor is obscure: they come across as merely gauche. The score contains a duet called *I Remember It Well,* in which the protagonists recall an earlier time—and recall it differently. Lerner had a habit of returning to old ideas, and he would return to this one in *Gigi.* A character named Miss Ideal Man delivers this interesting line: "After all, when you find a man doesn't live up to your ideal, there's nothing to do but get rid of him and keep looking." Applied to women, and remembering Lerner's father's dictum that the woman is always wrong, it sounds like the formula of Lerner's life.

And of course the premise of the show is preposterous, that a hundred and fifty years ago the love life of a family was simple and pure and it has deteriorated with the Industrial Revolution. A hundred and fifty years ago the life of the average man was arduous and brutal, haunted by diseases that decimated the large families necessary for survival and weighted by cruel long hours of labor. Romantic love was hardly the norm of the common man. Indeed, the whole play makes it obvious that Lerner knew about as much about the common man as Cole Porter, and his occasional attempts to characterize the lower orders would always prove inept.

Whatever the show's virtues or shortcomings, it was indeed a precursor of much that was to come in the theater. At times the score sounds like a pre-echo of Stephen Sondheim's *Company,* which also deals with the detachment of contemporary life, though far more brilliantly than *Love Life.*

Love Life would be the first and last Lerner and Weill collaboration. Weill died of heart disease April 3, 1950, only fifty years old. Lerner said, "Shocking. Just terrible. And I knew something was going to happen to him. The day he had his heart attack, he received a letter from me. I was out in California. I said, 'Dear Kurt, I'm worried about you. Please come out and visit me.' And the letter arrived right after a heart attack.

"He was a melodist, of course, which will sustain any composer in any language. And the whole dying of German romanticism in the 1920s is embodied in Kurt, and all the work he did with Brecht and George Kaiser. And then he came over here. Kurt more than anyone, which very few people realize, was responsible for the change in the American musical theater with the accent on good books. Because that's what he did in Germany. He was the one who got George Kaiser, who was a first-rate playwright, into the musical theater. And when he came over here, he was the one who got Maxwell Anderson into the musical theater to write

Knickerbocker Holiday. He got Moss Hart into the musical theater to write *Lady in the Dark.* And it was out of that came *Oklahoma!* and then the whole change in musical theater. But Kurt did it, and I think we all owe him a debt, besides all the wonderful music he's given us." (TT)

Lerner and Fritz Loewe resolved the tensions in their relationship to write *Paint Your Wagon.* How and why is not known, although many of their acquaintances said that they always went back together because the results of their collaboration were so good. They kept a curtain over their relationship. Benjamin Welles said that Lerner was the dominant force in the team; Marion Bell said Fritz was the strength of it. Perhaps, in a sense, they are both right, and therein lay the cause of the clash.

Paint Your Wagon, which opened November 12, 1951, has a California gold rush setting. We shall have occasion to discuss it in more detail when we come to the movie version of it that Lerner eventually produced. Suffice it for now to say that it was the only show they would ever write with an American story, and the score, which sounds like a collage of old Western-movie scores and snippets of Stephen Foster, shows nothing so much as that Fritz Loewe was not an American. Excepting *They Call the Wind Maria,* its songs were undistinguished and are rarely heard today. Lerner said, "I didn't realize until many years later that practically every song in it is about loneliness." (TT) The show opened November 12, 1951, and closed after 289 performances.

MGM optioned *Paint Your Wagon* at that time, and Lerner wrote a screenplay for it. The first draft, a copy of which now reposes at the Institute of the American Musical, says on its title page "Screenplay and Lyrics by Alan Jay Lerner, additional music by Arthur Schwartz." The film was not made, and the screenplay bears almost no resemblance to the one Lerner later wrote for Paramount.

Love Life eventually attained a certain cult status because of its pioneering techniques, which opened the form of the musical outward. Yet *Paint Your Wagon,* which ran only thirty-seven performances longer, is remembered, and eventually became an expensive motion picture. Why? For one thing, a recording ban called by James Caesar Petrillo, the dictatorial ruler of the American Federation of Musicians, was under way at the time *Love Life* appeared, and so no original cast album was made. There was no touring company of the show and no rights were released for other productions; it faded into silence.

After *Paint Your Wagon,* Lerner and Loewe parted again. Fritz, estranged from Tina, went to Europe to gamble, and Alan went to Hollywood.

Composer Burton Lane, who would be Lerner's collaborator there, said categorically, "Fritz Loewe, whom I got to know and like, *despised* Alan." André Previn doubts this. Though they had their disputes, and separated several times, their friends tend to characterize the relationship as love-hate, and André added, "He was very different from Alan, but I think Alan really truly adored him. I heard Alan play great compliments to a great many song-writers, but he reserved the final encomium always for Fritz. He said he was the best songwriter he had ever known."

five

AN AMERICAN IN PARIS

Through Lillie Messinger, Lerner knew Louis B. Mayer, the head of MGM. Mayer introduced Lerner to Arthur Freed, himself a lyricist with a long list of credits, and now head of one of several production units assigned to making musicals at MGM. His was considered the best.

Lerner, like others, found Freed to be a shy man with an obtuse and involuted way of communicating with his associates. It seemed to take him forever to get to a point. In spite of this, or perhaps because of it, he was noted for a quiet prowess with the opposite sex. After the success of *Brigadoon*, Freed urged Lerner to spend a few weeks in California to see if he could find a film project to appeal to him. The money was good, and Lerner went west.

Freed was looking for an idea for a picture for Fred Astaire. He and Lerner discussed the days when Astaire's dancing partner was his sister, Adele. The conversation led to a decision to do a film about a famous brother and sister dance team performing in London at the time of a royal wedding. This would permit the use of colorful footage of pageantry and crowds shot in London during the marriage of then–Princess Elizabeth to Philip Mountbatten, Duke of Edinburgh.

Freed suggested that Lerner write the songs for the picture with Burton Lane, composer of the music for *Finian's Rainbow,* whom Lerner knew slightly. Thus began a long and often uncomfortable association. Physically, they were an improbable pairing: at six-foot-two-and-a-half, Burton Lane loomed more than eight inches over Lerner. Lane, a serious and even somewhat somber man, himself has a reputation for being difficult to work with. He is capable of great charm, but he is said to be grumpy. Certainly he is an extraordinary melodist and he deserved more success in musical theater than the one hit show he had, *Finian's Rainbow.*

One night while they were working on the picture, which eventually would be titled *Royal Wedding,* Lerner had a dream in which Fred Astaire danced up the wall of a room and across the ceiling. The idea may have derived from a subliminal memory of the Rodgers and Hart song *Dancing on the Ceiling.* Lerner proposed the idea, and the special effects people said it was feasible to execute it. The sequence was among the picture's few distinctions.

The film contains one of Lerner's loveliest lyrics, and one of Burton Lane's best melodies: *Too Late Now.* Lerner told Tony Thomas that they wrote it over the telephone. He also said that another song in the picture, *How Could You Believe Me When I Said I Love You When You Know I've Been a Liar All My Life,* is the longest title in ASCAP history. The idea came to Lerner in a car as they were driving to the studio. Lerner thought the film was altogether too charming, and they needed something to take that curse off it. Lane said, "Well, give me a title. Let's write something ricky-tick." Lerner immediately gave him that delightfully funny phrase. Lane began to hum a melody. Before they reached the studio, work on the song was well advanced.

Lane told me, "I was not happy with Alan's work on the picture, even his lyrics, with the exception of two numbers, *How Could You Believe Me When I Said I Love You When You Know I've Been a Liar All My Life,* which was a funny idea, and the ballad, *Too Late Now.* I thought I had some tunes that deserved better, including *Every Night at Seven,* which was the opening tune, and *I Left My Hat in Haiti,* which was contrived."

And it was slapdash. Lerner at one point rhymed "clearly" with "near me." It is the sort of breach one expects in rock lyrics but not in the work of someone of Lerner's stature. Since no one knew

the "rules" of lyric-writing better than Lerner, one can only assume that he didn't care, possibly because he was in the throes of
a new romance. Even the lyric for the song used in the ceiling-
dance sequence, *You're All the World to Me,* is mediocre; Lane's
melody, by contrast, is superb. It is what is known in the profession
as a laundry-list lyric, the kind that rattles off a list of comparisons, a you-are-this, you-are-that song. And that kind of song was
wrapped up, ribboned, and sent by Cole Porter and Oscar Hammerstein, respectively, in *You're the Top* and *All the Things You Are.*
The Lerner lyric in that sequence isn't anywhere near their level.

Lerner, as we have already noted, was prone to the re-use of
phrases he had invented and polished, such as his remark about his
failed shows: "If you were away for the weekend, you'd have missed
it." An interesting phrase occurs early in *Royal Wedding.* Shortly
after their arrival in London, Jane Powell says to Fred Astaire: "I
wonder what the princess is doing this morning?" Long afterward,
a variant on it will become a song in *Camelot.*

The Cinderella theme is implicit in *Royal Wedding.* Jane Powell
marries a lord, played by Peter Lawford, and thereby acquires a
title. Fred Astaire, the big star of musical theater, marries Sarah
Churchill, a publican's daughter, who thereby attains comfort and
status.

When, later, Lerner referred at all to *Royal Wedding,* it was to
praise Lane and Astaire and disparage his own part in it. As he put
it, "My contribution left me in such a state of cringe that I could
barely straighten up."

"I must agree with him," Burton Lane said. "It was Alan's first
picture, and I thought it was dull. But *An American in Paris* was
wonderful. It was a marvelous script with wonderful ideas in it."

The American love affair with France, and more specifically Paris,
goes back at least to the time of Jefferson and Franklin. French
support for the Revolution inspired an affection for France and
things French that has continued, despite periods of friction between the two countries. Oliver Wendell Holmes said that good
Americans when they die go to Paris. There have been countless
American songs about Paris (though no comparable body of French
songs about America), and American authors have endlessly
romanticized the city. In the 1920s, Paris experienced an inunda-
tion of talented expatriate Americans, some of them there to write,
or learn to write, such as Gertrude Stein, F. Scott Fitzgerald, Ernest

Hemingway, Ezra Pound, and Henry Miller, and some to study painting, among them a young man better known for another talent, George Gershwin.

Not long after World War II, Arthur Freed saw a *Life* magazine picture layout about American veterans studying in Paris on the GI Bill. It stuck in his mind. Freed was in the habit of spending Saturday nights at Ira Gershwin's house in Beverly Hills, playing poker or shooting pool. Late one night Freed said, "Ira, I've always wanted to make a picture about Paris. How about selling me the title *An American in Paris?*" The piece of course was not a song but an orchestral suite, one of five orchestral works George Gershwin completed before a brain tumor ended his remarkable and still-promising career in 1937. Ira controlled his estate.

"Yes, if you use all Gershwin music," Ira said.

Freed said, "I wouldn't use anything else; that's the object."

MGM paid Ira Gershwin $300,000 for the use of the title and songs, and another $50,000 as a consultant. Freed went about putting the project together. He considered both Fred Astaire and Gene Kelly for the lead role as an American studying painting in Paris. Since he wanted to use the Gershwin orchestral work as a ballet, Kelly was the more logical choice. His background was ballet, not tap dancing. Besides, his was a newer face, and Astaire, associated always with top-hat-and-white-tie roles and the prewar years—indeed he had considered retiring—would have been wrong for the part of a young ex-GI. Freed also wanted to use in the film the humorist and sometime actor Oscar Levant, a formidable pianist who was Gershwin's foremost disciple and champion. He planned to base the character Levant would play on the composer David Diamond, because, as he put it in later years, "Dave . . . always got scholarships and went to Europe but never had enough money to come back." So whoever was assigned the task of writing the picture, he would have to deal with these materials, fleshing out Arthur Freed's concept.

In *The Magic Factory* (Praeger, New York, 1973), an oral history of the making of *An American in Paris* compiled by Donald Knox from the collective memories of the principals in the project, Freed said that he remembered that Gershwin had studied art in Paris. "That," he said, "made the character that Kelly would play a little bit of Gershwin." He continued:

"Now was the time to find a writer for the project. I talked to Vincente Minnelli about it and mentioned Alan Jay Lerner. Vincente was crazy about the idea, so I tackled Alan. I didn't think I'd get to him, because Alan likes to write the songs. But, when I told him the idea and the characters, he said, 'I'd love to do it . . .' "

Lerner thought that it was in the late spring of 1949 that Freed proposed the project to him. Alan went back east, then returned to California in September and began working on the script.

Alan, now thirty, was courting Nancy Olson, a promising twenty-two-year-old actress. She had made three movies, all in starring roles, though none of them had yet been released. Nancy Olson was born July 14, 1928, in Milwaukee, Wisconsin, the daughter of Dr. Henry J. Olson, a well-to-do physician, and grew up there. She had her first stage experience reading an essay she had written for an all-state oratorical contest, telling children how to bring up their parents and calling for a teenage bill of rights. It won her the prize. Then she appeared in a play at Wauwatosa High School, which apparently kindled an ambition to act. After high school, according to an interview she did with Sidney Fields in 1957, she spent "a year at the University of Wisconsin, where by her own description she was 'the country club kid of the Middle West,' achieving a record of thirty-two dates in one month." She also majored in dramatics, and for a time attended the respected drama school of Northwestern University.

Her family moved to Los Angeles, when her father became a professor of obstetrics and gynecology at the University of Southern California in Los Angeles. Nancy moved to UCLA, to major in radio acting. While she was in a student play there, she was noticed by a talent scout from Paramount. The studio signed her to a contract, put her on salary, and forgot her. She continued at UCLA for several months until she was cast in a loan-out from Paramount to play the lead opposite Randolph Scott in *Canadian Pacific*, and then played an even bigger role in *Sunset Boulevard*. The picture, written by Charles Brackett and directed by Billy Wilder, was a dark exposé of Hollywood.

One of the pillars of the studio system was typecasting, and Nancy Olson always played nice girls. She had a fetching catch in her voice, a vulnerable sound, soft and breathy, and Paramount cast her as the Nice Girl who loves William Holden and tries to draw him back from the Fate Worse than Death as the kept young lover of the harpy ex-queen of the movies played by Gloria Swanson. The picture was grim, gritty, moody, and ground-breaking for its dark sardonic realism. It had an enormous impact, and so, in the role of Nice Girl Betty Shaffer, in demure clothes, did Olson.

Benjamin Welles said, "Nancy was rather clean-cut, and Scandinavian, a very nice milk-fed American girl." Columnist Sidney Skolsky described her: "She is five-feet-six inches tall, weighs 120 pounds, has honey-blonde hair and blue eyes. She has high Scandinavian cheekbones, fair skin, small features." She rapidly become known as "wholesome Olson." In his column of March 20, 1956, Walter Winchell wrote: "Mike [*Hollywood Reporter*] Connelly's skewp [*sic*]: That actress Nancy Olson's panties are initialed NO."

After *Sunset Boulevard,* Olson was cast opposite Bing Crosby in *Mr. Music.* All three films were on the shelf, unreleased, when, she said, she met Lerner through friends who, she told Sidney Fields in 1957, "were trying to fill his loneliness while he was in Hollywood, writing *An American in Paris.* The friends went down the list and when they reached Nancy's name, they said, 'You won't like her. She's dull and too straitlaced.' Alan looked at her picture and said: 'I want to meet this dull girl.' "

"When they invited me to their house," Nancy told Fields, "I said, 'Who's Alan Lerner?' They told me he had written *Brigadoon,* and I thought it was going to be a big party for this celebrity. It was only for the two of us." She said that ten days after they met, they were engaged.

Burton Lane said, however, that it was during the work on *Royal Wedding* that Lerner met Olson. Lane said, "Alan was a very complicated fellow. Every time I would start to work with him, he was divorcing one wife and marrying the next one.

"You get very close to somebody very quickly when you're working with them. It's like a father-confessor relationship. Alan was that kind of fellow, looking for someone he could talk to.

"One day he came to my house and said, 'I met the most wonderful woman last night.'

"I said, 'What?' It was Nancy Olson.

"I said to him in the friendliest way, 'Alan, you've been married twice already and getting a divorce. Take it easy.' "

Lerner was still married to Marion Bell, who said with a small, tolerant chuckle, "Alan was like that. If he liked somebody, he didn't think about whether he was married or not. It didn't occur to him."

Lerner began making regular trips to Nevada to establish residence there so that he could divorce Marion Bell. Benjamin Welles remembered, "He was flying back and forth from Hollywood to Reno. Every night he would fly over, and check into his hotel, and then come back the next day, so he could build up the six weeks' residence." Burton Lane said Lerner made the trip only three times a week, and to Las Vegas.

Marion Bell told me, "Alan and I were very good friends. He came to me and told me that he wanted to marry Nancy Olson. So I stepped aside. He never got any objection from me.

"I was just interested in not taking anything from Alan. When we were divorced he deposited six thousand dollars in the bank for me. Otherwise I didn't take anything from Alan." Bell said that when, some time after their divorce, she needed gynecological surgery to enable her to have a child, Alan paid for it.

And of all Lerner's wives, she seems the most fragile: a fey, delicate, gentle, self-effacing creature who loved him enough to give him up if that would bring him happiness. Interestingly, she and Ruth Boyd had become friends and remained so. "I thought the world of Marion," Ruth told me.

It was through Nancy Olson that Lerner formed one of the longest business associations and closest friendships of his life.

Stone (Bud) Widney was working toward a master's degree at U.C.L.A. He had begun as a philosophy major and then switched to the theater department. At the time he was writing a thesis on the Mexican Americans. Widney had directed a student musical in which Olson had appeared.

"Alan was writing *Paint Your Wagon,*" Widney remembered. "He had changed the leading character from a Swede to a Mexican and didn't know much about Mexicans, so Nancy suggested that Alan talk with me, because that's what I was studying at the time. I was doing it for the film department but the sociology department sat in on it. I had become very familiar with the mentality and the psychology of the Mexican in America in the struggle with the people who took his land from him. Alan wanted to know more about that and she arranged a meeting and the two of us started talking and we just continued talking for thirty years.

"It would have been 1949. He was dating Nancy as he was getting a divorce from Marion. It was the combination of events, the fact that I had done a musical for her, knew the field and also knew about Mexicans. That's how we met."

Born in 1926 in Los Angeles, he was of a family prominent in the city's history. Indeed his grandfather, Judge Robert M. Widney, had assembled a group of people who founded the University of Southern California and, together with his brother, Joseph P. Widney, had played a major role in establishing the city as a terminus of the Southern Pacific Railroad and in developing the harbor at Long Beach.

After graduation from U.C.L.A., Bud Widney would join the faculty of the U.C.L.A. film department, where he remained for a year. Then Lerner would ask him to come east and work as his production assistant, in which capacity Widney continued until Lerner's death.

"What attracted Alan," Widney said in May 1990, "was not that I had done a musical or that I had a knowledge of the Mexican-Americans. What attracted Alan was that I was a philosophy major and he wanted somebody he could talk to and bounce ideas off, somebody who would listen to him and help develop those ideas."

Given the materials he had to work with, Lerner struggled to find an idea for *An American in Paris* for what seemed like a long time. He told Donald Knox: "When I say 'a long time,' I am speaking of California, where the days go slowly and the weeks go fast, especially for one who does not live there. . . .

"When you are really concentrating on something, I think that you have another mind working. Time after time, people go to sleep and just wake up with an idea. Just the night before, that person would be faced with a problem that he didn't think he would ever be able to solve. That happened to me here, for finally I had one idea. It must have been some time in November when I finally got some notion of what I was going to do. And that was that a kept man falls in love with a kept woman. . . . Arthur cautioned me that the girl could not be kept per se, so with this idea I began to write, and by Christmas I had the first act completed."

We note here that though motion pictures are not divided into acts, Lerner continued to think in stage terms. But this is hardly the most significant element in that paragraph of reflection. It is possible that even Lerner was not aware of what he revealed. Whatever the case, he gives us here the first inkling of a theme that would recur in his work: that of the courtesan. As the script to *An American in Paris* evolved, the heroine works in a perfume shop. She is engaged to marry a music hall star, played by Georges Guetary, who has protected and kept her during the war after the death of her father, killed in the Resistance. Even in its final form, and with the girl wearing the mask of a respectable job, we sense that she is somehow the property of Guetary. The painter played by Gene Kelly is more obviously kept—by Nina Foch, the rich American who buys his pictures, sets him up in a studio, and keeps him as a sort of house pet.

Lerner's opening scene introduced the main characters, to be played by Kelly, Levant, Leslie Caron, and Guetary. Lerner had wanted not Guetary, who was unknown in America, but Maurice Chevalier as the music hall star. Chevalier was unavailable. Yves Montand was considered for the part, but rumors reached the studio that his politics were of the left. Apparently no one was bothered that Chevalier had been accused of being a collaborator in entertaining the Germans. Caron told Knox:

"I remember once Louis B. Mayer making a speech on the steps of the Thalberg Building, and we were all down below on the street. It was the weirdest scene. He was very short, so he needed a few steps to put himself on the same level as everyone else. This was at the beginning of the McCarthy era, so the whole studio was asked to come and listen to Mr. Mayer's speech on how we had to be good Americans."

Lerner's reaction to the speech—it is unlikely that he was unaware of it—and to the veto of Montand have not been recorded, but one can imagine what it was.

six

OSCAR
NIGHT

teve Allen defined radio as theater of the mind (and television as "theater of the mindless"). The form of direct address that Lerner used to introduce his characters in *An American in Paris* would have been unremarkable in a radio drama by Norman Corwin or Arch Oboler. But this violation of the proscenium, in which the characters address us directly, this acknowledgment that the audience exists and is observing the action, which would be dangerous in a play, is even more so in motion pictures, essentially a realistic medium.

One of the purposes of this opening scene was to set the style of the piece, for, as Lerner quoted Thornton Wilder, "More plays fail because of a breach in style than for any other reason."

Lerner established in the opening sequence that the picture is fantasy, not reality. He accomplished this by a device that may have derived from his experience in writing radio drama. The camera shows the *quartier* in which much of the story is set. Gene Kelly is heard, voice over, directly addressing the audience and telling us his name is Jerry Mulligan and he's an ex-GI and a painter who lives here. Then we see him, and he is established. Then Oscar Levant's voice is heard, telling you that his name is Adam Cook, and he is a pianist, and we see him. Similarly Georges Guetary introduces himself as Henri Barrelle, and he too comes into view.

Lerner took the risk. Vincente Minnelli staged the film's opening sequence beautifully, and it works—a clever bit of writing that sets the tone of the picture as a modern fairy tale.

"As I continued to write," Lerner told Donald Knox, "I indicated generally certain songs that I thought might work. I kept giving the work to Vincente and Gene, and they seemed to feel that I was on the right track. The script was developed so that a choice of numbers could flow from it. For example, with just a small change in the screenplay, I could have my choice of *Our Love Is Here to Stay* or *Love Walked In.* They could have the choice of either song and not affect the characters in any way. As I wrote, I automatically started thinking that at certain places I had to have music. My instinct tells me that it is right. Then I begin to think of the music, and it should all balance because the whole technique of writing a musical is to try to make the emotional requirements be such that they demand the kind of music that will balance the screenplay. If you have a romantic moment with a slow ballad, you cannot have another one right away. The whole idea is to make the story unfold so that right after that moment somebody will be feeling something that will bring in a gayer song. Also, you must balance the score from the standpoint of solos, duets, choral numbers, large numbers, small numbers, and so forth.

"I got about forty pages done before Christmas, and then I went home for the holidays. At that time, I had no idea how that story was going to end. I came back to Hollywood and went through January and February without figuring out how I was going to end it. Meanwhile, Frederick Loewe had come back, and we began to think about another musical. Also, I was going to be married in March and go on a honeymoon, and still I had not gotten an idea about how I was going to end the story. The night before my wedding, I sat down at eight in the evening and wrote sixty pages. Somehow I ended it and I never changed anything. That is what is so strange about it. The answer to why I wrote it then is that I had to." If Lerner's memory was correct, the script was completed on the evening of March 18. He and Nancy Olson were married March 19, 1950.

He turned in his work and left on his honeymoon. After that he made only one minor change before shooting began. Vincente Minnelli called him in New York and said, "We need one speech before the big ballet begins."

"I wrote the speech and mailed it in," Lerner said. "As far as I can remember, that was the only rewriting that I did. Small adjustments may have been made, but that was just a matter of editing."

Minnelli said, "Alan is marvelous at devising things like *An American in Paris.* The whole scheme he had for the book he got pretty much the first time through. It only needed the changing of certain things going in and out of numbers. . . .

"Alan Lerner completed the script, and I thought it solved the problem marvelously. The problem was: how do you make a picture using all of Gershwin's songs and finish with a ballet? That's quite a problem. But he came in with a very fresh idea and a wonderful set of characters, and it worked just right."

For the part of the girl in the story, Freed and Gene Kelly decided on a seventeen-year-old dancer named Leslie Caron, the child of a French father and an American mother of French descent who had herself been a dancer. Kelly had seen her two years earlier when she was a premiere dancer with the Ballet des Champs-Elysees, playing the small role of the sphinx in a ballet called *Oedipus and the Sphinx.* Kelly had shown some pictures of the girl to Freed, who asked him to fly to Paris and make a screen test with her. Kelly was adamant that the part should be played by a French girl, not an American girl affecting a French accent.

Caron made the test and forgot it. She was astounded when, two weeks later, she was asked to be in Hollywood in three days. She recalled that, "as I always do in the case of complete panic, I started making clothes for myself. That was the best thing I could think of doing. I didn't read the papers, so I didn't know much of MGM, but all the same, America and a film, so I was quite excited. I made myself a dress, a blue dress."

Caron had been anemic in childhood, and suffered—as did almost all the French—from food deprivation during and after the war. For all the suppleness of her dancing, she was in fragile health. Her arrival in America produced something bordering on shock. She said:

"I think I arrived in L.A. on Saturday morning, June 3, 1950, and my new agent . . . waited for me at the airport with some photographers and some studio executives. From the airport, a limousine took my mother and me to a hotel, the Beverly Wilshire, and the agent advanced us . . . about five hundred dollars and told us he would come and pick us up for dinner. Anyway, the next thing I knew was the dinner, at LaRue, and there was so much meat on my plate. I ordered like I would in France, pâté to begin with, then a steak, a vegetable, and a salad.

"When it came, the portions were like for four people. I couldn't believe such wealth. . . . After the pâté, I already had enough to eat. I couldn't bear to leave the rest, so my agent had to get a doggy bag."

Caron and her mother were horrified at the cost of their room, and promptly moved into a cheap hotel in Culver City.

"The next thing that happened is Gene Kelly invited us for the afternoon on Sunday. We arrived at his house and everybody was terribly nice. There were all sorts of movie people, and it was very free and very casual, which was very new for us. I was used to the formality of French houses, which is almost like in Spain, where someone is only admitted to the home after long knowledge of the family. For a long, long time, I couldn't get used to this kind of informality.

"Then, on Monday, I met Arthur Freed and Vincente Minnelli and Alan Jay Lerner in Arthur's office, and they were terribly nice. I was immediately conquered by them."

The character Gene Kelly plays in the film is a lot like Kelly in reality. It seems likely that Lerner wrote him that way: he had a remarkable flair for tailoring parts to his performers, and he would repeat the trick in tailoring the role of Professor Henry Higgins to Rex Harrison. He was right to make the young painter in *An American in Paris* Irish. Kelly has a cocky Irish grin and a half-teasing charm with which, more than thirty years after the film was made, he could make women of all ages melt. He is a literate and cultivated man who speaks fluent French with a slight echo of Italian accent, a hint that he spoke Italian before he learned French, which he did in the Italian neighborhood of Pittsburgh where he grew up. The thumbprint of his cosmopolitan qualities are all over *An American in Paris*, along with Minnelli's stunning sense of the visual. And, though she was only seventeen, Caron was well aware of these qualities in the man who had lifted her from the comparative obscurity of her life as a dancer in Paris to what would soon prove to be movie stardom in Hollywood.

The shooting of Lerner's opening scene led to a funny moment that Caron always remembered, along with Kelly's unfailing solicitude toward her and his concern for her anemia, which left her without energy and frequently in depression. He would arrange for her to take rests, even entire days off, whenever possible in the grueling rehearsal schedule they faced together.

Lerner said, "I wrote into the script the basic idea that Guetary at this point describes Leslie to Oscar. It was Vincente's idea, not mine, that in describing her, Guetary and Levant misunderstood each other. But in terms of the script, I indicated that Leslie should be introduced in a dance at this point, and left it open for Minnelli to figure out how precisely to do it.

"I wrote that Guetary starts to talk about her and that there was going to be a mirror, and you would see her. She was a dancer. It was important, therefore, to show her dancing before we showed her doing anything else. Stylistically, that was very important. The audience had to accept her as a dancer. We weren't worried about people like Gene Kelly as a dancer, because nobody is surprised when he dances. But, if there is some character that you have never seen, and all of a sudden you see that person dance, it may shock you. . . . With Leslie Caron, who was a beautiful dancer, I felt that it was important that you see her dance before you know anything more about her."

Vincente Minnelli suggested that *Embraceable You* would be a good song to use at that point. And he had the idea of showing the girl in different period settings. "It sounds terribly simple," Kelly said, "but it was a brilliant idea, the kind that choreographers can really use."

It is the mark of Kelly's choreography that he always uses other dancers to their best advantage, even in scenes in which he is the dance partner, and in bringing Lerner's mirror scene to life, he devised some stunning and very sensual choreography for Caron. She remembered:

"That sequence of introduction numbers was particularly hard for me to do. I was frightened to death—little me, all by myself on this big stage with all those men. . . . Gene was really the director for those things. He'd say where to place the camera, which was the best angle and the best cuts, and so on.

"When we got down to actually shooting . . . I did it one day in bed, one day shooting, one day in bed, one day shooting. It was about like that. Those days of shooting were so horrendous. You know, in the legitimate stage you practiced one hour and then you danced on the stage what amounts to ten or twenty minutes at the most. You don't dance all the time in a ballet. When I was filming, however, I danced for practically eight hours. Those days were just exhausting.

"Now, one of the numbers I liked was the modern dance with the chair, what they called the 'sexy number.' I remember it was a blues, sort of heavy, nearly bump and grind, and that to me was great fun. It was all American jazz, and I thought it was terrific."

Problems derived from the fact that Caron, in a dark blue dress with a panelled skirt that is double split in front, spread her superb legs and slips the chair into her crotch, hardly a subtle symbol.

"We did this number once," Caron remembered, "and then I started hearing rumbles about it. It was shocking, it was going to be censored. There was trouble. So onto the set came the censor, a very sexily dressed female censor, and she was shown the number.

"Then I remember the whole performance that went on: Gene practically seducing her on the set and she being thrilled with all the attention. Eventually, she decided, if we trimmed it a bit here and a bit there it would be all right. So we reshot it and made it a little less provocative.

"But the appearance of this censor lady was just the wildest thing. Everybody was sort of giggling in corners, and Gene was doing his whole number with her It was very funny."

It is worth noting that in this montage introducing the girl, whose name is Lise, Lerner has Guetary say that she could dance all night. Further, the magnificent sequence in which Jerry Mulligan and Lise fall in love as they dance to *Our Love Is Here to Stay* on the Quai de la Tournelle, at the rear of Notre Dame, ends when she asks with alarm what time it is. He tells her it is eleven o'clock. And she turns and runs back to her reality in an echo of the Cinderella myth that underlies *My Fair Lady*.

That scene is one of the most romantic ever put on film, as Kelly—both as choreographer and dancer—breathes life into Lerner's script. The body language he imposes on himself and Caron, particularly when she tries to flee from him and he seizes her hand and almost shyly draws her back, and when they walk in graceful slow unison toward the camera as she rests her head on his shoulder, accumulates into one of the most exquisitely lyrical portrayals of the timidity and vulnerability and gentleness of deep sexual encounter in the whole history of art.

The portrait of the girl suggests that at that time—this would change—no one was more susceptible to the image of The French

Girl than Lerner himself: she is all the things that American men tended, particularly in those early postwar years, to think of the French female as being—the embodiment of Marianne, as the French call the symbol of their national identity. Caron's memories of the period indicate that as young as she was, she was already a typically French female in her thrift (always looking for a cheaper place to live), her skepticism, her horror at American excess, and her realistic appraisal of the world and the people around her. Her recollection of columnist Hedda Hopper is an example:

"One day, something happened which is all part of Hollywood's history. Hedda Hopper came on the set, and it was like Queen Elizabeth was coming. There were whispers, 'Hedda Hopper is coming. Where are we going to sit her? We don't tell her this. We don't show her this. We're going to show her this. We're going to do this scene for her and tell her this.' It was a great hullabaloo. So this extraordinary creature arrives, with an umbrella for a hat. There was more hat than you needed to shade an elephant. It was an enormous thing with fringes, and there were jewels and there was lipstick and shining glitter and scent, and she had rings and varnish and so forth, and they sat her in the director's chair, and then I was brought to her. You know, I was still a convent girl, and I was still used to curtsying to people, especially to elderly ladies, and I curtsied to her. That was my education, but everybody thought it was so quaint—this quiet little girl who curtsied. So there was the whole afternoon that Hedda Hopper came and gave her blessing. Everyone flirted with her and brought her coffee, I mean it was a big deal. Once you were big enough to tell her to go to hell, she was perfectly all right. You could then be very sharp with her and tell her, 'Oh, Hedda, get off it; that's none of your business.' But, for beginners, she was a terrifying bird of some other plumage."

Curiously, the big ballet to the music of Gershwin's tone poem that gave the picture its title almost was omitted from the picture. The concept was to stage it in sets resembling the work of painters the Jerry Mulligan character supposedly admires, Rousseau, Monet, Renoir, Van Gogh, Toulouse-Lautrec, Utrillo, and Dufy among them. This presented enormous challenges to Preston Ames, the art director, and Keogh Gleason, the set designer, and their workers. The problem was compounded by the fact that Vincente Minnelli, who had a commitment to direct another film at the time, would not be there to complete the picture. That duty would devolve on Gene Kelly, who had great respect for Minnelli's eye and taste and who already had the responsibilities of choreographer and dancer. Caron would be in much of the ballet, but Kelly had to be in all of it.

The cost of the sequence shocked the studio heads. Dore Schary, then executive vice-president in charge of production, recalled:

"The budget . . . was very high for a musical at the time. . . . We began to hear from New York: 'Expensive picture. Ballet? Whew! Half a million dollars for one number. . . . Dore, it can't sell.' Nick Schenck, president of Lowes, Inc., our parent company, had Joe Vogel in charge of sales. He was a Schenck man, and he and I had had many disagreements before and after that. He just said, 'Dore, you're making a terrible error. Nobody's going to see it; we'll cut it out of the picture.'

"I said, 'No, you won't cut this out, because we might as well junk the picture, and we're not going to do that.' "

Lerner told Knox, "At that time, the idea of spending $500,000 on a ballet was a very adventurous decision, to say the least. In terms of this ballet, Mayer played a key role in making the decision to keep the ballet in no matter what the cost. As a matter of fact, that decision was probably one of the last major picture-making decisions he was to make. I remember that Louis B. Mayer left the studio some time before *An American in Paris* was previewed. All during the time of the making of the picture, there was a lot of animosity between Mr. Mayer and Dore Schary, a lot of infighting. It had to do with Dore working more closely with the New York office. I never really understood all of what was happening, nor did I care to get involved. Anyway, I remember very clearly the day that Arthur Freed went up and discussed the whole thing with Mr. Mayer. Freed then came right down and told me that it would be all right. Louis B. Mayer had okayed the money for the ballet."

Lerner was as proud of *An American in Paris* as he was ashamed of *Royal Wedding.* He said: "When I came back to California, I saw the rough cut of *Royal Wedding* the same day I saw a rough cut of *An American in Paris.* . . . Well, when I saw *Royal Wedding* I was ready to commit suicide. I realized what an amateur I was as far as that film was concerned. But, when I saw *An American in Paris,* I turned to my friend Lillie Messinger and said, 'It's going to win the Academy Award.' I told her that it was the best musical that I had ever seen."

But Lerner was to take some lumps for the film. Arthur

Freed said, "The reviews were pretty good, but the critics didn't like the story line. They said it was weak. Myself, I think it was the right story line for the Gershwin music." *Newsweek* on October 8, 1951, said, "On the debit side is a silly story by Alan Jay Lerner . . ." Bosley Crowther wrote in the *New York Times*, "Mr. Kelly's the one who pulls the faint thread of Alan Jay Lerner's peach-fuzz script into some sort of pattern of coherence and keeps it from snapping in a hundred pieces and blowing away." *The New Yorker* said, "Never too tightly confined by its slender story, [it] skips from love in the moonlight to handsome ballets with the greatest of ease."

Lerner told Knox, "The criticism that I remember was about the sentimentality of it. There has always been the kind of critic that views the musical as being the intellectual brothel. They can go and see the girls and the pretty legs; they don't want to be bothered by the story. They don't want to be asked to feel anything. They want to go and get their jollies. Every time you write a film or a play, you get two hundred reviews. After a while, you get immune to them. . . . But I would rather not have bad reviews, thank you very much."

Lerner had the last laugh. He was one of the many participants in the vast and complicated enterprise by which *An American in Paris* was to receive Academy Award nominations. He did not expect to win, because no screenplay for a musical ever had won.

He could not attend the award ceremonies. He was called back to New York.

Lerner's father had lived with cancer for seventeen years, and fought it all the way, surviving interminable surgeries at Memorial Hospital in New York. Eventually his tongue had to be removed, an ironic fate for a man who loved language and used it with wit and style. Thenceforth he communicated on a note pad, yet never lost his sense of laughter, nor his taste for the company of women.

Burton Lane remembers seeing him once in a theater, well before he knew Alan. "He practically had no face left: it was cut away. It was all covered, in a mask. Apparently he broke the record for the number of operations. He was with a woman he was writing notes to. That was Alan's father."

Through the writer Damon Runyon, a patient in an adjacent room, Joseph Lerner met Cardinal Spellman, with whom he became close friends. Spellman used to visit him, according to Alan, at least once a week. Alan eventually asked him what he, a Jew, had in common with the Catholic cardinal. The elder Lerner smiled and immediately wrote on his pad: "We have a great deal in common. We're both in the chain-store business."

Even facing death, Joseph Lerner never wavered in his atheism. A few days before the Academy Award ceremonies that year, Alan's brother Bob visited their father in the hospital. Joseph Lerner wrote on his note pad:

"What religion are your children?"

Bob Lerner said, "I don't know. Whatever church is on the corner I'll send them to."

Joseph Lerner nodded and wrote: "It's all a lot of apple sauce."

He was facing yet another bout of surgery. When he signed the official form permitting the operation, he read: "Number of operations: 49." He wrote beneath it, "When it gets to fifty, sell."

Alan flew back to New York to be near him during the operation, after which Joseph Lerner was returned to his room under heavy sedation. He was not expected to regain consciousness before morning.

Alan went home to listen alone—new wife Nancy was in California—to the Academy Award ceremonies on the radio, which went on the air at 11:00 P.M. New York time. He sat on the floor, leaning against a sofa, holding a cup of coffee in his hand.

An American in Paris was sweeping the awards. Preston Ames won for art direction, Johnny Green and Saul Chaplin for art direction, and Alfred Gilks and John Alton for cinematography. Charles Brackett announced, "An honorary Academy Award is given to Gene Kelly for his extreme versatility as an actor, singer, director, and dancer but specifically for his brilliant achievement in the art of choreography on film." Finally the picture was named best film of the year and the award presented to Arthur Freed, who also picked up an Irving Thalberg award as the best producer of the year. It was the first time a producer of musicals had ever received it.

In New York, Alan Lerner heard the voice of Clare Boothe Luce reading a list of five movies, all but one of which is now virtually forgotten: "The last category is 'story and screenplay.' The writers of the following took blank sheets of paper, their own experience or some historical event, and transformed those blank pages into the text of a finished picture. The nominees are *An American in Paris*, Metro-Goldwyn-Mayer, story and screenplay by Alan Jay Lerner; *The Big Carnival*, Paramount . . .; *David and Bathsheba*,

20th Century–Fox . . .; *Go for Broke,* Metro-Goldwyn-Mayer . . .; *The Well,* Harry M. Popkin, United Artists. The envelope, please.

"The winner is Alan Jay Lerner for *An American in Paris.*"

Lerner exploded, flinging up his hands and bouncing his coffee cup off the ceiling. Then he heard his wife's voice saying "On behalf of my husband, I want to thank all of you, and congratulations, darling."

Lerner went immediately to Memorial Hospital. He asked his father's nurse to tell Joseph Lerner, if he should awaken, the news. She said, "Oh, he knows."

"How?" Alan asked.

She said, "Well, at five minutes to eleven he came out of his coma, reached over, and turned on the radio." After hearing of Alan's victory he turned it off again and went back into the coma.

The summer after *An American in Paris* was released, Gene Kelly and Arthur Freed were in Paris on vacation. They arranged for Raoul Dufy to see the film in a screening room of the MGM Paris office. They were well aware that the design of the fountain in Place de la Concorde in the ballet sequence was based on Dufy's style, though Dufy had never painted that scene.

Kelly recalled, "Dufy arrived on time and was wheeled into the room by his nurse, for he was very old. The four of us—Dufy, his nurse, Arthur, and I—watched the picture. Now, Arthur and I were literally sweating with fear. After all, here we were, showing one of the great painters of the world our treatment of his work. Well, he just chortled. He was so pleased. After the house lights went up, he asked if we would show him the ballet again, which we joyously did. He thought we had all done a wonderful job."

Viewed today, *An American in Paris* is as fresh as it was at the time of its release. Gene Kelly thinks that his next important musical, *Singin' in the Rain,* has stood the test of time somewhat better than *An American in Paris,* but they are both brilliant movies. It is hard to see why anyone faulted Lerner's script: it is slight and slender because it had to be, a structure to support the music, which told most of its story. To imagine telling the story through music and leaving the air and space in which the rest of the collaborators on the project could do their work was a remarkable achievement. The script is notable for its grace and, when it is called for, wit.

It is something else: it is America's ultimate love letter to France.

Not long after Lerner won the Academy Award, he was wheeling his father's bed into an elevator on the way to yet another encounter with the surgeons. Joseph Lerner wrote on his pad:

"I suppose you're wondering why I want to live." Alan nodded a melancholy agreement. His father wrote an answer that he pushed into Alan's hand. After delivering him to the operating theater, Alan returned to his father's room and only then thought of reading the note. It read: "Because I want to see what happens to you."

His wish would be denied. A month after Joseph Lerner died, Alan Jay Lerner, now thirty-four, and Fritz Loewe began writing *My Fair Lady.*

seven

PASCAL AND PYGMALION

*I*t is not known how Gabriel Pascal, a penurious Ruma-nian émigré who claimed to be Hungarian, talked George Bernard Shaw into assigning him the movie rights to several of his plays. Pascal had almost no experience in or knowledge of the movie industry. Shaw was hostile to the very idea of adapting his plays to film, and efforts by figures as important in the movie world as Alexander Korda had failed to persuade the playwright that they would be faithful to his work.

Shaw was always mindful of money. One of the legends of show business holds that Samuel Goldwyn tried to get the rights to a play, assuring Shaw it would be treated as a work of art, to which Shaw is alleged to have said, "Well, that is the difference between us. You are interested in art and I am interested in money." The story may be apocryphal.

Unabashed flattery figures in most of the stories of how Pascal talked Shaw out of the movie rights to *Major Barbara.* The version that Alan Jay Lerner liked is this:

A man rang the doorbell of Shaw's cottage in Ayot St. Lawrence. When Shaw's maid answered, the man said he was here to see Mr. Shaw. The maid said, "Who sent you?"

"Fate sent me," said the man. Shaw heard this and came to the door.

"Who are you?" he inquired.

"I am Gabriel Pascal. I am motion picture producer and I wish to bring your works of genius to screen."

"How much money do you have?" said Shaw.

"Twelve shillings," Pascal said, removing them from his pocket.

"Come in," said Shaw. "You're the first honest film producer I have met."

When Pascal left that day, the story has it, he carried with him a paper assigning him the motion picture rights to several Shaw plays, which he converted to films: *Pygmalion* with Leslie Howard as Professor Henry Higgins and Wendy Hiller as Eliza Doolittle, *Major Barbara,* with Rex Harrison and with Wendy Hiller in the title role, and *Androcles and the Lion. Pygmalion* and *Major Barbara* were made in England; *Androcles* in Hollywood. It was during the making of *Androcles* that Pascal first approached Lerner.

In Hollywood in early 1952, while he was working on the screenplay for *Brigadoon,* Lerner got a phone call from Pascal, whom he had never met. Pascal asked Lerner to have lunch with him. Two days later Lerner met a rotund man with a shrill voice and "an accent that defied any known place of national origin" and without definite or indefinite articles.

He ordered spaghetti for himself and Lerner. He poured the contents of raw eggs over the plates and began:

"I want to make musical of *Pygmalion.* I want you to write music."

Lerner explained that he was a librettist and lyricist, not a composer. "Who writes music?" Pascal asked.

"The composer—Fritz Loewe."

"Good," Pascal said. "We will meet again and you will bring man who writes music."

Lerner told him that Loewe was in New York.

"Good. You will tell him to come out here."

Pascal devoted the rest of the lunch to a discussion of Shaw's sex life, which he said was nonexistent, and Mahatma Gandhi's, which he said was extensive. Then they left the restaurant and ordered their cars. What happened next left Lerner, the parking attendants, and other departing diners silent and wide-eyed with amazement.

Without pausing in the conversation, Pascal opened his fly, took out the contents, relieved himself, zipped up his pants, and without so much as a good-bye got into his car and drove away.

About this time, Lerner's new wife did an interview for Irene Thirer's *Screen Views* column, published January 23, 1952, in the *New York Post.*

"If you're going to be an actress, and I always aimed for it," Nancy Olson said, "you're bound to keep on learning until you retire or die. It's pretty difficult to retire, because you're never quite satisfied. It's tempting when you don't have to be a breadwinner." Thirer noted that Olson was wearing a seven-karat diamond and a mink coat, adding "doubtless she has more gems and furs at home." She quotes Nancy as saying "I've taken time out to have a baby, and now I'm ready to resume [work]."

Olson described her daughter, Liza, three months old, as looking "just like the baby in the food ads. Her cheeks are so plump they hang over. Her eyes are huge, her mouth is small. And already she weighs sixteen pounds.

"She's a lovely, sweet baby," Olson said, "and I realize when I go back to Paramount, I'll have much less time for her. But movies are fun, and especially when one can be independent. Of course, Paramount has the right to throw in an occasional role which doesn't please me particularly, to counterbalance all the good roles I've had."

Lerner and Loewe at this point had no next project in mind, either. With the filming of *Brigadoon* under way, they would be looking for one, and Fritz was due in California shortly to discuss it. Because of Loewe's talent for characterizing locales and past historical periods, Lerner thought *Pygmalion* would be an ideal project. As soon as Fritz arrived, Lerner contacted Pascal, and the three men had lunch several times at the gloomy neo-Spanish house Pascal had rented in Westwood. Pascal, exercising his gift for unctuous flattery, told the two men that only they could fulfill his dream of a musical version of *Pygmalion;* they didn't bother to tell him they knew he had already approached Rodgers and Hammerstein, Howard Dietz and Arthur Schwartz, Cole Porter, and E. Y. Harburg and Fred Saidy, all of whom had turned the project down as fraught with insoluble book problems. They told Pascal they would consider the project and agreed to meet him in New York.

Lerner remarked to Tony Thomas, "The number of people who had tried to do *Pygmalion* reads like a roster of the theater. After we had it and abandoned it, Frank Loesser had it for a while. Moss Hart had it for a while."

For the record it should be noted that Harry Warren, one of the great intuitive melodists in American music, always insisted that Lerner first approached him to do the show. When, later, he reminded Lerner of this, he said, he found that Lerner simply had forgotten about it. With all the principals dead, there is no way to verify the story, but it is widely known.

Rodgers and Hammerstein were correct in their evaluation of the difficulties inherent in *Pygmalion.* It was considered imperative that a musical be built of two story lines. Since musicals were then almost entirely romantic, these consisted of a foreground love story between the two main characters and a background love affair between secondary characters, the latter as often as not comedic figures who could be played for laughs. This arrangement allowed the main characters to get offstage for a time to rest voices and bodies while the secondary characters advanced the overall tale. *Pygmalion* permitted no such structure, since it had a one-line story, that of the relationship between Higgins and Eliza. And that relationship was not a love story but a Shavian polemic on the English language, the expert in which was the linguistic scholar Higgins and the butt of which was the Cockney flower girl Eliza. Aside from letting Shaw deliver through Higgins lectures on language, the play also permitted him to show that social stratification and suppression are enforced through dialect.

The play's major disadvantage, as Lerner and Loewe both saw clearly, was that it is a drawing-room comedy of interminable talk that offered no logical placement points for songs, certainly none for choral scenes, which, the conventional wisdom held, were essential to the structure of a musical comedy. The cast of *Pygmalion* was small, and there were no massed scenes.

The play, then, was a non–love story, "and how, I may ask," Lerner said, "does one write a non–love song?"

Lerner was in a state of malaise at that time. "It was during that period," he wrote in *The Street Where I Live*, "that I, slowly but irretrievably, began to feel myself sinking into a stagnant sea of self-doubt. I was thirty-four years old, I had won a Drama Critics' Award in 1947 and an Academy Award in 1952 and yet, for reasons perhaps logical, perhaps illogical, I had begun to feel an ever-widening separation between myself and the times in which I lived." His reasons, in fact, for this alienation, to use a word that later became fashionable, were sound. The culture was undergoing a change whose nature was not yet obvious; in retrospect it seems to have come about with bewildering speed. The three major radio networks, CBS, NBC, and Mutual, were slowly closing down as these corporations hastened to set up their television operations, which were immensely more profitable. Cut off from high-quality network programming from New York, Los Angeles, and Chicago, the affiliated stations turned more and more to records and began a scramble for ratings that placed a premium on repetition and a short "play list" and sought the lowest common denominator of public musical taste. Rock and roll was arriving.

It is worth examining the major hits of 1932 and those of 1952, two decades later, to perceive the change that was taking place in the culture and the reason, or part of it, for Lerner's emotional state. The year 1932 produced:

Alone Together, April in Paris, Brother Can You Spare a Dime, Darkness on the Delta, Fit as a Fiddle, A Ghost of a Chance, Grenada, How Deep Is the Ocean, I Don't Stand a Ghost of a Chance with You, I Gotta Right to Sing the Blues, I Guess I'll Have to Change My Plan, I Surrender Dear, If I Love Again, I'll Never Be the Same, I'm Getting Sentimental over You, Isn't It Romantic?, It Don't Mean a Thing If It Ain't Got that Swing, I've Got the World on a String, I've Told Every Little Star, Keepin' Out of Mischief Now, Let's Have Another Cup of Coffee, Let's Put Out the Lights and Go to Sleep, Louisiana Hayride, Lullaby of the Leaves, Mimi, My Silent Love, Night and Day, Please, Rise 'n' Shine, Say It Isn't So, A Shine on Your Shoes, Smoke Rings, Soft Lights and Sweet Music, The Song Is You, Street of Dreams, Take Me in Your Arms, Try a Little Tenderness, We Just Couldn't Say Goodbye, Willow Weep for Me, You Are Too Beautiful, and *You're an Old Smoothie.* Many of these songs are in the repertoire of the better singers nearly sixty years later, and seem likely to remain so.

Nineteen fifty-two produced only one song that is still performed, a French adaptation at that: *When the World Was Young,* which has in its English incarnation a magnificent Johnny Mercer lyric. It produced two more that deserve to be heard, *That's All* and *Somewhere Along the Way.* For the rest, the hit parade of that year of Lerner's discontent contained such ephemera as *Botch-a-Me, Bunny Hop, I Saw Mommy Kissing Santa Claus, I Went to Your Wedding, Takes Two to Tango,* and *Your Cheatin' Heart.* The following year was leavened by a few Cole Porter songs, because of the release of the movie *Can-Can,* but 1953 was also the year of *How Much Is that Doggie in the Window* and *That's Amore.* Two years later, Bill Haley's *Rock Around the Clock* made the hit parade; in January 1956, Elvis Presley recorded *Heartbreak Hotel* for RCA. If Lerner could not quite grasp the nature of the vast cultural change that was occurring in America, he was not alone: few who lived through the era could.

All that summer of 1952, Lerner was disturbed by the predatory demagoguery of Senator Joseph McCarthy, who was affixing the label "Communist" to anyone in public life with even mild liberal tendencies. And the newspapers of the country, whose owners almost to a man were Republican, were desperate for a Republican president. Republicans in the arts, Lerner noted, were rare.

As repugnant to many people as McCarthy himself was his young chief counsel, Roy Cohn. Despite Lerner's interest in the occult, no eldritch premonition came to him as he watched the McCarthy hearings on television that he would one day have two scarifying courtroom encounters with Roy Cohn.

Lerner devoted at least half his time that summer to the presidential campaign of Adlai Stevenson, organizing Democratic party rallies in New York State. On May 13 the *Herald-Tribune* reported that he and Nancy Olson were members of a newly formed Rockland County Stevenson for President Committee, along with Columbia Records pop-music producer Mitch Miller. On May 30, the *New York Times* reported that "The Women's Division of the Rockland County Democratic Committee attracted 5,000 bidders, including many Republicans, to its annual auction today." Among the auctioneers, the newspaper noted, were Bill Mauldin, Mitch Miller, and Nancy Olson.

Lerner agreed to recruit entertainment-industry people for the Stevenson campaign. and, according to Doris Shapiro, who by then had been his assistant for four years, he spent a great deal of time that summer on the telephone, setting up their appearances in the campaign.

During the final rally, held in Madison Square Garden in early November, Lerner and Oscar Hammerstein talked about *Pygmalion.* Hammerstein said that he and Richard Rodgers had spent more than a year trying to solve the problem of the book and described precisely the same difficulties Lerner and Loewe had encountered. Within a month Lerner and Loewe abandoned *Pygmalion.*

Nancy Olson continued to accrue publicity, including a column by Sidney Skolsky, which said the Rockland County house where she and Alan lived had been inhabited by the Marquis de Lafayette and General Mad Anthony Wayne. She and Alan slept in a double bed. When she wasn't working on a picture, she retired around two in the morning and slept until noon, in nightgowns in hotels and pajama tops at home. She liked interior decorating, ice skating, scarves, costume jewelry, buying clothes, playing piano, playing croquet, playing charades, taking long walks, watching football on television, and eating Spanish food, curry, smorgasbord, Swedish meatballs, garlic bread, on which she was inclined to lunch constantly, and milk in great quantities, though she drank neither tea nor coffee. She read avidly, fiction and non-fiction, kept up on the current plays, and liked attending the theater. Her sartorial taste ran to simple formal wear for going out, and, when she was in the country, jeans and tailored sports clothes. She kept her clothes a long time. She didn't consider herself beautiful and thought she didn't photograph well.

Skolsky's column contained this perhaps revealing statement: "She would not enjoy living on a too-confined income and fortunately has never had to face this prospect." Whether this is her comment or Skolsky's is unclear.

The column also said that she was interested in politics and believed actors should be able to express their political viewpoints as ordinary citizens. That actors are not ordinary citizens apparently escaped her attention. And, like everyone else, she did not foresee a time when television would blur the borders between image and reality, between imitation and life, between pose and politics, and one of her Hollywood colleagues would posture himself all the way to the White House.

Uneasy about a half-sensed change in the culture and deeply disturbed by McCarthyism, Lerner passed through that summer at loose ends. He was discontented with his past work and doubtful about what, if anything, he had to contribute to the future. Fritz Loewe had left him to work on a new musical with lyricist Harold Rome. Then Lerner came down with encephalitis, which evolved into spinal meningitis. He spent several weeks in hospital, suffering through a period of delirium and a paralyzed left leg. As his health improved, he approached composer Burton Lane about collaborating with him on a show based on the Al Capp cartoon *Li'l Abner.*

Lane, like Lerner a native New Yorker, had among his credits the score for the 1947 musical *Finian's Rainbow* and songs that included *Everything I Have Is Yours, Howdja Like to Love Me?, The Lady's in Love with You, There's a Great Day Coming Mañana, How Are Things in Glocca Morra?, That Old Devil Moon, When I'm Not Near the Girl I Love,* and *Too Late Now,* written with Lerner for the film *Royal Wedding* the previous year, 1951. Lerner asked Herman Levin to produce the proposed show. Levin's credits included *Gentlemen Prefer Blondes* and *Call Me Mister.* But after many months, Lerner was unable to find an approach to a book or songs, and Al Capp grew impatient.

And then in the summer of 1954, Gabriel Pascal died. Reading the obituary, Lerner found himself thinking anew about the abandoned *Pygmalion* project, and called Loewe to discuss it.

"We started thinking about it, and then we did do it," Alan told Tony Thomas. "I don't know why. The times changed. What we felt a musical should be had changed. Suddenly a lot of the problems that we had originally were nonexistent.

"I'd gone to school in England and spent a lot of time there. As I was in the case of Barrie, I was a great Shavian fan. I had very strong feelings about Shaw and his work, and it gave me an opportunity to put them into effect and see if I was right."

One of the things that had changed was the "rule" of musical construction requiring a subplot. It had faded. Lerner advised Herman Levin that he was not working on *Li'l Abner* and wanted Levin to produce *Pygmalion,* by whatever title the musical version might eventually acquire.

At that point, no one knew who owned the rights, whether they belonged to Pascal's estate or had reverted to Shaw's. The task of seeking them fell to Irving Cohen, Lerner's attorney and close personal friend, who represented among others Rodgers and Hammerstein, the producers Cy Feuer and Ernest Martin and, significantly, Moss Hart. Lerner wrote of Cohen in *The Street Where I Live:* "Irving refuses to this day to accept a fact of legal life which is automatically assumed by every other lawyer I have ever met, i.e., that there is a wide difference between what is right and what is legal." Lerner's bitterness toward attorneys is manifest in the next sentence: "In a profession that has distinguished itself by having sixty-three of its members indicted in the Watergate scandal, where an ever-increasing number of ambitious young men go to law school and study law in order to learn how to evade it, whose Bar Association constantly rallies to the defense of any scurrilous member under public attack and only raises its voice in censure when one of them has finally been caught red-handed and sent to jail, and where legal victory is seldom encumbered by truth or morality, Irving Cohen with every passing year becomes one of its loneliest members."

The musical rights to *Pygmalion,* it was discovered, belonged to Pascal's estate, and that estate was being contested by two women, his widow and the Chinese mistress with whom he was living at the end of his life. Any transfer of the rights required, by the terms of Pascal's agreement with Shaw, the approval of Shaw's executors in London.

The Chase Bank (later the Chase Manhattan) was the executor of the Pascal estate. Lerner got a call from an executive of MGM, advising him that MGM intended to acquire the rights to *Pygmalion,* and that since massive amounts of the company's money were at the Chase, the bank assuredly would not anger so powerful a depositor by letting the rights go to anyone else. In short: forget it. Lerner never did learn what prompted the call, but chances are that Irving Cohen's inquiries into the condition of the Pascal estate set off alarms in MGM's executive suite. In any event, such naked uses of power are by no means uncommon in show business, particularly the movie industry.

But, as chance would have it, the Chase executive in charge of the Pascal estate was also the executor of Lerner's father's estate. This didn't assure that the rights would go to Lerner, but it gave cause for hope. Fritz told Alan: "My boy, there's only one thing to do. We will write the show without the rights, and when the time comes for them to decide who is to get them, we will be so far ahead of everyone else that they will be forced to give them to us."

The course of action was astonishingly foolhardy: Lerner and Loewe could have ended up with a finished book and a score for a show they could not present. But they went ahead. They decided they wanted Oliver Smith, who had worked with them on *Brigadoon* and *Paint Your Wagon* and with Herman Levin on *Gentlemen Prefer Blondes,* to design the sets, and Cecil Beaton to design the costumes.

Lerner was convinced that Henry Higgins was Shaw's fictional projection of himself, a man who concealed his shyness behind a screen of language and sublimated his sexuality into wit, living his love life through the mails—a view shared by most Shavian scholars. The casting of Higgins was critical. Lerner says in *The Street Where I Live* that "the first person I thought of was Rex Harrison."

Stanley Holloway, in his own autobiography, says otherwise. He says that when he was approached about playing Doolittle by a representative of Lerner and Loewe, he was told they were after Noël Coward to play Higgins. When they couldn't get him, they thought about Michael Redgrave. Then, Holloway says, "the name of George Sanders was carefully considered." The late Richard Maney, the exuberant and extroverted publicist who worked on *My Fair Lady*, supported the Holloway version of events. He once told Herbert Whittaker, drama critic of *The Globe and Mail* in Toronto, that Harrison was chosen for the part "only after every other actor in England had been asked to play it, starting with Noël Coward and ending with John Gielgud."

It is interesting to speculate what *My Fair Lady* would have been like with anyone other than Rex Harrison. He seemed to have been born for the part.

His imperious air was remarked by one colleague after another. Many of them have noted that he could be arrogant, rude, insensitive—and irresistibly charming when he chose to be. There is no indication in his autobiography that he ever thought he was wrong in his six marriages and various other liaisons. One of his ex-wives, Rachel Roberts, and one of his mistresses, Carole Landis, committed suicide. But he walks through the scenario of his life like, well, Professor Henry Higgins, admitting of no defect of character, expressing no sorrow. Like Alan Lerner's father, he is never wrong.

The source of Harrison's grandfather's riches, according to family legend, may have been the nineteenth-century slave trade. His grandfather owned a large house called Belle Vale with stables, a tennis court, and a cricket field, and was in the custom of shooting on the Scottish moors. William Harrison, the father of Rex, grew up in all the advantages of privilege, including a Harrow education. When he met and decided to marry Edith Carey, his father still held the family fortune, but somehow lost it, declaring bankruptcy. Belle Vale became a jam factory.

Yet William Harrison, a mechanical engineer by training, drifted through life with charm, a sense of his own superiority, and a lofty indifference to work. He fathered two daughters and then, on March 5, 1908, in Huyton, Cheshire, a son who was named Reginald Carey Harrison. The daughters, Marjorie and Sylvia, were then eight and four. Young Reginald was pampered by his mother, his sisters, and a small army of female cousins.

Reginald contracted measles, which left him almost blind in one eye. He could not read the school blackboard and was usually at the bottom of his class. "I had no real education," he said long after-ward, "largely because I wasn't capable of taking one in." After seeing his first pantomime—the panto, as they call it in England—he put two chairs in front of a bay window and started practicing bows. He adopted the name Rex shortly after World War I because he hated the nickname Reggie. He was surely not unaware that *rex* is the Latin for king. He entered Liverpool College at age eleven and joined the school's Junior Dramatic Society. When the students were asked by a teacher what they wanted to become, most of the students were unable to answer. Harrison, however, said, "I want to go on the stage in musical comedy."

He apprenticed in British repertory companies among mediocre actors in worse plays, revealing a touch for comedy. He first sang onstage in 1932, when he was twenty-four, in a farce by H. F. Maltby called *For the Love of Mike*. A correspondent for *The Stage* wrote that "singing is not the company's strongest point."

A friend described Harrison as "always very smart. Beautifully groomed in lounge suits, very suave, an elegant walker. He had tremendous ambition and sacrificed everything to his acting. Except the girls. . . . He was a great one for living secondhand. If he didn't have a car, he knew girls who did. He was always considered dangerously attractive."

Late in 1933 Harrison toured in a musical comedy called *Mother of Pearl* with another young actor with a gift for light comedy, Robert Coote, who would become one of his lifelong friends. He made his first New York stage appearance in January 1936 in the play *Sweet Aloes,* with leading lady Evelyn Laye, who long after-ward described him as "very highly strung and nervy . . . He was, and always has been, insecure. It was all bubbling up inside him. He was quite nice, but self-possessed—a difficult man to know and to get inside."

"I am always indecisive at the beginning of anything and I spend a lot of time making up my mind," he said of himself. "I was always like that, even when I was a young man and I was offered the lead in *French without Tears . . .*" The play was a triumph for Harrison and its writer, Terence Rattigan, putting them at the top of their professions.

In 1940 Harrison was offered the role of Cusins in Pascal's pro-posed movie version of George Bernard Shaw's *Major Barbara.* The part had been declined by Leslie Howard, who, interestingly enough, had been highly successful in the role of Professor Higgins in the film version of *Pygmalion.*

Pascal's *Pygmalion* had been a success, and Shaw encouraged him to film another of his works. In July 1939 they decided on *Major Barbara*. Such was Pascal's ego that he decided he should direct it himself. He had never directed a movie in his life.

In July 1940, Harrison joined a cast comprising Robert Newton, Robert Morley, Sybil Thorndike, Emlyn Williams, a very young Deborah Kerr—and Stanley Holloway. In the title role was Wendy Hiller, who had played Eliza Doolittle opposite Howard in *Pygmalion*. The costume designer was Cecil Beaton.

The noise of German air raids slowed work on the film. Shaw, then eighty-four, followed its progress closely, even visiting the set. Pascal had Harrison and Hiller read through a scene for him. Shaw offered some suggestions for the playing of the scene, gave Harrison some tips on another, and left. He apparently approved of Harrison as having the right light touch for his plays. This may in part explain Harrison's reverence for Shaw, which would create a problem for Lerner.

Harrison was at that time in love and living with a young German Jewish actress, Lilli Palmer, who was classed, ironically, by the British bureaucracy as an enemy alien, and seeking a divorce from his first wife, Collette.

He had tried to enlist in military service, but, like Lerner, had been debarred from it by his damaged eye. Finally, in 1942, he was accepted by the Royal Air Force, assigned to officers' training, and eventually became a Flying Control Liaison Officer. That summer his divorce came through, and early in 1943 he and Lilli Palmer were married. In 1944 he was honorably discharged from service and joined the cast of the film version of Noël Coward's play *Blithe Spirit*. Then he made a film with Dean Jagger and Anna Neagle. The experience caused Neagle to comment, "I do say categorically that he [Harrison] is the most brilliant actor that I have ever worked with. I've liked others very much more, but it is not unusual for a very great and very talented person to be self-centered—and Rex is very self-centered."

Shortly after the war, he was offered a seven-year contract at $4,000 a week by 20th Century–Fox in Hollywood, with his first film to be *Anna and the King of Siam*, based on the Margaret Langdon book. In Hollywood, Harrison and Lilli became part of Darryl F. Zanuck's circle of friends, which included Moss Hart. Harrison's next film was *The Ghost and Mrs. Muir,* one of whose supporting actors was his old friend Robert Coote.

During this sojourn in California, Harrison proved susceptible to the sexual offerings of various movie beauties, an indulgence Lilli Palmer viewed with sophisticated tolerance. One of these affairs proved disastrous, his relationship with the actress Carole Landis, whose faltering career contributed to her neurotic insecurity. After Harrison told Landis he was going to New York to play Henry VIII in Maxwell Anderson's *Anne of the Thousand Days,* she committed suicide with barbiturates. The Hollywood press corps went after Harrison with all the venom at its command, and Hedda Hopper wrote that his career was "as dead as a mackerel." A few months later, in November 1948, she had the painful duty of presenting him with the Antoinette Perry Award—the Tony—for his triumphant performance in the play, which was a huge hit.

Rex and Lilli at this time were spending a good deal of time with the Vincent Astors and with Maxwell Anderson and his wife in Rockland County, where Alan Lerner had a 220-year-old farmhouse, painted blue and white. His studio was in a small house nearby. It was at Anderson's home that Rex and Lilli met Alan, who recalled, "Rex used to come up to Max's house at the weekend and we used to play a penny poker game. I saw them frequently and many times Lilli would stay over an extra day and I would give her a ride into New York with their little boy."

Lerner was at that time working on *Love Life* with Kurt Weill. While they were walking a country lane, Weill said, "You know what I would love you to do, Alan? I would love you to do a proper English version of the *Three-Penny Opera.*"

Lerner said, "Who could play Mack the Knife?"

Weill said, "Rex."

"Rex doesn't sing," Lerner replied.

"Yes, he does," Weill said.

"How do you know?"

Weill said, "I just know. He sings well enough for that."

Weill's remark stuck in Lerner's mind, and he even told Fritz Loewe about it.

Weill was not the only composer to think Harrison might make at least a serviceable singer. When *Anne of the Thousand Days* came to the end of its long run, Richard Rodgers and Oscar Hammerstein approached Harrison. They had, apparently, been impressed by his performance in *Anna and the King of Siam,* and asked him to reprise his role as the monarch in their musical adaptation of the story under the title *The King and I.* Harrison, committed to a film in London, had to turn down the role, thereby opening it to Yul Brynner who helped make the show a hit, played it five years later in the movie version, and continued to play it in revivals until the end of his life. Harrison was to return to Broadway in November 1950 in John Van Druten's *Bell, Book and Candle*, with Lilli as his costar. They next appeared on Broadway in Christopher Fry's *Venus Observed,* a personal success for the Harrisons though it ran only eighty-six performances, then in Peter Ustinov's *The Love of Four Colonels,* which Harrison directed. Costarring with them was Robert Coote.

Harrison's next major affair was with the beautiful young actress Kay Kendall, who at twenty-six was twenty years his junior. Despite knowledge of the affair, Lilli appeared with Harrison in a London production of *Bell, Book and Candle,* under Harrison's direction. Indeed, the affair was such an open secret that one wag referred to the production as *Bell, Book and Kendall.* Rex and Lilli had built a house at Portofino, Italy. Lilli sensed that there was another woman in his life. Eventually, unable to stay away from him, Kendall, with a friend—Carol, William Saroyan's estranged wife—went to Italy and called him. He invited the two women for dinner at his home. Lilli knew immediately that Rex and Kay were having an affair. As she wrote in her autobiography, "All at once, there it was. In the open, clear as daylight. The impact hit me full force."

It was during this time that Lerner, with Kurt Weill's comment about Harrison in mind, first approached the actor about the role of Henry Higgins in a musical version of *Pygmalion.* Lerner phoned from New York to ask if he, Frederick Loewe, and their producer, Herman Levin, might meet Harrison in London to discuss it. Harrison thought them mad. Lerner did not tell the actor that the rights to the show still had not been cleared.

Uncertain and noncommittal as he usually was when offered a new project, Harrison told them to come ahead.

eight

THE
CREATION OF
A CLASSIC

Songs in musicals serve certain specific functions. One of these is declamation, exemplified by *Get Me to the Church on Time* and *Why Can't the English?* But the most important is the soliloquy. Since the dawning of supposedly realistic proscenium-framed theater with Ibsen, the soliloquy as a means to express a character's inner state and to clarify the definition of his or her persona has seemed unnatural to audiences. But the conventions of the musical, that body of expectations that facilitate the suspension of disbelief, make it possible for the audience to accept soliloquy when it is presented in song. Eight of the sixteen songs in the score of *My Fair Lady* are soliloquies, including *Wouldn't It Be Loverly* (which, though sung in the presence of other characters, is a statement of Eliza's inner yearnings), *I'm an Ordinary Man, Just You Wait, On the Street Where You Live, A Hymn to Him, Without You,* and *I've Grown Accustomed to Her Face.* Even *With a Little Bit of Luck,* though it is sung by Eliza's father to his cronies, is essentially a soliloquy.

Lerner saw that the key to adapting *Pygmalion* as a musical was to be found in the film, not the original play. He perceived that the way to break it out of its chamber-theater confinement was to present in musical form parts of the story that happen offstage in the Shaw play. And he moved one of the locales: events of the tea party were shifted to the races, providing the excuse for *Ascot Gavotte,* one of the first songs written for the show. The idea apparently was Fritz's. Said Franz Allers: "Fritz told me that he had gone to Ascot and got the idea for the scene then and there." Alan and Fritz also wrote, at this early phase, *Just You Wait 'enery 'iggins,* as well as three songs later abandoned, *Please Don't Marry Me,* designed to express Higgins' misogyny, *Lady Liza,* intended to reassure Eliza before the ball, and *Say a Prayer for Me Tonight,* expressing Eliza's insecurities as she faces her ordeal.

Lerner said in *The Street Where I Live* that when news of the show leaked to the press, Mary Martin, then appearing in *Peter Pan,* and her husband, Richard Halliday, said they would like to hear the songs Lerner and Loewe had written to date. He wrote that Mary Martin was never considered for Eliza Doolittle.

But Stanley Holloway, in his memoir *Wiv a Little Bit o' Luck,* said, "Lerner and Loewe both wanted Mary Martin, even though she isn't English. In fact, at first they decided not to write the show unless they could get Mary.

"When she eventually turned it down the writers suggested Deanna Durbin." The next actress considered, Holloway says, was Dolores Gray. Finally someone suggested Julie Andrews.

Lerner's version is that it was out of courtesy that he and Fritz acceded to Halliday's request and demonstrated the five songs they had come up with thus far to Halliday, who said he loved them.

Shortly after that, they performed them again at Lerner's mother's apartment for an audience consisting of Halliday, Mary Martin, and their friend the couturier Mainbocher. The small audience listened in silence and dispersed almost immediately.

A week later, in Lerner's account, overcome by curiosity about Martin's silence, he called Halliday, who gravely suggested that they have lunch. At the Hampshire House, after ordering, Halliday began the exchange:

"Alan, you don't know what a sad night that was for Mary and me."

"Why?"

"Mary walked the floor half the night saying over and over again, 'How could it have happened? How could it have happened? These dear boys have lost their talent!' "

Shaken, Lerner sat silent. Halliday continued:

"Alan, *Just You Wait* is simply stolen from *I Hate Men* in *Kiss Me, Kate* and the *Ascot Gavotte* is simply not funny. It's just not funny at all."

Lerner ate quickly. Halliday said, "I'm so sorry, Alan. We're so sorry."

And Lerner left. Heading up to Rockland County, he told Fritz Loewe of the encounter. With that sangfroid that remains one of his most interesting characteristics and probably a blasé continental shrug, Loewe said, "Well, I guess they didn't like it."

Lerner says in his book that Martin, at forty-two, was too old for the character, whom Shaw describes in the text as "perhaps eighteen, perhaps twenty, hardly older," even if Mrs. Patrick Campbell had originated the role in 1914 at the age of forty-nine. Lynne Fontanne had played the role at thirty-nine in 1926, and Gertrude Lawrence was forty-four when she played it in 1945. Lerner said he and Loewe both thought it would be refreshing to cast a girl in the role who was somewhere close to the character as written. Furthermore, given the challenge of mastering two English accents, one of them cultivated and the other down-on-the-cobblestones Cockney, Lerner wanted an English girl for the part.

A nineteen-year-old Julie Andrews was playing in *The Boy Friend,* a parody of 1920s musical comedy, a few blocks away from *Peter Pan.* Whether she was the first choice or, as Holloway says, the fourth for the role of Eliza, Lerner and Loewe became fascinated by the girl, who had a powerful four-octave voice of accurate intonation, the kind of clear projecting enunciation beloved by lyricists, and that indefinable extra quality that is the mark of stardom, the inexplicable ability to command interest just by standing there. Even those who possess it do not understand it. In a biography titled *Julie Andrews* (New York, G.P Putnam's Sons, 1970) Robert Windeler painted this portrait: "Julie Andrews was not conventionally pretty, and at the start of her career her major asset seemed to be her singing voice—still her strongest asset twenty-two years later. She is tall, five feet seven, her legs are too thin . . . her feet too big (size eight A) and her swooping nose is covered with freckles. She was not the sort of lady who was inundated with marriage proposals." He added, "With her large frame (125 pounds), boyish hairdo, and a prominent jaw, she was surprisingly sexy, dainty, and feminine." But her very features, her long nose and large jaw, helped her project over the footlights, whereas those with the delicate features beloved of fashion photographers tend to get washed away in the burn of stage lights.

"She had," Lerner wrote, "a composure and ease beyond her years and I was curious to see if, perhaps, there might be some indication of how much feeling lay buried beneath her . . . coating of middle-class niceness." He and Fritz told her of their pending project and their interest in her.

"Lovely," she said, and they left her, to pursue their other problems with *Pygmalion.*

She was born Julia Elizabeth Wells in Walton-on-Thames, which is in Surrey eighteen miles south of London, on October 1, 1935, the daughter of Ted Wells, a teacher of woodworking and metalcraft, and Barbara Morris Wells, who ran an evening dancing school and played piano part time. At the age of three, she appeared in the school's production of *Winken, Blinken and Nod.*

In the summer of 1939, as Adolf Hitler moved his armies, Barbara Wells was engaged to play piano in a variety show, the star of which was a Canadian tenor named Ted Andrews. Barbara and Ted Andrews joined the British equivalent of the USO to entertain the troops. Julie's parents divorced and Barbara married Ted Andrews. Julie disliked her new stepfather, and the family lived in one of London's more tawdry slums. But the vaudeville act of Barbara and Ted Andrews began to catch on, and the family moved up in their vaudeville billings and their living. Julie's stepfather sent her to a voice teacher, who discovered that the child could sing. Andrews later described herself as a "bandy-legged buck-toothed child" but remembered that, with her enormous range, she sounded like "an immature Yma Sumac."

Her stepfather forced her to practice, which she loathed, although later she would express gratitude for the discipline. She would often go to the theater to watch her mother and stepfather perform, and then, at the age of ten, she began making occasional guest appearances in the family act, standing on a beer crate to sing solo into a microphone. Pushed by her stepfather, she made her first professional appearance in a show at the Hippodrome not long after her twelfth birthday, singing the aria *I Am Titania* from *Mignon.* She earned the equivalent of two hundred dollars a week.

She later described herself as a "hideous" child with crooked teeth (which were soon fixed) and "very bad legs." Like Lerner and Rex Harrison, she had a problem with her vision. Her eyes were not coordinated. She corrected the condition with exercises.

At thirteen she performed on the same bill with Danny Kaye in a royal command performance at the London Palladium before then—Queen Elizabeth, the mother of the present queen. At fourteen she began touring music halls, sometimes working with Ted and Barbara Andrews but mostly as a single. Then she went into radio and television. As her career advanced Julie, now earning up to five hundred dollars a week, began to support the family, including her two stepbrothers. A neighbor of the family said that her mother and stepfather "were always drunk—on liquor that she had paid for. It was sad." She spent as much time as she could with her real father, Ted Wells.

She played in pantomimes, touring companies, and vaudeville, all the while continuing her voice studies until she was eighteen, when Cy Feuer of Feuer and Martin, getting ready to mount the New York production of *The Boy Friend,* heard about her. He took a train to Leeds to watch her in a play with music. Feuer later recalled, "She started to sing, and her pitch was perfect and her voice was delightful. Later, we went to dinner, and she was thrilled and excited at the prospect of starring in a play on Broadway."

But she was also apprehensive. She said, "Oh, good Christ, the idea of leaving my home and family—I couldn't do it. I had toured on my own all through England, but suddenly the idea of two years in America was too much." Ted and Barbara Andrews encouraged her to take the offer, and so did her real father, Ted Wells. Feuer said of her, "Most performers at that age are very amateurish, but even then she had great equanimity and poise. She didn't rattle. She had a very good dramatic ability even then; she was an instinctive actress." She signed on with Feuer for one year, arriving in New York in August 1954.

The Boy Friend opened at the Royale Theater on September 30, 1954, to excellent reviews. Alan Lerner, who with Fritz Loewe and Herman Levin was in the audience one night, found, to his puzzlement, that at the end of the first act, when boy loses girl, he found himself "embarrassingly unhappy" about it.

Lerner contacted Andrews to see if she would be available to play Eliza Doolittle. Andrews recalled, "I thought, 'What are these Americans going to do to poor George Bernard Shaw?'" thereby, without even realizing it, manifesting a typically English condescension. Despite misgivings, she auditioned for Lerner and Loewe, reading scenes from different plays. They told her they were interested in her and asked that she make no commitments until they had obtained the rights to *Pygmalion.*

If MGM had tried a power play against Lerner, he and Fritz now made one of their own. Given that Lerner had a friend at the Chase—his father's estate executor—the bank decided in its wisdom that an artistic decision was beyond its competence and petitioned the court to let it appoint the literary agent Harold Freedman to make that decision for it. When Lerner and Loewe were advised of this, they promptly asked Freedman to become their agent.

Soon after that, Freedman recommended to the court that the rights be awarded to Lerner and Loewe, and on the advice of Irving Cohen, Lerner's lawyer, also told the court he was their agent. "To the kind of court we have in New York City," wrote Lerner, "this seemed eminently satisfactory, because it proved Mr. Freedman was indeed a man of great intelligence whose judgment could be trusted."

MGM got the shaft and Lerner and Loewe got the rights.

But they didn't have a director, and they didn't have a star. Lerner made plans to take himself, his wife, Nancy, Fritz Loewe, Herman Levin, and Irving Cohen to London for talks with Rex Harrison. The visit might last several weeks, and cost a great deal of money.

Alan's father left an estate of $3,389,495 in New York and $200,000 in Florida, according to an application for letters of administration and letters of trusteeship that had been filed in Surrogate Court in New York.

The *New York Times* reported:

Mr. Lerner, who was chairman of the board and founder of the Lerner Stores, Inc., died last January 18.

The petition disclosed a bequest of $20,000 to the Museum of Natural History, $20,000 to the Federation of Jewish Philanthropies of New York City, and $10,000 to "my good friend" Cardinal Spellman for charitable purposes.

The will also directed that Mr. Lerner's wife, now Mrs. Edith A. Lloyd, of 480 Park Avenue, receive $60,000 a year in compliance with an agreement entered into by the couple in December, 1944, and that his three sons, Richard M. Lerner of Newport Beach, Calif., Alan J. Lerner of Pomona, N.Y., and Robert W. Lerner of Encino, Calif., share equally in the remaining estate.

But the money had not yet been distributed, and despite the earnings from *Brigadoon* and *Paint Your Wagon*—and no doubt because of his lavish spending habits—Lerner did not have the money for the trip. Why Fritz Loewe didn't have it either has never been explained; possibly his gambling had eaten up his profits. In any case, Lerner began casting about for money for the trip.

During their adolescence, Joseph Lerner had purchased stock in a gold mine for Alan and his brothers. Since it was their property, the stock did not have to be held until the disposition of the will for distribution: it was handed to them shortly after their father's death. By this point, Lerner was so determined to see the *Pygmalion* project through that he would have been willing to mortgage his house and anything else to make the trip. He sold the mining stock for $150,000 and left with his party for London, arriving on a cold January night in 1955. It was the first time Lerner had been east of the Atlantic since returning to America from prep school in 1937.

Lerner telephoned Harrison to make an appointment for dinner after the show. Backstage, Lerner and his party could sense tension. After visiting Harrison, he visited Lilli, who was reserved. "Later," Lerner wrote, "I found out that despite the fact that they were costarring together and playing love scenes in the most convincing fashion, offstage it was 'goodbye' until the next performance. They were separated and Rex was in love with Kay Kendall, whom he joined every night after he and Lilli had taken their curtain calls. This rather prickly situation was covered in a cloak of secrecy so large it could be seen for ten miles."

Nancy Olson said later, "It was the first time I had met Rex. I found him very English, the perfect image of the English gentleman. He was also ideally Henry Higgins: he was very independent, very opinionated, very judgmental, very male and arrogant—but in the best sense of the word. He knew who he was."

Said Lerner to Tony Thomas, "Rex is the embodiment of the Shavian hero, which is one of the things that facilitated it for me. Shaw skillfully took his own shyness and evolved it into a philosophy of life. Although Rex is not shy—I wouldn't say that—he has that male pomposity and male vanity which is so typical of Shaw and Shavian heroes."

nine

FEARS AND HESITATIONS

Rex Harrison was doubtful about playing the part of Henry Higgins, and for good reason. It is a truism that the artist must know his limitations, and his air of imperious authority notwithstanding, it appears by all the evidence that Harrison knew his. He has never been a master dialectician, like Peter Sellers, Laurence Olivier, Marlon Brando, or Richard Attenborough. He has never had anything approaching the reach of Alec Guinness. He works for the most part in his own voice and in parts that suit him. He is brilliant when he is impeccably cast, allowed to play a character who is at bottom himself. Examples abound: the king in *Anna and the King of Siam*, the imperious spectral sea captain in *The Ghost and Mrs. Muir*, Henry VIII in Maxwell Anderson's *Anne of the Thousand Days*, and of course his greatest performance of all, Higgins. His failures have always come about when he essayed anything too far from himself, as in his portrayal of Caesar in *Caesar and Cleopatra* with Elizabeth Taylor and Richard Burton. His politics are of the right, and it would be difficult to imagine him in the role of someone outside his caste.

When Lerner, Loewe, and company arrived in London, Harrison expressed his misgivings. The barrier was Leslie Howard. Harrison thought Howard's performance in the Pascal film version of *Pygmalion* was definitive.

After that first meeting, Lerner and Loewe avoided the theater. Lerner was uncomfortable seeing Lilli Palmer, with whom he maintained a friendship, so they had their conversations with Harrison elsewhere. In Fritz Loewe's room at Claridge's hotel, Harrison did something unusual for a performer of his stature: in essence he auditioned, singing *Molly Malone,* accompanied by Fritz on the piano. After only a few bars, Loewe stopped him and said, "Fine, that's all you need." Alan too was convinced he could do the role. He and Fritz performed two of the songs they had written for the show.

Harrison said, "I hate them." Instead of being dismayed, Lerner and Loewe agreed with him. Alan immediately saw how they should write for Harrison. They assured him that they were in the early phases of the writing, and better songs would be forthcoming.

Fritz later told Miles Kreuger, in an interview for WBAI-FM in New York, that later, when he and Lerner were writing *Camelot,* he was able to assign Richard Burton a few sustained notes because he could sing a little. "In the case of Harrison," he said, "it was not possible. He doesn't have one note in his entire system, although he's incredibly musical, enormously rhythmic. In the case of *My Fair Lady,* an entire new way of presenting numbers had to be invented. It's what is called in German *sprechtgesang.* In this case it was really interwoven with all sorts of things, because the patter songs in *My Fair Lady* are not just rhythmical patter songs, they have a character and a melody of their own. And that is what made it different. It is the combination of the lyrics and *sprechtgesang* that made a new form. Up to then, patter songs had no melody to be distinguished. Also they made no attempt in characterization of the character. I have tried to picture within the music anger in, for instance, *Just You Wait 'enery 'iggins.* Then she becomes sweet in the middle when she dreams about her revenge. Or when Harrison sings *Why Can't a Woman Be More Like a Man*—well, all his songs—I attempt characterization in the music, as well as in the lyrics."

But much of that work lay ahead. For the present, Harrison still had reservations about taking the role. For one thing, Kay Kendall was making a film and he would have to go to New York without her. One evening he said to Lerner, revealing a touching (but selfish) naïveté: "You see, it isn't how much I will miss her that bothers me. But what will I do for fun?"

Lerner confronted Harrison's trepidations about the Leslie Howard performance by screening the film. Lerner, Nancy, Fritz Loewe, Levin, and Harrison watched it together. After Eliza's triumph at the ball, for which Higgins is taking all the credit, she says, "But what is to become of me?"

Higgins responds, "Oh! That's what is worrying you, is it?"

Lerner told Harrison that in Leslie Howard's reading, it is obvious that Higgins knows quite well what is bothering her. He said that he thought Howard's reading was wrong, that Higgins genuinely should *not* know what is bothering Eliza. Harrison began to agree that Howard had given away too much about the character too soon.

There exists an essay by Maxwell Anderson on the nature of drama, which Joshua Logan used to circulate in a manuscript photocopy to his friends. Anderson describes the moment of self-revelation of the central character without which, he argued, no play could succeed. In *My Fair Lady*, Lerner illustrated Anderson's point—and since he and Anderson were neighbors and friends, it seems like that they had discussed it—in Higgins' discovery that he has grown accustomed to her face. The song of course had not yet been written. But in making Harrison see that Leslie Howard made the insight arrive too soon, thereby weakening the story, Lerner opened the way for the actor to see that he might indeed have something to add to the role of Higgins.

Lerner did something more: he shifted the character of Higgins closer to Harrison's own personality. In Harrison's autobiography, and in the biography by Roy Moseley and Phil and Martin Masheter, it is evident that Harrison has no more insight into a woman's needs and nature than Higgins himself. He did not understand Carole Landis, Kay Kendall, Lilli Palmer, or any other of the women in his life. In the redefinition of that one line, Lerner shrewdly tailored the suit to fit Harrison exactly.

While they waited for Harrison to come to a decision, Lerner and Loewe met with Cecil Beaton, who agreed to do the costumes for the show, and with Stanley Holloway, Lerner's choice from the beginning for Doolittle. Lerner had remembered Holloway's performances in music hall from his own schoolboy days in England and had asked him, more than a year before, if he would be interested in the role. Holloway had nothing like Harrison's hesitation about the play: he loved the idea of the flamboyant role of Eliza's father. He met Lerner, Loewe, and Herman Levin for lunch at Claridge's. Lerner says that when Holloway was asked if he could still sing, he fired off a baritone note that rattled the dining room crockery, and that was that.

The story is colorful, but again Holloway has a different version of events. He says that in Fritz Loewe's suite, Levin said to him diffidently, "Look, before we go any further, would you have any objection to letting us hear you sing in a theater—preferably a big one, like Drury Lane?"

"Not a bit," Holloway said.

An observation of André Previn's is pertinent to these variant versions of the Holloway audition: "You know how John Ford says, 'If there's history and there's legend, show the legend.' If Alan had to edit the facts a little to get a good story, he told the story. Always. Always."

Levin left to discuss terms of the contract with Holloway's agent. In their absence Fritz moved to the upright piano he had had installed in the suite and began playing a few chords. Holloway joined him to sing "some bits and pieces," as he put it. Levin and the agent returned, smiling over their agreement on the contract, and Levin said, "Well, when can you get across to the theater?"

Fritz looked up from the piano, raised a hand, and said, "No, there is no need. It is quite all right. His singing is perfect and there's no need for him to go to the theater."

Still Harrison could not make up his mind, and the money Lerner had derived from the sale of his gold mine stocks was draining away, although Herman Levin used the time to clear up some details of the rights to the play with the British Authors' Society.

Lerner encountered an old friend, the film director Lewis Milestone, who suggested that if they were going to do the Shaw play, they should visit Covent Garden, the natural habitat of Eliza Doolittle.

Benjamin Welles, then a correspondent in the London bureau of *The New York Times,* remembered the night of that visit. He said, "Alan and Fritz came to our house at Wilton Place in London. We had a piano, and I had a few friends come in to meet them. Attractive people. Three or four young couples. Fritz played the piano and Alan sang. Fritz played beautifully. He was a very accomplished musician. I loved the songs. When they left our house about twelve-thirty, they were going down to Covent Garden to get some atmosphere, some mood. That's the night—I think—when they finalized *Wouldn't It Be Loverly.*"

In a damp early morning cold, Lerner and Loewe explored the area for three hours, observing a group of costermongers warming themselves by a fire. Once Alan gave him the title, *Wouldn't It Be Loverly,* Fritz wrote the melody in an afternoon.

On a Sunday in February, five weeks after their arrival in London, Harrison called and asked them to go for a walk in Hyde Park. They made an incongruous trio, Harrison over six feet tall and long-legged, Loewe only five-foot-five, and Lerner five-six-and-a-half if he was that. Lerner said that he and Fritz had to jog-walk to keep up with him. This curious performance lasted nearly three hours, with Harrison chatting about everything but the play. Was he working up the nerve to turn it down? Suddenly he stopped, turned to face them, and said, "All right, I'll do it."

They left the park. Harrison said to Lerner as they finally parted, "I don't know why, but I have faith in you." Lerner would remember the remark for years. Fritz went back to their hotel for a nap, awaking, according to Lerner, two days later.

When Lerner and Loewe and party returned to New York in the middle of February, they had commitments from Harrison, Holloway, and Beaton, and the musical rights to *Pygmalion* for seven years. And Harrison went about preparing for the role of Higgins. "I went to a singing instructor," he said. "And I realized in two short lessons that I'd never be able to sing, or it would take me seven or eight years—far too long, so then I gave up the singing lessons." He approached Bill Low, the musical director of the English company of *Guys and Dolls.* "He taught me the initial things," Harrison said. "He taught me how to talk on pitch. And that is what I did . . . I do use the notes, but I speak-talk . . . I picked it up quite quickly, because I've got a sense of rhythm and it wasn't very difficult, and then I worked on my own after that, and I evolved my own technique of doing it."

On March 10 there occurred one of those alignments of stars that occur not infrequently in the small world of show business. Julie Andrews appeared with Nancy Olson in a musical version of Maxwell Anderson's *High Tor* made for television. It had been at Anderson's house in Rockland County that Lerner met Rex Harrison and Lilli Palmer. The music for this version of *High Tor* was by Arthur Schwartz, who also produced the show. The lyrics were by Anderson. Bing Crosby played the role of a man in love with the

112

ghost, played by Andrews, of a Dutch girl dead for two hundred years. Olson played his fiancée.

Nancy complained about her part in it, telling a *New York Times* writer, "I'm pleased, naturally. But in *High Tor,* as in most of the movies I've made, I'm just a reactor. Bing has a charming song that he sings to me. It's called *Living One Day at a Time.* And Everett Sloane sings to me, too. But I have to just stand there and just react. I went mad trying to find something to do."

High Tor had a budget of $300,000, unprecedented in television at that time. Filmed in twelve days in November of 1955, it was broadcast Saturday, March 10, 1956. Nobody seems to have been very happy with it.

Lerner's house in Rockland County had its own ghost, he wrote in *The Street Where I Live.* The house had been built in 1732 by the father of Mad Anthony Wayne, and was reputed to be haunted by the shade of Mad Anthony himself. Given his interest in the supernatural, Lerner hoped to have a brush with the spirit, but in the seven years he had lived there not so much as a wisp of ectoplasm had appeared.

Fritz Loewe, however, reported a strange experience. In October 1954, shortly after they had auditioned Julie Andrews, Fritz was sleeping in one of two double beds in the guest room; his current lady was asleep in the other. He was awakened by the sound of heavy footsteps, approaching in the hall, then coming through the locked door into the room, which turned cold. At that moment his friend Virginia, hiding beneath the covers in the next bed, cried out, "Go away! Leave us alone! What did we ever do to you?"

The footsteps passed through the wall and the chill left the room. Fritz turned on a light and observed that the door was locked. And there was no question in his mind about it: both he and Virginia had heard the steps and felt the chill.

On New Year's Eve the footsteps returned, this time passing through into the adjacent bathroom. Then Fritz and Virginia heard the toilet flush. Without waking Lerner, they packed and drove back to New York. Fritz left a note to explain their departure, which concluded:

"Dear boy, a ghost who wakes me up in the night is one thing, but a ghost who goes to the bathroom and takes a crap is more than I can stand. I will call you tomorrow. Fritz."

Though the guest room was still available to him, Loewe refused to sleep there and rented a house on a nearby hill from actor Burgess Meredith to work on the show.

Now that the rights had been cleared and Harrison had agreed to do it, Herman Levin told Julie Andrews, who had held herself available in spite of several offers for shows, that he was ready to sign an agreement with her agent. The show still did not have a director, and the money had not been raised. Given the scope of it, the sets by Oliver Smith and costumes by Cecil Beaton, and the salary of Harrison, it was going to be expensive.

The Lerner and Loewe group held the musical rights to *Pygmalion* for only seven years. This meant that if the show was not adapted to some other medium by the end of that period, they would lapse. They could solve the problem only one way: get financing from a company able to turn it into a movie or a television show at will. Lerner called an old friend, Robert Sarnoff, the president of NBC, the parent company of RCA Records. He and Fritz contacted Goddard Lieberson, vice-president of Columbia Records, a division of CBS. Both companies were in a position to record the show in an original-cast album, as well as to present it on television.

Lerner got a call at the Rockland County house as he and Fritz were working on the score. It was Lieberson, who said he was about to lunch at "21" with Bill Paley, the president of CBS. Goddard couldn't remember which Shaw play they were adapting or who had been cast in the roles. Lerner quickly reminded him of the details. That afternoon, Lieberson called back to say that Paley—who by happy circumstance was a friend of Rex Harrison's—was excited by the project and wanted to discuss it further with Herman Levin.

Levin and Paley quickly reached an agreement in principle that CBS would finance the entire production, with rights to the original cast album going to Columbia Records. The show was now budgeted at $400,000. Not only was this the largest budget for any Broadway show ever mounted up to that time, it was the first time anyone could remember when the financing of a show had come from a single source. The deal made trade paper headlines.

The package was almost completed. Lerner and Loewe had the rights, their producer, their stars, their set and costume designers, and the financing. They seemed to have assembled the perfect team, excepting one member: they had no director.

They had immediately of course mentioned Moss Hart, but Hart was working on a musical with Harold Rome, and they did not at first think it was worth contacting him.

Moss Hart is one of the major figures in American theatrical history, both as a director and as a writer. He wrote books for shows with almost every major Broadway songwriter, including the Gershwins, Rodgers and Hart, Irving Berlin, and Cole Porter, as well as six plays in collaboration with George S. Kaufman, one of which, *You Can't Take It with You,* took a Pulitzer Prize in 1937. He was famous for his wit and for his grand style of living. When he acquired a farm that was devoid of trees, he had workmen plant hundreds of fully grown pines, which prompted George S. Kaufman to remark that the place now looked the way God would have done it if he'd had the money. Doris Shapiro remembers him wearing a mink-lined vicuña coat. Hart was married to the actress and singer Kitty Carlisle.

He could be scathing when provoked. Lerner remembered that once, as they walked down Fifth Avenue, a man confronted them, delivering a variant on the line that is resented by everyone famous: I'll bet you don't remember me. This man went further. He said, "Well, if it isn't the great Moss Hart. I'll bet you're too big and famous to remember me."

Hart, who had risen from terrible poverty that he never forgot, said, "No, you're quite wrong. I remember you very well indeed. We went to school together in the Bronx. You bored me then and you are boring me now."

And he and Lerner walked on, the latter almost speechless with admiration.

Lerner said that Hart, Joshua Logan, and Vincente Minnelli were the only directors he had encountered who understood lyric writing.

But thus far, though Lerner was in the custom of talking to Hart almost daily on the telephone, he had not approached him about their show. Alan and Fritz continued working on the score in Rockland County, tidying up *Wouldn't It Be Loverly,* scrapping *Please Don't Marry Me* and replacing it with *I'm an Ordinary Man,* and writing *Why Can't the English?* The two songs took them about six weeks to write.

Whenever they completed a song, they would go searching for what Fritz called "customers"—people to listen to it and give them a reaction. They toured the neighborhood with their proud new possessions and got universal approval. Satisfied with this early response, they held a meeting in the New York office of Herman Levin, who said they had nothing to lose by approaching Moss Hart. The worst he could do was say no. They called him, and to their surprise he said he would be interested indeed in hearing the score thus far.

There are two versions of what happened next. Lerner wrote that they auditioned the songs for Hart in Levin's office. Kitty Carlisle Hart in her autobiography says they did it at Beach Haven, New Jersey, in a comfortable house whose every room faced the ocean. She and Moss had bought the house and moved there after Hart had suffered a heart attack on the Fourth of July weekend of 1954. "Summer is not summer," Hart said, "unless you get sand up your ass."

He had lots of it at Beach Haven, a lonely windswept strand lying between the Atlantic Ocean and Barnegat Bay, innocent of vegetation other than sea grasses and reeds. "It was paradise to Moss," Kitty Carlisle wrote. "I think he loved it so much because when he was growing up in the Bronx, the family's two-week vacation started with a trip on the subway with the pots and pans and the cat, and wound up in the overcrowded Rockaways."

Carlisle had found an old gap-toothed upright piano in the house of two spinsters who ran the local kindergarten during the school year. The local grocer had told Carlisle his daughter wanted to learn to sing. She took the girl on as a pupil, along with a boy whose ambition was to sing in the school choir and a couple of actors from a nearby summer-stock theater.

"And then," she says, "that miserable piano was elevated to an instrument of historic importance. Alan Lerner and Frederick Loewe came down to the beach to persuade Moss to direct their new musical based on Shaw's *Pygmalion.*" Lerner's memory, however, was that they went to Beach Haven to play some of the later songs *after* Hart had agreed in Herman Levin's office to direct the show. Whichever story is correct, Carlisle says that "the minute I heard Fritz Loewe play the first two songs, *I Could Have Danced All Night* and *Why Can't the English?* I looked at Moss, and I knew he felt that no matter what was at stake, he had to do that show. It had the inevitability of a great love affair."

The musical Hart was working on was in its early stages, whereas the *Pygmalion* show was nearing completion, with its principals and designers already under contract. Whether it was in Herman Levin's office or in Beach Haven that he agreed to do the show, agree he did, and in a state of euphoria over his decision, Fritz and Alan flew to London to play the new songs for Rex Harrison who, to their relief, was delighted with them and began to learn his material.

A second reason for the trip was to introduce Harrison to Julie Andrews, who had returned to England on the completion of her one year in *The Boy Friend.* Harrison had serious doubts about her because of her inexperience. Lerner and Loewe hoped to reassure him that she was capable of performing the role.

Andrews said later, "I was shaking at the thought of working with him—one heard awful things about Rex, how rude he is and all that."

Harrison accepted her casting as Eliza with as good a grace as he could muster. And he made a valuable suggestion for an important role that had not been filled—his old friend Robert Coote for Colonel Pickering—that Lerner and Loewe immediately accepted.

They went home to work further on the book and score, and Harrison continued preparing himself for his role. Meanwhile Cecil Beaton was working on the costumes. He said later:

"Rex is a perfectionist and demands minute attention. . . . He is like a dog with a rat and will worry details at enormous length. If given the opportunity, he will work himself up into a state of alarm. . . . I cannot say that Rex is the easiest boy in the class. But he has good taste and knows when something is not right for him. If it is wrong, he can become wild. One morning, he ripped off in anger his first-act long coat because it was too tight under the arms. The seams split and the expensive stuff frayed. The 'straitjacket' was thrown to the floor."

Harrison was, Beaton said, "a martyr to indecisions and doubts."

ten

THE SHOW
DOES
GO ON

Lerner described Cecil Beaton as "the only one I know who can design clothes that are both witty and beautiful at the same time." He also said of him that it was difficult to decide whether Beaton had created the Edwardian era or the era had created him. Beaton was almost manic in his perfectionism, and once sent a representative to India to find materials for the costumes of a Noël Coward play.

Beaton was the first member of the British contingent to arrive in New York. He selected some exquisite pastel fabrics for the ballroom scene. Lerner and Moss Hart loved them. Abe Feder, who had been engaged to light the show, said, "I'd like to show you the kind of light that is going to hit those costumes." He switched on a lamp. The colors in the fabrics vanished. Beaton resumed his search for materials. Hart, Lerner, and Loewe had meetings with Michael Kidd, who had choreographed *Love Life*, and Gower Champion, but settled finally on Hanya Holm as their choreographer. It was a foregone conclusion that Franz Allers would be the conductor.

One of the most painful ordeals in the development of a musical is the auditioning of the ensemble. Nor is there any way to avoid it. Young hopefuls turn up in scores, nervous and desperate for the few jobs available, standing in the wings and watching their competitors display their abilities and guiltily wishing them bad luck, then following them into the light of the naked stage lamp to show their own. These cattle calls are as painful to those making the choices as they are to the applicants, because the process is cruel, humiliating to everyone involved. Hanya Holm began auditioning dancers, selecting twenty-two from among more than a thousand. Over a period of two weeks, Franz Allers endured the vocal auditions, listening to two or three thousand hopefuls, culling that number to two hundred, at which point Fritz joined him, cutting that number in half. (Others in the company found it vaguely disorienting that Franz and Fritz carried on their discussions in German.) Hart, Loewe, Lerner, Beaton, Holm, and Levin made the final selection of sixteen singers.

One young actor was brought to the attention of Hart and Lerner by Bud Widney, Alan's friend and production assistant: Miles Kreuger, trained as an actor at Bard College. The meeting was the beginning of a long association with Lerner, for whom Kreuger would for a number of years work as public relations director. Kreuger's ambition was to become a historian of American musical theater, which in time he became. He is now head and virtually the entire staff of the Institute of the American Musical in Los Angeles, where he has amassed an astounding treasury of theater memorabilia and documentation. Widney introduced Kreuger and Lerner in the room of Herman Levin's office Lerner used as his own. In February 1990 Kreuger recalled:

"Alan had the strangest-looking office within Herman Levin's office. I don't think it was his own taste. I think it was decorated by Levin. The whole thing was done from parts of an elephant. The wastepaper basket was the paw of the elephant, with the big toenails on it. And behind the seat on which he sat were two tusks that crossed. The desk wasn't Moroccan leather, it was elephant leather.

"I remember vividly the first time I ever laid eyes on him. I somehow thought he would be a young man, he would look very handsome. Instead he had a very drawn face. All I could think of was Roland Young as Uriah Heep in *David Copperfield*. I did not then know that he had only one eye, and that eye wasn't even very good. He was hunched over his desk with his nose practically on the paper, with a pen in his hand, writing. He couldn't have been any closer to the paper. Bud Widney introduced us. He looked up with that strange kind of cockeyed way that I was to become very accustomed to, because he only saw you with one eye. He would always give you a slightly sideways look. And he said, 'Are you an actor?'

"I said, 'Yes, I acted in twenty-four plays in Bard College.'

"He said, 'Yes, you're just what I'm looking for for Freddy.' "

During that encounter, Kreuger heard part of the score.

"Fritz sat at the piano and Alan sang, roughly six songs. It was just incredible. After hearing these wonderful, wonderful songs. Moss Hart was there, and Biff Liff, who was to be production stage manager—now he runs the William Morris agency in New York—was there."

Kreuger was asked to read for the part of Freddy Eynsford-Hill, for which Bud Widney had apparently suggested him. "I read with Biff Liff throwing me the cues," he said.

"Moss said, 'You have the part, as far as I'm concerned, in terms of the acting. Can you sing?"

"And I said, 'I was a tenor soloist in our college choir, I sang the tenor part in *The Messiah*, I sang Richard in *Ruddigore*.' Moss said, 'There's a song called *On the Street Where You Live*. The music is going to be written to the voice of whoever plays the part. But Fritz has it in his mind that he wants it to crest at an A. Can you hit an A?'

"I said, 'Effortlessly, I'm a high tenor.' It turns out now that the song doesn't hit an A. But I was so painfully shy that I couldn't get up on the stage of the Mark Hellinger, where we had the auditions, and sing. *Ankles Away*, the Sammy Fain musical, was still running. They would roll away the scenery. The actor who was auditioning would give me his name and I would tell Biff Liff and he would tell everyone out front. One time he had to go off for an hour, and I had to go on the stage. Suddenly I was in what seemed like a Leni Riefenstahl airport where those movies like *Triumph of the Will* were shot, because the Mark Hellinger stage was huge compared to the one at Bard College. I was so tongue-tied that I could hardly talk, let alone sing. Moss really wanted me to be a protegé, and would always afterward say, 'Why didn't you sing?' "

So Kreuger was passed over for the role of Freddy. The meeting, however, resulted in a long association with Lerner, and he remained close to *My Fair Lady*, observing much of what went on.

One major role had yet to be filled, that of Higgins' mother. It was widely agreed that Cathleen Nesbitt would be perfect but the role was too small for an actress of her stature. Moss Hart said he was going to try nonetheless to get her. Long afterward Lerner was in awe of the way he went about persuading her.

Hart said, "Cathleen, the role of Mrs. Higgins was never a great role and it is even smaller in the musical version. Furthermore, I want you to know it will not get any bigger and might even become smaller on the road. But we want you very much. Cecil has designed some ravishing clothes, you will look beautiful, and you will receive your usual salary. Also, Cathleen, I beg you to consider this. For years now you have been appearing in very large roles in very bad plays, to which all your friends have come out of loyalty and suffered through the evening. I believe they will have a very good time at this play and I think you owe it to them to give them a nice evening in the theater."

The next day Nesbitt joined the company.

The cast was complete. The score was not, nor was the book.

One day after auditions, Alan and Fritz were walking to their office. They decided that the sequence concluding Eliza's lessons should be a song in which she does correctly everything she got wrong before. Since her greatest difficulty had been the letter A, Lerner suggested a song called *The Rain in Spain.*

After a moment's consideration, Fritz said, "Good, I'll write a tango." The decision was a little odd. The tango came to Europe from Argentina, not Spain. But it works for the show, and, according to Lerner, the two wrote the song in the office, two lines at a time, in about ten minutes. It came so easily that they were doubtful of its value until Moss Hart reassured them.

"That summer of fifty-five," Ben Welles recalled, "before it opened, I went to see Alan and Nancy at a house they had down in Sands Point. I was about to go back to London. He was out somewhere, and I was talking to Nancy. He'd had the terrible failure of *Love Life* with Kurt Weill. Nancy looked at me sadly, and she said, 'Oh, Ben, he needs a hit so badly! He really needs it.' "

As summer ended, Alan and Nancy bought an apartment in New York and returned to the city. Fritz moved into the Algonquin Hotel with his lady of the moment. By mid-November, Lerner had a libretto, though he had further revisions in mind.

Moss read it. He telephoned Lerner and said, "If you have any plans for this weekend, cancel them. We're going away together."

"Where?" Lerner asked.

"Atlantic City. And we're not leaving until you have finished the book and we have had time to discuss every scene together."

In 1955 Atlantic City was a shabby remnant of a former glory. The great rococo hotels were running to ruin. The famous five-mile boardwalk, once crowded with the elderly wealthy and young lovers, was all but deserted. The Steel Pier, where once the big bands had played, was run down; the bands had vanished from the landscape of American show business and the memory of spinning jitterbugs was fading. No more remote broadcasts by Tommy Dorsey and Benny Goodman and Duke Ellington emanated from its ballroom. The city's shabby streets were strewn with flattened soft drink and beer cans and paper, and graffiti defaced the brick walls of its old alleyways. Many of its windows were covered with plywood, looking like blinded eyes. Hart could hardly have chosen a more desolate place for their work, but it had the advantage of seclusion. The hotel he selected had only four guests, and for a paltry rent he reserved its penthouse. As Lerner drily put it, "Even when slumming he wanted the best."

Lerner would get up and start writing by seven-thirty. Hart would wake about eleven and phone him. Alan would show him what he had done. In the afternoons they would go for long strolls in the chill sea wind on the boardwalk and discuss the show from beginning to end, with Hart making suggestions for the writing. This routine continued over a period of four days. Moss judged the book completed and said he hoped he and Alan would do another play together someday. Lerner always treasured that compliment. Kitty Carlisle Hart mentions that trip to Atlantic City in her autobiography, saying, "Later on, when I asked Moss why he didn't get [writing] credit—the wife is always more royalist than the husband—he said he was hired as the director, and the fact that he was a writer-director didn't make any difference."

Early in December Alan and Fritz wrote *Get Me to the Church on Time* and *I've Grown Accustomed to Her Face,* the latter providing the play with that moment of self-revelation that Maxwell Anderson said was requisite to a great play. Fritz Loewe's conscious command of theatrical craft is seen in a description of the song to Miles Kreuger. He noted that the song was twenty bars long, not the usual thirty-two, and that it was not in conventional AABA or ABAB form. He said, "The scene goes into organized song, then goes away from the lyrics musically. He speaks while the music just attempts to underpaint the scene, and then drifts back to the rhythm with the lyrics, which at no time waits for a second chorus or something like this or a second verse or a repetition."

By this time Lerner would occasionally note a look of pain on Loewe's face. He had no idea what was causing it, and more or less dismissed it from mind.

Bell, Book and Candle had continued to do well in London, but its producer, Hugh (Binkie) Beaumont, had agreed to close it down to free Harrison in return for a payment of $50,000 and the rights to the British production of *My Fair Lady.* Beaumont had cast Kay Kendall in the touring company of *Bell, Book and Candle.* It is believed by some that he did this in order to prevent her going to New York and thereby distracting Harrison from his preparation for the show, in which Beaumont now had a vested interest.

Rehearsals were set to begin January 3, 1956, which allowed the British members of the company to spend the holidays at home, but Kendall, in tears, saw Harrison off at Heathrow Airport three days before Christmas and he arrived in New York anxious and ready for work.

Julie Andrews was at home in Walton-on-Thames with her family. She had a copy of the script. Lerner thought her initial tryouts had been very good. He wrote of her in *The Street Where I Live:* "Julie had no sense of being a star, none of that sense of obligation that a star has toward a play. The others, Rex Harrison and Stanley Holloway, turned up . . . ahead to talk over their parts. Not Julie. She sent us a letter from London saying she would arrive on the day rehearsals began, not before, because she had promised to take her two little brothers to a pantomime. It was so different, so unbelievably unprofessional, that we were amused rather than annoyed."

Right up until rehearsals, Lerner remained unhappy with one of his lines in *I Could Have Danced All Night,* which he wrote in twenty-four hours. He did not like the phrase "All at once my heart took flight," promising Fritz he would find a better one. He never did, and ever afterward the line bothered him. (Oscar Hammerstein felt the same way about the penultimate line of *All the Things You Are*—"I'll know that moment divine, when . . ."—but he never found a replacement for it.)

Alan still thought Fritz did not look well. Soon Loewe was walking in a bent posture. Finally Alan virtually forced him to see a doctor, who promptly put the composer in a hospital for the removal of his appendix. Fritz was furious.

Nancy Olson said, "Alan's relationship with Rex was much closer than with Julie. I don't think Rex was truly interested in women the way many men are. I felt that he did not feel comfortable with women. He was never flirtatious with me—he had a great friendship with Alan which was very important to him."

One day Harrison and Lerner went for a stroll down Fifth Avenue, past its stores of famous names—Bonwit Teller, Saks, Lord and Taylor, Tiffany's—past Rockefeller Center and St. Patrick's Cathedral. Presumably some heads turned with recognition of Harrison, but New Yorkers are used to the sight of the famous in their midst and usually do not intrude on their privacy. The conversation turned to marriages, past and present. "It is a melancholy fact," Lerner wrote, "that between us we have supported more women than Playtex."

But this was not so at that time. Though Harrison would in time accrue six wives to Lerner's eventual eight—a total of fourteen between them—Lilli Palmer was only his second wife. And thus far he had shown no intention of marrying Kay Kendall. She was merely the latest of his affairs. Any disinterested examination of the evidence leads to a conclusion that for all her charm and wit, she was extremely aggressive in her pursuit and determination to wrest him from Palmer.

Actress Diana Dors recalled a weekend, not long before Harrison left for New York, when Harrison and Kendall arrived in his chauffeur-driven Rolls-Royce at Dirk Bogarde's home in Buckinghamshire. Later they left in Dors' Cadillac for a fashionable hotel in a nearby village. In the course of the drive, Kendall raised the subject of marriage, prompting Harrison to explode, "Oh come along, Mousey! For God's sake, don't let's start all that bloody nonsense again."

"This rattled Kay," Dors said. "And, despite his obvious annoyance, she made matters worse by fawning around his neck, begging him to say he loved her. It was all done with a general air of half-amusement, but the conversation came to a very unamusing and sudden stop when Rex clouted her on the ear." In the hotel restaurant, Dors said, Harrison repeatedly told Kendall to shut up and said she was behaving like "an untrained puppy dog."

The incident may offer further indication that Harrison was perfectly typecast for Higgins, but it also shows that he had no intention of divorcing Palmer. Through this period and long afterward, if we are to judge by Harrison's own biographers, as well as other sources, Palmer's behavior—her tolerance, her forgiveness, and her disinclination to make heavy financial demands of him—bordered on the saintly.

Whatever transpired in that conversation on Fifth Avenue, and though their joint tally of wives at that point was only five, Lerner's memory is probably accurate about the crest of it: Harrison stopped still and said in a firm voice that startled people around them: "Alan! Wouldn't it be marvelous if we were homosexuals?"

It was, Lerner said, this conversation that gave him the idea for *Why Can't a Woman Be More Like a Man?*

The company began to assemble. Julie Andrews, despite her status as its least experienced member, was the last to arrive. She got to New York precisely on time for the start of rehearsals.

The press was invited to witness the first day and do interviews. Moss Hart had set up sketches of the scenery and costumes around the stage, with rows of chairs in midstage for the company. After about an hour, everyone but members of the company was asked to leave. The exception was Kitty Carlisle, who wrote: "Moss always asked me to come to rehearsals. He also arranged for me to come to the first reading of the play, which was trickier—outsiders were not welcome; they made the actors self-conscious. Moss knew I loved every aspect of the theater, but the best part was watching the pieces of the mosaic put into place and seeing the whole picture emerge. To me the empty theater with one work light on stage was wonderfully romantic. I loved sitting there in the dark, watching the actors fumble their way to perfection, or as near to it as they could get."

The cast read through the script, with Lerner and Loewe performing the songs. As they proceeded through the second act, a dark expression came over Harrison's face. He said he thought the character of Higgins was getting lost. Moss Hart agreed. Alan and Fritz decided he needed another song, but they had no idea yet what it should be.

Hart focused his attention on Harrison for the rest of that week, while Hanya Holm worked with the dancers and Allers with the chorus. Hart spent every evening with his star, rehearsing the staging of his numbers. Meanwhile, Lerner and Loewe sought another song. Alan and Fritz started work on *Why Can't a Woman Be More Like a Man?*, which eventually was retitled *A Hymn to Him*. They showed it to Hart and Harrison eight days into rehearsal.

Harrison listened unsmiling. Then he said, "Quite right! You're absolutely right!"

During that first week of rehearsal, Stanley Holloway announced that he couldn't continue without his afternoon cup of tea, and Moss Hart decreed that the British contingent, Holloway, Harrison, Andrews, and Cathleen Nesbitt, could observe the national custom: rehearsals would be halted for a half hour each day for the tea Julie Andrews brewed backstage. Herman Levin recalled that English biscuits were always served.

All the while, according to Bud Widney, Moss Hart's sense of humor kept the company in good spirits. "He made it his business to arrive every day with a new joke," Widney said. "He took on that responsibility. And he kept everybody laughing."

Though Andrews had become a sort of young den mother to her countrymen, Harrison was disconcerted by her habit of walking into the theater singing scales. She also had an unsettling habit of laughing in his face when he was playing a dramatic scene with her. He said, "It was a form of nerves, I think. She was really only a kid at the time, and it must have been a frightening experience for her. I always asked her why she laughed, and she never did tell me." And he continued to doubt her ability to play the role, though in later years he was to praise the way she went about preparing for it.

The insertion of *A Hymn to Him* caused friction between Harrison and his old friend Robert Coote, because it stepped on one of the latter's best scenes, the one in which Pickering calls his old friend Boozie at the foreign office about the missing Eliza. "For a long time," Harrison admitted later, "our friendship was strained."

Harrison continued to irritate various members of the company. Cecil Beaton seems to have been the most annoyed. Beaton said that Harrison became increasingly agitated. "Rex was by now extremely tense: never having appeared in a musical before, and doing something so utterly different, he felt that he could not rehearse enough." Beaton continued, "Rex's continuing egotism upset me to such an extent that only by a miracle was I prevented from making an ugly scene."

Hart said in defense of Harrison, "The key to Rex is he's not a frivolous man . . . What he achieves he gets from digging. Once I discovered this, I could forgive him a good deal." Still, Hart admitted that "there were tremendous rages and stalkings off stage."

Harrison would repeat lines from his songs over and over and over, wearing the rest of the company down to exhaustion. When the scene arrived in which Eliza throws his slippers in Higgins' face, the line between fantasy and reality slipped and, Beaton said, "the entire chorus applauded from the stalls."

But Andrews was herself a problem. She could not get a fix on her role. She said that she knew what Hart wanted but when she tried to give it to him, something would happen and she would feel as if she were a crab clawing at a glass wall with Hart on the other side. Hart said, "She was charming, but it seemed to me that she didn't have a clue about playing Eliza. About the fifth day I got really worried that she was not going to make it." Years later Andrews said in a *Playboy* magazine interview, "I knew I was the worst, and if not for Moss Hart . . . I'm sure I would have been sent back to England. Talk about Pygmalion and Galatea; Moss was my Svengali!" She was about to enter on what she later called "the days of terror" and "the now famous, dreaded weekend."

As Moss and Kitty drove home after one particularly discouraging rehearsal, he said, "What do you think of Julie?"

"She needs a bit of help," his wife said.

"Yes," he said. "If I were David Belasco I would take Julie to a hotel for the weekend. I'd never let her out. I'd order up room service. I'd keep her there and *paste* the part on her."

Carlisle said, "Why don't you do it?"

He didn't take Andrews to a hotel. He dismissed the company for two full days and took Andrews to the New Amsterdam Theater. Hart remembered, "It was the sort of thing you couldn't do in front of a company without destroying a human being. We met in this silent, lonely, dark theater and I told her, 'Julie, this is stolen time, time I can't really afford. So there can be no time for politeness and you mustn't take offense, because there aren't any second chances in the theater. There isn't time to sit down and do the whole Actors Studio bit. We have to start from the first line and go over the play line by line.'"

They worked from two in the afternoon to six, then from eight to eleven. Andrews said, "He bullied and pleaded, coaxed and cajoled. He made me be Eliza."

He told her, "You're playing this like a Girl Guide. . . . You're not thinking, you're just oozing out the scene. . . . You're gabbling."

Andrews probably believes to this day that there was no witness to her ordeal. There was: Miles Kreuger.

"Moss Hart was the Pygmalion of *My Fair Lady*," Kreuger said, "I watched him, before my very eyes, create a performer named Julie Andrews, when I wasn't supposed to be in the theater.

"As I remember it, the show had reached the very end of the last full week of rehearsals and they were going to go to New Haven midweek of the following week. Rex Harrison was very, very restive and unhappy with Julie Andrews, who had very little experience as an actress. She had never played a book part, ever, and she was following in the footsteps of Wendy Hiller and Mrs. Patrick Campbell. That's rather a daunting thing for a poor young girl barely nineteen or whatever she was.

"I remember Rex Harrison stormed out of the theater, saying, 'If this bitch is here on Monday, I'm quitting the show!' Finally Moss had Biff Liff dismiss everybody. And two hard-back chairs were set up on the stage. They put two scripts down. Of course the scripts had been out of their hands for weeks now. And I was sitting there, 'way in the back, in the bowels of the theater, and I wasn't supposed to be there. Everyone had been dismissed, but I couldn't leave, because I had a feeling something historic was about to happen. I was drinking coffee, and I didn't leave until I had to go to the bathroom. I sat there for an hour, and they were up to page ten or eleven, with a whole script to go, and I was desperate, squirming. I knew that the second I walked out, a shaft of light would come from the outer lobby and they'd know someone had been there and I wouldn't be able to get back in. I stayed as long as I could, and I watched as Moss Hart went through the script line by line, explaining every joke to Julie Andrews. If you've ever had to explain one joke to somebody who didn't get it, that's difficult enough. But to have to explain an entire script—Lerner out of Shaw—to someone. Finally I couldn't bear it any longer and I had to leave.

"All I can tell you is that Julie Andrews had it all in there, way down deep somewhere, because it was like lifting the veils. And two days later, when rehearsals resumed, Julie Andrews was, full-blown, the Julie Andrews we know today—that uninhibited, wonderful comedienne who can give so much and do screwball things, do everything."

Andrews, who ever afterward treasured the memory of that weekend, said that "at the time he made me infuriated, and scared and mad and frightened and in awe and full of inferiority complex, while knowing I could do it. . . ." She did not, apparently, reveal these feelings to Hart, who recalled, "She was neither affronted nor hurt. She was delighted. We were both absolutely done in. But she made it. She has that terrible English strength that makes you wonder why they lost India."

Carlisle said that for some time she could hear Hart's inflections in the way Andrews read her lines, but then the part became her own.

Harrison said that one of the most difficult things for Andrews—

and he said it was also difficult later for Audrey Hepburn—was to get "the gutter quality in Eliza." Andrews was coached on her Cockney accent by Alfred Dixon, an American actor and dialect coach. Later, they had to modify it for New York audiences, who couldn't understand it. (Eventually they would have to restore it for London audiences who could.)

Harrison continued to be difficult, insisting on fidelity to Shaw's original play. He kept a copy of the Penguin edition of *Pygmalion* near at hand, and if there was any doubt about a line, he would call out, "Where's my Penguin?" Lerner purchased a stuffed penguin from a taxidermist and presented it to Harrison in front of the cast, sending them into fits of laughter. Harrison kept the stuffed bird in his dressing room throughout the run of the play.

Lerner said he made a mistake when Harrison asked him the source of the speech that goes, "Oh, Eliza, I know you are tired. I know your nerves are as raw as meat in the butcher's window, but think . . ."

Harrison said, "That's a damn fine speech. Where in Shaw did you find it?"

Lerner said, "I wrote it."

After that Harrison, encountering a new line, would say, "Is that yours?" And Lerner, having learned his lesson, always said he had found it somewhere in the body of Shaw's work, in prefaces to plays or letters or something of the kind. Some time later, Harrison told an interviewer from the London *Times* that there were only six lines in the play that weren't Shaw's. This is the source of the belief that almost everything in it is Shaw's. It simply isn't so. One of the remarkable things about the play is the fidelity to Shaw in tone and sentiment with which Lerner was able to invent both dialogue and the shimmering lyrics. The flow back and forth between his material and Shaw's is almost seamless.

After the evenings Hart had spent working on Harrison's performance, and then the weekend with Julie Andrews, Stanley Holloway took umbrage. Herman Levin arrived at the theater to rattle the whole company with the news that Holloway wanted to leave the show.

Hart's blarney came to the rescue. He took Holloway aside and said, "Now look, Stanley, I am rehearsing a girl who has never played a major role in her life and an actor who has never sung on the stage in his life. You have done both. If you feel neglected, it is a compliment." Holloway burst into laughter and withdrew his resignation.

The show still did not have a title, and it was time to place ads. Lerner suggested that of all the names that had been suggested, they use the one they all disliked the least, which turned out to be *My Fair Lady.* It is drawn not from the play or any lyric in it or for that matter even from Shaw: it is from the children's chant *London Bridge Is Falling Down.*

During the last week of rehearsal before departure for New Haven, Harrison presented a new difficulty. He had said several times that he had no intention of standing passively on a stage while Julie Andrews sang *Without You.* As he put it, "I'm not going to stand up there and look like a cunt while this young girl sings a song at me."

When Lerner and Loewe asked Hart what they were to do, he said, "I'll tell you precisely what you are going to do. Nothing. At least until everything else in the play is rehearsed. You can't fight every day of your life or you dissipate your strength and it becomes a way of life."

The company did a final run-through of the show, though without costumes and sets and without orchestra. Harrison still refused to be onstage when Andrews sang *Without You.*

The next day the company assembled in little groups in the brass-and-marble cavern of Grand Central Station, then trailed out to the platform to board their train. Partway through the journey, Moss Hart slipped into a seat beside Harrison to discuss the schedule for rehearsals at the Shubert Theater in New Haven. Harrison was adamant that he would not remain onstage for the performance of *Without You.*

Hart said, "Well, I think you should at least give me the courtesy of seeing how I would like to stage it—because the song is going to get sung, don't make any mistake about that. It's going to be sung! Now you can walk offstage while it's being sung and walk on again when it's over, but you will look like the biggest horse's ass in the history of the theater. So I would suggest that you at least come to the rehearsal and see how it could be staged."

Harrison reluctantly agreed, but to placate him, Lerner and Loewe wrote a codetta for the song. At the end of it Higgins says, "I did it! I did it! I said I'd make a woman and indeed I did!" The line is a topper, stealing the applause from Andrews and handing the attention back to Harrison. It made him more comfortable, and it stayed in the show.

The New Haven rehearsals began on Monday. The scenery and lighting had been hung and adjusted. A special preview performance had been scheduled for Saturday. Friday evening was set for the first rehearsal with an orchestra numbering thirty-two musicians. Kitty Carlisle had warned Harrison that the first time he tried his songs with full orchestra, rather than only a pianist in accompaniment, he would find it extremely disconcerting. No one, however, was prepared for the extent of his discomfiture.

"At two in the afternoon that Saturday," Franz Allers told me, "I had the orchestra there for a final brush-up. I said to Rex then, 'If you sit right next to me, we'll go through the numbers slowly. We have hardly thirty minutes of music to go and we have two and a half hours.' We had a very solid rehearsal. After that he said he would go on. Then he was so nervous that he said, 'No, I can't do it.' That's why one sequence of *You Did It, You Did It,* was never done. It was never done until 1980, at the revival, because he couldn't learn it and said, 'I won't do it.' That was just the way Rex was, or still is."

With only hours until the curtain time, Harrison announced that under no circumstances would he perform that night. He said that he needed all of Sunday to rehearse with the orchestra and ready himself for a Monday-night show. He was adamant. Everyone with any influence or authority in the company tried to talk to him. Kitty Carlisle was home with the flu, but Hart told her later that Harrison said, "I never *liked* musical com! And I won't do musical com!" Nancy Olson said, "He just went to pieces and locked himself up in the dressing room. He was terrified."

Finally Moss dismissed the company, and Bernie Hart—Moss' brother, and the show's assistant stage manager—began placing hourly bulletins on local radio stations that there would be no performance that night. Apparently none of the ticket holders heard them.

The weather had turned bad. At five o'clock the manager of the Shubert Theater learned that there was to be no performance. Outraged, he confronted Alan, Fritz, Moss, and Herman Levin in the lobby and said, "There's a raging blizzard outside. People from miles around have already left their houses to mush through to the theater. I can't head them all off even if I get on the radio now. There will be a riot in this lobby at seven-thirty when I announce that there won't be any performance. You people leave here next week and move on, but I have to face this same audience every week, and I depend on them to fill my seats. I have no choice but to announce that there will be no performance tonight, and the reason is that Rex Harrison refuses to go on."

eleven

MY FAIR LADY

Accompanied by Herman Levin, Harrison's agent strode to the star's dressing room. Nancy Olson said, "He pounded on the dressing room door, saying, 'Come out! Come out! You'll never work again, Rex! You've got to do this!'" Harrison was told that the manager had no intention of abetting the fiction that the cancellation was due to "technical difficulties" and was determined to make a public announcement of the true reason for it.

In his biography of the actor, Roy Moseley says Harrison reached the agonized conclusion that he owed it to the rest of the company to go on. Lerner thought that Harrison's fear of the consequences overcame his fear of the thirty-two musicians in the pit and the orchestrations by Robert Russell Bennett and Phil Lang. An hour before the curtain, Achilles came out of the tent: Harrison unlocked his door. "I don't think I've ever been as frightened before or since in my life," he admitted in his autobiography. But he had arrived at this change of heart a little late. The company had been dismissed for the evening and had dispersed. Bernie Hart hastened out into the blizzard to look for them. Slogging through the streets, he went to every nearby movie theater and asked the manager to interrupt the film and raise the house lights while he stood in front of the blank screen to shout, "Everybody from the *Fair Lady* company back to the theater: we're opening tonight!" He went to restaurants. He went to health clubs, and according to Kitty Carlisle, "People were jumping off massage tables, flinging their sheets onto the floor, and heading for the theater."

Incredibly, he managed to find everybody. Carlisle says that not one member of the company was missing as curtain time drew near.

The manager opened the doors and the audience poured in. There was not an empty seat when the curtain rose at eight-forty. Harrison was in his place, behind a pillar and out of the audience's view, when Viola Roache, in the role of Mrs. Eynsford-Hill, and Michael King, as her son Freddy, came through the Covent Garden crowd, looking for a taxi. We can only imagine Harrison's emotional condition at that moment. The dialogue between Julie Andrews, in her shabby clothes as Eliza, Mrs. Eynsford-Hill and Freddy, and then Robert Coote as Pickering, proceeded at due pace. Harrison stepped into view and heard the protocol applause a star always receives. He entered on the dialogue with Pickering and Eliza. The music started in the orchestra. He began his *sprechstimme* and moments later he had finished *Why Can't the English?* A delighted audience roared applause, and this time not from protocol. He began to relax.

Stanley Holloway said, "From the moment the curtain rose I felt that we were on a winner. You could sense the cordiality coming up from the audience in waves. There was an electricity in the atmosphere. You realized that everything was falling into place. Yet oddly enough, it wasn't till the interval that I was gripped by that completely sure feeling that this was a terrific hit."

Holloway's performance of *With a Little Bit o' Luck* stopped the show, but *Come to the Ball,* which had been foreseen as Harrison's big number, simply lay there like something dead. The first act was twenty-five minutes too long. There were technical difficulties. But the second act went well, and when the final curtain fell, the audience rose instantly to its feet and cheered. The stars took their bows as the thunder continued. Lerner had a funny memory of that moment: Cecil Beaton rushing past him backstage, saying, "That bitch! I told her that hat had to be pulled forward." He hurried away before Lerner could explain that he and Moss had told Julie Andrews to pull it back so that her face could be seen when she sang.

Kitty Carlisle, in bed at home, was counting the minutes. At twelve-thirty the phone rang. "How did it go?" she said, and held her breath.

A muted Moss Hart said, "It's some kind of a hit. I don't know how big."

The dressing room in which Harrison had been hiding alone only hours before was crowded now with friends and fans, and the actor greeted them with beaming smiles. Curiously, in all the recollections of these events—Kitty Carlisle's, Lerner's, that of Harrison biographer Moseley, even the biography of Julie Andrews by Robert Windeler—there is no mention of what happened to Andrews that night.

The rest of the week at the Shubert in New Haven was a triumph. Moss Hart and Fritz Loewe wanted to dump *On the Street Where You Live.* Fritz had never liked it anyway, and evidently never changed his mind about it as long as he lived. Lerner defended it. It had not gone well, but a new verse improved its effect. *Come to the Ball* was scrapped, along with *Say a Prayer for Me* and a ballet in the first act.

Harrison's dressing-room visitors continued to praise him. One of its members, however, stood quietly, waiting for a chance to talk to him alone. When all the others had gone, Lilli Palmer told him she wanted a divorce so that she could marry actor Carlos Thompson. Thompson was a well-known American film actor of the second tier.

Harrison would not hear of it. "How can you want to marry a man younger than you are?" he demanded. "In any case, we belong together and we have our son and our work."

Palmer stayed far into the night, trying to persuade him, but the most Harrison would grant her was a separation. He told her that this "thing with Carlos" would run its course and end. Clearly he had no intention of marrying Kay Kendall.

The week in New Haven drew to a close, and the company moved on to four weeks at the Erlanger Theater in Philadelphia, as word went ahead that a huge hit was coming in, that Julie Andrews would be the newest star of Broadway, and that Rex Harrison was unimaginably brilliant as Higgins. By now he was in command of the part.

Lerner says in *The Street Where I Live* that audiences are always dazzled by the appearance onstage of chandeliers, and the three that descended from on high in the first act produced a collective orgasm. One night one of them was lowered too far and snagged Harrison's hairpiece. When the stage manager corrected the mistake, raising the chandelier, the hairpiece went with it, dangling in full view of the audience. With unshaken aplomb, Harrison continued as if it were still in its rightful place. But at the end of the act, he demanded that the guilty stagehand be brought to him. Otherwise, he said, he wouldn't go on for the second act.

Jerry Adler, the stage manager, said, "No, Rex, I won't bring him here. He's a brute. You'll insult him and he'll kill you." After expressing his fury to Moss Hart on the telephone, Harrison went on in the second act.

Lerner records that one night during the second act, Harrison had an overwhelming need to break wind. He controlled it until the script called for Higgins to pass behind the flowerpots at the rear of the stage. Then he relieved the pressure. "Unfortunately," Lerner wrote, "there was more wind in need of egress than he had contemplated and from behind the potted flowers came one of the loudest farts ever heard in the history of the theater."

The audience maintained its composure, even when Cathleen Nesbitt as Mrs. Higgins said, "Henry, dear, please don't grind your teeth."

Still the audience behaved itself. But then, at least a full minute after the eruption, Harrison delivered the line, "My manners are the same as Colonel Pickering's," and the dam broke. The roar of laughter eventually diminished, but recurred in scattered pockets through the scene and into the next.

By now rumors about the show were circulating in New York. Mail-order sales were announced three weeks before the Manhattan premiere—and the orders poured in by the canvas-sackful. The box office opened two weeks before the premiere, and all day every day a queue stood before it. Burglars, it was reported, hit upon a ruse of sending tickets for the show to people and then robbing their homes in their absence. Such was the demand on the show's principals for tickets that in Philadelphia, both Harrison and Andrews cut off their telephones, with a particular charge to their hotel switchboard operators not to let long-distance calls through. Lerner was nervous, doubtful that any play could live up to such expectations. Andrews too remained reserved, saying, "We still haven't opened in New York."

The tumult only grew when at last the play opened March 15, 1956, at the Mark Hellinger Theater. Extra police had to be posted outside to control crowds of sightseers. Lerner paced back and forth at the rear of the theater, as was his wont, watching the audience, anxious over every line. And as was *his* wont, Fritz Loewe dipped in and out, stepping out into the lobby to pull on a cigarette during dialogue, returning when the music began.

At the intermission, Lerner went to Harrison's dressing room, which was crowded with enthusiastic friends. Nancy Heyward, wife of producer Leland Heyward, noticed the continuing look of anxiety on Lerner's face; after all, the newspaper reviews were not in. She seized his arm and pulled him out of the dressing room. She said firmly: "Alan, listen to me, and listen to me well. What is happening in this theater is incredible. It is something that has happened to few people and will never happen to you again. So for Christ's sake, stop worrying and enjoy it. Do you hear me? Enjoy it!" And after a hug she left him. But he couldn't enjoy it.

The second act went off flawlessly, and after the curtain fell and the players had taken interminable curtain calls, the backstage response was even more ecstatic than it had been in New Haven and Philadelphia.

When, in his crowded and noisy dressing room, Harrison saw T. S. Eliot, in whose play *The Cocktail Party* he had appeared in London, and asked what he thought, the poet drily commented, "I must say, Bernard Shaw is greatly improved by music." Charles Laughton said that in all his life he had seen "only a handful of performances to match Rex's." Noël Coward said, "Rex Harrison and Julie Andrews are wonderful, the score and lyrics excellent, the decor and dresses lovely and the whole thing beautifully presented."

There was no opening-night cast party. Lerner wrote in *The Street Where I Live* that he and a small group went directly to "21," but Doris Shapiro in her book insists that he stopped first to see his mother, Edie, in her Park Avenue apartment. Shapiro describes her as resembling the "large Wagnerian mother with a voice that shatters glass," as Lerner put it in the lyric to *Let a Woman in Your Life.* It was in her dining room, Shapiro says, that Lerner saw the first newspaper reviews. His mother issued her judgment:

"What, my son, can you ever do to top this?" Shapiro said the remark haunted Lerner ever afterward.

In any event, Lerner ended up at "21" in a small room reserved for his party, Moss Hart and Kitty Carlisle, Rex Harrison, Goddard Lieberson and his wife, and his producer friend Irene Selznick. Reading the reviews, Harrison flew into a brief rage because, in his opinion, the *New York Times* had not given Alan sufficient credit.

Fritz was not with them. Calmly confident of what the reviews would be, he had gone to Sardi's restaurant. So had Julie Andrews, on the wings of applause for the eight songs she had sung. Still, like Lerner, she awaited the reviews warily. "When I saw the big sheaf of newspapers coming in, my heart stopped," she remembered.

They were uniformly ecstatic. Praising Lerner's lyrics and Loewe's "entrancing love music," Brooks Atkinson in the *New York Times* called it "a wonderful show." Walter Kerr in the *Herald-Tribune* proclaimed it "a miraculous musical" and said, "Miss Andrews descended a staircase looking like all the glamour of the theater summed up in an instant."

The gathering at "21" dispersed. When Alan and Nancy entered the elevator at their apartment, he said, "What a night."

"Did you like my dress?" he recalled her saying.

"Beautiful," he said. "Beautiful."

Lerner and Loewe were now royalty of the theater, Andrews was established as a star, and, as Roy Moseley later wrote, "For Rex Harrison it was the crowning achievement of his entire career—a definitive characterization which firmly placed him among the ranks of the legendary Broadway stars."

The success of the show provided Harrison with a moment of delicious retribution. Hedda Hopper, who had pronounced his career ended after the Carole Landis suicide, came to his dressing room, all smiles. She was a woman absolutely detested in the movie and theater community for the arrogant rule of terror that her newspaper column, with the obsequious acquiescence of the movie studio heads, had permitted her. Harrison got a little back for all the actors and actresses she had ever hurt when he slammed the door in her face.

At 10:00 A.M. on the Sunday after the opening, most of the cast gathered in the famous old converted Gothic church at 207 East Thirtieth Street that was Columbia's most resonant studio, ready to record the full score under the supervision of Goddard Lieberson. The session started with a jubilant Stanley Holloway performing *With a Little Bit o' Luck.* Lerner had to change a lyric line: in that vanished era, it was thought that some people might take exception to "for God's sake get me to the church on time," so it became "be sure and get me . . ." According to Franz Allers, the session went to 3:00 A.M. Monday.

The record cover had already been designed, and three days after the session Columbia shipped a hundred thousand copies of the album—an extraordinary figure in that time only a year after the rise of Elvis Presley. As summer progressed, the sales of the album mounted. Lines at the box office grew longer and would continue for eight years. A queue of people with sleeping bags and food in paper sacks began forming each midnight to await the opening of the box office at 9:30 A.M. They were after the forty standee tickets that could by law be sold at the Mark Hellinger. Seats for the show were sold out two years in advance. By September the album was at the top of the sales charts, where it was to stay for two years.

In March 1957 Lerner was in Rochester, New York, for the opening of the national touring company of the show. Brian Aherne and Anne Rogers had the lead roles in the road company. They would be followed by a long line of successors. Ray Milland several times played Higgins in summer theater. The show would be translated into eleven languages. The Spanish-language production in Mexico City featured as one of the buskers a young tenor named Placido Domingo. The producer was Alan's younger brother, Bobby Lerner, who took residence in Mexico City and became an important producer of Spanish versions of American musicals.

In its first year after release, the recording became the best-selling album in the history of Columbia Records and the best-selling original cast album of all time, with a million copies sold for $5 million, thereby outgrossing the show itself. In England, where the album was not released—in anticipation of sales that would follow when the London company was established—copies brought in by airline stewardesses and pilots went for fifty dollars each. In the next fourteen years, the various versions of the show, including the movie, grossed $85 million. But no one could foresee any of that. Hearing the album the day after the recording session—at fifty-four minutes and twenty seconds, an unusually long album—Lerner phoned Lieberson to thank him, saying, "Goddard, it's terrific. If it sells fifty thousand albums I'll be satisfied."

Moss Hart had left town. The preparation of *My Fair Lady* had been an enormous strain on him, and immediately after the opening he and Kitty left for a vacation on Barbados.

One night, according to *The New York Times*, Fritz enjoyed a leisurely dinner and then decided to drop in and see the latter half of the show. The paper reported: "He instructed the driver to take him to the Mark Hellinger Theater. The driver checked his watch, turned to the composer and proceeded to berate him for having the bad taste to arrive so late for one of the great musicals of our time. Mr. Loewe gave him no argument and a very lavish tip."

Thoroughly enjoying his status and the money that went with

it—and remembering the lean years—Fritz went to Paris, where, after two weeks at the chemin de fer tables in a gambling club off the Champs-Elysées, he headed south to Cannes and more gambling at the Palm Beach Casino. One of his friends remembered Fritz dropping enough money in the casinos of the Hotel Internationale in pre-Castro Cuba to open a casino of his own. And that was before *My Fair Lady.* One can only imagine how much money he dropped at Cannes that summer of its early and stunning success.

When he was not at the chemin de fer tables, he was busy at his other hobby, and proving, Lerner said, Marc Connelly's maxim that the only known aphrodisiac is variety. As Lerner put it in his book, "Fritz's reaction to it all was uncomplicated, total, uninhibited, and enviable. He joyfully flung open his arms, clasped the bitch-goddess to his bosom and danced all night."

Maurice Abravanel said: "After the success of *My Fair Lady,* Fritz told about the great life on the Riviera. He would tell the concierge, 'Get me a good-looking girl, a tall one.' After a while he would call the concierge, and say, 'Get me a dark one.' He said he did it all night. Whether that was bragging or not, I don't know.

"Goddard Lieberson said that when he was giving Fritz a royalty check, he said, 'Fritz, who in your opinion is the best composer these days? Hindemith, Stravinsky, all of them?' Fritz said, 'No question about it, me.' Lieberson smiled and said, 'No, in serious music.' Fritz said, 'I am the best composer.' And he was serious about it."

twelve

MAYBE THE CHANDELIERS

Rex rented an apartment in Manhattan and a house on Long Island, and in April—a month after the opening—Kay Kendall arrived. Kendall's sister, Kim, who was married to an American banker, thought Harrison was "a real egotist" but Kay, she says, "knew how to cut him down to size. She would say, 'Come along, you stuffy bugger' or something like that to him—which he was."

The Lerners were often with them, and Nancy remembered their volcanic fights. "When Rex and Kay had a row," she said, "it was like a contest to see who could be the most outrageously nasty but with an undercurrent of such amusement with it all and tremendous fun. It was not lethal venom, but theatrical venom. They played the part well and enjoyed their own performances." For all the energy of these fights, she and Alan noticed that Kendall did not look well. One night after the performance, they went back to Harrison's dressing room to decide where the four of them would dine. Nancy said, "Kay suddenly sat down and looked in the mirror and said, 'God, I'm so pale. Look at the circles. I have no energy. I'm absolutely tired all the time.'" This is one of the early hints of Kay Kendall's illness.

On March 11, 1957, Sidney Fields published a curious interview with Olson, in which she bemoaned her problems as one of the stars of *The Tunnel of Love,* including the tryouts in New Haven, Boston, and Philadelphia, which she said made her morose. It was her first Broadway play, and her costar was Tom Ewell, who, like Olson, had studied at the University of Wisconsin. She told Fields that during tryouts she just kept yelling, "I quit! I'm retiring!" But the moment she read excellent reviews in New York, she began to think, "Now my next part is going to be . . ."

The first hairline fractures in the Lerners' marriage are evident in that Sidney Fields column. Olson told him, "We've been married seven years," she said, "and I'm just getting the hang of being Mrs. Lerner. Everything at home is so vital. The things every young mother has to learn! And now I have to manage a husband, a house, children, and get to the theater eight times a week. Oh, if only the kids were at college and Alan were peacefully writing his memoirs." Lerner by now had three children, his daughter Susan (by his marriage to Ruth Boyd) who sometimes came to stay with him and Nancy, and two daughters by Nancy, Liza and Jennifer.

Nancy recounted friction in her relations with the writers of *The Tunnel of Love,* Joe Fields and Peter de Vries. She was complaining to them and to Lerner about how tough it was, with all her responsibilities, to get to the Royale Theater on time and dress and don her makeup.

Lerner said tartly, "Why don't you get there a little earlier?"

Olson told Sidney Fields (not to be confused with playwright and director Joe Fields), "I'm starting a Joe Fields Fund, to buy him a one-way ticket to Nassau and get him the hell out of New York, and rehearsals."

Olson said, "[Alan] is dedicated to the stage. I'm not." And all through the rehearsals of the play, according to the interview, Lerner had told her, "If you're going to do this, do it right or not at all." When the show opened, he said, "You've improved a lot since you opened in New Haven."

"The trouble is he thinks I should go on improving," she said. "He tells me by September I should really get this part down polished like a little gem—if I keep working at it. But by September I'm leaving the show."

The Lerners at this time were living in a duplex fourteen-room apartment on the Upper East Side. The May 5, 1957, *Herald-Tribune* carried an interview, bylined Helen Ormsbee, in which Olson's tone is somewhat subdued. It is reasonable to conclude that Joe Fields had taken offense at her comments about him, and undoubtedly her husband had, too.

She told Ormsbee that, aside from one brief visit to New York for theatergoing during her early movie years, she had first come to the city with Alan. "I came here as a bride," she said.

"At first I kept on with pictures. While Alan was working in Hollywood I'd do a film, and then when he came to New York I'd pack up and come, too. Sometimes, though, a picture took longer than I'd thought it would. This wasn't very satisfactory, especially now that I have two children. And so I didn't renew my film contract. Not that I won't go on working, but I must fit it in with my husband's commitments. I'm perfectly clear about one thing—his career comes first."

About her work in *The Tunnel of Love,* she said:

"There's something very stimulating about comedy. You've got to hold it all freshly in your mind, as if the lines you say had just that moment come into your thoughts. Tom Ewell is an expert at that—and delightful to work with."

Her remarks about Fields are quite different from those in the earlier interview.

"Then there's Joseph Fields, who directed our play besides being co-author of it. Every now and then he watches the performance and comes back with notes and comments for us. We like that. It keeps us on our toes.

"One day last summer my husband and I were talking. He looked at me and said, 'Nancy, maybe you'd be the right one for a part in that show.' And he told us about it. Afterwards I had to audition for the part, though. I felt as if I were back in school, but when I finished they said, 'Guess you'll do.' "

She said that the break-in tour of *The Tunnel of Love* had been hard. "Five weeks away from the children seemed so long. Liza is five now, and Jennifer three." Though the reporter noted the size of the Lerners' apartment, she did not say how large a staff they had to run it. Olson said, revealing perhaps more than she realized, that when her daughter Liza was playing with her dolls one afternoon, the child put them to bed and said, "Now be good and go to sleep. I'm going to rehearsal."

She continued, "Being married to Alan, I live in the theater vicariously. Even when I'm not playing. For instance, one night he and Fritz Loewe were writing songs for *My Fair Lady.* I'd gone to bed in the room upstairs over the studio.

"At two or three in the morning, the buzzer woke me. It was Alan, wanting me to come downstairs. I crawled into a robe and went down. Fritz was at the piano and Alan in the middle of the floor. 'We've finished that song!' they cried. 'We've got it! Listen.' So they did it for me, with Alan dancing around and leaping up onto a chair. It was *The Rain in Spain.*" The trouble with that story is that Lerner is absolutely specific about the origin of that song: in *The Street Where I Live,* he said that he and Fritz developed the idea while walking back from auditions, and wrote it in about ten minutes in the office.

As the summer passed, there was no sign of diminution of public interest in *My Fair Lady.* On the contrary, the excitement mounted. Rex Harrison recalled the electric sense of audience expectancy every night, every matinee. "And this kept you keyed, this kept you up more than anything," he said.

Lerner's memory was that at times Harrison walked through the part, though if he knew there was a significant celebrity in the house, his performance came back up to standard. Kitty Carlisle, on the other hand, said she never saw him give anything less than his best. She said, "On the stage he is a god—there is nobody like him."

By August Nancy Lerner had seen the show in New York twenty-seven times, not to mention rehearsals and performances in New Haven and Philadelphia. An interview with Marjorie Farnsworth in the *New York Journal American* of August 8, 1956, notes that she and Alan lived in their apartment in New York City and a house on Long Island.

"To return to Nancy's role as Mrs. Lerner," Farnsworth wrote. "She loves the excitement, the glamour, and even the hectic activity of opening nights. She is of course referring to the Lerner stage openings. What she could do without (and nicely thank you) are the days when Alan gets far removed from the world. When, to get him to down a lamb chop, get his hair cut or wear two shoes that match, she has to keep gently urging him, 'Come back, come back.' " This is a curious statement: Lerner was always fastidious about his clothes.

"Then on the BIG night (and it's always the same)," Farnsworth's story continued, "they quietly drink a glass of champagne 'to festive hopefulness' and leave for the theater where Mr.

Lerner never sits down and Mrs. Lerner slips into a seat usually next to someone near and dear to her. They meet at intermission, smile at one another and their tensions pass when the final-act curtain goes down."

The story describes Olson as Lerner's own "fair lady." (The dedication page of the printed edition of the show reads "For Nancy with Love.") Farnsworth's portrait is idyllic, the writing gushy in the manner of women reporters of the period, but a careful reading of the story betrays tensions in the marriage.

Rex Harrison's contract in the show was for nine months, not for run of the show. Though the terms of that contract have never been made public, we can make a reasonable surmise about its character. In addition to salary, the major figures in a musical receive a percentage of the box office, referred to as "points" in the show. Normally the lyricist, librettist, and composer receive two to three points each, though as lyricist and librettist Lerner may have settled for a total of five. Julie Andrews, who was receiving a salary of $2,000 a week, probably had no points in the show, but Moss Hart had at least some. And Harrison undoubtedly had points. If the points in a show rise too high, it becomes impossible to stage it at all. So some sort of compromise was reached, and whatever the terms of the contract, Harrison at this point could have made more money by leaving the show to return to movies. But Higgins was then—as it is to this day—the best role of his career. So Herman Levin had no trouble getting him to agree to stay on through the end of 1957.

All the while Kendall was growing weaker and suffering from headaches. Harrison's doctor did some blood tests on her. Just before Christmas, he telephoned Rex to say he wished to see him privately, but Harrison delayed the meeting until after Christmas. The holidays seem to have been particularly happy for them. After Kendall left for California to work in the film *Les Girls* with Gene Kelly and Mitzi Gaynor under George Cukor's direction, Harrison went to see his doctor at the Harkness Pavilion. The doctor said that since he did not know Kay's family, he had no choice but to tell Rex the results of the test, and let Harrison bear the burden of the knowledge. Kay Kendall had myeloid leukemia, a cancer in the bone marrow that prevents the production of blood cells. She would be dead in three years.

Harrison wrote to his wife, who was skiing with their son Carey in Austria. She flew to New York, where Harrison's doctor explained Kendall's condition to her. It was a peculiar situation: the wife of the woman's lover was being told her condition when her own blood family was not.

In the altered circumstances, Harrison not only was not opposed to divorce, he asked Lilli to give it to him as quickly as possible so that he could marry Kay Kendall and take care of her. In her autobiography, Palmer recalled her conversation with Rex at the Plaza Hotel, where she was staying.

Harrison said, "I cannot do it. You know how I feel about death. I cannot do it."

She said, "Well, you've got to consider it like a war mission. You've got to do it."

"I could only do it," Harrison said, "if I knew that you would come back to me and that there is some light at the end of the tunnel."

"But I'm going to marry Carlos," she said.

"Well, you can—you can," Harrison said. "And when you get that out of your system, then you can come back to me because we belong together."

Palmer said that she did in fact promise to return to him, to which he responded: "Well, if you change your mind, don't let me know."

Palmer filed a petition for divorce in Juarez, Mexico, on February 4, 1957, on grounds of incompatibility. An insight into how perfectly Harrison was typecast for Higgins, or how shrewdly Lerner had tailored the lyrics to fit him, came in a statement Palmer made to reporters in London when word of the divorce leaked out. She said:

"Let's face it, Englishmen don't like women, at least not in the way that Italians or Frenchmen do. Englishmen don't ever really look at a woman. The greatest compliment Rex could ever pay me was to say that being with me was as good as being with a pal."

On April 21 *My Fair Lady* received the Antoinette Perry Award—the Tony—as best musical of the year. Harrison received the award for best performance in a musical by an actor. Moss Hart received one as director, and Tonys went to Cecil Beaton for costume design, Oliver Smith for scenic design, and Franz Allers for musical direction, making a total of six for the show.

Though history would adjudge it one of the finest musicals in the annals of American theater, and some critics and scholars go beyond that to call it the pinnacle of the form, the best musical ever made, it did not receive the Pulitzer Prize.

In May 1957, a forty-foot-long piece of machinery weighing several tons came crashing down on the stage while Harrison was performing, narrowly missing him. In the confusion, the orchestra stopped playing and the man who had been afraid to open in New Haven calmly continued reciting his lyrics until the musicians found their places and rejoined him.

On June 23, after the evening performance, Reginald Carey Harrison and Kay Kendall were married at the Universalist Church of the Divine Paternity at Central Park West and Seventy-sixth Street, twenty blocks north of the theater.

On the evening of December 23, 1957, Harrison gave his last performance—his 750th—in the original Broadway run of the show. That night Kay Kendall made the only appearance of her life on an American stage. With the connivance of everyone in the company, she changed places with the actress playing the Queen of Transylvania in the first act. Moss Hart did a walk-on as her escort. In the second act Kendall played Higgins' mother's maid.

Harrison gave a party onstage for the company. For the American cast who had shared this adventure the fact that Harrison wasn't the only one leaving rendered the moment the more poignant. Julie Andrews, Stanley Holloway, and Robert Coote would soon be going, too. Edward Mulhare, who had substituted for Harrison during an illness and again during a vacation, was to take over the role of Higgins the next night, and British actress Sally Anne Howes would make her American stage debut as Julie Andrews' replacement in February.

My Fair Lady was by no means over for Hart, Lerner, Harrison, Andrews, Holloway, and Coote. On the contrary, they were only getting a break from it. Binkie Beaumont, who had bargained for the rights to present the show in London when he released Harrison from *Bell, Book and Candle,* had set the West End opening for the end of April. Lerner noted that it would be theatrical suicide to do the show there without Harrison, Andrews, Holloway, and Coote in their original roles.

They were to leave for London to begin rehearsals. After a vacation, Andrews arrived in London, having become, as she put it, "comparatively rich." Robert Windeler, in his biography of Andrews, wrote that she was accompanied by 260 pounds of excess baggage and a canary that had been given to her by the company of *My Fair Lady.* He said, "The girl who had flown to New York

for *The Boy Friend* four years before with just two battered suit-
cases, arrived in [an] Alaska sealskin coat . . . a pearl-and-gold
ring . . . clinging American-designed white wool dress and a
seed-pearl-and-gold locket, another gift from the *My Fair Lady*
cast." Seven trunks of clothes and other belongings followed her.

Stanley Holloway, the first of the team to arrive in London, caused
a stir when, in an interview in the *Sunday Express,* he excoriated
Rex Harrison. The newspaper quoted him as saying, "Rex and I
certainly had nothing in common. In fact, he didn't once come to
my dressing room during the two years we were in the show together. Nor did I go to his. . . . Well, you know, in *My Fair Lady*
Rex really plays himself. For Professor Higgins is arrogant and
rude. But charming . . . He's got amazing charm, that man. The
chorus girls were wild about him." When he was asked if the
members of the company had liked Harrison, Holloway said, "I can
only tell you that when Rex was leaving the show he gave a small
cocktail party for the cast and stagehands. Not a single stagehand
turned up."

Holloway later claimed that he had been misquoted. Lerner believed, however, that he must have said something the reporter
could hang a story on. Harrison was in Paris with Kay Kendall
when it broke. He told reporters, "Holloway and the *Express* made
me look like a beast. It was such a happy company in New York and
everyone got along so well. I didn't even realize Holloway had a
gripe." Harrison said he was prepared to sue Holloway. "I've noti-
fied my solicitors in London. I have to take steps. Perhaps he'll
have to turn over his salary to me at the end of each week."

Lerner, who was also in Paris, received a call from a friend at the
Daily Express in London, saying that the paper would like to help
repair the damage and promising that if Harrison would consent
to an interview with the paper's Paris correspondent, he would be
treated fairly. Lerner arranged for the paper's Paris man to be
invited to a cocktail party that Alan and Rex would attend. The
reporter predicted, "The moment Rex hears I'm a reporter, I know
he'll turn to me and say, 'Fuck off.' " So Lerner took Harrison aside
and convinced him that he could trust the man. Harrison and the
reporter began to talk, and the conversation took on a pleasant
tone. Kay arrived. Rex introduced her to the man, saying, "He's
from the *Express.*"

Kay said, "Fuck off," and the interview ended.

When Harrison returned to London, Stanley Holloway apologized for the *Express* story, apparently to Harrison's satisfaction, and rehearsals got under way. Andrews remembered that she had to "brush up my Cockney and put back the heavy accent that I had had to tone down" for the New York audiences.

The furor over the show was unprecedented, with newspapers headlining "Five more days" and then "Four more days" and people flying to London from all over Europe and America for the opening. Implicit in all the interest was a predictable raised-eyebrow curiosity about what "the Colonials," as Americans are secretly and sometimes not so secretly referred to by the English, had done to "their" Shaw. The fact that Shaw was Irish had long since been obscured in that process by which the English appropriate the products of Celtic creativity as their own. "The British," reported Kitty Carlisle, "felt that it was Shaw and Eliza Doolittle coming home."

The opening night was April 30, 1958. The audience, in white ties and dinner jackets and formal gowns, accorded the cast a four-minute standing ovation, bringing eight curtain calls that were brought to closure only when the orchestra played *God Save the Queen.* The critics were almost universally impressed, and those who had seen the show in New York predictably thought the London production was better.

One minute after midnight, the original New York cast album—previously withheld—went on the market in England, becoming an immediate best-seller.

A command performance occurred on the Monday following the show's opening. Moss Hart worked with the Queen's equerry on protocol for the evening. The show continued in its triumphant London engagement. Moss Hart and Kitty Carlisle returned to America on the *Queen Elizabeth.* Given his lavish spending habits, he had never really known unshakable financial security, and *My Fair Lady* gave it to him. And waiting for him in the stateroom was one of the first rave reviews of his memoir *Act One,* which would become a best-seller.

The London cast of *My Fair Lady* went into the studio on a rainy February day in October 1959, to make a second album of the score. The transition from mono to stereo had occurred since the recording of the first album, and the new version was made in both formats.

Warner Brothers purchased the film rights to the show, which would be released in this new version in 1964. Jack Warner thought Julie Andrews had insufficient international name for the part of Eliza Doolittle. Warner didn't even want to use Rex Harrison in the picture, preferring Cary Grant. Lerner objected, saying that there was "an unmistakable Cockney strain" in Grant's English. Lerner was wrong. Though he quoted himself confidently in *The Street Where I Live,* he betrayed that his ear for accents was not good. Grant's accent has nothing to do with London and the Bow Bells. Grant was born in Bristol, which is Celtic country. The city is directly across a narrow river from Cardiff, Wales. Grant's accent is essentially a synthetic one, carefully cadenced, that he developed after settling in the United States, and to British ears he sounds American. To the extent that he retained traces of his origins, his voice echoes the west country, which scholars think may be the source of the "standard" American accent. In any event, Grant declined the part, saying that only a fool would follow Rex Harrison in the role. Warner then suggested Rock Hudson, causing Lerner to say, "A fine actor, but all wrong."

"Why?" Warner asked. "He's not Cockney."

"Neither is Marcello Mastroianni," Lerner said, "but that doesn't qualify him to play Henry Higgins."

Warner finally did accept the inevitability of Rex Harrison in the role, but he replaced Julie Andrews with Audrey Hepburn, whose singing abilities were minimal. Marni Nixon, a Los Angeles studio singer almost unknown to the public but legendary in the profession for her musicianship and an almost eerie ability to match the vocal sounds of other people, sang Eliza Doolittle's songs. Hepburn then synchronized her lip movements to Nixon's voice tracks.

Lerner hated the movie version of the play.

There exists a tape of the scenes involving Julie Andrews, made by her understudy, Lola Fischer, very early in the run of the show. A member of the backstage crew recorded it so that Fischer could study those scenes. But that tape, as crude as it is, gives a glimpse into what Moss Hart's direction gave the show.

Miles Kreuger said, "The film is like a caricature of the original work. What characterized the original was Moss Hart's brilliant sense of timing. The show was crisp and cool. It was not a warm and loving show. I remember that in rehearsals, Rex would try to sing. And he was trying to be funny. One time Moss said to him,

'We have a cast full of comedians and we have a cast full of singers. I want you to speak the words, and I don't want you to be funny. You are the acerbic edge of this show.' The minute Moss Hart's back was turned, Rex Harrison started to soften that edge by singing a little, by being charming. If you compare the original 1956 Broadway cast album with the 1958 London cast album with the 1964 movie soundtrack, you hear the performance of Rex Harrison growing blunter and less sharp and immensely less adequate. He is the only major actor I have ever heard of who grew progressively incompetent in a major leading role, for which he was world-famous."

One thing that the early tape of the show reveals is the brilliance of the performance by Julie Andrews, who makes her flower girl a gutsy, unintimidated, admirable creature. Andrews' disappointment at losing the role to Hepburn was assuaged when the Disney studio signed her for the role of Mary Poppins, which established her as a major international film star. Ironically, Harrison and Andrews were onstage together in Hollywood to receive Academy Awards, he for Higgins, she for Mary Poppins. She gave her only public sign of bitterness at being passed over for the film role of Eliza. She approached the microphone and said, "My name is Marni Nixon."

Lerner told Tony Thomas, "I felt that *Fair Lady* should have been the best musical ever produced, because it had everything to do it with. It had been a successful film with Leslie Howard, the score was what we had wanted it to be, and we had an ideal cast. It should have been a perfect film. But again it started off on the wrong foot by not being shot in England. And to me that deprived it of its ultimate glory."

Harrison played Henry Higgins in the London production until March 18, 1959. He declined to make a curtain speech. Lauren Bacall, who was in the audience, recalled it as "an exciting moving evening" and noted that Kay Kendall had tears streaming down her face.

Harrison was engaged in a desperate deception. He had conspired with the doctors to keep Kendall from learning the nature of her illness, convincing her that the blood transfusions she was receiving were for anemia. He nursed her through her work in Paris on the film *Once More with Feeling* opposite Yul Brynner. When the film was completed, he took her to Italy, then to Switzerland.

Despite her weakness, her wit and verve for life were unflagging. Finally Harrison took her back to England and put her into the London Clinic. She whispered to Harrison, "I love you with all my heart," and slipped into a coma. At 12:30 P.M. on Sunday, September 6, Kay Kendall, gifted, funny, and beautiful, died. She was thirty-two.

Julie Andrews had left the London company of *My Fair Lady* a month earlier, on August 8, 1959. The cast gave an ovation after her final performance, and she stayed in her dressing room for an hour, weeping.

The original New York run of *My Fair Lady* ended on September 29, 1962, six and a half years after its opening.

Abe Lauffe, professor emeritus of English at the University of Pittsburgh and a scholar of musical theater, wrote in his book *Broadway's Greatest Musicals* that the show "broke records not only for number of consecutive performances and gross receipts in New York, but also, possibly, for number of performances given all over the world. Within a few years the show became internationally known, with companies in Australia, Sweden, and Mexico. Four years after the show had opened on Broadway, it was running simultaneously in London, Oslo, Stockholm, Melbourne, Copenhagen, and Helsinki. It was also presented in Amsterdam, Moscow, and Israel." There were companies in Spain and South America.

It became the third longest-running show in Broadway history, exceeded only by two nonmusicals, *Tobacco Road* and *Life with Father.* Its 2,717 consecutive performances made it the longest-running musical on Broadway up to that time, and it has been exceeded only by *Fiddler on the Roof* with 3,242 and *Hello, Dolly!* with 2,844. And, Lauffe noted, "many showmen wondered why the producers closed the show, since it was still playing to profitable houses."

Lerner wrote, "In Germany . . . where every major city has a state theater, there are over five hundred performances a year, second only to Wagner—much to Fritz's amused satisfaction."

Miles Kreuger observed, "The importance of *My Fair Lady* can't even be measured against shows of today, in terms of the public being preoccupied and fascinated by it. The only other shows I can think of like that would be *H.M.S. Pinafore* in 1879 and *The Merry Widow* in the period from 1905, when it opened in Vienna, and 1907, when it finally got to Broadway. It made the front page not of the entertainment sections, but the front page of major newspapers when Lola Fischer had to go on in place of Julie Andrews."

The score was recorded in the language of every country in which the show appeared, sometimes several times. In the first two years of its Broadway run, it grossed $12 million and Lowal, the corporation held jointly by Lerner and Loewe, owned 30 percent of the show. By 1970 approximately sixty albums of the score had been made. The show was revived on Broadway in 1975. By 1978 CBS had made $42 million on its $400,000 investment. In 1965, when the film version had been in release for a year, Warner Brothers estimated that the gross revenues of the albums and the first year of the film came to $800 million.

Lerner was always puzzled by this. "The songs of *My Fair Lady* are good songs, and I know they are," he wrote, "but the quality still falls short of explaining why its popularity ascended to such an unprecedented height. I have no answer and I am grateful for my ignorance. It would corrupt my soul and destroy my creative life if I did."

He thought that the right people had come together in the right circumstances and the right vehicle at the right time, but he was never quite sure. He said to Herman Levin, "Who knows? It may have been the chandeliers."

thirteen

GIGI

After the success of *An American in Paris,* Arthur Freed had signed Lerner to a three-picture writing contract. The first of these was the 1954 film version of *Brigadoon,* with Gene Kelly and Van Johnson, and directed by Vincente Minnelli. Lerner was disappointed by the picture. The film is quite wooden, for all the teaming again of Kelly, Minnelli, and Lerner. Lerner said, "That was unfortunate. Arthur Freed was the producer, and he was and for all I know is the best producer that ever was, and he taught me everything I ever learned about being in films. He was marvelous. He created the Hollywood musical in the best sense of the word. But it was one of those mistakes, putting it on a sound stage instead of doing it in Scotland. I suppose, when I think about it, it takes genuinely talented people to do something really bad." (TT)

The next picture under the contract was to be a musical version of *Huckleberry Finn,* with music by Burton Lane. Freed had at first planned on using lyricist Yip Harburg, with whom Lane had written the score for *Finian's Rainbow.* Lane said:

"Alan and I had just finished *Royal Wedding* for Arthur Freed. He signed me and Yip Harburg. This was at the time when the blacklist started. Yip made a deal with Metro that he could write a couple of songs for it. He had a show called *Flahooley* in New York. He would go back to New York, then come back to finish the score. But Yip got caught in the blacklist. Arthur Freed said to me, 'How would you like to do this with Alan Lerner?' I said, 'Okay.'

"We did a score that everybody was crazy about. They were looking for a new kid to play Huckleberry Finn. William Warfield was going to play Jim. Gene Kelly and Danny Kaye were going to play the Duke and the Dauphin, though I thought it was wrong to have two big stars in such secondary parts.

"Because of Alan's peculiar thinking, he would go off and not come back. He was doing *Paint Your Wagon* in New York. I was guaranteed a certain amount of money every week whether we wrote anything or not. I made more money on *Huckleberry Finn* than I ever made in my life, because of Alan not being there to do the job and finish it up.

"Danny Kaye was supposed to start *Hans Christian Andersen* at the Goldwyn Studios, and they suddenly realized that Gene Kelly would not finish *Singin' in the Rain* in time to do *Huckleberry Finn* in the time they had. It got all snagged up in schedules. The picture was called off and the songs reverted back to Alan and me. We talked about doing a stage version. But we never did it."

The blacklist was terrorizing the entire movie industry. Lane had been signed as both a composer and producer by Paramount.

"Y. Frank Freeman, the head of Paramount, was the guy who cleared everybody for all the studios," he said. "He was the center, working with the American Legion. I wanted to do *Finian's Rainbow*. Freeman said, 'That was written by that Communist Yip Harburg.' He apparently didn't associate me with it.

"I said, 'Mr. Freeman, Yip wouldn't join the Automobile Club. I've known Yip since I was fifteen years old. Yip is not a Communist.'

"I finally said, 'There's something wrong here in Hollywood. You're going to let the American Legion tell you who you can hire? You know that you can't make a good picture without talented people, and everybody I want to hire, I can't hire. I'm getting a lot of money here, but you're throwing your money away, because I cannot produce if I don't have the talented people to work with.' "

The accumulating pressures of the blacklist so frustrated Lane that he left Hollywood and returned to New York, where he would in due course write two more stage musicals with Lerner.

Lerner had thus written two pictures under the terms of the deal with Arthur Freed, one that he disliked and one that never got into production. He owed Freed another film, and Freed flew to Philadelphia during the tryouts of *My Fair Lady* to suggest that they make a musical film from Colette's novel *Gigi.* In August of 1956, with *My Fair Lady* sold out two years in advance and looking for his next project, Lerner flew to Los Angeles for a further meeting with Freed.

The novel is about a young girl being trained by her two aunts in the social graces so that she may become a courtesan. A rich young man falls in love with her and transforms her life. The story thus embraces two of Lerner's three thematic preoccupations: the courtesan and the Pygmalion or Cinderella transformation.

Lerner was particularly eager to have Maurice Chevalier play one of the key roles in the story. He said that Chevalier was one of four stars he had always worshipped and wanted to work with; the other three were Fred Astaire, with whom he had worked on *Royal Wedding,* Katharine Hepburn, who would eventually perform for him the title role in *Coco,* and Cagney. He wrote in *The Street Where I Live:* "James Cagney has retired, and so I will have to wait for another lifetime." Another lifetime: the choice of phrase is interesting.

Lerner was anxious to write the score with Fritz Loewe, who was inevitably gambling at the Palm Beach Casino in Cannes. Lerner knew quite well that Fritz wanted nothing to do with movies—he was interested only in writing for the stage. Earlier Alan had cabled Fritz to ask him to work on a film that in any case failed to materialize, a musical based on *Gone With the Wind.* Loewe's reply that must have been dictated, probably over a telephone, to a French telegraph clerk, since it arrived in his Viennese accent: *"Vind* not funny. Love Fritz." To Lerner's disappointment, Loewe now turned down the projected *Gigi.* Alan advised Freed he would write the film with someone else, on two conditions: that they try to get Chevalier for the role of Honoré Lachailles and that Cecil Beaton design the sets and costumes.

In New York that autumn, Lerner completed a first draft of the screenplay. He returned to California to show it to Freed, who was enthusiastic about it. But by November they still had no composer. Burton Lane was now at Paramount, coping as best he could with the problems created by the blacklist. Fritz was back in New York,

155

and Alan returned to make a last effort to interest him in the film. Loewe read the script and, to Lerner's vast relief, agreed to write the music.

They were to fly to Paris to begin work. The usually punctual Loewe was forty-five minutes late getting to what was then called Idlewild Airport. Only a year later did Lerner find out why. He tells the story with wry amusement in *The Street Where I Live.*

Before leaving for the airport that morning, Fritz had gone to see their accountant, Israel Katz, to examine their books "in order," Lerner wrote, "to reassure himself, I suppose, that I had not been raiding the till."

Lerner described Israel Katz as "a Merlin in the metaphysical world of the Internal Revenue Service," a man who spoke English and "taxasian." He wrote, "Israel, one of his assistants and I can be having a chat about my affairs, when suddenly he will turn to his assistant, address him in the language of 'taxasian' and I might as well be in Outer Mongolia." A few years after writing that, he may well have wished he had bothered to learn "taxasian" and that he had taken Loewe's suspicions seriously instead of dismissing them as illustrative of a quaint quirk of character. It was a year later that Israel Katz, "one of the kindest and most human beings I have ever known," asked him with a chuckle whether Fritz had made the plane that Saturday. He then explained why Fritz had been late.

Settling in at the Georges Cinq Hotel in Paris, Alan and Fritz started work on the first of Chevalier's songs, *Thank Heaven for Little Girls.* Then they made a trip to Belgium to see Chevalier, who was performing in a one-man show in Ostend. After the show Chevalier made a comment that lodged in Lerner's mind. He said, "At seventy-two, I am too told for women, too old for that extra glass of wine, too old for sports. All I have left is the audience but I have found that it is quite enough." The remark was the source of the song *I'm Glad I'm Not Young Any More.* Again Lerner was tailoring material to a performer.

Lerner wanted Audrey Hepburn for the role of *Gigi,* which she had played on the stage, but she turned it down. He wanted Dirk Bogarde for the part of Gaston, but Bogarde was unable to get a release from his contract with J. Arthur Rank. Leslie Caron, with whom Alan had worked in *An American in Paris,* took the title role, and Louis Jourdan eventually signed on to play Gaston, the bored and wealthy young man who falls in love with Gigi and marries her, thereby saving her from life as a courtesan, as Higgins by his training saves Eliza Doolittle from life as a flower girl.

Completing *Thank Heaven for Little Girls,* Lerner and Loewe moved on to I *Remember It Well.*

Fritz said of his career with Lerner, "All the songs that we wrote are dramatical ideas. We never attempted to write a song for the song's sake. Lerner had the idea for the song and gave me the title. I did the title. From then on it was developed dramatically. Whatever was needed to develop dramatically I would follow musically, which we did through our entire career. The one exception that I remember was *Say a Prayer for Me Tonight.* In that case I had the melody first, and Alan found the title, which fitted beautifully into *My Fair Lady.* We tried it out in New Haven. It was a charming song and Julie Andrews did it beautifully. But it laid an egg, and we threw it out the very next night. We stuck it into *Gigi.* And that was the only time I remember that we did anything of the kind."

It was not the only time Lerner retrieved an idea from an earlier show. *I Remember It Well* is a direct lift from a song in *Love Life.* It is even metrically the same. Lerner apparently assumed that no one would remember the earlier version. And the second version of the song is better, with Fritz Loewe's music much more effective than Weill's. The lyric has a wry charm that the earlier song lacked. Lerner showed the two songs to Chevalier, who loved them. Arthur Freed and Vincente Minnelli arrived in Paris toward the end of April, and began, with Cecil Beaton, to scout outdoor locations for the film. Though the studio system of Hollywood was collapsing, and location shooting enormously expensive, Freed had somehow convinced MGM that the whole film should be made in Paris.

One evening when Lerner, Loewe, and some others of the company were sitting in a café, someone said, "I don't understand Freed. Why do you all think he's such a great producer?"

Fritz said, "We're all here, aren't we?"

Noting that *Gigi* takes place around the turn of the century, Fritz Loewe later said to Miles Kreuger, "Much of the music has to have a French character, or what one thinks is a French character. Now, when Gaston goes to Maxim's at that time, he would only hear Viennese music. *The Merry Widow* was ruling the world at the time. So when we did *She's Not Thinking of Me,* I was convinced that it could only be a Viennese waltz." Lerner agonized over the lyric of that song. He was always reluctant to show a lyric to anyone before he was satisfied with it, and his refusal to do so fired the curiosity of Arthur Freed, himself a lyricist. André Previn, who was music director, arranger, and orchestrater of the picture, recalled:

"Arthur Freed came to me and said, 'We cannot wait any longer for it. I know Alan's finished. And even if he wants to polish it later, I've got to have it. We've got to get going. And he won't give it to me. Here's what I want you to do. I'll get you a key to his apartment at the Georges Cinq and you go over there and steal it for me.

"I said, 'No.'

"Arthur said, 'What do you mean, no?'

"I said, 'No, Arthur, I am not going over there and sneak into his apartment and steal the lyric for you. But I'll tell you what I will do. I'll tell him it was suggested, and perhaps that will galvanize him.'

"Which is exactly what happened."

Fritz, by contrast, was always patient when Lerner was working on a lyric. If someone from the film asked where Lerner was, Fritz would reply, "The poor little boy. I have knocked him up." A variant on this was "Alan is pregnant." And Loewe was never more patient than during the preparation of *Gigi* in Paris, since the longer Lerner worried a lyric, the more time Fritz had for his girls and the chemin de fer tables.

Lerner noted that Fritz once looked in on him at six in the morning, when Alan had been working all night on the lyric to *Gigi*. Fritz had been not only up but out all night, gambling, drinking, and chain-smoking. One of the most difficult songs for Lerner was *I Remember It Well,* because of the sparsity of notes. The fact that he was reworking an old idea may have compounded the problem. Laymen often assume that the challenge to a lyricist is the wordy song with lots of notes, but it's not so. The simple melodies are harder, because one has so small a choice of words. Furthermore, since there are few notes, they are long notes, and that further restricts the choice: you must find words with long vowels to make it easier for the singer to sustain them. Lerner said, "The lyrics were terribly difficult because there were so few notes, only four syllables in each line. I was on it for about two weeks, day and night, despairing all the time. Fritz was delighted, he used to love me to be stuck on a lyric, because then he could go out and play. But I do like the song as it was finally finished." (TT)

Lerner wrote the first draft of the script in March. He repeated a device he had used in *An American in Paris.* As the characters in that earlier film introduced themselves in direct address to the audience, Maurice Chevalier looked into the camera and started telling you the story.

When Alan and Fritz had arrived in Paris, they had no songs and only that draft of the screenplay. Four and a half months later they had six of the planned eight songs for the film and a finished screenplay.

By then André Previn had begun prerecording. In making musical movies, it is the practice to record the songs first and then synchronize actions and lip movements to the music, but before that could be done, André had to write the orchestrations.

Previn is an extraordinary musician. He was born in Berlin in 1929 and raised in Los Angeles, where his parents moved as the Nazi persecution of the Jews deepened. He was recording as a jazz pianist by the time he was sixteen. At the incredibly young age of eighteen, he was head of the music department of MGM, which is to say that various brilliant composers, all of them his seniors, were reportable to him. I never met one who did not hold him in deep respect. In 1956, Previn made a best-selling jazz album of the music from *My Fair Lady.* He was equally adept as a film composer. Eventually he abandoned the movie industry to become one of the most distinguished symphony conductors of our time, although he still plays jazz on occasion. The late Johnny Green, who knew Previn well when he was a fellow composer at MGM, once said to me, in tribute to Previn's powers of analysis and memory, "If you have written a film score you don't want André to know all about, don't even walk by him in the parking lot carrying it in a closed briefcase." With all his accomplishments, Previn is devoid of airs or pretense. Multilingual and deeply cultivated, he has a gentle manner and speaks softly. But he is also very funny, and one can see how his kind of wit would readily accord with that of Lerner. André said:

"I knew Alan first. I did not meet Fritz until I arrived in Paris to work on *Gigi.* We were going into prerecording. I adored the score to *Gigi.* I thought it was wonderful. I had enormous admiration and respect for Fritz.

"He was the single most conceited man I ever knew. Well, I don't know whether that is the right word. Perhaps vain is a better word.

"When Fritz and I had worked together and I had listened to the score, I said, 'I must ask you a question. When you give me the piano parts of these songs, and I have orchestrated them, is it okay with you if I occasionally change a voicing or a spelling or a thing here and there, lighten it up and put things on the top that were on the bottom, to make it more orchestral? Would you mind that? Or are you conversant with orchestration, and want to go through it with me, like someone giving me a sketch?'

"And he said, 'You went to conservatory?'

"I said, 'Yes.'

"He said, 'Did they give you orchestration problems?'

"I said, 'Yeah.'

"He said, 'When you were given a piano piece by Brahms to orchestrate, did you change it?'

"I said to myself, 'Right! Oh-*kay.*' And I went back to my hotel room and did what I would normally do, I made arrangements to suit the orchestra. He never said anything. In fact he was very complimentary. But the equation with Brahms was extraordinary. Absolutely extraordinary.

"Another man who orchestrated on the film, Conrad Sallinger—a sensational musician and a lovely man—also asked Fritz whether he was very conversant with orchestration, as Kurt Weill was. Fritz really bridled and said to Connie, 'Do you know how much money I made last year?' It was an extraordinary answer.

"Fritz once asked me what I thought was technically the most difficult piano concerto of the standard repertoire, and I said, 'Brahms Two.'

"He said, 'I played that, you know.'

"I said, 'In public? My goodness, that's highly impressive. Can you still play it?' "

"He said, 'No, no, no. It would take me a month to get it back up.'

"And I thought, A month?

"Fritz was given to those things."

At a party in Paris that year, Alan met Micheline Muselli Pozzo di Borgo.

At the time she was thirty, and anyone who knew her then will attest that she was a breathtaking beauty, small, blonde, graceful, and speaking English with that Gallic accent so many American men find irresistible. Her Italian name derived from her Corsican background. Her father, a lawyer and a general in the French army, had died when she was young. She wanted to be an actress, an ambition she shared with four other Lerner wives. Her mother, without telling her, turned down a proffered movie contract.

"I was brokenhearted when I found out," she told a reporter. "So I decided I would be a lawyer. So I went to Joseph Pythan, one of the most prominent of criminal lawyers in France. He advised me and took me under his wing."

She studied at the Sorbonne, where she proved to be a brilliant student, and graduated. Her apprenticeship, which normally would have lasted three years, ended after a year when Pythan died. At the age of twenty, she became the youngest *avocat* ever called to the French bar.

She said, "The newspapers and magazines made a great deal about me being admitted to the bar at my age and I found myself in minor trouble with the authorities because it is unethical for a lawyer to gain publicity."

She became a defense attorney, handling the cases of rapists, thieves, murderers, and other criminals, and building a reputation, particularly for the eloquence of her addresses to juries. She was in the process of divorcing him when she met Lerner. Lerner, in a now-familiar pattern, began courting her while he waited for his divorce from Nancy Olson.

As we noted earlier, Lerner's superstition extended to the number thirteen. He told a reporter, "I know it sounds somewhat illogical, but our first success, *Brigadoon*, was packed with thirteens. There were thirteen principals, thirteen songs, and thirteen scenes. Since then, I've been greatly in favor of the number thirteen." Micheline considered the letter *M*, with which her first and second names began, to be a lucky number. Lerner said, "One of the talking points in proposing to her was the fact that 'M' is the thirteenth letter in the alphabet. This brought both our superstitions into line."

André Previn met her at this time. He said, "We were having dinner one night at a place called the Méditerranée, on the Left Bank. She left the table at one point, and Alan said, 'Isn't she wonderful?' And Fritz leaned across and said, no joke, 'Alan, my boy, *never* fuck lawyers!'"

Word of the new romance did not take long to cross the Atlantic. On October 15, 1957, *The New York Times* carried a brief United Press story datelined Milwaukee, Olson's home town: "Nancy Olson, actress, has separated from her husband, Alan Jay Lerner, who wrote the book for the musical *My Fair Lady*, it was revealed today. Mrs. Lerner said the separation occurred about a month ago. The couple were married in 1950 and have two children."

Principal photography on *Gigi* began in August, as planned. During that month, Parisians go on vacation, leaving the city almost deserted, except for tourists and moviemakers. It is the perfect time to shoot pictures there. Location shooting was completed by September.

With most of the picture on film, Lerner and Loewe headed for California. They stopped in London for a luncheon with Binkie Beaumont. Then occurred an incident that became distorted in the retelling, eventually turning up in newspaper stories as fact. In this version of the story, Alan and Fritz went to a showroom in London and bought two Rolls-Royces. When Alan reached for his checkbook, Fritz stopped him, saying, "I'll get this. You paid for lunch."

What actually happened, according to Lerner, is that he and Fritz stopped by the Rolls-Royce showroom on the way to the airport. Lerner had admired a Rolls convertible in Paris and wanted one like it. The salesman said it would take a year to fill the order. Lerner told him to order it, and from a color chart decided he wanted it in royal blue with a beige hood.

Then he told Fritz, "You must get one, too."

Fritz said, "What for? I don't want one."

Alan said, "Maybe you don't now. But when I have one and you don't you'll be sore as hell. Pick out a color."

Fritz chose a battleship gray, and Lerner told the salesman, "That's it. The gray one for Mr. Loewe and the blue one for me. We have no more time to discuss details. We have to catch a plane. Louis Dreyfus will be in touch with you." Dreyfus was co-owner of Chappell Music, publisher of the Lerner and Loewe music.

It is true, therefore, that Lerner and Loewe bought two Rolls-Royce convertibles in five minutes. When Dreyfus confirmed the order, the salesman was promoted to sales manager.

Gloria Messinger, managing director of ASCAP, the performing rights society through which Lerner and Loewe received their immense earnings from performance of their songs in movies and television, gave another example of Lerner's spending habits. "I was shopping for a fur coat in a shop on the East Side," she said. "The salesmen said, 'Excuse me, we don't usually do this, but would you mind if I left you alone for a few minutes? One of our best customers just came in. Already this year he's bought two fur coats for himself and three for his wife. It's Alan Jay Lerner.' And I thought, I'll bet it's Alan Jay Lerner."

Tenants of a house he had inhabited in Los Angeles found in a closet financial records that showed he thought nothing of spending $40,000 in 1960s money on clothing, jewels, and various whatnots in an afternoon's browsing through the shops on Rodeo Drive.

Said Benjamin Welles, no stranger to wealth himself, "I was there for weekends time and time again at his house at Center Island in Oyster Bay, sometimes with my wife and children, sometimes alone. Sometimes Kitty [Carlisle] would be there, sometimes Sidney [Gruson, of the *New York Times*] would be there. There were five or six servants all the time. That runs into money. There was an Alsatian butler and his Spanish wife and her Spanish sister, and Tony the chauffeur, and more. There were flowers galore and big apartments everywhere and later on he was always flying Concorde. Alan chartered a little seaplane and ran it like a taxi, to bring his friends out from New York. You could get there in fifteen minutes. It went back and forth all the time."

Burton Lane said, "I would like to have just what he spent on plane trips to Paris every year."

André Previn said, "Alan was very easy to criticize because he was larger than life. He didn't conform terribly easily. He lived a *very* rich and selfish life. And he had his own kind of morals and mores and predilections, and I'm sure they angered a lot of people. It was easy to snipe at him, but if you knew him, it was very hard to resist him. He was a terribly nice man. And generous.

"The enthusiasm Alan had for the theater, and the very wicked sense of humor! And the adoration of gossip. God, if you wanted to make Alan happy, you told him some kind of dopey gossip. He was like a chorus boy. He loved it.

"I really admired Alan's work a lot. I liked him as a friend enormously. He was great fun to be with. He had an indecent amount of charm. Working with him—it was never dull, by God."

The last two songs of the picture, *The Night They Invented Champagne* and *I'm Glad I'm Not Young Any More,* were recorded in California. The film was finished in October. The post-production work, orchestration, recording, and editing were completed by January 1958, and the picture was shown to a preview audience in Santa Barbara. The next day Lerner and Loewe discussed the film's shortcomings. It was too long and would have to be cut. But certain scenes, including that in which Chevalier and Hermione Gingold sing *I Remember It Well,* needed reshooting. This would mean reassembling a cast that had dispersed to various parts of the globe. Arthur Freed projected that the changes Lerner and Loewe wanted to make would cost $330,000. A meeting with Benny Thau, head of the studio, was arranged. Alan and Fritz had decided on their strategy.

When Thau refused their request for additional shooting, Lerner and Loewe said they would like to buy 10 percent of the film for

$330,000. Thau called Joe Vogel, the head of the company, in New York. Vogel came immediately to California and said that studio policy did not permit outside investment. Besides, he thought the picture was good as it was.

In Vogel's office after lunch, in the presence of Benny Thau and Arthur Freed, Lerner said, "Joe, Fritz and I would like to buy the print of *Gigi* for three million dollars." Vogel, after a long silence, asked if he, Arthur Freed, and Benny Thau might be excused to discuss the matter.

Lerner and Loewe went to the men's room, where, according to Lerner, Fritz said, "Dear boy, where the fuck are we going to get three million dollars?"

"We don't know. Don't you remember?"

"Don't remind me," Fritz said.

"What about Bill Paley?" It was Paley who, as head of CBS, had financed *My Fair Lady*.

"Bill Paley? Put three million dollars in a picture which isn't very good? My boy, he's not an idiot. Who would make such an offer?"

"We just did."

Fritz said, "That's because we don't have three million dollars. Bill Paley has. That's a big difference."

As amusing as this dialogue is, there is something disingenuous about it. The court record of Tina Loewe's separation from Fritz states that he was earning $450,000 a year from royalties. Thus from song royalties alone, Lerner and Loewe had a combined income of $900,000 a year. Lerner had more, with theater royalties on the libretti of both *Brigadoon* and *My Fair Lady*, as well as his earnings as a screenplay writer, not to mention the money he inherited. "Alan once let it slip," Benjamin Welles said, "that he had made fifteen million dollars by the time he was thirty-five." He was approaching forty when he had that men's room conference with Fritz. So there can be little doubt that, for all the profligacy of Alan's spending and Fritz's gambling, they were good for the money: on the security of their song royalties alone, they could have borrowed it from a bank.

A few minutes later, in his office, Joe Vogel said that since Lerner and Loewe felt so strongly that reshooting was needed, the studio would put up the additional money. *Gigi*, with the repairs completed, opened that spring in New York to excellent reviews. Lerner and Loewe prepared to go to England for the London opening of *My Fair Lady*, set for April 30. Shortly before they were to leave, they were given a testimonial dinner at the Lambs Club, where they had met. Maurice Chevalier flew in to perform.

Meanwhile, Lerner had brought Micheline from Paris. Doris Shapiro rented them a lavish apartment at the Stanhope Hotel, overlooking Fifth Avenue and Central Park from the fifth floor. Shortly afterward, she says, they moved to the St. Regis, then to a large furnished apartment on Sutton Place. She writes: "Alan changed houses easily. He simply had others come in and pack and move. He could leave an old home without nostalgia."

This paralleled his attitude to his collaborators and his wives. One wonders if there was anything in the world to which Alan Lerner was truly attached. Given the loveless home he grew up in—for all he adored his father, there is little evidence that the love was truly requited—and the fact that he was educated like a British public school boy, living away from home much of his childhood, this is perhaps not all that surprising. In all the Alan Jay Lerner canon there is not one true song of deep loss and longing. He might abandon women; they never abandoned him, with the possible exception of Micheline. Every writer works out of his own experience; even in selecting material, he chooses that which accords with his own inner imperatives and aesthetics and understanding. And Lerner never touched that chord in his lyrics. The pain of terrible loss was apparently not in his repertoire of emotional materials.

On Christmas Day in New York City—two months and ten days after Nancy Olson announced her separation from her husband— Micheline Muselli Pozzo di Borgo became the fourth Mrs. Alan Jay Lerner. This time he had married not a socialite, an aspiring singer, or an ingenue actress. He had married a lawyer, and she would not leave with the acquiescent docility of her predecessors. Kitty Carlisle detested her, and never made a secret of it. A *New York Times* article published September 21, 1988, said:

"She has liked just about everybody she has known, [Carlisle] said. Two notable exceptions: Cecil Beaton ('arrogant and snobbish') and Alan Jay Lerner's fourth wife, Micheline. 'I once hauled off and smacked her,' Mrs. Hart recalled with a touch of glee." Carlisle was offended, as she makes clear in her book, that when Micheline arrived in New York for the wedding, she did not know who she and Moss were. She tells us that Micheline said to Alan, "Oo *are* zees pipple, ze Mosses?"

On the evening of Tuesday, February 26, 1959, Fritz was having dinner at the Lambs. According to *New York Herald-Tribune* columnist Hy Gardner, he told a dinner companion (presumably female; Gardner didn't specify) that he felt nauseated and had a chest pain.

"It would be just my luck," he said, "to get a heart attack just when I'm at the peak of success in this rough business."

He returned to the Algonquin Hotel, and shortly after midnight he suffered a coronary attack. Lerner remembered that he got a call about three in the morning from the night manager of the Algonquin, who told him that Fritz had been taken with severe chest pains to the Medical Arts Center on West Fifty-seventh Street. Lerner dressed quickly, called his own doctor, Milton Kramer, a heart specialist at New York Hospital, and grabbed a taxi. "I arrived at the hospital," he remembered, "to find Fritz in pain, weak, and a ghastly shade of white. I demanded that he be placed in an oxygen tent at once. The hospital said they did not think it necessary, but I made so much noise they finally agreed. Shortly after, Dr. Kramer arrived and upon examination he informed me that Fritz had suffered a massive coronary. He could not evaluate his chances of survival, but said the first three days would be crucial." (Withal Alan's fixation on thirteen as his lucky number, he apparently did not notice that it is thirteen blocks from the Algonquin to the Medical Arts Center.)

The next day all the New York newspapers reported the story. One of them noted that Fritz was "recently divorced."

On February 27 the *New York Daily News* reported: "Loewe's lyricist, Alan Jay Lerner, spent most of the day with the composer, who was in an oxygen tent. Lerner was supposed to fly to Paris last night to spend a week with his French wife. Plans had called for Lerner to get together next week in London with Loewe, who was to have sailed Saturday on the *Queen Elizabeth* in the company of *Fair Lady* producer Herman Levin and director Moss Hart."

On February 28, in his *Little Old New York* column in the *Daily News,* Ed Sullivan wrote sentimentally of the composer as if his demise were imminent.

There is a certain quality of bounce and gaiety peculiar to the Viennese and it distinguished [sic] Fritz Loewe . . . now in the hospital after a heart attack. Through the oxygen tent, I'm certain

*that Fritz is regarding the world with as much gay impertinence
as he regarded the bouncing dice at Las Vegas. He'd discovered the
game of dice last September: "utterly charming," he told me. When
I rolled the dice, Fritz enthusiastically would rub my back for luck
and he insisted on the same massage when he rolled them. The
massage cost him a lot of money but didn't faze him a bit. We ran
into him at Henri Soule's a few weeks back. He was with the Moss
Harts but he came over to our table and said wistfully: "Can't we
go back to Las Vegas soon?" This isn't the first time he has been
hurried to a hospital. After the first reading of* My Fair Lady, *he
suffered an emergency appendectomy. While he was hospitalized,
he continued to compose his brilliant music. He always has had the
vivacious wit and philosophy of the true Viennese.*

*A critic suggested that his partner and lyricist, Alan Jay Lerner,
was lucky. "Indeed he is," said Fritz. "And the harder he works,
the luckier he gets."*

Sullivan was wrong about the remark. Its author was Lerner's
father.

A few days later the *New York Times* reported that Fritz was
"coming along nicely" but would be in the hospital for several
more weeks. It noted that Lerner had recently left for London with
Herman Levin and Moss Hart to complete casting for the West End
production.

Long afterward, Loewe told an Associated Press reporter: "If you
live through it, a heart attack is absolutely the best thing that can
happen to you. I never enjoyed life until I had my attack. I drank
from five at night until five in the morning. I smoked three, four
packs of cigarettes a day. It was a senseless, futile existence."

When he came out of his oxygen tent, his first questions were
about the London production of *My Fair Lady*. Told of its success,
he eased back in his bed in satisfaction, then said, "Goddamn it!
That son of a bitch Lerner got all my house seats."

On April 6, 1959, at the Academy Awards ceremony in the RKO
Pantages Theater in Hollywood, *Gigi* took nine Academy Awards,
including Best Screenplay based on material from another medium, Best Song, and Best Picture, along with a Special Award to
Maurice Chevalier. It was the largest number ever won by a film
in the thirty-one years of the Academy.

Lerner had two more of the golden statuettes to stand beside the one he already owned for the screenplay of *An American in Paris*. Receiving his statuette for Best Song, Fritz said, "I want to thank you all from the bottom of my somewhat damaged heart."

fourteen

THE ROAD TO CAMELOT

oris Shapiro remembered that when Fritz was released from the hospital to move into a suite at the Essex House, he was being trundled into the hotel in a wheelchair, wrapped in a blanket, looking "like a small immigrant getting off the boat." He spent the summer of 1958 at Cannes, trying to be moderate in his indulgences. By fall he was back in Manhattan.

In March 1956, in Philadelphia, after it became apparent that *My Fair Lady* was a hit, Lerner, Loewe, and Hart had taken an oath to work together again and begun to look for a project. They considered doing musicals based on *Children of Paradise, Father of the Bride,* and others, rejecting them all. Now Lerner and Hart thought they might be onto the right project. Lerner read Fritz a *New York Times* review praising T. H. White's *The Once and Future King,* yet another retelling of tales of the court of King Arthur.

"You must be crazy," Fritz said. "That king was a cuckold. Who the hell cares about a cuckold?"

Lerner pointed out that the tales of Arthur had persisted for a thousand years.

Fritz said, "That's only because you Americans and English are such children."

The legends of King Arthur come to us largely from Thomas Malory's *Le Morte d'Arthur*, which Caxton published in 1485. During the Renaissance, it was common for artists to paint biblical subjects in the costumes of their own times, not biblical times, and, similarly, Malory and other contributors to the Arthurian canon were not bothered by imposing the trappings and practices of their own eras on that of Arthur. The prior source of the stories, and the one that spread Arthur's name throughout Europe, was the *Historiae Regnum Brittaniae* (c. 1135) of Geoffrey of Monmouth, who was no more scrupulous of fact than Malory. He attached all sorts of classical precedents to the stories. The still earlier source was the Welsh antiquary Nennius, who between 796 and approximately 830 compiled or revised the *Historia Britonum*, in which he listed twelve victories ascribed to Arthur. The tales of Arthur were popular in the eleventh century in Wales, whose people saw him as a hero on horseback, holding back the advance of the hated Saxons. If an archetype for Arthur ever lived, it was around A.D. 500. Malory clothes his knights in articulated armor, which was not developed until almost his own time. And armored knights did not leap off spirited Arabian steeds and engage in sword-fighting, as they do in the movies: plate armor weighed as much as its wearers, who had to be helped onto their horses and, when they were felled, were almost as helpless as a turtle on its back. The horses bred to carry this combined weight were huge.

Some scholars date the emergence of knights as early as the eighth century, others as late as the tenth. At any rate, they were not around in the hundred years after the the Romans left Britain. It was an age of decline into savagery, and it has been largely lost to history. This made it possible for later writers to populate the vast reaches of dark virgin forest that covered much of Britain with dragons, griffins, giants, sorcerers, and enchantresses, and fill their tales with magic castles and ships that move without crews.

As Frances Gies observes in *The Knight in History* (New York, Harper & Row, 1984), "In England and America the popular image of the knight is preponderantly English, thanks to the overpowering appeal of the King Arthur story. Real knights, however, originated in France and were unknown in England until the Norman Conquest. The French-Welsh-English creators of the Arthur literature, who grafted onto a grain of historical fact a mass of legend about a sixth-century British chieftain, ended by creating a bizarre time warp in which knights in gleaming plate armor galloped anachronistically through the primitive political countryside of post-Roman Britain."

Even if one accepts White's setting of the story in *The Once and Future King* in the twelfth century, it is not a twelfth remotely in accord with historical reality. By then the Normans had come. Although they ruthlessly confiscated the lands of their new Angle and Saxon and Celtic subjects and wrought terrible hardship on them, they also gave the land a sense of legal order. William the Conqueror completed the work of civilizing that Alfred the Great had begun and unified the country, so that it was never again subject to the incursions of foreign ravagers. He, and his nobles, both French and Norman, imposed their language on England, and French remained the language of privilege and the courts for three hundred years; indeed, 60 percent of the vocabulary of the English language even now is French. Thus if White's Arthur and his knights are mostly Norman, then Lancelot du Lac of France cannot have an "accent" in the story: for Arthur and all the court would also speak French, not the language of the conquered Saxons.

The novel, actually four novels totaling more than six hundred pages, partakes of that English tradition of gentle whimsy that produced A. A. Milne's *Winnie-the-Pooh* and Kenneth Graham's *The Wind in the Willows.* The White novel has been called a satire, but the term seems inappropriate. At least a modicum of malice is implicit in satire, and *The Once and Future King* is devoid of it. And Fritz Loewe precisely delineated the problem: the bright romanticism of the play's first act would have to give way to the dark drama of the second, when Arthur understands that his wife Guinevere has taken his beloved friend Lancelot as her lover. It is comparatively easy to go from dark to light in music or narrative, but it is extremely difficult to go from light to dark. The problem would never find a solution, and the search for it would help put both Lerner and Hart in the hospital and open a great breach between Lerner and Loewe.

Fritz didn't finish reading the book, but in view of the enthusiasm of his two friends, he agreed to compose the music for the show when his doctor gave him permission to work again. He told Lerner: "My boy, I'll try it one more time. But if it's too tough or if I start to worry so much I can't work the way I want to, the next will be my last."

According to Kitty Carlisle's book, to Moss Hart's delight Lerner had asked him to collaborate with him on the libretto. The Harts were in Jamaica on a winter vacation when they received a letter from Alan saying that he had changed his mind and wanted to write it alone. To soften Hart's disappointment, Carlisle said, "You're well out of that. There's no way *Camelot* can ever be as good as *My Fair Lady* and you'll be the one who gets the blame. Just do what you did on *Fair Lady:* direct it, and help as much as you can." After they returned to their home at Beach Haven, New Jersey, they received Lerner's first draft of the script. Both of them judged it unworkable.

At this remove it is hard to tell when Lerner wrote what. But the final script shows an indifference to historical consistency that rivals Malory's. While Lerner is quite right in asserting that theater is not a realistic medium, it nonetheless must deal with credibility—and the "voluntary suspension of disbelief" without which no narrative can function. You cannot expect an audience to sit still for it if, to invent a preposterous example, Jesse James pulls out a pocket calculator to divide the spoils of a train robbery. It isn't that you cannot stage the fantastic and the magical, as witness *One Touch of Venus, The Wiz,* and for that matter *Brigadoon.* But the style must be consistent. The audience must be willing participants in the premise, and to sustain their participation, the premise must never be violated.

White's novel looks at the story of Arthur as if through a telescope from the twentieth century. He revels in anachronism. Merlin lives his life backward and remembers the future, when Malory and Tennyson will write of Arthur's deeds. For example, White says that Merlin possesses all sorts of weapons that have not been invented yet. He brings Robin Hood into the story, which he says airily takes place in "the twelfth century, or whenever it was." Yet later he has Lancelot say that the Holy Shroud was discovered in 1360, which sets the story in the fourteenth or later. The novel is not so much anachronistic as achronic. White mentions the Declaration of Independence, Freud, and Einstein. With its adulteries and betrayals and slaughters and necromancers and magical beasts and talking birds and historical distortions and keen psychological insights, it is like a mixture of Jerzy Koszinski, William Faulkner, Mickey Spillane, Lewis Carroll, and Doctor Seuss. It is long, sprawling, and complicated. The very effort to put White's fantasy onto the stage presented a series of problems that were never solved.

Lerner never even solved the problem of language. The trick in writing period fiction is not to use the language of the story's time—even Malory requires translation for a modern audience—but to avoid language that is conspicuously of our own time. And Lerner scrapes the sensitive ear in *I Wonder What the King Is Doing Tonight* when Arthur refers to himself as "a king who fought a dragon, whack'd him in two and fix'd his wagon." That last phrase is conspicuously modern slang, and American at that. Guinevere asks at one point, "Can you stay for lunch, Arthur?" There are other references to lunch as well. But "lunch" as a term for the midday meal is American usage, and recent. Into modern times the English referred to that meal as dinner, and the evening as supper; some people still do. (Guinevere says she must change for dinner, meaning the evening meal.)

Morgan Le Fay is tricked into temporarily imprisoning Arthur by Mordred's promise of chocolates. Chocolate was first seen in London in 1697, just thirty-five years before George Washington was born.

To be sure, just about every version of the Arthurian legend has been anachronistic, from Malory's translations in the Late Middle Ages of the French tales until the present. Mark Twain had fun with anachronisms in *A Connecticut Yankee in the Court of King Arthur,* and so did Rodgers and Hart in their musical version of that novel. But these were comedies. In comedies the anachronisms are part of the fun. But *Camelot* is essentially a tragedy, and the anachronisms breach the style of it, the very pitfall Lerner so consciously tried to avoid in his work.

The book and the play end with Arthur telling a boy named Tom of Warwick to go and spread the story of Camelot's glory. Thomas Malory came from Warwickshire, and was elected to Parliament for Warwickshire in 1445. He died in 1471. So the boy at the end of the play is Thomas Malory, and the play in essence has Arthur commissioning him to a career as his press agent. Thus if the story happens not in misty mythological time but between the twelfth and the fifteenth centuries, a period crowded with more or less known history, including that of Edward IV, who sent Malory to prison for the political error of backing the wrong side. Arthur seems to be about sixty by the end of the novel; but on the book's internal evidence the story has occurred across a span of three hundred years.

If Lerner meant these references and anachronisms to be funny, they don't work. White's book is a fantasy, in which they do work;

Lerner's play is a romantic tragedy about two men who love each other and love the same woman and by a painful accommodation share her, physically and otherwise. The germ of this plot is found in *An American in Paris,* in which the American painter Jerry Mulligan and the French singer Henri Barrelle both love the girl Lise and have affection for each other. In *An American in Paris,* however, they are unaware that they are sharing her. In *Camelot,* both men know it. In White's novel, Lancelot tells Guinevere, "In fact what you really want is two husbands." This theme had a powerful appeal to Lerner. He made it the spine of his play, and, as we shall see, returned to it repeatedly in later works.

Lerner felt strongly about Thornton Wilder's admonition that "more plays fail because of a breach in style than for any other reason." Yet that is precisely what was wrong with *Camelot* from the beginning. It wasn't just too long; it was and still is full of breaches of style.

But the most serious problem of the play lies in Lerner's alteration of the character of Lancelot. While he was writing, he was, as we shall see, going through a period of terrible tension with his French wife. In *Camelot,* Lerner projects the French knight Lancelot as a man of great physical beauty and insufferable vanity. He makes a fool of the character in the song Lancelot sings to introduce himself: *C'est moi.*

White's Lancelot, by contrast, is physically ugly and devoid of a sense of his own worth. He is constantly indeed striving to be worthy. He does not consider himself good, much less saintly; he only aspires to such an estate, and not with much hope. In his childhood he is ignored by his family, except for his Uncle Dap, who trains him in the arts of combat. White shows him to us as he examines his image in a piece of quartz: "So far as he could see— and he felt that there must be some reason for it somewhere—the boy's face was as ugly as a monster's . . . He looked like an African Ape." As the eldest son of his family, he knows he will someday be knighted, but he refuses to think of himself as Sir Lancelot. He decides as a child that when he grows up he will call himself the "Chevalier Mal Fet—the Ill-Made Knight." White tells us, "The boy was disabled by something we cannot explain," and he "hated himself." And, later, when he is grown:

"The best knight in the world: everybody envied the self-esteem which must surely be his. But Lancelot never believed he was good or nice. Under the grotesque, magnificent shell of a face like Quasimodo's, there was shame and self-loathing which had been planted there when he was tiny, by something which it is now too late to trace. It is so fatally easy to make young children believe that they are horrible."

If Lerner had left Lancelot as White portrayed him, we would have far less trouble understanding Arthur's forgiveness for and even tolerance of his affair with Guinevere. Indeed we would have less trouble understanding why Guinevere loves him. By altering Lancelot, Lerner changes both Arthur and Guinevere, because we are always defined by what (and whom) we love. And they love an incomparably beautiful but egotistical, shallow, vapid prig. That Arthur loves such a man leads the audience inexorably to an uncomfortable conclusion about the king.

That, more than anything else, was what was wrong with *Camelot.* It still is. It is there in the script. Why did Lerner have to make his Frenchman a fool? The answer to that question will, in due course, suggest itself: we shall see how the artist, consciously or unconsciously, works his personal life into his art. White's ugly, self-despising Lancelot becomes the vain and beautiful Frenchman during that time when Lerner is going through a turmoil of troubles with his vain and beautiful French wife. Doris Shapiro quotes him as saying: "Micheline's religion is getting too much. She's a devout narcissist, you know." The conclusion that his narcissistic Lancelot is an expression of his hatred of her is all but inescapable. This very subjectivity destroyed the play, successful though it was.

Strangely, the play is dedicated to Micheline.

Lerner, Loewe, and Hart discussed possible producers for the show, and then, as Lerner put it, "opted for greed and decided to produce it ourselves."

The rights to the last three books making up *The Once and Future King*—those to the first book were held by the Walt Disney organization—were duly obtained from the author, who lived on the island of Alderney, one of the Channel Islands. Julie Andrews and her husband, scenic designer Tony Walton, had a house nearby. And she was first choice for the role of Guinevere. She was still appearing in the London company of *My Fair Lady* at the time.

Andrews later said that after her long runs in the New York and London companies of *My Fair Lady*, her voice "was in a ragged state from night after night of belting. Then I had my tonsils out—at age twenty-three. I thought I would never sing again. I very tentatively and timidly took on *Camelot*. It was an enormous period of anxiety about my voice. The next eighteen months were a miracle to me—I got my voice back."

She said, *"Camelot* was just about my size and weight, a good level for me, and I enjoyed it so much more than *My Fair Lady."*

Moss Hart suggested Richard Burton for the role of King Arthur. Hart had written the screen adaptation of *Prince of Players,* in which Burton had played the actor Edwin Booth, brother of John Wilkes Booth, and knew him. Burton was then thirty-four. His face, pocked by childhood skin eruptions, was at once sensitive and manly, and he was compellingly attractive to women. With his classical training, great vibrant voice, and experience as a player of kings, he was the perfect Arthur.

But could he sing? Lerner wrote that "at birth when a Welshman is slapped on the behind, he does not cry, he sings *Men of Harlech* in perfect pitch." Burton was amused by this ethnic cliché, as one hears in an interview with Tony Thomas for the Canadian Broadcasting Corporation. On the tape, made in Toronto when the show was in rehearsal, Burton says to his Welsh countryman Thomas with a chuckle of shared understanding:

"Camelot. There's a Welsh name. It must be a Welsh story. It's about King Arthur, and the Scots claim King Arthur, and the English claim him, and the Welsh claim him, although I think the Irish let him go. King O'Arthur, I suppose he should be. We have a mountain in the north of Wales which is called Arthur's Seat, if you'll pardon the expression, so we have some claim. And we always think of Merlin as a Welsh magician.

"Had I ever sung professionally?" Burton said. "No, I had sung a couple of songs on the stage in the course of a play. But apart from the feeling that all Welshmen can sing—we should explode that myth; I know a few who can't, let me tell you, I know a few who, when they're singing *God Save the Queen,* sound as if they're singing *The Minstrel Boy to the Wars Has Gone.* They really don't know what they're singing.

"Now I got the job in an extraordinary way. Messrs Lerner and Loewe came to Hollywood to pick up their twenty-five Oscars or whatever it was they got last time, and they called and said they'd like me to be in their new musical. So I said I'd be enchanted, of course. I said, 'But what about singing?' And they said, 'Oh, we know you can sing.' And I said, 'How?' They said, 'Because we heard you sing at Ira Gershwin's at a party, we heard you sing a duet with Laurence Olivier.' And I said, 'You did?' And they said, 'Yes.'

"Well, Sir Laurence happened to be staying with me at the time, so I went home, and I said, 'Have we ever sung a duet together?'

"And he said, 'Not as far as I know, dear heart.' [On the tape, Burton's imitation of Olivier's voice and speech cadence is impeccable.]

"So I said, 'Lerner and Loewe think I have, that we did sing together, and they want me to be in a musical.' And he said, 'Say nothing and carry on.'

"So I said nothing and carried on."

Lerner, however, said in *The Street Where I Live* that he heard Burton sing Welsh folk songs not with Olivier but with Burton's wife Sybil.

Burton gave another version of the story to his brother, Graham, who recounts it in his book about the actor. In this account Lerner told Burton he needn't worry about singing: he could talk his way through the songs, as Rex Harrison did in *My Fair Lady*. Burton replied, "But I can't do that. What would they say at home to a Welshman who was in a musical and wasn't allowed to sing? I'd be classed as a traitor."

Whatever actually happened, Burton was being less than honest. He had sung in competition in Wales as a boy. He liked a good story and he was prone to embellish his tales. Julie Andrews later said that his stories were wonderfully entertaining for three weeks and then he began to repeat himself.

In the end, Burton told Lerner and Loewe he would think their offer over, then accepted the role for one year. He was to receive $4,000 a week and a percentage of the box office receipts.

The next actor cast was Robert Coote, who was still playing Pickering in the London company of *My Fair Lady*. When he was asked on the telephone if he had heard of *The Once and Future King*, he said, "Got it by my bedside. My favorite book. Want me to play Pellinore?"

"Yes."

"Love it. Absolutely love it. All that rusty armor. Couldn't be better."

Roddy McDowall, who pleaded for the part, was cast as the evil Mordred, Arthur's illegimate son.

Auditions for the part of Lancelot went on all that winter. One day Lerner and Hart were walking up the aisle, on the way out of the theater, when a young man in blue jeans (or in white ducks, by another account) walked onstage and began to sing. Lerner, Hart, and Loewe, who had been coming up another aisle, all stopped, then returned to their seats. At the end of the song, Fritz asked the handsome young man to sing another, which he did. After that he recited some Shakespeare. Lerner said they thought he was French Canadian because of his name, but learned later he was from Lawrence, Massachusetts, and "had only gone to Canada to work." Lerner was wrong. Though he was born in Lawrence, Robert Goulet had lived in Edmonton, Alberta, since his early adolescence, had been trained at the Toronto Conservatory of Music, and had accumulated a good deal of experience in radio, television, and theater in Canada. Goulet, who was on his way back to Toronto from Bermuda, was signed within the hour for the role of Lancelot. It would make him famous.

Lerner and Loewe went to Europe to work on the show. An Associated Press report by Robert Musel, filed June 22, 1959, catches a glimpse of the work in progress:

There's a certain hotel chambermaid in Paris who is humming a tune that belongs to the hit parade of 1960.

It snuggled into her ear while she was passing the suite of an American gentleman who spends a lot of his time coaxing melodies from the keyboard of a piano.

Frederick Loewe, composer of My Fair Lady, *is writing the most important music of his life—the most eagerly awaited musical comedy score in years.*

And the blandishments of the three cities in which he is working—London, Paris, Cannes—are as nothing compared with the challenge of weaving once more songs the whole world will want to sing (including the French chambermaid who has a head start).

Writing a smash hit musical is difficult enough at the best of times. But Loewe and his brilliant lyricist-librettist, Alan Jay Lerner, are working in Europe under an additional mental hazard such as few writers have had to face.

As the authors of My Fair Lady, *one of the most fabulous successes in the history of the stage, they know that everywhere it has played—which means practically everywhere—people will be wondering whether they can repeat the unprecedented.*

They are in the strange position of having set themselves such an extraordinary standard that what would pass for a great hit from anyone else might be reckoned a disappointment coming from them.

So the songs are taking shape on the manuscript paper with infinite care. Latest bulletin: six songs completed. And Lerner is still scribbling notes for the dialogue to come on sheets of yellow

*paper, folded in half because he says he cannot stand to see so much
empty space waiting to be filled.*

*The new musical, as yet untitled, is based on a satire on the Court
of King Arthur and his gallant knights of the round table by British
author T. H. White, a forthright chappie who wouldn't leave his
home in the Channel Islands even to sign the contract that would
make him rich.*

*Instead, agents, producers and technicians had to fly in a spe-
cially chartered plane to get his signature on the essential documents. White's book,* The Once and Future King, *concerns that
chivalrous triangle, King Arthur (who will be played by Richard
Burton), Queen Guinevere (Julie Andrews), and Sir Lancelot (Canadian newcomer Robert Goulet).*

*During one of his few breaks from the labor of creation Loewe
wandered into London's exclusive Les Ambassadeurs Club with a
friend who had heard three of the new songs.*

"Great," confided the friend. "Just as good as Fair Lady.*"*

*A mild-mannered thoughtful type, Loewe would not confirm or
deny this assessment. But he did not look unhappy . . .*

The show presented an obvious problem to Fritz in that there was
no stylistic model on which he could base the score. As he later said
to Miles Kreuger, "I probably have a kind of adaptability to locale.
I never do any research. It may also have to do with my background, which was serious, studying Chopin as well as Beethoven
or Bach or Ravel and Debussy. And so you get a general feeling for
music. Now the nationality of it, one just has to close one's eyes
and dream about it. I would say that if we had ever gone to Scotland, we would never have written *Brigadoon.*

"As for *Camelot,* Purcell is the earliest English music you can
go to. And this is much much earlier. And so there is no music,
you just have to make it up."

I Wonder What the King Is Doing Tonight?, we should note in
passing, is an example of the way Lerner would rework earlier
ideas: it derives from the question "I wonder what the princess is
doing this morning?" which occurs in *Royal Wedding. If Ever I
Would Leave You*—enumerating the seasons and circumstances in
which Lancelot could never leave Guinevere—is a classic laundry-
list song, and a lovely one.

Lerner had rented a château at Antibes because, he said, Fritz
wanted to be near the chemin de fer tables at Cannes. There he
installed his wife Micheline, their infant son Michael, his visiting

Fritz arriving at the Majestic Theater for the Broadway premiere of Camelot, *December 3, 1960.* (UPI/BETTMANN NEWSPHOTOS)

Fritz and Alan just after the opening of My Fair Lady *in 1956.*
(AP/WIDE WORLD PHOTOS)

Alan in 1983, just before the opening of Dance a Little Closer, *his thirteenth musical. He held to a belief that thirteen was his lucky number. The show, which closed in a night, was the end of his Broadway career.*
(AP/WIDE WORLD PHOTOS)

Fritz and Alan take a bow May 15, 1979, at a gala tribute to their work at the Winter Garden Theater. (UPI/Bᴇᴛᴛᴍᴀɴɴ Nᴇᴡsᴘʜᴏᴛᴏs)

On the set of Paint Your Wagon, *Alan and his fifth wife, Karen, strike an American Gothic pose. The movie was the most expensive musical ever filmed up to that time.* (BOB WILLOUGHBY)

Karen and Alan on the dock in front of the house at Center Island.
(WALLACE LITWIN)

Alan shares a joke with actor Lee Marvin on location for Paint Your Wagon. (BOB WILLOUGHBY)

*R*ichard Rodgers and Alan in April 1961. Rodgers was one of a number of composers Lerner worked with after Fritz Loewe retired. The new team, much heralded in the press, would never complete a show. (UPI/BETTMANN NEWSPHOTOS)

*A*lan leaves the Shubert Theater with Liz Robertson on January 30, 1986, after a memorial service for Yul Brynner. Brynner made a television commercial to be shown after his death of lung cancer, cautioning the public against smoking. Lerner, also a heavy smoker, would be dead of the same dread malady a little more than a year after this picture was taken. Robertson would later devote time and energy to the cause of fighting the disease. (UPI/BETTMANN NEWSPHOTOS)

Sir Laurence Olivier visits Alan and Liz Robertson, Lerner's eighth wife, backstage at the Minskoff Theater, where Dance a Little Closer *was in rehearsal. April 22, 1983.* (UPI/BETTMANN NEWSPHOTOS)

Alan with Liz Robertson, examining a model of the set for Dance a Little Closer *on March 7, 1983, just after the first rehearsal. The set, elaborate as most sets for Lerner shows were, turned out to be one of the musical's problems.* (UPI/BETTMANN NEWSPHOTOS)

This photo of Fritz Loewe, who had just turned thirty-six, was taken July 7, 1936, five days before the opening of Salute to Spring *at the St. Louis Municipal Opera. The lyricist was Earle Crooker, and it was the only show Loewe would write with any collaborator but Lerner.* (AP/WIDE WORLD PHOTOS)

Alan with Nancy Olsen in Hollywood, December 13, 1949. They were married—Alan for the third time—immediately after he completed work on the script of An American in Paris. *(AP/WIDE WORLD PHOTOS)*

Alan with Julie Andrews and Richard Burton backstage after the opening of Camelot *in New York. Burton is still in makeup.* (AP/WIDE WORLD PHOTOS)

Fritz in his apartment in New York, March 17, 1961. People were beginning to take him seriously when he insisted that he had retired. It had been three years since his heart attack. (AP/WIDE WORLD PHOTOS)

Alan and Micheline—his fourth wife—in 1964. Their divorce would fill more newspaper space than all his other divorces put together, and cost him more money. (UPI/Bettmann Newsphotos)

Alan and Fritz give a press conference in San Francisco, where they opened the stage version of Gigi *in 1973. It was their last collaboration for the stage.* (AP/WIDE WORLD PHOTOS)

*A*lan and Fritz with Rex Harrison in May 1979. They were planning a revival of My Fair Lady with Harrison in his old role as Higgins. (UPI/Bettmann Newsphotos)

daughters, Susan by Ruth Boyd and Liza and Jennifer by Nancy Olson, as well as nurses, servants and others. He invited Moss Hart to come over and work with him. When the Harts arrived, Lerner was not there: he had sailed off to Capri on his yacht. Fritz and Moss had no choice but to wait, as Burton Lane had waited through Lerner's absences from the work on *Huckleberry Finn*.

At summer's end, the party returned to New York, then at the coming of winter went to Palm Springs, California, where Fritz had acquired a house and would spend much of the rest of his life. Meanwhile, more of the team from *My Fair Lady* had been signed: Oliver Smith to design the sets, Abe Feder for lighting, Hanya Holm for choreography, and of course Franz Allers as conductor. As with *My Fair Lady,* financing of the show—the budget had been set at $400,000—came entirely from CBS.

In March 1960, on the fourth anniversary of the opening of *My Fair Lady,* a large ad in Sunday's *New York Times* announced that the new show, which by now had acquired the title *Camelot,* would open in November. Three-quarters of a million dollars worth of tickets were sold within a month.

And Lerner still had not produced a workable script.

Early that summer he moved to Sands' Point, Long Island, and invited Moss to come out for a few days. Kitty Carlisle says that it was apparently difficult to work with Micheline in the house: "She would waltz into the room where he and Moss were working, saying, 'I want to lerne about ze zeatre.' "

Whenever she quotes Micheline, Carlisle exaggerates the French accent in transliterations that are not always accurate. She says that Micheline would sit in the room while Hart and Lerner were working, making just enough sound to be distracting, and that when Fritz was working on a new melody, she would call from the next room, "Oh, zat sounds just like ze leetle Frrench folk song I used to zing." The French know perfectly well the difference between voiced and unvoiced fricatives, even in English; s and z are pronounced the same in both languages.

"To understand what happened that summer and subsequently on the road during the tryout period, it will be necessary to mention a few details about my health," Lerner wrote in *The Street Where I Live.*

"To understand the details concerning my health, it will be necessary to mention a few details concerning my private life."

He mentions his marriages, then says: "Ruthie was a lovely woman. All my wives were, with one aberrational exception. Her name will not appear in this book, but the havoc she wrought that summer must."

His nerves, he says, were so bad that work on the show slowed to a crawl. In July Micheline told him she was taking their son Michael, then two, to Europe for a while. She left. (They seem to have referred to the boy equally as Michel and Michael.)

Lerner soon was writing again. Then, he says, he got a call from her saying that she would never return to him and if he wanted to see Michael, he would have to do it in Europe. For three days, he says, "I felt torn, trapped, and helpless. I lost all control of my tear ducts and other bodily functions and could not get out of the chair." As July ended, he visited a psychiatrist, who prescribed a powerful medication—Lerner doesn't say what—and within two days he was back at work. He worked day and night, with little sleep, and only three days before rehearsals were to start in September, he had a completed script. His personal life was left in suspension as he dealt with the pressures of the show.

The first in a series of the troubles and tragedies that were to haunt the production arrived: Adrian, who had come out of a retirement caused by ill health to design the costumes, died of a heart attack before completing the task. A protegé, Tony Duquette, finished the work.

The show went into rehearsal, with Julie Andrews brewing her tea for the company and Richard Burton repairing to his dressing room for harder stuff. Coming from his coal-mining workingman background, Burton looked on womanizing and the ability to down immense quantities of liquor as evidences of manhood. Though his wife Sybil was often around, her presence did not impede his sexual explorations. Her tolerance of his philandering is like that of Lilli Palmer's toward Rex Harrison's, which leads one to reflect that perhaps women attain this largesse when large amounts of money are involved. At first Burton focused his attentions on M'el Dowd, who played the minor role of Morgan Le Fay.

Robert Goulet, according to Lerner, developed a severe crush on Julie Andrews, who was devoted to her husband and turned Goulet aside with grace and good humor. He went to the master, Burton, for advice, and got none. Burton told Lerner, "Why did he come to me? I couldn't get anywhere either." He later said that Andrews was one of the few leading ladies he had never slept with, which prompted from her the retort, "How dare he say such an awful thing about me?"

Graham Jenkins—Burton's name at birth was Jenkins—wrote in

Richard Burton, My Brother, "Rich never ate before going on stage but he drank copiously, starting with vodka and ending with a can or two or three of Budweiser beer. This was in the days when my brother's drinking was treated as a joke. Because however much booze he got through it never seemed to affect his performance. Colleagues who might otherwise have delivered a friendly warning indulged his choice of relaxation."

Burton, by all accounts, dominated the cast from the first moment of rehearsals. The dancers, actors, singers, and crew adored him, and he soon had a dedicated entourage that followed him everywhere, among them Goulet and John Cullum, at that time a member of the chorus and, like Goulet, making his first appearance in a major musical. Burton's power over the company was hypnotic. They would need his strength. Without it, according to Lerner, the show would never have reached Broadway.

fifteen

TROUBLES
IN
TORONTO

After five weeks of rehearsal in New York, *Camelot* moved to Toronto to inaugurate a huge new 3,200-seat theater, the twelve-million-dollar O'Keefe Centre, named for one of the divisions of Canadian Breweries Ltd. It had been donated to the city by E. P. Taylor, who had built the company by absorbing many smaller breweries and become one of the wealthiest men in Canada in the process.

Security around the theater was so tight during the rehearsal period that a guard almost tossed Taylor out. He said, "I'm sorry, sir, but you can't stand around here." Later the guard said, "I was polite to him, but I was ready to make him get out if he resisted." Taylor apparently took it with good grace. Every doorway had a guard, and every backstage passage had more guards. Newspapermen and photographers were barred from the theater, interviews with performers were forbidden, and no one was allowed to enter the building without a pass. In charge of all this security was Norman Rosemont, now an important film producer who then had been working with Lerner and Loewe for five years and managed Alfred Productions, the corporate entity through which they conducted their business affairs. Meanwhile, Robert Goulet was in bed with the flu; Moss Hart had it too.

Lerner, Loewe, and Hart all knew that new theaters are hazardous. It is widely believed that theaters absorb sound vibrations, that they become "tuned" by years of performances until they take on a living quality. New theaters are cold. The backstage crew, furthermore, is unfamiliar with the technical equipment. "Hanging the show"—that is, setting its scenery in place—which is difficult under the best of conditions, becomes a nightmare. There was already rumor about the hall's shortcomings. The consortium of businessmen who had built it took Tyrone Guthrie, director of the Stratford (Ontario) Shakespearean Festival, on a tour of the place, after which he said, "Well, gentlemen, a theater that is built for all purposes is a theater that is built for no purpose at all." Christopher Plummer, Lorne Greene, and other Canadian actors and directors had looked on it with dismay. Why, then, did such experienced theater people as Lerner, Loewe, and Hart consent to open a large and difficult show at the untested O'Keefe?

The major factor was money. Lerner said in his book that Hugh Walker, the manager of the new theater, had approached him some months before about opening the show there and offered the use of the theater free. Since the cost of out-of-town openings—moving the scenery, housing and feeding the cast, travel expenses—is enormous, the offer was tempting indeed. Help the show assuredly needed. With huge sets and an equally oversized cast and technical crew, it was easily the biggest production ever designed for Broadway. Furthermore, they thought they could, in Toronto, avoid the attentions of the "dear shits," as Lerner called them, the "wrecking crew" in Carlisle's term, from New York: the smiling people who wish you well while yearning for your failure. To Walker's offer Lerner had replied, "On one condition. And that is that no critics come up."

"We should have realized," Lerner wrote, "that the O'Keefe Brewery Company"—he had the name wrong—"and the city of Toronto did not intend to allow their new toy to be unveiled in secret. It was a national event. Planes were chartered to fly people in from all corners of Canada and the United States. Not only did we not escape from the theatrical horde of 'well-wishers,' but they were cordially invited, all expenses paid." Lerner went so far as to tell his friend Ben Welles that he had been double-crossed.

Lerner's account of events is not accurate. In any case, it is hard to see how he could ever have expected the directors of the O'Keefe to open a show in secrecy. It was precisely to draw attention to the new theater that they made him so generous an offer.

One of the witnesses to all that unfolded is Mary Jolliffe, who was publicist for the theater. An articulate and intelligent former Latin teacher born and raised in China, she had for six years prior to that been publicity and public relations director of the Stratford Festival, and later worked for the Metropolitan Opera. Jolliffe told me, "The person who did arrange for the kind of exposure that Lerner ostensibly did not wish was Alexander H. Cohen." Cohen, a highly intelligent and beautifully spoken man, is a prominent New York theatrical producer. "He was hired by Canadian Breweries Ltd. to be both a producer for the O'Keefe Centre during those first years as well as a booker," Jolliffe said. "So he wore two hats.

"It was Alex Cohen who loaded all the heavies from New York. He brought in the media from the outside as well as all the producers, because he wanted to get more bookings for the O'Keefe, he wanted to show it off to producers for his own future bookings. He was more interested in producers than journalists. I remember him calling me as the plane took off from New York, and saying, 'If this plane were to go down, Mary, New York would lose its whole theatrical infrastructure." Jolliffe said that, with Canadian Breweries Ltd. paying the bills, Cohen's out-of-town contingent was housed in the top floors of the Royal York Hotel, which is within walking distance west on Front Street from the O'Keefe. The *Camelot* company itself was lodged there and at the King Edward Hotel, also nearby.

Hugh Walker said, "Alexander Cohen wanted to bring in a lot of people who would say nice things about the theater, and he did so at my request and with my blessing. Alfred Drake, David Susskind, Walter Prude, assistant to Sol Hurok, and his wife, Agnes de Mille, were among the people who came." The out-of-towners also included singers Carol Channing, Jayne Morgan, and Giselle MacKenzie, and dancers Marge and Gower Champion.

This is Alex Cohen's account to me, thirty years and three weeks later, of the events leading up to that opening:

"About six months before the building was completed we naturally began to turn our attention to what would open this building. I was the theatrical consultant to the building of the theater, to the operation of the theater, and I was the booker. And I had the right to book anything into the theater that I wanted to book.

"Along about a year before they opened, I insisted that they have subscription. Subscription is the key to opening a theater on the road even in 1989, as it was in 1959. If you have the ability to guarantee an incoming attraction a couple of hundred thousand dollars a week for two or three weeks, you obviously get the attraction, and if you don't have that ability you lose a lot of attractions. So we went for subscription, then we decided we had to open this theater in the most flamboyant possible way. And that was my assignment.

"I went to a meeting in New York with Alan Lerner, whose offices were then I believe in 120 East Fifty-sixth Street. I had arranged to meet with Moss, Alan, Fritz, and Bud Widney.

"I had to have that show," Cohen said. "I knew that show had to open at O'Keefe Centre. But before going to them, I made a deal with the theater. I said, 'I want you to play the engagement of this show without rent. We don't get a nickle out of it. They just come here and play and they get all the marbles.' And they agreed.

"In those days theater terms were different than they are today. They were what we call sharing terms. The average deal was seventy-thirty, with the attraction getting seventy and the theater getting thirty. So in effect I made them the best deal that has ever been offered to any attraction, and if they'd turned it down they'd have been very foolish. They took the deal. They were very, very impressed that anybody cared enough about the show at that stage in its life to gamble the opening of a theater on it. They thought we were brave, and we thought they were very brave. We loved each other at the time.

"So we wrote this deal giving them a hundred percent of the gross. It hadn't been done before and it hasn't been done since. When we signed a contract, it is absolutely true that I was in charge of circusing the opening of the show. My interest was the theater and in showing people this majestic piece of work they had done there. And so we had marching bands, we had grandstands, we flew a plane from New York, with a full load, we flew another from London, with sixty or seventy people.

"Just about everybody in the business came up from New York."

Mary Jolliffe recalled meeting a train from New York at Union Station, a pillared limestone landmark across the street from the Royal York, to pick up two of the actors. "It was my mission to get Richard Burton and Bobby Coote to the King Edward," she said. "En route I took them into the O'Keefe. They were funny as hell, both of them. I think they'd sat up all night drinking. Burton took one look around that great cavernous hollow and said, 'Jesus, think of the hangovers that went into this.' And of course I fell about laughing."

To add to the tension, Lerner received two unexpected visitors not long before the opening, which was set for October 1, 1960. Micheline returned to Lerner with their son as abruptly as she had left.

One newspaper reported that two weeks before the opening formal wear rental shops began doing a brisk business, with women renting furs and gowns and men reserving dinner jackets. Limousine leasing services were similarly affected. Opening-night parties had been planned all over the city, which has long been sardonically referred to by Canadians as Toronto the Good, and sometimes Hogtown. The city at that time was grimly provincial, far from the sophisticated theater and film center into which it evolved in the 1970s and '80s. Curtain time was eight-fifteen.

"The opening night had its magic," Jolliffe said. "Everybody wanted a ticket. The publicity had mounted and mounted. It was an electric night. It was covered live by television, CTV and CBC, and all the radio stations. There were interviews with the guests. Canapés and champagne had been arranged, to be served at intermission to all the guests. It was opulent.

"The money poured into it by the Canadians gave *Camelot* the impetus to keep it going. We were the tryout. That show wasn't ready. Naturally, we thought it was wonderful in Toronto. It brought a glamour that this city had not known. There was a glamour about the occasion and the names and the event that was alien to this city. It wouldn't be now, of course. But something like it had not been seen—the Klieg lights, the red carpet, the names, Burton, Julie Andrews, Moss Hart, Lerner. It was harried, and it was exciting."

Twenty policemen directed traffic in front of the O'Keefe, which covers a full city block, moving the limos and taxis on as they disgorged their well-dressed occupants under the wide front-door canopy, which reaches out over the street. The front face of the building was lit with floodlights, and cameramen fired enough flashbulbs to compete with even that great white glow. An estimated 2,500 spectators stood on Front Street to watch the celebrities.

Lerner, Loewe, and Hart went to the theater early, leaving Kitty Carlisle to escort Micheline to the O'Keefe. Carlisle says in her book that when Micheline did not appear, she went on to the theater alone. She found the three men backstage with Micheline, who, she says, was "berating Alan unmercifully":

" 'Ow could you let me walk zroo ze strits of Toronto in zis beautiful dress alone? 'Ow could you be zo zoughtless?' "

Carlisle wrote, "She was working up to hysteria over the lack of escort, which had been her own idiotic fault. Alan was distraught."

Carlisle said she grabbed Micheline by the hand and dragged her down a hall, opened a door, and found herself on a fire escape. She said Micheline was raving uncontrolledly. "I hauled off and smacked her," she said. This was the incident she recalled with apparent pleasure to the *New York Times* writer in 1988.

She said Micheline stopped crying, and quoted her as saying sweetly, "Ees my drress rreally all rright? Do I look prreety?"

"Yes, really lovely."

"But ees too many petticoats, no?"

"No."

"Oh yes. You help me take one off?"

"Sure."

In an empty dressing room, Carlisle said, she got down on her knees and unhooked one of Micheline's petticoats and said, "Step out of it."

Then, Carlisle says, she rose to her feet and gave Micheline the petticoat. The latter said, "Zat ees ze wrrong one."

It is worth noting in passing that Carlisle never in her book attempts to transliterate Fritz Loewe's accent.

Doris Shapiro has another version of what happened. She writes that ten minutes before curtain, she found Micheline sitting on a tall wooden stool in the backstage confusion, wearing turquoise silk, pointing a finger at Alan and berating him. She said Alan was on one knee, looking up at her and pleading: "Forgive me, darling. Please forgive me. You're right. It was my fault."

According to Shapiro, Micheline said, "You know the woman doesn't speak English. How could you do that to my mother? She's an old woman."

"I just forgot. Forgive me."

"She's sitting there in the hotel room waiting to be picked up, and all the while you didn't send the car for her."

"I'll send it now. But, darling, it's almost time . . . We have to go."

You can take your choice of the two versions of what happened, Shapiro's or Carlisle's. This may help: the O'Keefe Centre has no fire escapes.

Mary Jolliffe has a different memory of Micheline. She said Lerner's wife was considerable help with the publicity: "She was very elegant and very gracious. We held a successful fashion gathering, to which she lent her presence, a luncheon for a group of fashion columnists and writers, hosted by the O'Keefe. All you had to say was *Camelot* and O'Keefe, and you had the press coming in droves."

Alex Cohen said, "I remember Micheline. She was an extremely bright woman, marvelous conversationalist—a bit of a flirt, I thought."

"She sure was fun to be with," Bud Widney said. "You could see why Alan fell into it."

The theater was packed. Cohen said, "Moss came out on the stage and welcomed everybody to the theater. He said, *'Camelot* is lovely, *Camelot* is going to be glorious, *Camelot* is long.' He said, 'You're going to be a lot older when you get out of here tonight.'

"I thought to myself, 'Well, that's either shrewd or very unnecessary.' Why tell them about it in advance? But he did, that was a conscious decision that he made. The play opened and it obviously was going to be a success because you were dealing with pros who would know how to cut the show." Mavor Moore, writing in the *Toronto Telegram* the next day, took note of Hart's announcement and said he wished Hart had not apologized.

Present during all of this was John Springer, the prominent New York publicist who had recently been engaged by both Lerner and Loewe. He had two more clients in the show, Richard Burton and Roddy McDowall. "I was standing in the back. It went on and on and on and on and on," he remembered.

Jolliffe had her own problems opening night: "The escalator caught fire." The building was safe, but the management feared that the smell would cause a panic in the audience. The hall was packed, all 3,200 seats. Two truckloads of firemen arrived and found that the escalator motor had merely overheated, and there was no real danger. Jolliffe said, "Then I was standing there in my long dress with an aerosol can to get the smell out."

Alex Cohen said, "The fire was smelled out by Paula Lawrence in the theater. She said to my wife, Hildy Parks, 'Something's on fire.' I got up and went out into the lobby. The fire department came during the performance." But there was no panic; indeed most of the audience never knew there had been a fire.

The show ran four and a half hours, instead of the normal two hours and forty or so minutes, the curtain at last coming down at twenty minutes to one. Lerner wrote, "Only *Tristan and Isolde* equaled it as a bladder contest." It was humorless and heavy, and the "dear shits" smiled broadly afterward.

Lerner found the Toronto critics to be kind, on the whole. He was lucky. The Toronto critics had, and still have, a reputation for reflexive gratuitous viciousness such that some performers simply will not play the city. One critic did praise the show for "helping considerably to shorten the winter"; another called it *"Gotterdämmerung* without laughs." Probably the reason the press was kind is that they were, at that time, still in awe of anything American. The late Nathan Cohen of the *Toronto Star* wasn't enamored of the show. Cohen was tough, cultivated, and uncompromising. But he was comparatively kind to the show in his review, as were the others. He and the critics on the city's other two dailies took up what seemed like a hobby for the next week or two: advising Lerner and Loewe and Hart how to fix their show. In New York, thanks to the two planeloads of the "heavies," the word was out that it was a disaster.

The next day Alan, Fritz, and Moss Hart frantically began to repair it, seeking to excise at least an hour and a half. Jolliffe remembered, "Moss Hart was working very hard, and I remember Kitty Carlisle coming in with sandwiches and beer for him, and the rehearsals being endless. Kitty was very much the *grande dame*, elegant, and very conscious of her position. Lerner was urbane. He was a specialist in charm—it came out in waves—and in dominating the environment. He would always enter through the front of the theater. He was much in evidence around the theater. You never saw Fritz Loewe. He came in by the stage entrance and he did his work and he left. He never went to any of the social things. As staff, we were not allowed to go in to watch rehearsals."

Hugh Walker said, "Fritz knew how to relax. If he felt himself getting worked up, he seemed to have the gift of saying, 'I'm not going to do this.' Alan would only get more so, pacing up and down like a caged tiger."

A *Globe and Mail* reporter described Moss Hart on the morning that followed the opening: "With his wife, Kitty Carlisle, he stood smiling, dark and flinty-eyed in the spanking new backstage quarters."

Hart told him, "The audience was so wonderful and warm. But I have to watch the show surgically later in the week. All the good things are there. It only needs tightening."

The reporter's next paragraph would prove prophetic: "The room eddied and swirled with newsmen and photographers, jostling well-wishers and asking Mr. Hart to pose. Miss Carlisle gave her husband a worried glance and looked as if she would like to take him and give him a sedative."

By Monday the curtain came down at midnight, and the hall's acoustics had been improved. But after that performance, Lerner began having dizzy spells. He consulted a doctor, who told him he was bleeding internally. He was rushed to Wellesley Hospital, which is about a mile north of the theater, where he learned he had a bleeding ulcer. Lerner told the doctor he would have to be back at work in three days at most. The doctor filled a syringe. Lerner woke five days later, on Saturday, only to be told he would have to stay in the hospital another week. Moss Hart sent a message that the show was going as well as could be expected and said he would not touch the writing of the play until Lerner returned. The following Saturday Lerner was told he could leave the hospital. As he waited with a nurse for an elevator, he saw a bed being rolled into the room he had just vacated. In the descending elevator, the nurse told him the new patient was Moss Hart, who that morning had suffered his second coronary thrombosis.

"That night," Jolliffe said, "the press kept phoning from all over the world. A friend of mine, who was drama critic for the Canadian Press, just stayed with me all night, taking the calls."

When Kitty Carlisle reached Hart's bedside, he told her, "Go immediately to Alan's room and tell him to take over the direction of the play until I'm well enough to come back, and not to look for anyone else." Hart would spend three weeks in the Toronto hospital. Carlisle said she later learned that Micheline telephoned the producer Irene Selznick to say, "Moss has had a heart attack. Who can we get to direct the show?"

Carlisle wrote that Micheline evidently had no faith in Hart's judgment or Lerner's abilities as a director. But Micheline was not the only one to doubt Lerner in this capacity. So did Fritz Loewe. Fritz said that it would be impossible for Alan to work on the rewrites and direct the show, that they needed a fresh mind to help them. Lerner felt it was imperative, for various technical reasons, that he, and not a new director, open the show in Boston. Fritz insisted that they find a new director immediately and left the room. "It was the first time," Lerner wrote in *The Street Where I Live,* "that the seams of our collaboration had begun to pull loose."

That is not so. There are too many witnesses to Fritz Loewe's determination not to work with Lerner again after *Brigadoon.*

Lerner went to Richard Burton, telling him that he would be directing the show himself for at least two weeks. He quotes Burton as saying, "Don't worry, love. We'll get through." And then: "Why don't you direct it yourself? Anybody else who comes in is liable to muck it up."

In *Burton* (G. P. Putnam's, New York, 1986) Hollis Alpert recounts something Lerner fails to mention in his own book. He says that Burton told Lerner, "Listen, luv, you're not going to have time to rehearse the understudies, so I'll take that for you." And from then on, Alpert says, Burton rehearsed them. Lerner did say that he couldn't recall an actor who was as much loved by a company as Richard Burton.

Tony Thomas got to know Burton fairly well during this period. As was often the case, Burton was doing two (or more) things at once: even as he worked on *Camelot,* he was performing in a two-hour radio drama for the Canadian Broadcasting Corporation.

Thomas, now a writer, film historian, and television producer in California, was one of his fellow actors.

"Every time anyone did a Welsh drama at CBC radio, I got a call," Thomas said. "They needed a few Welshmen around to do that lingo. I had met Richard twice before, and he and I being Welsh, and it being such a small club, we got along. They rounded up all the Welsh people and the other English types in Toronto to do this two-hour piece about the First World War, starring Burton. We did it in three or four days.

"Richard was rehearsing *Camelot,* so I went down to the O'Keefe quite a lot to watch them struggling through it. And it was a hell of a struggle. It wasn't in shape, it was so long, and it floundered, it waffled, and they didn't seem to be able to get a grasp on it. Moss Hart was looking very sick, and then he had the heart attack. It must have been the strain of it all.

"Lerner was a man of tremendous ego. And such people cannot admit to the areas in which they don't function well. His genius was lyricism, the poetry of words and ideas, but not structure. I don't consider that a fatal flaw in a writer unless he can't deal with it.

"It was logistically a terribly difficult subject to make into a musical. The glory of that musical is the music and the lyrics. The characters aren't all that great. You could see it in that month they were struggling through it at the O'Keefe. I saw the weariness. They were like men playing tennis in the dark. They were all on edge, trying to get a four-hour-and-more show down to two and a half."

"About a week after the opening," Alex Cohen said, "I was in the Royal York Hotel where Alan and Fritz were staying. They had the largest suite in the hotel, naturally. It's got a lot to do with people in the theater. We all get the largest suite in whatever hotel we're in. I was walking down the hall toward the door of Alan's suite, which was open, a big double door, probably because they had just ordered room service trays or something. And I could hear Alan yelling, 'Just wait till I get my hands on Alex Cohen! I'll kill him!'

"And I thought, What the hell is that about? I walked right into the room. Whatever it was about, he said nothing to me. There was a bit of being flustered, but there was no complaint. And in point of fact, there shouldn't have been, because they had a sold-out engagement, from which they kept a hundred percent of the receipts. There wasn't a seat to be had. They did us proud, but we did them proud. In a major way we were responsible for giving *Camelot* global publicity on its opening night in one city, in Toronto, which had been a dead-assed town. The year before O'Keefe opened the Royal Alexandra theater played five weeks, and that was it. O'Keefe played fifty-one weeks in its first year.

"Nathan Cohen of the *Toronto Star,* among others, disliked *Camelot.* He thought it was a mess. And at the time it was. But when you have a basic story, and Lerner and Loewe, and Moss Hart, and Richard Burton, and Julie Andrews, and Bobby Goulet, you have a hit show, and you know it. All you have to do is cut time. And they did. There never would have been any complaint if the notices had been good—none of that hollering if Nathan Cohen had said '*Camelot* is great.' Then Alex Cohen would have been the world's greatest hero.

"In later years, Alan came to me on several occasions, and his anger had evaporated."

The gulf between Alan and Fritz was growing. Lerner thought of a director who might be satisfactory to everyone in the company: José Ferrer. But Ferrer turned out to be unavailable. Lerner hoped that his call to Ferrer would at least prove to Fritz that he did not oppose finding another director. Loewe took no consolation from it.

In *The Street Where I Live,* Lerner wrote: "By the end of the week Fritz and I were seeing less and less of each other. Irritations and differences between us that had been long forgotten and were of little consequence at the time had now become the subject of questions by interviewers. Our replies traveled from mouth to mouth and by the time they reached us they were unrecognizable distortions. If we had stayed steadfastly and constantly together as we always had in the past we would have laughed, rowed, or shrugged but in the end gone on about our business. We did not. I do not know why we did not. I may have thought I knew then but whatever I thought, I am certain I was wrong. I have a feeling the reason was something far more insidious, something of which neither of us was aware and which affected each of us in different ways. I have a feeling it may have been too much success."

Or maybe a composer who didn't want to do *Camelot* in the first place was losing patience with a man who imperiously threw out his first two melodies in any project, had no real grasp of structure, and now saw himself as a director. The chasm between them was a silence. Lerner, in describing it, quoted two lines from a Noël Coward play:

"Do they fight?"

"Oh no. They're much too unhappy to fight."

Rumors got rolling to New York and Hollywood that *Camelot*, which was now two weeks behind schedule, would be closed in Boston. Lerner was deeply disturbed, and in an interview set up by his publicists told the *Globe and Mail* that nothing less than an atomic bomb would prevent its opening in New York. The rumors, Lerner said, "are absolutely untrue."

He said, "And I know where they started. The ladies in the theater parties got a bit hysterical and started spreading rumors that the show was closing."

Before it left Toronto, *Camelot* ran up another casualty: Hugh Walker, the O'Keefe's manager, also came down with an ulcer, and was carted off to Toronto General Hospital for surgery. Yet, for all its problems, the show closed out at the O'Keefe with a for then huge weekly gross of $110,161, up more than $4,000 from the previous week.

Then it moved on to begin four weeks at the Shubert Theater in Boston. Fritz refused to sit with Alan during the technical run-through. He hovered at the back of the theater and left before it was over. Later they had a confrontation about the lack of a director. Lerner said they were arguing in a vacuum: "And in a vacuum we remained."

Burton continued to be the strength of the company. He was in every way the opposite of the frightened Rex Harrison preparing for *My Fair Lady*. He had gone through doubt about taking a singing role in the first place, according to his brother Graham, but having done so he was determined to make it a triumph. Rich, as his family and close friends called him, accepted one scene change after another without complaint, learning replacement dialogue in his dressing room in an afternoon and integrating it easily into the show that night. Far from seeking reassurance, he was constantly dispensing it to other actors when morale sagged. He would make the rounds of dressing rooms, regaling his colleagues with his jokes and stories, easing their nerves, keeping them on course. John Springer said, "Richard was marvelous. He was the rock of Gibraltar. Richard was so positive. He was such a strong personality and strong presence." In *Richard Burton: A Life* (Boston: Little, Brown and Company, 1988), Melvyn Bragg wrote: "Fellow actors emphasize and insist that he was not a stealer of scenes, an upstager, did not throw his weight about. Particularly not to those he liked. They were 'family' and although he would rough and tumble he was just as willing to hold out a hand."

And even as they praised Burton, the people who were involved in *Camelot* always made comment on another stabilizing force in the show, Julie Andrews, operating her little tea stand backstage. In the four years since her terrified weekend with Moss Hart on *My Fair Lady*, she had become an accomplished and consummate professional. Indeed, the performers—Burton, Andrews, Coote, McDowall—seem never to have been the problem. The problem was Lerner's vast, clumsy script, the script he had chosen to write himself rather than in collaboration with Moss Hart.

By now a *Time* magazine crew had come aboard, working on a cover story on Lerner and Loewe. The magazine dispatched correspondents to interview *Hasty Pudding* colleagues Benjamin Welles and Stanley Miller in Washington.

In those days *Time* was not in the practice of giving bylines to its writer. But one of the reporters in Boston was Joyce Haber, later a well-known columnist. The writer in charge was Henry Anatole Grunwald, who later became editor-in-chief of Time, Inc., and still later was appointed ambassador to Austria by Ronald Reagan.

"Lerner smokes," the story noted, "and has a habit of twirling the ignited cigarette in his fingers like the active end of a turbo-prop." It said that Fritz had quit smoking but kept an unlighted cigarette in his hands, which he flattened and shredded as he talked. It recorded that he demolished a pack of cigarettes a day in this way, and that he fingered a piece of jade, as if it were a string of Greek worry beads, to calm his nerves.

The show's personal problems and tragedies continued to accumulate, the death of Adrian and the hospitalization of Lerner and Hart among them. The husband of a wardrobe mistress was found dead in their apartment. The show's chief electrician went into the hospital with a bladder problem. A chorus girl ran a needle into her foot onstage. Fritz Loewe said, "We will all be replaced tomorrow by hospital orderlies." Lerner had taken to calling him Sir Aggravate. It was a pun on the name of Sir Agravaine, brother of Sir Gawain.

In Boston Lerner had Apartment 1004 of the Ritz Carlton, with Micheline and two-year-old Michael in a suite across the hall. Two floors up, in 1204, according to the *Time* cover story of November 14, 1960, Fritz Loewe "broods under the fond eye of his current, 24-year-old girl friend. He calls her 'baby boy,' she calls him 'baby bear.'" Actually, Fritz called her Tammy boy. The story described the two men at this stage of their lives: "Short, lean, with the sallow skin of the heart patient, Loewe is fifty-nine and looks it; about the same height . . . with small bones and an unweathered complexion, Lerner is forty-two and could pass for a graduate student." Lerner was a devotee of psychoanalysis; Loewe scorned it. Lerner was dapper, Loewe was rumpled. Lerner lived on the telephone, and according to Fritz picked it up before he was fully awake in the morning. "Half the time he doesn't even know who he's going to call," Fritz said. Loewe hated phones because, he said, he picked one up in his childhood and learned a favorite uncle had killed himself. It is a story he told many times. "Bad news I don't want to hear, and good news I don't need anymore." He said that many times too: like the stories of his past, the line sounds rehearsed.

Doris Shapiro described Fritz's girlfriend, Tammy, as a young actress who didn't wear makeup. She said Tammy had a long, white, narrow face with large dark eyes and straight black hair combed back from her forehead. She said Tammy was in love with him, but Fritz wouldn't marry her because of their age difference, expecting that sooner or later she would turn to a younger man. "Fritz took better care of himself in love matters than Alan did," Shapiro wrote.

The *Time* story quotes Lerner as saying, "I don't bet." But Fritz, it said, "thinks the second biggest thrill" was to lose $30,000 in a night at the casino tables. It left it to the reader, titter titter, to figure out what the first biggest thrill was. The story noted that Lerner and Loewe had yachts on the Mediterranean, villas on the Riviera; Lerner had a town house in Manhattan and Fritz "an airy glass pleasure dome" in Palm Springs. It took note of the two Rolls-Royces. It said that when Lerner married Marion Bell, Fritz had an affair with her understudy. (That would mean he had the affair when he was still married to Tina.) Fritz said he couldn't stand the crying of children, which was why he didn't have any. He said that he treasured privacy and quiet more and more as he grew older.

He said: "What's the point of seeing people—those poor, sad, beautiful faces with all their heartbreaking troubles?"

John Springer said: "Fritz followed the line of least resistance. He was cool, relaxed. If they were going to get a cover story in *Time*, he couldn't have cared less. Alan was gung ho. That's when I was first involved with them. Since I handled Richard, and Alan and Fritz, and Roddy McDowall, I was very involved with that story. Joyce Haber was getting all the dirt possible, and she loved to get all the dirt possible."

The *Time* team of Grunwald and Haber learned nothing of the schism between Lerner and Loewe, saying in the final story that they were "marvelously meshed" in contrast to such love-hate teams as Gilbert and Sullivan. Nor did they uncover any trace of the troubles in Lerner's marriage. The article includes a photo by Milton Greene of Micheline and Michael. She is beautiful. So is the child.

And by this time Alan's problems with Micheline were enmeshed with his problems with Fritz.

Doris Shapiro wrote:

"Despite the troubles with *Camelot* and the ailing Lerner and Loewe attachment, Fritz was always ready for a gag. One night in his hotel suite he disappeared into another room, leaving me with Tammy sitting on the bed. When he reappeared, he was wearing Tammy's nightgown, his big head and chin peeping mischievously out of a Peter Pan collar, his legs and feet bare. . . .

"One day Alan committed the worst breach of faith imaginable. In an effort to appease Micheline and keep her from leaving again, Alan told Fritz he was going to allow her to sit in on their sacred creative sessions. Stunned, Fritz countered: If Micheline was going to join them, he would bring Tammy as well. Hardly a solution for *Camelot.* I watched Fritz approach the breaking point.

"One night the rift climaxed. I can remember cringing . . . on the bed in the Ritz Carlton Hotel as we listened to Fritz's all-night outburst of fury and pain down the hall. Luckily he didn't have another heart attack."

This is the only instance I have ever found of Fritz Loewe completely losing control. Several persons have told me that Fritz held Micheline at least partly responsible for the dissolution of his partnership with Lerner. Some of them said that Fritz hated her.

Shapiro wrote that during these estrangements from Fritz, Alan began to depend more and more on Bud Widney in story conferences, which did not escape Fritz's attention. He resented it, Shapiro said. Later, Burton Lane too would complain of Lerner's reliance on Widney's judgment.

Widney said that Fritz more than threatened to bring Tammy to a conference. He brought her. Yet, like everyone else, Widney was unable to specify the exact cause of the growing schism between Lerner and Loewe.

He said: "Even as close as I was, I have to do some kind of speculating about what it was. Specifically Alan was having a terrible time in Toronto and Boston with Micheline. The blowup came in Boston because Alan was trying to get his wife back and make her part of something that was going on, he allowed her to come into sessions that she had never been in before. Suddenly there was a third person in the middle of a creative work session, so Fritz brought his girlfriend Tammy into it. But that was only part of it. It provoked an anger that was going on prior to that. Fritz thought that in some way Alan was doing one-upmanship on him, maybe chiseling him out of money or hiring Norman Rosemont to do publicity about the two but it was only coming out about Alan. None of which was true. But Fritz was paranoid about it.

"There's a third-party thing that happens in story meetings, and it saves an enormous amount of time. You know in the theater that what you're confronted with is an audience. You're confronted with something that's got to land, a joke that's going to make people laugh or not, a character or situation that's going to tug at your heart or it isn't. You find out right away. That was necessary to Alan. Fritz couldn't sit through it as the years went on, yet he was sort of envious that he wasn't asked."

I told Widney that no one had ever told me what it was that destroyed the working relationship between Lerner and Loewe. "No," Bud said, "and I don't think you'll find anyone who can. Some specific dramatic thing, I don't think you'll find anything. It was an accumulation of things."

The *Time* magazine team ended their researches in Boston and went back to New York to write their cover story. Grunwald and

Haber missed still another part of the story. Neither they nor any of their associates turned up the fact that Lerner had become a heavy and habituated amphetamine user.

The show lumbered on to Philadelphia: the scenery, which had come from Toronto in a caravan of vans, left Boston by train. It occupied eight baggage cars; the company comprised more than two hundred people, including ten musicians (who would be joined by thirty-one local musicians in each city) and fifty-six actors, singers, and dancers. By the time it reached New York, its freight charges and railway fares ran to $35,000. Its Broadway nickname was *Costalot;* and with all the problems it had encountered, it was being referred to as a medical, not a musical.

A short walk away from the Majestic, *My Fair Lady* was still running—it would run for nearly two more years—and the comparisons were inevitable. Its very success was an additional pressure on everyone involved in *Camelot.* On the other hand, advance ticket sales for *Camelot* had piled up to $3 million, prompting the prediction by a press agent that the show could be the first flop in history to run two years.

In the late afternoon of December 3, 1960, Lerner sat low in a dim-lit desert of empty seats in the Majestic Theater as Abe Feder made last-minute adjustments to the lighting. The curtain was to go up at 6:45. About 4:30 Lerner crossed the stage to leave. A stagehand was sweeping the floor. Lerner touched him on the shoulder and said, "Good luck, kid."

The young man paused in his work and said, "Mr. Lerner, you don't need any luck. There's too much love on the stage." Lerner left. In the alley outside he began to weep.

sixteen

CAMELOT RECOVERED

The audience was full of celebrities that Saturday night. The opening song, *I Wonder What the King Is Doing Tonight,* did not elicit the chuckles Lerner expected. The pallid laughter and scattered applause disconcerted the cast during the first act. Even Burton got only perfunctory approval. At intermission, Lerner stayed in the manager's office, as was his habit. Robert Goulet stopped the show at the start of the second act with *If Ever I Would Leave You.* The show still ran long. Benjamin Welles said, "I remember Fritz looking at me that night, saying, 'How'd you like the score?' I said, 'Lovely, Fritz, one of your best.' I think he thought I was being a little reticent. The more I hear it, the more lovely it is, and the lyrics are superb. It's a lovely score, one of the most beautiful Fritz ever wrote."

Burton, with his gift of mimicry, had vividly limned Noël Coward on an opening night, patting people on the shoulder and saying, "Mahvelous, darling, mahvelous," and Coward did precisely that to Lerner. Though he made it a practice to avoid opening-night parties, Lerner attended the one held that night at Luchow's restaurant. The first reviews came in. Howard Taubman of the *Times* liked Richard Burton and Julie Andrews and the first act; he didn't like the second act. Fritz simply shrugged. Then the show's press agent got off the telephone and said that Chapman of the *News* loved the show. Lerner went home. The next day Walter Kerr of the *Herald-Tribune* gave the show a mixed review. He praised the songs but not the play. The evening papers gave the show good reviews.

But there was no lineup at the box office. Advisers to William Paley at CBS, which had funded it, predicted that the show would close by May. Lerner thought that much would hinge on the success or failure of the original cast album. He went off to Switzerland to ski for a couple of weeks.

For Richard Burton, however, the show was the triumph he had determined to make it. He was being called the King of Broadway. His dressing room backstage, which acquired the name Burton's Bar, became a gathering place for actors, among them Alec Guinness, Tammy Grimes, Lauren Bacall, Jason Robards, Jr., and Robert Preston. Preston, one of Burton's drinking companions, bet him that he could not down a fifth of hundred-proof vodka during a matinee performance and another that night without showing signs of it. Burton took him on, and others in the company made side bets. Burton later recounted, "I popped off the stage every so often, and there was a glass waiting for me. The unknowing judge was Julie Andrews." At the end of the night, Burton asked her how he had been. "Rather better than usual," she said, and Burton collected from Preston.

Burton's brother Graham said that after a good performance, Rich was always anxious to go on the town. When he got standing ovations, he would use an expression picked up from their miner brother Tom: "I reckon I've filled my ten drams today." A dram was a coal cart, and ten drams brought a bonus. Perhaps this is the secret of the difference between Burton's relations with his cast and Rex Harrison's. Harrison thought of himself as a scion of the rich; Burton was of the working class, and fiercely proud of it, and did not see himself as better than his fellow players: they were his colleagues, fellow conspirators, and friends.

Graham says that Sybil Burton was reconciled to his philandering, which he no longer even attempted to hide. He speculates that after an affair Burton had had with Susan Strasberg, "any lesser indiscretion could be treated as incidental." Graham reminded him that he used to say he hadn't a care in the world, and asked, "So what's happened to you?"

Rich said, "I don't know, Gray. It's just that, well, all this, it's not what I expected."

Graham Jenkins says Burton never missed a performance during his time in *Camelot*. Lerner says he missed one or two shows. He adds that John Cullum, a native of Tennessee, so idolized Burton that at that time in his career he had absorbed Burton's technique, his manner, even his patterns of speech, and once or twice went on to creditable effect in Burton's place.

An Evening with Nichols and May was running at the theater next door, and Mike Nichols had become one of Burton's cronies. Nichols told Hollis Alpert, "I was good friends with Julie Andrews, too. Our group would sometimes include her, and sometimes Elaine May. Robert Goulet and Roddy McDowall were with us often. We would do things after the show. One place we went to a lot was a small restaurant, Mont St. Michel, which Richard loved. He had a lot of girls. None of us knew whether or not Sybil knew. I think there was a way in which Richard managed it without her knowing. It seems hard to believe, because it was so open, and there was so much talk about it."

But as Graham Jenkins makes clear, Sybil did know.

Another of his friends recalls that Burton also liked a bar just west of the theater district, on Eighth Avenue—Downey's. It was an actors' hangout, the repository of countless stories of the theater and the actors who started coming there as unknowns and in later years came back as stars. The place was full of young actresses and chorus girls, and Burton had the pick of them. M'el Dowd evidently had been replaced. Burton was frequently seen in Downey's with Pat Tunder, a blond and beautiful dancer from the Copacabana.

For all the beauty of the songs, and the brilliance of the performances, *Camelot* was tottering toward failure.

But by now Moss Hart was back. Three months after the opening, he went to see the show, and urged Lerner to do something that is almost never done in theater: revise a show that is already running. Lerner corrected flaws that were obvious to Hart, investing a week in rewrites. Two songs were cut. The show was finally down to size.

And then occurred what Lerner called "the miracle."

Ed Sullivan, who was wont to pay tribute to songwriters on his television show, wanted to do one on Lerner and Loewe for the fifth anniversary of the opening of *My Fair Lady.* Lerner and Lowe asked Sullivan if they might be permitted to present a little of the material from *My Fair Lady,* a lot from *Camelot.* Sullivan agreed. Burton, Andrews, and Goulet did twenty minutes of *Camelot* high points on Sullivan's show, which was immensely influential at that period: indeed, a few years before it had been instrumental in launching Elvis Presley and not much farther into the sixties would establish the presence of the Beatles in America.

The next morning Lerner got a call from the manager of the Majestic, telling him he'd better get down there and have a look. When Lerner arrived, he viewed a line stretching halfway down the block. And the audience that night saw the enormously improved show that Moss Hart had that week rehearsed. The show was a hit.

It would run two more years on Broadway and two more on the road, then two years at Drury Lane in London in a production starring Laurence Harvey, and more than two years in Australia. The film rights were sold for a million dollars, and the play was botched by Joshua Logan, who directed it, into a bad film starring Richard Harris as the King and Vanessa Redgrave as Guinevere. For sixty weeks the original cast album was the biggest seller in America. The soundtrack of the movie sold two and a half million albums.

Burton did not stay with the show for the full year of his contract. One man who saw *Camelot* was producer Walter Wanger, who invited Burton to lunch with him. Wanger asked Burton to costar, in the role of Mark Antony, on a second billing, with Elizabeth Taylor in a film to be directed by Joseph Mankiewicz: *Caesar and Cleopatra.* By one of those turns of destiny common in the theatrical world, which is a small and incestuous community, Rex Harrison was to play Caesar. But Burton's *Camelot* contract had three months to run.

Wanger and 20th Century–Fox were willing to buy him out of it. On Burton's advice, Lerner asked for $50,000 and got it. Burton suggested his own replacement, a Shakespearean actor and (naturally; Burton was intensely loyal) fellow Welshman named William Squire.

"But a musical," Moss Hart said doubtfully. "Can he play a musical?"

"If I can," Burton intoned, "he can."

Squire was brought to New York. Burton introduced him to all the cast, then showed him his dressing room, the most capacious and luxurious Squire had ever had. "And this," Richard said, "is all yours."

Camelot took four awards in the New York Drama Critics' Annual Poll: Richard Burton was voted the best male performer in a musical, Oliver Smith the best set designer, Adrian and Tony Duquette the best costumers, and Alan Jay Lerner the best lyricist. It outran the other three hit musicals of the 1960–61 season with 837 performances.

Lerner went to Europe that summer of *Camelot*'s success. Fritz returned to Palm Springs. Moss and Kitty Hart decided to move there too. A few days before Christmas, as Carlisle was backing the car out of the driveway to take Moss to the dentist, she heard something fall. Hart was lying on the lawn, dead of his third heart attack. One of the first visitors was Fritz Loewe. Carlisle, who had given up smoking, reached for a cigarette. Fritz said, "Don't." But she smoked it anyway.

Shortly after Alan in New York had received the news from Carlisle, the *New York Times* asked him to write an article about Hart. He wrote it in two hours through a mist of tears.

(Kitty Carlisle wrote that after Hart's death, Lerner and Loewe and Herman Levin gave her a small percentage of royalties on both *My Fair Lady* and *Camelot* in appreciation of his work. "This is," she notes pointedly, "an example of generosity quite rare in the theater, or anywhere else for that matter.")

The partnership of Lerner and Loewe, except for a 1971 film score that constituted a brief codetta to their careers, was essentially over. There was no dramatic termination of their entente, no ceremonious farewell. Fritz was, Lerner wrote, "only sixty, and a vigorous one at that, both vertically and horizontally." Fritz took what at first seemed to be a long sabbatical. It would lengthen into his retirement from the stage.

It was not for another two years, Lerner said, that he began to understand the true nature of their partnership. He was at work on a new musical, eventually to be known as *On a Clear Day You Can See Forever.* Lerner said that he came to realize that he and Fritz Loewe had built a protective fortress around their working relationship. "A collaboration as intense as ours inescapably had to be complex," Lerner wrote. "But I loved him more than I understood or misunderstood him and I know he loved me more than he understood or misunderstood me."

On September 22, 1962, the *New York Herald-Tribune* carried a column about Fritz by John Crosby. Crosby wrote:

He quit, and you see him from time to time taking it easy at Cannes, Paris, Palm Springs and other watering holes.

He passed through Paris the other day and I asked him if he didn't miss the excitement of opening nights. I must have been the 12,000th person who has asked this question, because the answer comes out very fast, very polished.

"Nothing surpasses the excitement of sitting down to a well-ordered dinner," said Mr. Loewe, "and ordering a good wine. Everyone talks about the excitement of opening nights. But they forget—or else never knew—that opening nights are the culmination of 18 months of agony. Ever since I was a child I've wanted to live real good.

"Do you think it's living real good to be in a hotel room in New Haven—have you ever seen a typical New Haven hotel?—eating stale sandwiches and drinking cold coffee, all because there's something wrong with the second act that only God can fix?"

The New Haven hotels get terrible notices from successful playwrights. I can't remember how many times I have heard complaints about the dreadfulness of the rotten coffee and the lousy sandwiches in a hotel while trying to fix second acts at New Haven tryouts. Thousands of young playwrights would give the blood of their veins to be in New Haven drinking rotten coffee and trying to fix the second act. This is what they would consider the very last word in living. If he's not fixing second acts, how does he spend his time?

"There's so much that's interesting connected with the art of living," said Mr. Loewe. "When I get up in the morning I say, 'Whom am I going to have lunch with?' and 'What am I going to eat?' I plan no further."

Well, I asked, didn't he miss the creative process?

"I have discovered the bedroom," said Mr. Loewe.

"The bedroom is the most neglected room in the house. Everyone pours everything into the living room. Why not the bedroom? You're born there. You make love there. You're sick there. If you're lucky, you're going to die there.

"Why do we just put a bed to lie down there instead of surrounding it with the most luxurious things in the house?"

Mr. Loewe is pouring all his enormous creative gifts into fixing himself a bedroom that will be as memorable as the score of My Fair Lady. *His bedroom in Palm Springs is on the top of a hill with a lovely view of the mountains and desert and it sports a bar, a library and a fireplace. The bed turns on turntable so that if he gets sick of one view he can select another. The view of the mountains is superb.*

It sounds wonderful if you like to look at mountains.
But for excitement . . .

"Look," said Mr. Loewe, "do you know what you have to go through to get the excitement of an opening night? There's a year and a half of doubt, disappointment, deception and total physical exhaustion."

I must say he looks wonderful, youthful, good-humored and full of the joy of living. There must be something in all this rest and mountain-looking.

After the assassination on November 22, 1963, of Lerner's Choate and Harvard classmate, John F. Kennedy, America took on an inchoate and unspoken belief that something had changed forever. Whatever Kennedy was or was not as a president, he had given America an optimism unlike anything it had known before, a sense of restored aspiration. The tales of his dalliances had not emerged, though it seemed everyone in show business was aware of his affair with Marilyn Monroe. He seemed like the golden knight, come to lead America to a higher destiny, and when he was shot it seemed that "they" could and would crush any hopes the people might have. Theodore White, who had been in that same class at Harvard with Lerner and Kennedy, went to Hyannis Port to interview Jacqueline Kennedy for *Life* magazine. She told them that at bedtime Jack had liked to play records, his particular favorite being the title song from *Camelot*. The lines he loved were those that come at the end, when the Round Table has been dispersed and Arthur's life and kingdom are in ruins. White wrote that she kept coming back to those lines, then saying, "And it will never be that way again."

The interview was quoted extensively in newspapers. Lerner was startled to see his quatrain in headlines on the front page of the *New York Journal American.* He was dazed. He walked on past his house, not noticing he had done so for another twelve blocks.

Lerner wrote in *The Street Where I Live* that the road company of *Camelot,* with Louis Hayward in the role of Arthur, was playing the three-thousand-seat Opera House in Chicago at the time. "When [Hayward] came to those lines," Lerner wrote, "there was a sudden wail from the audience. It was not a muffled sob; it was a loud, almost primitive cry of pain. The play stopped, and for almost five minutes everyone in the theater—on the stage, in the wings, in the pit, and in the audience—wept without restraint. Then the play continued."

If the incident happened, it was not in Chicago.

Miles Kreuger said, *"Camelot* opened in Chicago December 3, 1963. I went out on the road and visited the show before that, when it was playing Cincinnati, because we were having troubles with Katherine Grayson. This was the first time she played a big stage part and she had no discipline for appearing in theater. She simply could not sustain an evening's performance emotionally. Not that she couldn't creatively, but emotionally she couldn't. In making movies, she was accustomed to playing a scene and they'd say, 'Cut,' and then she'd go off to the dressing room. It was extremely difficult for her to sustain a show. So she would miss many performances and the understudy would do them, a wonderful girl with red hair from the New York City Opera named Jan Moody."

On October 15, 1963, the Associated Press reported that Grayson had been unable to perform in St. Louis and had been replaced by her understudy.

Kreuger said, "Alan sent me out because the people were furious at Katherine because she so often didn't appear. It was a big event to have a movie star come to your town. Katherine toured with a woman and her husband, and two big black poodles. The woman acted as a personal secretary and confidante and the husband carried the luggage. I remember walking those poodles on the main street of Cincinnati.

"The show would close in town A on Saturday night. Sunday was used for traveling to town B. Monday morning the core of musicians and the conductor would rehearse with the new orchestra. And then they would have a runthrough with the principals so that the soloists could get a sense of the acoustics of the auditorium and perform with the new orchestra. That evening the show would open.

"Katherine never showed up for any of this. She would arrive in the new city around five or six o'clock, demand and usually receive a police escort directly to the theater, and while the bags were being unpacked and her costumes laid out and her makeup was going on, she would eat her usual chili, and then go on to the stage and not perform very well because she had no idea what the acoustics were like or even how big the theater was or where to place her voice. In her extraordinary naïveté, she believed, and she told me so, the press releases from MGM saying that someday she was going to sing at the Metropolitan Opera House.

"Without any predictability, in the middle of songs, while dancers were midair, she would suddenly go into coloratura runs. In *The Lusty Month of May,* and things like that, she would start trilling all over the place. All these dancers, who were choreographed by measure, suddenly had no more measures. There was no more time being beaten, you see. And they would collide in midair. And when they came down, they had no idea what to do because they had no idea how long she was going to continue trilling. It was truly a nightmare for everyone.

"A friend of mine was understudying Joel Grey in *Stop the World, I Want to Get Off,* around the corner from the Taft Auditorium. I went around to see it. I sat down and heard people behind me whispering, 'I didn't know *Camelot* had closed!" I thought, 'Oh my God, what does this mean? I turned around and there was the star of our show, dressed to the nines in her jewels, watching a competitive show around the corner. She had taken off the evening.

"I told Alan and the next day she received a very harsh warning from Actors Equity that she dare not ever do it again. I left Cincinnati right after that, and I believe the show then went to Chicago."

On October 25, 1963, an AP story from Cincinnati said that Grayson had collapsed during a performance there and was not expected to return to the show. In fact she did play Chicago.

The resolution of the conflict must be left to Bud Widney, who also was in Chicago for the opening there. "Alan was a storyteller," Widney said with a chuckle. "He would take stories from life and make them a little more glamorous.

"I think he got that story from me, after the opening in Chicago. It was in Chicago that we got word that Jackie had connected *Camelot* with the Kennedy administration. I saw the newspaper headline.

"We were playing in a terrible theater, the Chicago Opera House, and all the company was downcast. I told them about the headline and emphasized the importance of what we were doing. And later I told Alan what had happened. I can't say with certainty that the incident of the collective groan didn't happen, but I don't know that it did." Widney chuckled again and added, "Alan always embellished the truth beautifully."

Lerner wrote in 1978 that he never saw a stage performance of *Camelot* again. He said he couldn't bear to.

At this point in his life—he was forty-three—he had a town house on East Seventy-first Street in addition to his various other residences, among them an eight-room apartment at the Waldorf-Astoria. The marriage with Micheline was deteriorating. The house would soon be the site of a tasteless confrontation and the cause of vicious battles in a courtroom.

"You are a funny little boy," Fritz said to Lerner of his many marriages. "You build a nest and then shit in it."

seventeen

FRITZ WALKS AWAY

In a March 1961 interview with United Press International writer Jack Gaver, Fritz Loewe said that he had decided "I will do absolutely no work for at least a year, and it is more likely that I will relax for eighteen months.

"Some persons think this is a little odd of me, but it is the only reasonable thing to do. I will be sixty years old next June 10, and I have actually been in the theater in some manner or other most of the time since I was nine years old. At that time I wrote a musical sketch for my father's use on the stage.

"And once you have felt that tap on your shoulder, you begin to think a little." He referred of course to his heart attack. Loewe spoke of his gourmet tastes:

"I simply apply myself to them in moderation. And I drink only as much as my physician allows me. A good wine with meals, of course. But I haven't smoked since my illness. Now, I just borrow a cigarette from a companion and sit with it in my mouth. The only trouble is that when I'm in a public place, someone, usually a waiter, is always trying to light it for me."

Lerner made an interesting point about Fritz: "There are two kinds of composers, in a way. There are those who compose in their fingers, in other words who improvise, and there are those who sort of compose in their heads, the way Kurt Weill did. Fritz was a finger composer, and he really sweated it out. He was afraid that the passion that he put into composing was a strain on his heart. Now whether it was or not is immaterial, because as long as he thought so, that could do the damage. And with good logic he said, 'Why should I go through this? And why should I agonize?'" (TT)

Fritz was living at that time in a penthouse apartment of the Dorset Hotel at 80 West Fifty-fourth Street. He was about to leave for Europe, and he next surfaced in print in a column from Cannes by Art Buchwald, who was also curious about the suspension of his career. Buchwald noted that Alan Jay Lerner had begun work on a new musical with Richard Rodgers. How did Fritz feel about this, and about the end of an eighteen-year "marriage" to Lerner?

"To answer these questions," Buchwald wrote, "we take you to Cannes, about four miles offshore on an anchored yacht where Mr. Loewe is seated on a deck chair looking through binoculars toward shore to make sure no one is tampering with his Rolls-Royce, which is waiting to take him when the long day is over to his rented villa which overlooks the Mediterranean."

Fritz told him, "I am truly happy. I am on a temporary permanent vacation. I have no deadlines, no telephone calls in the middle of the night. I go to Palm Springs in the winter, the Riviera in the spring, the Tyrol in the summer, and I might stop by in New York, providing that the weather is promising, to see shows I had nothing to do with." Countless authors and lyricists, he told Buchwald, were bombarding him with properties. He wasn't interested.

"When did you feel your marriage with Lerner was over?" Buchwald asked.

"I think we both felt it while we were writing *Camelot.*"

"Did Mr. Lerner inform you he was throwing you over for Mr. Rodgers?"

"No. I read it in the newspapers. Look, I'm not bothered by this at all. Mr. Lerner is a young man. I'll be sixty on June 10, the same date *My Fair Lady* will beat *Oklahoma*'s Broadway record.

"How can I be bitter when I don't want to work? I am a great admirer of Richard Rodgers and I think it was inevitable after Oscar Hammerstein's death that Lerner should become Rodgers' partner."

Lerner said in an interview, "When our lawyers brought us together . . . to discuss the possibility of collaborating, we discovered that we talked the same language. We hit it off right away. The thoughts he began, I'd finish, and vice versa. We realized we had the same attitudes toward the theater, the same ideas about casting, management, and breaking of theater molds." Rodgers had written his own lyrics for his last show, *No Strings.*

The collaboration certainly made the newspapers. As UPI writer Pat Herman wrote, it "left some New Yorkers as thunderstruck as if the Yankees had merged with the Dodgers." That was the era when there still was a Brooklyn Dodgers ball club.

Herman was in Lerner's office in the Waldorf Towers as the lyricist talked on the phone to Rodgers. "Dick," Lerner said, "there are a lot of jokes going around this office, and the latest is that we'd better do a good show tonight at *Camelot* because Mr. Rodgers is coming around to check on the tempo."

Herman wrote that the ease of the conversation "typified the relationship between the two giants of musical theater who will pool their talents beginning next fall."

After completing the call to Rodgers, Lerner said, "You asked if I had any trepidation about working with Dick, who with the late Oscar Hammerstein became a sort of legend." Hammerstein had died eight months earlier, on August 23, 1960. "No, not at all. My main emotion is a deep, excited curiosity, and I think that Dick shares my feelings."

The broker of the mating had been Irving Cohen, who was both Lerner's and Rodgers' attorney. "I was vacationing in Europe when Irving wrote me and suggested I get together with Dick. When I came home, we talked by telephone, and in March we met for drinks and decided to work together." He said that he and Rodgers had not settled on an idea for a show: "It may just be the life story of the dressmaker Chanel," Lerner said. It wouldn't be; that idea would come to fulfillment in *Coco,* a show written not with Rodgers but with André Previn.

Shortly after that, Rodgers was interviewed in his office, a few blocks away from Lerner's. The reporter said that the new collaboration was being called a "punctuation mark" in the history of musical theater. Rodgers' evaluation was more realistic than Lerner's. He said:

"You mean a question mark. You never know how a collaboration goes until the show is on. Alan and I are not the end of the line, you know. There is a natural qualm, when you embark on a new phase of your life, but it doesn't frighten me. I rather take it as a challenge."

Lerner was in for a shock in working with Rodgers. Josh Logan, who had worked with both Rodgers and Hart and Rodgers and Hammerstein, directing *South Pacific* for the latter team, said in his autobiography that he had given much thought to the question, What is a Richard Rodgers? His answer: "It is a brilliant, intelligent, theatrical, sound superbrain. It likes to work, it particularly likes to write music, which flows up plentifully from some underground spring. It plays the piano better than most composers. It's not given to smiling too much; yet when it scowls, I found that it does not indicate anything unpleasant: it is simply making a judgment, thinking things over, watching a private preview. It has a strong sense of discipline. It likes to be on time, to deliver work as promised. And when it works with an Oscar Hammerstein, that is accomplished frequently. But when it worked with a Larry Hart, well, that's when the scowl sets in.

"It pretends to hate business, and yet it is my theory that it is only really happy making contracts, haggling about royalties, salaries, and theatrical leases. I often believed it was a bit embarrassed about the ease of writing music, as though it were too easy, too soft a thing, for a man to do. Therefore it enjoyed being a hard-bitten businessman."

Rodgers was, Logan says, as tough as nails. Logan thought Lorenz Hart envied and therefore hated Rodgers' discipline, punctuality, and efficiency. Logan was being tactful: Richard Rodgers was alive when he wrote that. And Larry Hart had better reasons to hate Richard Rodgers. For one thing, Rodgers treated lyricists (and actors, and others) badly, never understanding that the writing of lyrics is a slow and painful process, one requiring infinite patience and a cruel self-criticism.

This fact underlies a famous story about Oscar Hammerstein's wife. At a dinner party, a woman said something about Richard Rodgers writing *Some Enchanted Evening*. Sweetly Dorothy Hammerstein said, "Mr. Rodgers did not write *Some Enchanted Evening*. Mr. Rodgers wrote dum-dee dum-dee dum-dum. My husband wrote *Some Enchanted Evening*." (Sometimes the story cites some other of the Rodgers and Hammerstein songs, but in any event the incident does seem to have occurred.)

Lerner told the UPI reporter: "Rodgers and Hart had a different voice than Rodgers and Hammerstein, and so it will be with us. If we do have different approaches, they will be resolved involuntarily . . . as we begin to work we will both shift gears instinctively."

Wrong. A clash between Lerner and Rodgers was inevitable.

They eventually decided on a subject. The new musical would be called *I Picked a Daisy,* Daisy being the name of one of the principals, an uneducated Brooklyn girl with extrasensory powers. The show would reflect Lerner's intense interest in "occult" matters, including reincarnation, for in the story the girl will turn out to be, under hypnotic regression, the reincarnation of an Englishwoman named Melinda Welles. (The surname was a small inside jest, that of Lerner's friend Benjamin Welles.) In *The Street Where I Live,* Lerner wrote, "I believe deeply there is a divine Order and that life is without end, but at times Fate deals with it so frivolously that it seems without meaning." So the play, then, would be a projection of his yearning for something beyond finite life, a yearning that one inescapably concludes is the consequence of his father's uncompromising irreligiosity. It would also reflect Lerner's awareness of social status. Again the story will be about a cultivated man acting to transform a street urchin of a girl, to save her from a sad fate, as Higgins does Eliza in *My Fair Lady,* as Arthur does in forgiving Guinevere in *Camelot,* as Jerry Mulligan does in *An American in Paris,* as Gaston does in *Gigi.* The omniscient male and the girl from the lower orders: every young romantic's dream of saving the whore.

They set to work, and Lerner soon learned about Rodgers and Rodgers learned about Lerner. Fritz Loewe's patience, his willingness to walk away with one of his girls or to the gambling tables while Lerner labored a lyric, must suddenly have seemed angelic by comparison with Rodgers' lack of it. Two years later, perhaps a half dozen songs had been written, and there was no completed book. On July 25, 1963, it was announced in the *New York Times* that the Rodgers-Lerner partnership had been dissolved.

Miles Kreuger later asked Lerner why this partnership had gone wrong. Kreuger reported, "Alan said, 'When two artists collaborate, they sit down and start working on something. And before I could sit down with Rodgers, I had to sign contracts, and we had to discuss subsidiary rights, and revival rights, and the movie version, and cast albums. By the time we'd discussed everything, there was no more show left to discuss. It was so enervating that I didn't have any more strength left to write a show with him.' "

According to the *Times* article, the production had been called off July 10 "because an insufficient amount of Mr. Lerner's lyrics blocked Mr. Rodgers from finishing the score." The story said there was a possibility that Lerner would continue work on *I Picked a*

Daisy with Burton Lane. Lerner was in Capri, the paper said, and unavailable for comment. Richard Rodgers said, ominously enough, "I have no idea whether there would be any legal complications to prevent Mr. Lerner from going ahead." But he took no legal action to stop him. Rodgers fired another barb at Lerner in a *New York Post* interview that noted that he had previously written with both Lorenz Hart and Oscar Hammerstein, who, he said, had something in common with Lerner: "not liking work."

And Rodgers, who was now past sixty, said something rather touching to a friend about Lerner: "How dare this young man take up a year of my life? I don't have that much time left."

It was at this time that Miles Kreuger became a member of the Lerner staff. As he recalled it:

"Norman Rosemont was director of public relations for Alan. Norman left. Bud Widney knew I needed a job, around the summer of 1963. Bud said, 'We're in the Waldorf-Astoria. Come on down.' We had lunch in the little coffee shop that was on the corner of Fiftieth and Lexington. He said, 'Alan needs someone to help him in public relations. Do you know anything about that?" I said, 'No.' He said, 'Well, come on up. Alan always talks about you.'

"We went upstairs. Alan had a suite, a whole suite, in the Waldorf-Astoria, on the fourth floor, on the corner of Lexington and Fiftieth, right above the coffee shop. I still have the key.

"I was sitting in this huge living room. There was a beautiful marble mantle. Alan came walking in and said, 'How are you, Miles?' It had been about a year or two since we'd seen each other. He said, 'What do you know about public relations?' And I said, 'Not very much.' And he said, 'Oh, what a relief. Norman Rosemont has left.' By then, '63, Norman was managing Robert Goulet. Alan said, 'Goulet is so enterprising, anything he touches turns to money. He's making more money than I am, with all the alimony I have to pay. I'd like to have you around because you don't know anything about public relations. But you do believe in my work, don't you.'

"And I said, 'Of course I do.' He said, 'That's all I want, you're hired.' I got a salary and I had, I guess, a literally limitless expense account, because whatever I wanted to do, I could do with no questions asked. I never took advantage of it, and I always felt self-conscious because there were no limitations. He'd say, 'Take so-and-so out to Pavillon.' And I'd say, 'But Alan, that's awfully expensive.' And he'd say, 'What do you mean it's expensive? Take her to Pavillon.' And Henri Soule would serve us, and it was lovely.

"I was always a little worried, because I still have the old work ethic and worry about spending other people's money. But he didn't care.

"I had the corner office, the master bedroom. I had the piano in my office, and I had a little bathroom. Outside it was a big living room, where Greg, the office manager, sat, and several other people. The public corridor ended in our suite. Alan was not in our suite. He had the next suite, so that he could be alone entirely if he wanted to be, and could write.

"Alan kept out of our way. The office consisted of Greg, the office manager, and a wonderful little lady, and then Felice Orlandi the actor, who was married to Alice Ghostley. It was a stable group, a wonderful little family, and we always had lots of laughs and good times. Alan was busy writing, and every day he'd try out a different title on me."

The writing of *On a Clear Day* took three years. The interruptions were interminable. Lerner had put work on it aside completely, leaving Burton Lane to fume, when he got a call from Washington, asking him to produce a fund-raising birthday party for President John F. Kennedy at the Waldorf-Astoria. Lerner had assembled a cast that included Audrey Hepburn, Leslie Uggams, Jimmy Durante, Ed Sullivan, and Henry Fonda. According to Doris Shapiro, Dr. Max Jacobson attended the rehearsal preceding the party, giving her and Alan their shot. The show was telecast. For its climax, it had featured Marilyn Monroe in a long dress so tight that it permitted her to do little but writhe provocatively as she sang in her little-girl's whispery voice, "Happy birthday, Mr. President . . ." In front of an entire nation, Monroe, the pathetic town punch of Hollywood, plaything of the powerful, was being offered up as a sexual birthday present to the president, a performance that remains one of the most tasteless displays ever to demean the office.

Rehearsals for *Clear Day* had been scheduled for January 15, 1964, with Barbara Harris in the lead. By September, the newspaper was reporting that the opening date had been pushed back to April. It would open, the *Times* said, at the Lunt-Fontanne Theater, with Cy Feuer and Ernest Martin, owners of the theater, as producers. The show was budgeted at $500,000. On April 7, 1965, the *World-Telegram and Sun* ran an interview with Lerner, who fired returning shots at Richard Rodgers. He said, "Dick just can't understand how it can take weeks to write the lyrics to one song. I think it would have been much better if we had tried an adaptation first, instead of an original. Then he could have done things on his own. With an original, he had to wait for me to write the book."

Lerner confirmed that Burton Lane had indeed contracted to write the music and that Louis Jourdan had signed to play the male lead in the show. "I wanted Louis from the beginning," Lerner said, "but Dick Rodgers preferred someone with a more legitimate voice." At Rodgers' behest, they signed Robert Horton. Barbara Harris, whom Lerner had wanted for three years, was to stay on. "The part was written for her," Lerner said. "I'm glad she waited. She's become a sort of underground star the last year or so. She's making her second movie and working on this show but no one has seen any of it."

Indeed no one had. There still was no score and no book. Compounding all the problems attending the show was Lerner's dependency on methedrine and Dr. Max Jacobson, who administered it in combination, apparently, with various vitamins.

There isn't the slightest question of Lerner's involvement with Max Jacobson. He denied that he had been getting drugs from the doctor, but there are too many witnesses to his habit, including wives Micheline and Karen, to believe him.

"While I was working with Alan," Miles Kreuger said, "he and one of his assistants used to go off to Max Jacobson's. One time I dropped Alan off there. He said, 'You must come in, this is the most fascinating doctor.' I said, 'I'm not ill, why do I have to go to a fascinating doctor?' He said, 'He does the most wonderful things. I don't know what he does exactly, but his treatment is just marvelous.' And he would disappear for a day or two. I would hear lurid stories about how patients would go there and he would stir up cauldrons, medicines. Whatever it was, it seemed cultish and eerie."

The assistant to whom Kreuger referred was Doris Shapiro, whose book extensively documents the visits to Max Jacobson with whom, Shapiro tells us, she eventually went to bed. Shapiro confirms that Lerner was always trying to proselytize his friends and associates into taking to Jacobson's needle.

Jacobson's office, in a white brick building on East Eighty-third Street, opened at five-thirty in the morning and, often, remained open until late into the night. Shapiro was herself habituated to Jacobson's "treatments" and she and Lerner visited their Dr. Feelgood at least daily, and sometimes three and four times a day. Jacobson had a taste for the company of the rich and powerful, particularly theater people, and often Shapiro and Lerner would encounter its denizens awaiting their injections in the small hours of the morning, women and men in evening dress, among them playwright Tennessee Williams. Jacobson liked to show a photograph of himself with President John F. Kennedy and Prince Radziwill, Jackie Kennedy's brother-in-law. He boasted that he had gone to the Carlyle Hotel to treat Kennedy, who had lost his voice just before an address to the United Nations. He showed another picture of himself on a movie location in Egypt with director Cecil B. DeMille during the making of *The Ten Commandments*. And it was, as Miles Kreuger said and Doris Shapiro confirms, all very cultish, with Jacobson selecting potions from his vials, including one marked "Meth" and blending his concoctions, like some medieval necromancer, and then slipping the mixture into the arm of his client, on whose face would appear a smile of beatific peace.

Shapiro gives a description of Lerner lying on Jacobson's table, looking "haggard and small behind his dark glasses" and holding her hand. "Do you want to work or don't you?" Jacobson fiercely demanded of Lerner.

"Yes, yes, I want to work."

Jacobson made up his mixture and slipped the needle into a vein. Shapiro writes: "Alan's eyes met mine in silence, and I could follow the journey of the heat through his body by the look in his eyes, which went heavenward and closed to receive the gift."

A moment later, she writes, Lerner sat up with a sigh of happiness, and Jacobson said, "Look at his face. He looks twenty years younger."

Then he gave Shapiro her injection.

And Lerner went back to work on *Clear Day*. It wouldn't open until October 1965, and by the time it did—at the Mark Hellinger—the budget would have grown to $600,000, and Burton Lane and Lerner would no longer be on speaking terms.

A further cause of the delay was the decay and death of Lerner's marriage to Micheline Muselli Pozzo di Borgo.

In *The Street Where I Live,* Lerner mentions moving into his "new digs" on his return from Europe at the end of the summer of 1960, after the success of *Camelot* had been assured. "Digs" seems a coy term for the house, whose purchase was deemed sufficiently important to warrant a news story, dated August 7, 1960, in the *Herald-Tribune,* under the headline

The five-story residence at 42 E 71st St. has been sold by Mrs. Alfred Rheinstein to Alan J. Lerner, lyricist for My Fair Lady. *The house, regarded as one of the finest in the city, and still in use as a residence, contains sixteen rooms and eight bathrooms. It was designed by Aymar Embury 2d, architect.*

The structure is one of seven on 70th and 71st Sts. between Park and Madison Aves., built in 1929 by the Rheinstein Construction Co. They were built to provide a 60×100 foot garden in the rear of the houses.

Francis R. Jaffin was broker in the sale for Mr. and Mrs. Rheinstein who plan to move to a new co-operative building being erected at 700 Park Ave.

The Lerners' next-door neighbor was David Sarnoff. The house on the other side was occupied by the Tunisian embassy. Doris Shapiro said that during the first year of the marriage to Micheline, while Lerner and his bride were off in Paris or Capri, a horde of craftsmen swarmed over the house, gilding the moldings and restructuring the bathrooms in marble, and vastly glamorizing the whole structure. "There was," she said, "a good deal of gold satin furniture and leopard print carpet. Micheline wanted Napoleonic splendor for her New York house and modern New York in the Paris flat."

The house was duly supplied with servants, most of them French-speaking. It was during the residence in this house that Alan's only son, Michael, was born. Doris Shapiro says the boy was the joy of Lerner's life. When she was there to take Lerner's dictation, she wrote, the boy would sometimes appear. The nurse would apologize for the interruption.

"That's all right," Lerner would say. "Come sit with me, Michael. He can stay with us for a while. What's your favorite word, Michael?"

"Island."

"What a beautiful word."

With three daughters already, Lerner seemed particularly delighted to have a son.

Lerner lived with Micheline in the house on Seventy-first Street for four years in turbulent conditions. Then on May 14, 1964, Micheline Lerner filed suit in the New York State Supreme Court for separation. The *New York Times* noted in its story: "Mrs. Lerner is a former Paris lawyer." It also noted that Mrs. Lerner was represented by Roy M. Cohn. Cohn, who had prosecuted Ethel and Julius Rosenberg and had been chief counsel to Senator Joseph McCarthy, was a man without a trace of moral principle. He would go to any length to win a case. Sidney Zion, who collaborated with Cohn on his autobiography, referred to him as "this rogue, this legal executioner, this notorious bastard who cared nothing for the conventions, who flouted the civil decencies." Micheline had acquired one of the most vicious hired guns of the profession.

At the same time, she obtained an order barring Lerner from the house on Seventy-first Street, which the *New York World-Telegram* said was valued at $500,000. State Supreme Court Justice Thomas A. Aurelio upheld the order, which would keep Lerner out of it at least through the weekend. "The court hearing," the *Times* reported, "was marked by acrimonious charges between Louis Nizer, who represents Mr. Lerner, and Roy M. Cohn, Mrs. Lerner's lawyer." It said that Mr. Lerner was permitted by the court to see his son Michael, now five years old, between 1:00 and 5:00 P.M. on the two days of the weekend.

The *New York Journal American* said the "lyricist and librettist of the most fabulous musical comedy in history, *My Fair Lady,* had three expensive homes to go to last night—but not his palatial Napoleon-decor mansion at 42 E 71st.

"Police were informed at 10 o'clock last night that the locks on all of his E 71st St. mansion's doors had been changed, that private detectives had begun a round-the-clock vigil and that Mrs. Lerner's lawyers had been instructed to institute suit for a legal separation. Right away."

The paper continued: "The incumbent Mrs. Lerner's decision to walk out on this walking-writing-Rolls-Royce-riding goldmine, it was learned early today, was the result of what Micheline considered insufferable marital cruelty: Micheline told friends she had only just discovered her credit at many fashionable Manhattan shops had been ordered cut off by her mate.

"Mr. Lerner this early A.M. had his choice of any of his other three homes: a luxurious Paris apartment, a large home on the French Riviera, or at the Towers of the Waldorf-Astoria, where the prolific writer also maintains an office and apartment. Expensive, of course."

"Among Mr. Lerner's countless creature comforts are five expensive cars, including a blue convertible Rolls-Royce; and chauffeurs, of course."

The May 15 *Daily News,* in its coverage of the story, said:

"The 45-year-old Lerner sneaked back [into the house] at 8:15 A.M. by way of Tunisia House next door, climbing to the roof and crossing over to his own roof. Then he descended, floor by floor, eventually surprising Micheline, clad in a white silk brocade lounge coat, as she was tending their 5-year-old son Michael.

"For a Choate and Harvard classmate of the late President Kennedy at both, he was very stubborn, refusing to budge even though a police sergeant, three patrolmen and six lawyers, three to a side, rushed to the scene.

"The sitdown deadlock was broken by Micheline's chief attorney, Roy Cohn, of Saxe, Bacon, & O'Shea, who obtained a show cause order why Lerner should not be given the heave-ho. Then, in an afternoon hearing that lasted almost two hours, he successfully defended the court edict against the application of Lerner's lawyer, Louis Nizer, that the order be vacated." The paper noted that former Supreme Court Justice Ernest E. L. Hammer had been retained as special counsel for Lerner.

The press was barred from the hearing, but the newspapers learned that Supreme Court Justice Thomas C. Chimera warned that if Lerner did not depart immediately, a deputy sheriff would remove him from the house. The judge said, "Here's a man who hasn't been spending much time at home, and all of a sudden wants to go home."

Roy Cohn planned to ask for an increase of alimony to $5,000 a week and $50,000 in legal fees.

On May 16 Louis Nizer said that Micheline was making "accusations ranging from drug addiction to tax evasion against this fine artist—a terrible injustice." But many of his friends knew that Lerner was an amphetamine user, and eventually the Internal Revenue Service would make the second accusation. Nizer said Lerner wanted to live in the house on Seventy-first Street so he could have breakfast with his son. Cohn said, "Night after night, he has slept at the Waldorf Towers. He never went near his home."

Nizer said the Waldorf apartment was used only as an office. He said, "Mr. Lerner will move out of the third-floor room to the fourth floor, which would separate them physically. He has been a loyal husband and father. So let him live in the house entirely apart from her and have breakfast with his boy every morning. I beg your honor to return Mr. Lerner to his house."

Cohn said, "Between September of 1963 and last January, Mr. Lerner did not live in his home at all. He was away from his home and during all that period he didn't see the child."

"It's not true!" Nizer shouted.

"We have an affidavit from the governess as to his absence from the home," Cohen shouted in return. (One is reminded of Maurice Abravanel's statement that Lerner kept a room at the Algonquin during his marriage to Ruth Boyd and called her only every week or two.)

The exchanges then become almost surrealistic. Cohn quoted the governess as quoting Michael, "Daddy doesn't love Mommy anymore. He's going to kick her out." Aurelio said he would give counsel ten days to file pertinent papers on Cohn's plea for $5,000 a week alimony and $50,000 legal fees.

Nizer shouted: "I deny all these charges against my client! They are untrue! There are no living quarters at the Waldorf."

Aurelio refused to let Lerner return to the house. He said, "I take it that a man with his money is not hard-pressed?" And he suggested that Lerner pay Micheline something "on account."

Nizer said that Micheline is "extremely wealthy."

Cohn said, "She is so wealthy that I had to lend her a thousand dollars."

"That shows how rich you are," former Justice Hammer quipped.

"But that doesn't mean he [Cohn] has to support her," Aurelio said.

"She has been given huge sums and has been sending them off to Switzerland," Nizer said.

"This is a four-time married man," Cohn shouted. "This morning one of the newspapers published a photograph of him with another woman."

"He was casting for a new play," Nizer shouted back.

"But he got home at four A.M.," Cohn rejoined. "This is his idea of casting."

Lerner was losing at every turn, with Nizer's protestations seeming curiously feeble. Reading the case all these years later, one is led to wonder what Micheline really did have on him. One thing is obvious: she and Cohn had plastered him with private detectives.

The *Daily News* posted photographers outside the house. On May 18 the paper ran a series of five pictures from the stakeout. The first shows Micheline carrying a large model sailboat as she and Michael return from Central Park Lake. The next shows Lerner standing outside his own door, cigarette inevitably in his right hand, as he waits for the boy. He is obviously unaware that a photographer, camera equipped with a long lens, lurks across the street. By the third photo, he has become aware of the camera, and looks away as he hurries east on Seventy-first Street. He wears a dark sports coat, light trousers, and beautifully cut loafers. The boy wears a light short-sleeved shirt and blue jeans. The fourth photo shows a boat floating on the Hudson, the cruiser *Betty G,* where Alan and Michael spend the afternoon. Finally there is a photo of Micheline, seen from behind, coming to the dock at the Twenty-third Street boat basin, with a sweater the boy forgot. There is something terribly sad about these pictures, which are spread across two full pages of the paper.

On May 20 Aurelio awarded Micheline possession of the house and temporary custody of Michael pending the separation hearing. Lerner was given visitation rights with the boy.

With this victory behind her, Micheline that very day gave an interview to the *New York Journal American.* It took place in the fifth-floor drawing room of the house. On a shelf behind her, the reporter noted, stood Lerner's Oscar statuettes, the two for *Gigi* and one for *An American in Paris.* On the wall were two framed gold records for the albums from *Gigi* and *Camelot,* with a third (probably for *My Fair Lady*) tucked behind a book. Micheline was wearing a sea-green silk brocade dressing gown and small white slippers. The reporter said that five-foot-two-inch Micheline "would have looked almost childlike except for the deep-set lines around her eyes."

She quoted Micheline:

"I'm not contemplating a divorce, only a separation. I thought maybe with a clean break, the bitterness and resentment would disappear. Maybe my husband will come back to the wonderful man he was when I married him.

"I am very hurt.

"I still love him. I never wanted to break up my home. But I had no alternative.

"My husband has acted like a man who wanted to drive a woman to separation and divorce. You don't put a detective on a woman's trail for a year if that is not your intention. I have been living for two years in fear that my husband would seek a divorce. He's been wanting to push me to that step."

Micheline crossed the room and pushed back a concealed door in the blond paneling in front of the Oscar statuettes. She pointed to gouges in the wood, saying, "That is where detectives found wires installed to listen in on what was said here. If I went to the country with our child for the day, there were six men searching my room.

"My only concern is for our five-year-old son. He cannot live under this tension. The only way to protect him was to go to court.

"I hope we can keep an agreeable relationship in front of the child. I hope that when his father comes to see him, he could be nice to me to make it easier for Michel.

"Always I will say to Michel his Daddy is marvelous, talented. I will make excuses when my husband cannot see him."

The question remains: why did Micheline grant the interview? No one submits to questions by a newspaper without a motive, the expectation of publicity that in some way will advance his or her cause, whatever it may be. Was she trying to soften her image before an unseen public?

Roy Cohn continued to pound Lerner in the courts, winning one victory after another for Micheline. On June 4, Aurelio gave her sole possession of the house pending her separation suit. Lerner retained visitation rights with his son. On June 24 Aurelio awarded Micheline $1,500 a week, which at that time was a record alimony judgment for New York State, as well as $15,000 for legal fees. The justice said he had taken into consideration the parties' "station in life" and Lerner's "reluctance to make a true disclosure of income."

Not without irony, the judge said that though the "copious papers" filed in the case "demonstrate a reasonable probability of the plaintiff's success in the action, the contested claims as to financial needs and resources of the parties are in sharp conflict.

"This is not unusual in matrimonial actions. The abused wife never minimizes her needs or preseparation standard of living. Nor does the harassed husband exaggerate his financial resources and ability to pay alimony." (In view of Lerner's spending habits, he could hardly claim convincingly that a $15,000 legal fee or $1,500 a week meant much to him.)

Later in the month the Appellate Division overturned Aurelio and restored the home to Lerner, ordering him nonetheless to continue the $1,500 weekly alimony payment and saying that Aurelio must direct Lerner "to provide adequate living and housing expenses for the plaintiff and her infant son during the pendency of the [separation] trial." In September the Supreme Court cut the alimony payments to $850 a week.

Micheline moved out of the house. Lerner gave her consent in writing to take Michael to California to escape the New York summer heat, with the understanding that they would return by August 5. Lerner went to California twice that summer to visit the boy in Beverly Hills.

On August 13 United Press International moved an item saying: "Alan Jay Lerner, the lyricist, and his wife Micheline, have reconciled and are staying in a cottage at the Beverly Hills Hotel.

"Mrs. Lerner said, 'Yes, we are reconciled,' when reached at the cottage. She said their 5-year-old son Michel was with them. But she would not comment further on the family's plans or the reconciliation."

The reconciliation was short-lived. On September 29, Lerner went to court to force her to return to New York so the boy could enter school. In October a New York Supreme Court justice ruled that it was in the child's best interests to stay in California. In November the full five-man Appellate Division ruled that neither Lerner nor his wife had been exactly forthright about their incomes and resources, and raised Lerner's alimony payments back to $1,500 a week. In December, according to the *New York Times*, Lerner was cited for contempt of court for failure to pay $9,000 in back alimony and ordered to turn over, within ten days, $7,500 in lawyer's fees for Roy Cohn. State Supreme Court Justice George M. Carney said that failure to comply could result in a jail term for Lerner. He also ordered Lerner to send Micheline's and Michael's clothes to them in California, adding: "Defendant's unwarranted withholding of the personal clothing demanded was picayune, vindictive and ill-befitting a man of his stature."

Thus 1964 drew to a humiliating close for Alan Jay Lerner, who had received more concentrated personal publicity in New York during the past eight months for his marital troubles than he ever had for his writing. One can only wonder what he felt at all that he saw in the papers. Micheline had won not only all the court battles but the war of publicity as well. For Lerner, the year to come would be as bad. Worse.

Micheline remains the most controversial of all Lerner's wives. All the others seem to have been generally well-liked. The attitudes to Micheline are partisan. There are those who think well of her, such as Alexander Cohen, others who hate her, among them, by her own statement to the *New York Times*, Kitty Carlisle.

I have met Micheline only once. I spent much of an evening with her at a dinner party at the home of a mutual friend in Holmby Hills, one of those curious California affairs crowded with well-massaged, lined faces you seem to recognize and at last place as being the crepe masks of people who remain forever young in old movies. That was toward the end of the 1970s, when Micheline was in her early fifties. She remained an extraordinary beauty.

Lerner used to say that she was related to Napoleon Bonaparte.

Others say that this was an affectation, generated by Micheline herself. It is entirely possible that she is related to the Bonaparte family, which was prolific. A grand-nephew of Napoleon, a Baltimore lawyer, even founded the FBI. Corsica is a small island, and probably much of its population is related to the Bonapartes. I found, further, on making a few inquiries in Paris, that the name Pozzo di Borgo is a respected one there.

The now-musty testimony in her lawsuit against Lerner makes clear that unlike the troubled and gentle Marion Bell, Micheline Muselli Pozzo di Borgo had no intention of being passively and unprotestingly and impecuniously retired from her second title, Mrs. Alan Jay Lerner.

eighteen

DRUGS AND DIVORCE

On September 29, 1964, Fritz was passing through New York. Like Alan, he made the newspapers. The contrast in their lives could not have been more vivid. The *New York Times* carried a two-column headline October 1 that read: LOEWE FINDS HIS POT OF GOLD AND CEASES CHASING RAINBOWS. The story says the sixty-three-year-old composer "is having a loverly time not working."

The reporter described him as gray-haired and well-dressed. He was in New York so seldom now that he was giving up his penthouse apartment at the Dorset. He'd spent the summer cruising the coast of Italy in the yacht *Fatima,* which he maintained on permanent lease at the marina in Cannes. He said it has "a crew of five and the best cuisine in the Mediterranean." The reporter took note of his Rolls-Royce convertible, and the pool at the house in Palm Springs.

Fritz told him, "Too many people have gone in for this senseless chasing of rainbows. How many rainbows does one need?" He said he hadn't written a note since *Camelot*. And: "I haven't the slightest intention to write another note." He was "having a wonderful time and writing a show is no fun. There is no reason for me to work now. I don't need the glory, I don't need money. I can use the time better.

"I'm deeply grateful for what's happened to me and I would be an absolute fool to get all tensed up with another show. This, after all, is what we're striving for—to be happy.

"When I was doing the score for *Gigi* in Paris in 1957, for the first time in my life it became clear to me I had never seen anything. I never saw. I only heard. My eyes opened up."

He said he had given up gambling a few months earlier, in December 1963. "I had reached the saturation point," he said. "All of a sudden I saw the complete idiocy of it. I had become a member of that royal clique of gamblers, of great suckers. They're the kind of people who can come into any casino and say, 'Give me $50,000 in chips.' You just sign your name. You don't even have to give a check. At the end of the season you settle up. You can only get into this exclusive circle by losing steadily through the years until your credit is completely unchallenged."

The story said that Loewe had left the day before for Palm Springs, where he would as usual spend the winter. Loewe's sabbatical had settled into a determination to write no more, and denizens of the music business couldn't believe that anyone with his melodic gift could cease to exercise it. But Jean Sibelius had gone before him, putting the pen aside and writing nothing in the last years of his life. Umberto Giordano stopped writing after his ninth opera and spent his last years, as Loewe was apparently determined to do, enjoying the ease and luxury his writing had earned him. After the success of his opera *William Tell,* and at the peak of his fame, Gioacchino Rossini, only thirty-seven years old, had ceased composing, choosing to spend the last twenty years of his life as a chef. Bandleader and composer Isham Jones, whose compositions include *On the Alamo, Swingin' Down the Lane, I'll See You in My Dreams,* and *It Had to Be You,* broke up his band and stopped writing in 1934. In 1954, Artie Shaw put his clarinet away and never played again. And one of the shadowy figures in New York at the time Fritz made his decision was Greta Garbo, who had walked away from a legendary movie career. There was plenty of precedent for Fritz Loewe's decision. The *Times* interview is his been-here-and-gone song.

In the meantime, Lerner continued to struggle along on his ESP musical with Burton Lane, while battling Micheline in the courts.

The separation trial began March 3, 1965, in New York State Supreme Court. Louis Nizer immediately lost a move to amend Lerner's answer to Micheline's separation suit. He sought a divorce from her "on the ground of an alleged adulterous act in California," the *Times* reported. Lerner testified that his wife's opinion of him was that he was "a cheap musical comedy writer."

On March 5, the *Daily News* carried the story under a three-column headline, saying that after hours of "quiet and composed" testimony describing her life with Lerner as "sexless, violent, and complicated by his addiction to shots," Micheline Lerner broke down in tears.

She said Lerner had told her he had "the power, the money, and the influence" to get custody of Michael, now six. She said she'd told him, "This child is my whole life. If you take him away I will kill myself—and I would." Lerner said she had threatened to kill the child; she denied it.

Much of her testimony concerned Lerner's alleged addiction to "shots" given by Dr. Max Jacobson. She said Lerner had persuaded her to take them over a period of two months and she had given them up because they made her feel "bizarre, very high" and she was becoming addicted to them.

"Was there a sex problem with your marriage?" Roy Cohn asked.

"Yes, on my husband's part. I had discussions with him. He refused to come near me."

"Did he tell you what the problem was?"

"He told me that when he was very much in love with a woman his problem occurred. But he told me it will pass."

"Were there any occasions when he could not have sex?"

"Since he went to Dr. Jacobson he was getting worse and worse."

She said he became more and more violent, bit his nails, lost part of his already-impaired vision, yet told her he couldn't stop his shots because they helped him "write quicker." She said Lerner went to see Dr. Jacobson as late as four in the morning, and sometimes stayed there the rest of the night. (Jacobson's office at the time was a block away from their house.)

Micheline also testified that Lerner had an affair with a former airline stewardess. She said that in her presence, Lerner telephoned the girl and said, "You're a naughty little girl. You must have talked too much. My wife found out, and I must not see you again." But the affair continued, she said.

In Acapulco, in December 1963, Micheline said, Lerner "beat

me all over, arms, legs, everything. I said, 'What have I done?' He said, 'You looked at me with disgust this morning at the pool.' He said, 'If you open your mouth, I'll kill you.' So I did not open my mouth."

Lerner's attorney insisted that the lyricist got only vitamin shots from Dr. Jacobson, whom he described as "a highly regarded doctor." In view of later developments, Nizer's assertion is ludicrous. The drugs were already interfering with Alan's relationship with Burton Lane. Lane said, "He was a self-destructive fellow. He chain-smoked. He bit his nails. He ripped his fingers. He wore white gloves. He did not drink, but he did everything else." Lerner wore the gloves to try to break his habit of chewing his nails until his fingers were raw. Peter Levinson, who then worked for John Springer, Lerner's publicist, says, "I had to take his prescription down to Philadelphia to him during the tryouts of *Lolita.*"

On the third day of the trial, Friday, March 5, 1965, Alan and Micheline hacked away at each other in testimony, each accusing the other of marital misconduct. "Speaking with a heavy French accent," the *Times* reported, "Mrs. Lerner accused her husband of associations with 'disreputable' persons, including homosexuals."

(Of the occasional rumors of homosexuality, latent or otherwise, in Lerner, Benjamin Welles said: "I have nothing to support that. All it ever was, was women, women, women, women, women. I have never had any reason to believe that." And it should be noted that it would be impossible to work in musical theater without having homosexual acquaintances, friends, or professional colleagues.)

Louis Nizer quoted from a diary Micheline had kept in 1963, in which she expressed feelings for actor Peter Zorin, twenty-seven, their son's music teacher. Micheline retorted that her love for Zorin was as "a member of the family." Micheline was forced to read from the diary, in which she told of having to "defrost" Zorin and complained, "The part has to be played by the man, not the woman."

She read aloud, "One has to defrost Peter constantly and I get enough of that." She wrote at another point, "He comes after dinner and I have two husbands instead of one."

But she insisted in court that Zorin was "a very adorable friend" and that he took her out only twice, and because Lerner had insisted on it. She said, "My relationship with Peter was clear and clean and you know it. I have been in love with my husband until the last minute. I would not be here where I am now except that I am trying to protect myself and my child."

Nizer said, "Did Alan say Peter Zorin had revealed that he had a relationship with you?"

"No, sir."

"When Alan was in California, didn't Peter occupy Alan's bed and wear his bathrobe and other clothes?"

"I swear it is a lie. I loved Peter only as a friend."

Nizer asked her, "Did you taunt your husband, criticize him about his fingernails? Did you write that they 'repel me'?"

She said she could not remember. Nizer read from the diary: "His horrible fingernails tried to caress my leg . . . I have lost the habit of making love and certainly lost the desire." He asked her, "Did you ever write, 'Marriage is a prison and I want to get out of it'?"

Examining the entry in the diary, she said, "It was the truth at the time. It was the way I felt sometimes."

Roy Cohn then brought out that Micheline had objected to Alan's relationship with two actors. When Lerner took the stand, he said he had merely given the men jobs and fired them because of gossip. It is ironic, all these years later, to see Roy Cohn using an imputation of homosexuality to smear Lerner: after his death of AIDS, it was revealed that Cohn had been an active homosexual. Cohn's reputation was such that after his death a quip swept the New York gay community: Roy Cohn is the man who gave AIDS a bad name.

Micheline was questioned about clothing bills amounting to $45,000 in seven months, including $12,000 for Christian Dior dresses, thirty-three pairs of gloves, and cold cream worth $500. She said that $71,000 worth of jewelry had been a gift from her husband, and denied sequestering hundreds of thousands of dollars.

Two days later, on March 8, the trial ended when Alan and Micheline reached an out-of-court settlement, "ringing down the curtain on a . . . trial of counter-separation suits by the couple that had grown increasingly sensational and intimate over three days of testimony," as the *Journal American* put it. On June 25 they signed an agreement "that features a separation settlement well up in the six-figure bracket, plus alimony of upwards of $50,000 a year annually," the *Journal American* said.

By then Lerner had sold the house on East Seventy-first and was living at the Stanhope Hotel at Fifth Avenue and Eighty-first Street. "Under terms of the settlement," the paper reported, "Micheline—a petite, blonde, Corsican-born one-time Parisian lawyer who never lost a case in La Belle France (or the United States, for that matter)—is due to get the bulk of the valuable French antique furnishings of the Lerner home."

On August 31 the *Daily News* reported that Micheline was establishing Nevada residence at Lake Tahoe in order to file for divorce. Its headline read:

LERNER WILL LINE OUT A MILLION
TO SHED HIS FIGHTING FAIR LADY

She was the most expensive of all his wives to get rid of—and she wasn't finished with him yet, as he would learn.

All the while, he was working on, or not working on, as the case may be, *On a Clear Day You Can See Forever,* his increasingly erratic behavior proving more and more exasperating to Burton Lane.

Shortly before the divorce was announced, *Life* magazine ran a spread of photos on the yachting life of the very wealthy on the Mediterranean coast at Cannes, among them the Greek shipping magnate Stavros Niarchos, the Italian automobile manufacturer Gianni Agnelli, Prince Rainier and Princess Grace of Monaco—and Fritz Loewe. Fritz was seen in several pictures with a collection of his girlfriends aboard his boat, the seventy-five-foot *Fatima,* originally a German ketch that sailed the cold waters of the North Sea. One photo, taken from a low angle close to the water, showed a French model named Dominique Joos, in the prime of youth with perfect breasts and a pouting little belly, plunging feet first as Fritz looks approvingly on from the teakwood deck above. Fritz lived at a hotel in Cannes, not on the boat—which he rented in any case, because he didn't want the responsibility of ownership—and began each day at ten A.M. with a champagne party on the beach. Then he would take his guests out to the *Fatima,* sail up and down the coast a little, and serve a lavish lunch. When he wanted to anchor off another port, he would send the boat and its crew on ahead and follow by plane.

Another photo showed a beautiful young German tourist, drifting on an inflated raft near the boat. Fritz, who was a good swimmer, liked diving into the blue waters from the *Fatima.* The last photo showed Fritz, aperitif in hand, standing by a luncheon-laden table with a bottle of wine in a silver ice bucket in the foreground and another girl or two added to the collection.

The pictures are quite astonishing. They are not only a study in realized hedonism. They are every man's sexual fantasy.

nineteen

ON A
CLEAR DAY

When Burton Lane read in the newspapers that Lerner's collaboration with Richard Rodgers had ended, he wrote Alan a letter saying that he would be interested in working with him again. Before the letter arrived, Alan telephoned to ask if he would be interested in working on the show. Lane found the premise of the show, the outline, and the lyric (already written) *What Did I Have I Don't Have Now,* irresistible, and agreed to collaborate with him again. They had not worked together since the aborted *Huckleberry Finn.*

In his apartment on Central Park West in August 1989, Lane described the frustrations he experienced working with Lerner on the show. He said, "When I heard the idea of the show, I thought it was wonderful. I said to Alan, 'This is one of the best premises for a musical I've ever heard.' "

The Brooklyn girl of the story tells a psychiatrist she can make plants grow and tell when a phone is going to ring and where someone has left a set of keys that seem lost. She asks him to hypnotize her to help her by posthypnotic suggestion give up cigarettes. When he puts her under, he finds compelling evidence that she was an Englishwoman in another life, one with a cultivated accent. The psychiatrist falls in love with the "other" girl, the one in the past. By the end of the show he brings the two together, in yet another Cinderella transformation. Thus *Clear Day* brings together in one show all of Lerner's preoccupations: social status, the Cinderella/Pygmalion transformation, the male authority figure, the occult, and even his wish to quit smoking.

Lerner believed in ESP. He told Douglas Watt of the *New York Daily News,* "It's true. In a European experiment, two identical plants were grown in identical soil and cultivated alike by two different people. One flourished and the other didn't. Talk made the difference.

"It's not what you say, of course. It's the way it's said, the feeling behind it."

Later he told a *New York Times* reporter that he had read many books on psychic research, voodoo, and ghosts, and had during his Harvard days taken a course in hypnosis for a year. While he had never had an ESP experience himself, he said he knew people who had. "Anybody can make flowers grow by talking to them," Lerner said. "It's a fact. Take two flower pots with the same soil, the same seeds, the same amount of water and talk to one of the pots. You'll see for yourself.

"I know a man who finds lost objects, who, like the girl in the play, can tell her psychiatrist that the message he is looking for is in the dictionary under 'X.' And I know people who will tell you the phone is going to ring before it actually does.

"You know, many of the plays I've done somehow have disregarded the boundaries of time. In *Brigadoon,* a town comes to life every hundred years. In *The Day Before Spring,* Voltaire, Freud and Plato came to life and advised the leading lady on what to do with her life. . . .

"To me there are several explanations for reincarnation or, as they say in the trade, the survival of human personality. Either there is such a thing as genetic memory or there is a thing of being able to tune in on sounds of a bygone age or something related to that.

"The weight of evidence is that we all have a vast latent extrasensory perception. Quite obviously, the human being has not completed his development. After all, if you're only using one quarter of your brain, well, there is hope."

Burton Lane said, "Alan was into drugs. It was a very difficult period.

"On a Clear Day had its faults, and I blame those faults on Alan. But how that score ever turned out as good as it did is a mystery to me. I've never had anything like this—the worst two years of my life. I don't know how to deal with people who are on liquor or anything else.

"I'm a very organized writer. I would make appointments with Alan to be here at ten o'clock in the morning, and the next morning he would be on his way to Paris, and I wouldn't see him for three or four months. While we're working on a score. Sometimes I wouldn't see him for *six* months.

"When I was at Metro, the first time I worked with Alan, and he was taking these trips back and forth to Las Vegas, he still at least was doing his job. I was getting paid and he was getting paid. We weren't depending on the show. But with a show, if it was a great success, we'd make money, and if it didn't it would be all for nothing. It didn't bother me that much. When you work with a lot of different lyric writers, you get accustomed to adjusting to the various personalities. Not that everybody's difficult, but everybody's different.

"But *Clear Day* was the worst, because of this business of making appointments and not keeping them and going off somewhere . . . It was endless.

"Alan's judgment was very faulty, although the guy had a fantastic talent. I think in *Clear Day* there are some lyrics which are absolutely fantastic—and others that are awful. *What Did I Have That I Don't Have?* is one of the best lyrics ever written of its kind. He had that title when he called me on the phone and asked me to do the show. He told me the scene and I said, 'This is great. It is out of the top drawer.' Then when I came in and he showed me a lot of lyrics that he had written with Dick Rodgers, I didn't like any but one. It was *Come Back to Me.* And there's an example of the frustrations I had with that show.

"Alan had a very extravagant suite at the Waldorf Hotel. He must have had eight or nine rooms—unbelievable expense. One night we had come out of a meeting at the Waldorf at twelve-thirty at night. I said, 'Alan, I have an idea for *Come Back to Me.* I told you that I thought that was the best lyric of all those that I saw.' Dick Rodgers had written a melody which I still have never heard.

Alan heard my tune. The room in which he had a piano must have been forty feet long. He started to pace the room. Tears came out of his eyes, he was so moved by the tune. The ending had to be changed. If I'd been working with Yip Harburg, the lyric would have been changed in two minutes. Four and a half or five months later, I still did not have the lyric to the last two lines. You go out of your mind.

"We went into rehearsal with practically half the score not written. And I was forced to take lyrics that he had written when he was working with Dick Rodgers and set them just to give the actors something to do at rehearsal, knowing that they would not remain in the show, because I wouldn't let those tunes go in the show.

"When I came into the picture, Alan wanted to produce it—and direct it. I said, 'Alan, you must be kidding. When you're doing a show, you need all the help you can get. If you're a director, and have to do a lyric overnight, or in two nights, who's going to write that lyric while you're directing?'

"So at my behest we got Feuer and Martin to be the producers. And Bob Fosse was going to direct.

"Feuer and Martin and Bob Fosse finally had to give up, because they could see that he wasn't writing, and he was not coming through. Cy Feuer had to beg me not to resign from the project. I was ready to walk away half a dozen times. It was awful.

"But, you know, Alan was a great writer. He had a tremendous talent. And you go along with this, you are drawn in because of this talent, and then you find yourself in quicksand, where you're dragged down."

During the writing of the show, and despite the divorce he was going through from Micheline, Lerner embarked on yet another love affair. Doris Shapiro writes: "Even during the divorce proceedings the intimate bond that had developed from his Kennedy connections turned into a romance. She was a well-known married public lady, almost as prominent as Jackie Kennedy. For the purpose of this book, I will call her Frances Douglas." In the middle of the show, Shapiro says, Alan told her he was taking "Frances Douglas" to Venice for a few days. He said that Frances had never been in love until then. Later Lerner chartered a yacht to be anchored in the St. Charles River in Boston during the tryouts of the show "so that Frances could come once or twice and stay overnight discreetly without running into everybody at the hotel."

After the Venice trip, Alan told her in some alarm that he had received a telephone call, apparently from Robert Kennedy, who said, "Listen, Buster, we've got a file on you. You're to stop seeing Mrs. Douglas. Or we'll fix your gondola," indicating knowledge of the Venice trip.

In their book *The Kennedys* (New York, Summit Books, 1984), Peter Collier and David Horowitz wrote, "Aggressively faithful to his own marriage vows, [Bobby] had been the Kennedy who tried to keep others from straying. It was he who was designated to talk to Steve Smith when rumors of philandering threatened to break up the marriage with Jean [Kennedy, second youngest of the nine Kennedys]; he tried to keep Peter Lawford in line when the same kinds of rumors surfaced." And, Collier and Horowitz wrote, "In the sexual heat of the New Frontier, Steve Smith had nonetheless kept his marriage with Jean together . . ."

During the tryouts Lerner met Karen Gundersen, a dark-haired, very pretty, slightly freckled journalist of Norwegian descent. Gundersen is the daughter of Sven Gundersen, who was born in Lacrosse, Wisconsin, one of seven brothers, six of whom became doctors. Members of her family founded the Gundersen Clinic in Lacrosse, an institution akin to the Mayo Clinic, staffed by approximately 290 doctors. Nine close relatives graduated from the Harvard Medical School—more than any other family in America. It is widely thought to be the biggest medical family in the country.

Karen's father, however, never practiced in Wisconsin or at the clinic. Rather, he practiced in Boston, then New Hampshire. He went to see President Kennedy to urge the establishment of Medicare, ironically while his brother was president of the American Medical Association, the most conservative organization in American medicine. "My father's always been a socialist," Karen said. "His brothers were very conservative."

Gundersen herself was born in Cambridge, Massachusetts. She was graduated Phi Beta Kappa from Vassar and then worked for *Life* magazine as a science reporter. She left *Life* to work in the campaign of Perkins Bass, a New Hampshire congressman running for the U.S. Senate. After he lost, she worked briefly as a freelance writer, then joined the *Newsweek* editorial staff. She worked on features on Andy Warhol, Truman Capote, narcotics addiction, and the pollution of the Hudson River.

Burton Lane remembers their meeting. "She and Mel Gussow had come up to Boston. She was trying to get material for a story on Barbara Harris. My wife was with me. We were in Boston, four, five, six weeks. She went to Barbara Harris.

"Barbara Harris is a marvelous performer but a very fragile

person, who is hurt very easily. Barbara went to Alan and said, 'This woman is driving me up the wall. You've got to get her off my back. She's after me all the time.' Alan said, 'I'll take care of it.' "

Benjamin Welles recalled:

"In 1965, I'd been up in Maine. My wife and I were coming down and stopped in Boston. Alan had a new show, *On a Clear Day.* He'd chartered a big yacht and kept it out on the Charles River. That's where we all lived. We'd shuttle in to the theater. I loved the show.

"The night that it opened, I saw him pacing up and down outside, the way he did. I said, 'I love it. I think it's terrific.' He was a little somber. He said, 'I'm not sure, I'm not sure, I'm not sure.' That night after the opening, there was a tremendous party for the cast. They started to dance with a wonderful abandon and sing those wonderful Burton Lane songs.

"I didn't see Alan after that. My wife and I went on to Washington. The next time I saw him, he had Karen Gundersen with him."

Karen said:

"I was assigned to the story by Jack Kroll, at that point senior editor for all the critical departments, movies, art, books, and so forth. It was to be a cover story on Barbara Harris that Mel Gussow was going to write. Mel is now the drama critic at the *New York Times.* I was going to do what I normally did for a cover story at *Newsweek*—interview all the ancillary people. Mel was going to interview Barbara Harris. But I was going to interview Herb Ross, the choreographer, and Alan, and all the other people, which I did do.

"We spent two or three days in Boston. Barbara was very upset with me because I wasn't speaking to her. Because that wasn't my job; Mel was interviewing her. Barbara got it into her head that I was going behind her back, and trying to find out dirt about her, which I wasn't at all. I was simply talking to other people, researching the story.

"Barbara went to Alan. Alan came to me and said, 'It seems you're the culprit.' He used that word. I said, 'What do you mean?' He said, 'Barbara's very upset, about your being behind the scenes talking to people.' I said, 'That's what I'm supposed to be doing. We split up our jobs here.' I liked Barbara, I thought she was wonderful in the play. Such a talented, fragile woman. She *is* a fragile person. She's absolutely lovely. But she was upset, and Alan had to support his leading lady.

"And I burst into tears. I was terribly upset. I said, 'I'm not doing anything devious here. I'm just getting the interviews with the people involved in the show, and I'm not interviewing Barbara, because that's what Mel is doing.'

"Alan said, 'Are you going back to New York today?' And I was. He said, 'Wait, and I'll go back with you on the shuttle.' And so we had a chance to talk a little more than we'd had when I was interviewing him. I got to know Alan a little bit then."

The house on East Seventy-first Street had been sold. When Lerner went up to Boston, he had left it forever. Doris Shapiro wrote, "He was striking another set.

"Alan was on first-name basis with the storage people. Like others who did things for him for money, they were protective of him. Through the years their workmen had come in and packed up the remains of his various households as they became obsolete. I don't think he knew exactly what pieces of his life reposed in the clean, dark, expensive warehouse. He had never had time to liquidate his stuff."

Burton Lane thought that *On a Clear Day* was a bad stage production in every way. Many of the critics agreed with him.

"The movie was different from the show, in that the past was slightly different," Lane said. "The show was much better than the movie. Barbara Harris was much better than Barbra Streisand, as a performer and as a believable character.

"I objected to the part of the show set in the past. Not that Alan shouldn't go back in time. But it was the way he was writing it. I said, 'This should be fun. It shouldn't be a serious story in the past.' I was just reaching out. I said, 'Gee, can't we make up a character that if it hadn't been for her, there wouldn't have been the United States of America? Let's have fun with it, let's treat the whole thing as a lark, this shlumpy little girl in the present who, when she's put under, is a totally different character in the past. And the doctor falls in love with her as she was in the past, and of course the two characters merge at the end of the show.' But I couldn't get Alan to move in that direction.

"I said, 'You should go into the past with no scenery. It should be like a mystery, so you wonder, 'Is she really in the past?' By the time we were into rehearsal, it was murder dealing with him. Our company manager went up to Boston when they were hanging the scenery. I hadn't seen anything of it, no designs. When Feuer and Martin left the show as producers, Alan took it over with Norman

Rosemont. That was Alan's partner. But Alan was really of course the boss. When the guy came back from Boston, I said, 'What does the scenery look like?' He said, 'There's no place to hang it. It's so massive, it's so big.'

"I said, 'We're dead. We haven't got a chance. If Alan went against what I said so completely that we have so much scenery we don't know what to do with it, we're dead.'

"One night, before the curtain went up, there was a terrible accident. Barbara Harris was standing on the stage talking to one of the kids in the show. They finished their conversation and walked off. And there was a crash. I was out front. People were coming into the theater. I went backstage, and I was told that a set hanging up in the flies had suddenly crashed down on another set—just where Barbara had been standing. The curtain went up, the show started. It came to the set in the past. Whatever fell had destroyed this over-large set. I said, 'That's what we should have had before! That's the kind of thing we should have had!' "

The show opened in New York at 7:16 P.M. Sunday, October 17, 1965, at the Mark Hellinger Theater on West Fifty-first Street. The audience numbered 1,600. The top ticket price was $11.90. Robert Lewis had replaced Bob Fosse as director. In the dim light at the back of the theater, near the entrance doors, Lerner, wearing a beautifully cut tuxedo, paced back and forth, glancing now and then at the stage. Milton Esterow of the *New York Times* wrote: "When Barbara Harris, the costar, was doing a number, he seemed somewhat like Prof. Henry Higgins carefully studying and admiring Eliza Doolittle. Her costar, in the role of the psychiatrist, was John Cullum, who had made his Broadway debut in the chorus of *Camelot.*

Burton Lane occupied an aisle seat in the last row of the orchestra. *Sotto voce* he sang the lyrics in unison with the performers onstage. He said he was unaware of this habit, except through others telling him about it. During the second act he left his seat to stand near Lerner, who continued pacing. Lane's wife said, "He's petrified."

The closing curtain fell at ten o'clock. There was the usual crush of people in and outside of the backstage dressing rooms. Alan's friends included Arthur Schlesinger, Jr., and sisters of the late John F. Kennedy, Mrs. Peter (Pat Kennedy) Lawford and Mrs. Stephen (Jean Kennedy) Smith. Mrs. Smith had invested $15,000 in the show. A woman hugged Lerner, saying "Alan, you should be thrilled to death."

The comments went on.

"Darling, you were wonderful."

"I adored it."

"The critics will love it."

Afterward Lerner did what he had done after *Camelot* and said he never did: he went to an opening-night party, this one again at Luchow's. There were seven hundred guests, and Jan Mitchell, one of Lerner's friends, who threw it, estimated that it would cost him $15,000. The guests at Lerner's table included Arthur Schlesinger, Mrs. Smith, Mrs. Lawford, novelist Irwin Shaw and his wife, and Goddard Lieberson of Columbia Records. At other tables were Senator Jacob Javits, David Susskind, and Arlene Francis.

Karen attended the opening in the company of George, Ethel Kennedy's brother. Alan was with Jean Kennedy Smith, who sat with him at the head table at the party held later that evening at Luchow's.

And therein lies the identity of the woman Doris Shapiro calls Frances Douglas, the "public lady" with whom she says Lerner was romantically involved. As it happens, a good many of Lerner's acquaintances knew who she was. She was the late president's sister, Jean Kennedy Smith. Shapiro leaves no doubt about it. She writes: "As the world knows, Alan never did marry the lady we are calling Frances Douglas, although she went so far as to appear with him in Boston several times and at opening night in New York."

John Cullum and Barbara Harris entered to a round of applause. A five-piece band played as many Lerner songs as its leader, pianist Derek Smith, could remember. Shortly after midnight someone said that the *Times* reviewer and some of the television critics had some good things and some bad things to say about the show.

Lerner said, "It sounds like quotable reviews. From the time the curtain comes down it's a crap shoot."

Gundersen said, "Because it didn't get good reviews, *Newsweek* decided not to make it a cover story. It ended up being a two-page inside story about Barbara Harris.

"It's too bad it wasn't a cover story. We had wonderful material."

On a Clear Day received one of the most peculiar endorsements ever given to a Broadway musical: that of Hugh Cayce, son of purported mystic Edgar Cayce and managing director of the Association for Research and Enlightenment in Virginia Beach, Virginia. Cayce recommended the show as a "carefully researched study of ESP gifts, telepathy, precognition, accelerated plant growth, clairvoyance and reincarnation." It was one of the few good reviews the show received, and despite an advance ticket sale of $1.2 million, it lasted only 273 performances.

"Alan believed in reincarnation," Karen said. "At Centre Island, he had a library of three or four hundred books about reincarnation and extrasensory perception. He was very preoccupied with Edgar Cayce. He loved Edgar Cayce. It doesn't go with a disciplined, Harvard-educated mind. To me, it doesn't fit. But that was Alan. He really believed in reincarnation. He wasn't just academically interested in it."

Later on the night of the opening, Lerner phoned Gundersen. "I think it was that night," Karen said, "around two or three in the morning. I later realized that he was up at those hours usually at Max Jacobson's office. I wasn't aware of what an evil influence Max was on Alan, nor was I aware that he was really addicted to the speed Max was giving him."

Alan continued calling her. In November 1989 she said: "We would see each other every once in a while. Alan would call me in the middle of the night. I was very excited, and kind of apprehensive about these midnight phone calls. I got to be really intrigued by him. I didn't fall in love with him instantly. I was just intrigued. I thought he was a very romantic figure. He was extremely funny, and he had a very romantic sensibility, as his work shows. I was totally captivated by him within about six months. His divorce from Micheline came through the day I met him in Boston. I think that was the longest time in his life he wasn't married, those fourteen months before we got married.

"We met in September of '65 and we were married November 15, 1966."

Ten days later, on November 25, 1966, the "Milestones" column of *Time* carried this item: "Married. Alan Jay Lerner, 48, Broadway lyricist-laureate . . . now finishing his libretto for a musical based on the life of Haute Couturiere Coco Chanel; and Karen Gundersen, 31, a *Newsweek* reporter he met during an interview last year; he for the fifth time . . . she for the first; in Santa Barbara, Calif."

Thus the dates of the Boston tryout and the *Time* story confirm that this was Lerner's longest courtship, except for his relationship with Ruth Boyd.

Ben Welles recalled, "I got a call from California. Karen was on the phone. She said, 'Ben?' I said, 'Yes.' She said, 'This is Mrs. Alan Jay Lerner.' I said, 'Not again.' But that's the way it was. He'd meet one, then lose interest. Or he'd marry her and lose interest and another one would come up over the horizon. He was always looking for something."

On their honeymoon, Alan took Karen to Bimini, where they visited his uncle, Michael Lerner, one of his father's brothers. Uncle Mike, as he was called, who commuted between that island, Miami, and New York, owned Lerner Marine Laboratory, with án aquarium on Bimini.

Lerner's fascination with the writings of Edgar Cayce extended to the point that he was convinced traces of the alleged lost continent of Atlantis could be found on the sea floor near Bimini. Cayce had written that the Atlantean civilization had been destroyed by its improper use of a mysterious force of energy that fueled all its activities. He said that the Atlanteans were now being reincarnated, and set the location of Atlantis in the Bermuda Triangle. Through his uncle, Alan obtained a two-man submarine and wanted Karen to go into the depths in search of it. Karen was somewhat less than enthusiastic about the venture, which in any event was canceled. "The submarine leaked," she said, "so we never went."

"Alan," Miles Kreuger said, "not only never knew how to mete out material, he also never knew how to leave out material. I was with him most of the time he was writing *On a Clear Day.* He was so in love with the idea of reincarnation that it was necessary for him emotionally to wedge into a very charming story a whole subplot about an Onassis kind of character paying the psychiatrist money so he could be sure of coming back and thus being assured of immortality. It should absolutely have been removed from the show. It had nothing to do with it. But he couldn't control himself, he couldn't leave it out. It became so important to him. This was a very basic weakness in his writing. Whenever he did an original he was in grave trouble."

Said Burton Lane: *"On a Clear Day* was such a disaster for me—a show with such promise. It was not a hit show. Through a connection I had, Paramount bought it. But Alan was very close to the guy who was head of the studio at that time, Robert Evans.

"When Paramount bought it, Alan was now a coproducer. His coproducer was kind of a weak producer, and Alan dominated the scene.

"My contract with Alan was that if a picture studio bought it, they'd have to ask me if I was available if there were new songs needed. Irving Lazaar, who had once been my agent and was the agent for the property, sent me a wire saying Alan did not want to work with me on any of the new songs. I sent a wire back and said,

'Then get another lyric writer.' And that was the end of that. I went out there finally and wrote two songs. I was the one to get Alan to rewrite the part about the past. But it was still a heavy, pointless kind of past."

The movie, in which Yves Montand awkwardly plays the psychiatrist and sings American music with discomfort, is not very good, and the ending is utterly unresolved.

Burton Lane said, "After *My Fair Lady*, Alan had a bigger reputation than I did. When you're working with somebody, it's either equal or it's no good. I don't try to dominate anybody, but I don't want anybody to step all over me.

"First of all, I have great faith in my judgment. I have the ability to stand back from my work and say, 'What I've done here I don't like.' And I keep working on it until it *is* right. And I'm the same way with lyrics and libretto. My interest in doing a show is not just to write the music but to see the whole thing is right. I came to Alan with a lot of suggestions, which he rebelled against or didn't agree with. And had he done his work we'd have had a hit show. There was every reason to believe that *On a Clear Day* would be a hit. We turned out a wonderful score. He had a marvelous premise. And he had a fantastic talent.

"He had a habit that drove me up the wall. Bud Widney was his production assistant. If I didn't like something in a lyric and said so, Alan would say, 'Bud likes it.' Bud was a yes-man for Alan.

"And he was getting shots from Dr. Feelgood, Max Jacobson. Alan used to say it was vitamins, but it wasn't vitamins.

"Alan and I didn't talk for a number of years after *Clear Day.*"

Widney, a warm and humorous man, said, "Alan's habits drove Burton crazy because Burton was a compulsive. He'd get the job done in a second. And Alan always made the mistake of saying he'd have it for you Thursday. About a year from Thursday you might see it."

Two months after the opening of *On a Clear Day You Can See Forever,* Bob Thomas, the Associated Press Hollywood correspondent, did an interview with Fritz Loewe on the occasion of his making an enormous donation to a hospital. Thomas wrote:

As soon as he walked in the door, Frederick Loewe kicked off his shoes and loosened his tie. "I'm not used to wearing these," he explained to a visitor at his palatial desert home.

Loewe had returned from dedication ceremonies at the Palm Springs Hospital, to which he has donated royalties that may amount to a million dollars, plus other gifts of cash. It was a significant interruption of the composer's daily routine, which is devoted to the pursuit of pleasure.

A small man whose energetic manner belies that fact that he suffered a massive heart attack eight years ago, Loewe sat down in his luxurious living room to explain his withdrawal from the musical theater.

He returns here for nine months amid the desert scenery he loves. He insisted on showing the visitor the 13½ acres he has transformed from a rocky wilderness into a minor Shangri-La. He proceeded at a lope, displaying with enthusiasm his automatic waterfall, a pond of goldfish that come when called, a garden where he grows roses all the year round, a grassy plateau overlooking the full sweep of the desert.

Loewe is up with the sun and by 6:30 may be pruning his roses or riding horseback through the chaparral. After lunch he naps, then listens to music, reads or walks about the grounds. He seldom goes out for dinner, preferring to entertain friends at his home . . .

He referred to his longtime collaborator, lyricist Alan Jay Lerner, whose On a Clear Day You Can See Forever, *recently opened on Broadway. It was the first work since* Camelot *for Lerner, who collaborated with Burton Lane after an unsuccessful attempt with Richard Rodgers.*

Loewe said: "You can't make a fine dinner merely by assembling the best of ingredients. Somebody must know how to cook it."

This cryptic remark is as near as Loewe had ever come, or ever would come, to public criticism of Lerner. To whom does he refer? Who is the missing chef? Moss Hart?

twenty

PAINT
YOUR WAGON:
THE MOVIE

Alan Jay Lerner's wives were all pretty, and in accord with the standard image of the American girl: wide eyes and cute lips and discreet noses, a look that is essentially Germanic. One was a journalist, Gundersen. Half of them were actresses. He ran into his most serious troubles when he departed from his pattern with Micheline, a lawyer, with a knowledge of the avenues, advantages, and appeals available to her calling. Still, she bore at least a stylistic resemblance to the others, though French by language and nationality and Corsican by background.

Micheline is almost certainly the cause for a peevish passage in *The Street Where I Live*—a seemingly sunny self-portrait of success that actually has a dark underpainting of bitterness—excoriating and deploring France and the French. *My Fair Lady* had never been produced in France. Lerner wrote, "Despite repeated requests from all my *confrères,* I refused, and they were kind enough to go along with me. My reason was that after living in France on and off for several years, I knew that the French regarded themselves as the cultural Supreme Court of the world, and that nothing irritated them more than to have something become successful before they had had an opportunity to pass judgment on it. Not only that, it is a linguistic impossibility to translate lyrics into French, or any of the romance languages for that matter. Economy is the soul of lyric writing and it takes one third more words to say in French what it does in English. (An English novel of three hundred pages, for instance, will be four hundred pages in French.) To my knowledge the only two successful translations of anything in English verse are Baudelaire's translations of Poe, which many consider to be superior to the original, and André Gide's extraordinary translation of *Hamlet.* After years of painstaking labor, Gide produced a translation of *Hamlet* that contains the exact number of lines as Shakespeare's."

Hurray for Gide. Most productions of the show contain cuts, frequently of material that has little meaning to a modern audience. Thus Gide's translation in the exact number of lines is one of those numbingly unimpressive achievements, like reciting the Gettysburg Address backward or whistling the *William Tell Overture* on roller skates. And Lerner needn't have chosen such exalted references. He could have looked at the cooking instructions on food cartons in Canada, where by law packaging is in French and English. The French instructions are a little longer, but by no means a third more.

At one point not long after the polite failure of *On a Clear Day You Can See Forever,* the trade paper *Variety* carried this item:

In an interview in a Parisian paper Alan Jay Lerner opined that the French do not like stage musicals, in fact he thinks they do not even like music. This is due to the fact that they do not distinguish between musical plays and operettas. However, the recent fine reviews and biz of the visiting Yank West Side Story *company is somewhat heartening but it seems to be the exception that proves the rule.*

Lerner thinks that translating a person into music and lyrics is too much for French logic. He is presently working on a musical based on the life of the French fashion designer Coco Chanel. However, he does not think it will ever play Paris, or, if it does, be a hit. Though she is known here, whereas she is mainly the name of a perfume in the U.S., he feels the Yank idiom of the musical would still find it hard going here. His Gigi, *though based on a French novel and with French players, did not go either. . . .*

Lerner also believes the literacy of many Yank musicals may make them difficult to translate. He thinks French is just not a good poetic or rhyming language.

This is the more puzzling in that Lerner had majored in French at Harvard and spoke the language well. French is an infinitely richer rhyming language than English. English indeed is very poor in rhyme, with only four rhymes for "love": above, dove, glove, and shove, with "of" forming an imperfect fifth. (In precise pronunciation it would rhyme with "suave.") French, by contrast, has more than fifty rhymes for *"amour,"* which makes it possible to say far more on the subject while maintaining a strict rhyme pattern. Then there is the device of liaison and the separation of vowels by the insertion of the letter *t,* both of which obviate the problem of avoiding the collision of consonants and vowels, which dogs every conscientious lyricist writing in English. In French the *s* falls silent in plurals not followed by vowels, and, within certain restrictions, the adjective can be placed before or after the noun; all of this further enriches the possibility for rhyme. For these and various other technical reasons, French is a superb language in which to write lyrics. English, because of its concision and precision, is far the better language for prose, but French is much superior to it for poetry and song.

Lerner's statement that it is a "linguistic impossibility to translate lyrics into French, or any of the romance languages" is astounding. The body of great song lyrics in French is perhaps the richest in the world. Surely he was not unfamiliar with those of Charles Trenet, Charles Aznavour, Raymond Asso, and Henri Contet, among others. If he did not know the Brazilian lyrics of such writers as Vinicius de Moraes and Newton Mendonça, a brilliant body of work, he was in no position to generalize about lyrics in the "romance languages." These attacks on France and the French puzzle Karen Lerner. She said, "He loved Paris. We were in Paris a lot. He took cracks at the French. But he loved Jean-Louis Barrault, there were many Frenchmen that he loved and admired and visited."

Miles Kreuger said, "We got a letter from a producer in Paris who wanted to have the French producing rights to *My Fair Lady.* Alan said, 'I'm turning him down.' I said, 'Why? Isnt he a prominent producer?' He said, 'Oh yes. But I'll tell you why I'm turning him down. I send my children to French school. I am a great Francophile. But I don't trust the French. Go back in your theater history since the end of the war. Every major American musical that was acclaimed and lauded everywhere else in the world was annihilated by the French because they're so capricious. They do it to show just how potent their good taste is and how superior they are to everyone else. While I am alive, I shall never permit *My Fair Lady* to be translated into French or performed in France.'

"And when Warner Bros. did the film and translated it into French, Alan was furious. But there was no way he could stop it."

Despite the fact that he wrote two beautiful films set in Paris—*An American in Paris* and *Gigi*—and a stage musical, *Coco,* also set there, he seemed, after the divorce from Micheline, to let fly at the French whenever the opportunity arose. To say such things to an interviewer from a French newspaper was hardly the way to endear himself to the French people or render them more receptive to his work. He is right of course that the French consider themselves the cultural Supreme Court of the world. But for the most part their criticism is about as substantial as a meringue; it is hard to take it seriously. Even Mozart complained about it. As for the French sense of themselves that Lerner finds so irritating, it's hardly worse than the self-admiration of the Americans and the English, and certainly the Germans. The French, however, became the bête noire of Lerner's later years, along with lawyers—Micheline was both—and his excoriations of them reflect a personality that seems to have been growing steadily more unstable.

On November 7, 1965, Lewis Funke of the *New York Times* reported that producer Frederick Brisson and Lerner were talking about "a musical based on the life of the French couturiere, Gabrielle 'Coco' Chanel."

"Both gentlemen," the *Times* said, "appear convinced that there is the potential for a lively, funny musical based on the more than 50-year saga of the woman who gave her name to the international byword, Chanel No. 5. The story would embrace the chronicle from her humble beginning as a seamstress in Marseilles to her fantastic success in her chosen work as well as in romance.

"Whether or not Mr. Lerner will continue his partnership with composer Burton Lane on this project remains to be seen." Not really. All the *Times* had to do was ask Burton Lane, at that point ready to tear his hair. Much of the time Alan would not even return his phone calls.

Karen Lerner said, "Alan hated talking on the telephone—unless he initiated the call.

"I was stuck answering the phone and having to deal with these people calling for the fifth or sixth time and saying, 'Why hasn't he called me back?' I'm talking about Freddie Brisson, or Burton Lane, or whoever he was working with. They'd say, 'It's urgent.' Alan said: 'I have one rule: I never return a phone call *particularly* if it's urgent. If it's urgent they'll have to figure out a way to deal with it themselves. They won't need me. By the time I call them back they won't even remember what they called me about.' "

The *Times* noted that Rosalind Russell was interested in playing the title role in the proposed musical, and that she was Freddie Brisson's wife. (Brisson, not one of the best-loved men in show business, was widely known as the Lizard of Roz.)

By January 23, the question of a composer for *Coco* had been resolved. Lewis Funke reported that Lerner's partner would be André Previn, "winner of four Oscars in Hollywood, his last being for his scoring of *My Fair Lady.*"

"It was Alan who brought up the possibility of collaboration," Previn told Funke. "We had worked together on the filming of *My Fair Lady* and *Gigi* and, let me tell you, if he had suggested, 'Let's do the phone book,' I would have seriously considered it. That's what I think of Alan."

The story said that the show would be ready for the 1966–67 season. It wouldn't.

The show had been Brisson's idea. He had suggested it to Lerner back in 1960. In the fall of 1966, Lerner was at Previn's home in Los Angeles trying to finish the show. He told a *Times* reporter that at one point he had despaired of it. "I struggled with it on and off but I just couldn't get hold of it. Finally I went to see Brisson to tell him how sorry I was to have tied up his idea for five years. He asked me whether I had any stray ideas on how it should be done, and I started to talk. I talked and talked and suddenly we all realized that we had a play here after all."

The *Times* story, by Peter Bart, says that Lerner "is holed up this week at the sprawling rustic home of his new collaborator, André Previn, hammering out the rest of the lyrics. As they worked, the two men paced incessantly across Mr. Previn's vast living room, whose walls are festooned with an impressive array of objets d'art. 'This is good working room for us,' Mr. Lerner said. 'We both need pacing space.' "

Lerner described his growing unease with the state of the music business. He said, "Music today is so strangely divided. I never remember a time when the sort of music you hear on the radio was so different from the music of the theater."

He said he disliked rock and roll but rather admired its "vitality" and its search for "a new sound" but the lyrics reflected a "revolt against language."

He made much the same point seven weeks later in an interview with a *New York World Journal Tribune* reporter, published New Year's Day, 1967. He said, "The music in the theater today bears no resemblance to the music that is popular on the outside."

Lerner clearly had no sense of the changes that were occurring in society. When he was growing up, there was a rich and healthy symbiotic relationship between network radio and the rest of the culture. It is not by accident that the era of the big bands and the golden era of Broadway music were coeval. The major figures who developed network broadcasting, such as William Paley at CBS and David Sarnoff at NBC, had simply put on the air whatever seemed culturally prestigious. Thus in the late 1930s there were dozens of programs of classical music, ranging from the light to the serious, on network radio, and the medium was able to make household names of James Melton, Arturo Toscanini, and Benny Goodman. The networks made the big bands and, similarly, made hits of the best songs of the Broadway theater.

With the coming of television, the radio networks were for all practical purposes dismantled. And since the radio stations of America could no longer get quality musical programming from the CBS, NBC, and Mutual networks, they turned to recorded music. Now the symbiosis in popular music was that of local radio stations and the record industry, rather than between New York networks and the theater. Lerner's bemusement, first expressed in the early 1950s, had only deepened. He simply did not understand the change that was occurring. Stephen Sondheim did. Sondheim saw that radio was no longer deriving material from the theater, and concluded there was no point in continuing to court airplay with songs written with two purposes in mind. Now it was possible, perhaps even necessary, to write solely for the theater audience. Even as Lerner was working on *Coco*, Sondheim was writing both lyrics and music for *Company*, a brilliant ensemble piece whose songs essentially cannot be detached from their context.

Coco continued to be postponed. Lerner broke off work on it to write the screenplay for the Warner Bros. film version of *Camelot*, which had been six years reaching the cameras. Jack Warner said it took so long because it took him two years to locate Lerner and two more years for Lerner to write it.

"Not true," Lerner said. "It took me five months to write it and

I am in the telephone book if anyone wants to find me." The statement is something less than ingenuous in view of his attitude to phone calls, particularly those that were "urgent." The film was not made with Richard Burton, Julie Andrews, and Robert Goulet—all of whom were now able to ask very high fees—but with Richard Harris, Vanessa Redgrave, and Franco Nero. The director was Joshua Logan, who was really at his best in theater, not films, as the ponderous screen version of *South Pacific* had already demonstrated. Harris had contacted Logan and offered to do a screen test for nothing to get the part of King Arthur. "His test was terrific," Lerner said. "And he's a good singer, too." Well, not really.

"Franco Nero, our Lancelot," Lerner said, "is unknown here. He brings the humor to the part that it didn't have before." He brought no humor, and even more important, he didn't bring a voice. The voice dubbed for him in the film was that of Gene Merlino, a respected Los Angeles studio singer. Richard Harris and Vanessa Redgrave did their own singing, under the supervision of Ken Darby.

Everything about the film was heavy, including Harris' acting, which had two levels, a hissy whisper and stentorian pronouncement, all of it given a peculiar pace by Brandoesque pauses and hesitations. Harris lacked, further, the haunting lyrical sensitivity that underlay Richard Burton's most macho readings and movements. There was a poetry in Burton, both in the man and his work, not to mention the perpetual utter rightness of his acting, that made you care about Arthur's heartache, no matter the seeming weakness of his character.

Logan's direction of the story is ponderous and dark. A coarseness in Arthur's image on the screen causes one to lose patience with him and eventually lose interest. Logan understood enough about film to know you could do in this medium what could not be done on a stage, but not enough to realize that you should not necessarily use its devices, and certainly you should not overuse them. He did. The film is an endless series of close-ups and two-shots, and much of its considerable length is wasted on long takes of facial reactions. His approach to the picture is cumbersomely literal. The song *If Ever I Would Leave You* is illustrated: when Lancelot sings that he could not leave her "in springtime, summer, winter or fall," Logan's camera in four misty slow-mo shots shows you Guinevere against seasonal bucolic backgrounds.

There is no grandeur about the picture, no sense of space and high purpose; it looks and feels as if it were shot mostly in the studio, which it was, and those interminable close camera shots give it a clogged and claustrophobic feeling.

The part of Merlin has all but vanished, and that of Morgan Le Fay has disappeared completely. As for choreography, it too has vanished; it is replaced by a good deal of jumping around by maidens at Maytime, and swinging on swings and bouncing on a teeter-totter. There is nothing that resembles dance. The anachronisms proliferate. Morgan Le Fay is not tempted by chocolate, since she is not in the picture, but Guinevere wants a cup of tea. Tea first appeared in London in 1697, the same year that chocolate did. There is a reference to tempests in teacups in a time long before food was served on plates; and certainly before teacups. There is a reference to "the doldrums," windless zones near the equator discovered by trans-Atlantic explorers in the fifteenth and sixteenth centuries. The term "barbecue" is used. The word has a comparatively modern American Spanish origin, *barbacoa,* derived from Haitian Creole. There is much passing of notes in a story about an age where paper was not yet known and few people other than priests and scholars—and certainly not the aristocracy—could read.

The story is about two men who love each other having an emotional and continuing physical relationship with the same woman, which after a time becomes obvious as a homosexual fantasy. There is one scene that is, for just that reason, clumsily and presumably inadvertently funny. It is hard to believe that Logan really wanted this effect. As Arthur soliloquizes about Guinevere's affair with Lancelot, the hilt and pommel of a sword cast a conspicuous vertical shadow on his face, camera right and stage left. It is an inescapable and perfect phallic symbol of exactly the right size just left of his mouth. It's an astonishing bit of film. If Logan and Lerner were unaware of it during the shooting, surely they saw it in what used to be called the rushes and now are known as the dailies. And if they did, why didn't they reshoot? It is unimaginable that the film editor and his people, constantly rerunning the footage on a Kem machine in the process of cutting it, did not detect it. Then, to put the cap on it, Mordred delivers this line: "Do you sometimes switch with Guinevere, Your Majesty?"

Meantime, *Coco* was still, well, in the doldrums. The *New York World Journal Tribune* reporter noted that "Lerner is in New York with his new bride (number 5, Karen Gundersen) for the holidays and will return to Hollywood shortly to watch the filming of *Came-*

lot and to work with composer André Previn on the songs for the musical comedy about Coco Chanel."

The delays piled up. The show was scheduled to open in February 1968. But by then Lerner had undertaken to produce the film version of *Paint Your Wagon.* Lerner's script departed so far from the original show, and from the earlier screenplay with additional music by Arthur Schwartz, that several new songs had to be written.

Karen urged Alan to go to Palm Springs to get Fritz to abandon his retirement to write these additional songs. "I wanted to meet Fritz, in any case," she said. "But my real ulterior motive was that I wanted to get them together again.

"We drove to Palm Springs from Los Angeles and spent a wonderful weekend with Fritz. Alan and I stayed at the Racquet Club, and Fritz entertained us extravagantly. We saw Frank Sinatra, who at that time was close to Fritz.

"It was a wonderful, happy reunion. Fritz said he didn't want to work on *Paint Your Wagon* but they did start talking of working together on something else, and I was happy about that."

Since André Previn was working on *Coco* with Alan, he was a logical choice to write the new songs for *Paint Your Wagon,* five in all. It was the first time André had worked with Lerner not as an arranger but as a composer. André encountered the same difficulty in getting lyrics out of Lerner that Burton Lane and others had. André said, "It drove people who worked with him kind of crazy that he could not release a lyric.

"I was under a very strange deal at Paramount. I would get paid by the song as I would hand it into the library. Alan and I would write very quickly, and then there would be, say, one line missing in the bridge." The bridge is the central variant theme in a song, particularly one in the AABA form. The B melody is the bridge; some musicians call it the channel. The French too call it the bridge: *le pont.* "And I couldn't get him to write it," André continued, starting to laugh.

"I was in Alan's office at Paramount way after hours. I said, 'Listen, Alan. I want the money. I want to hand in the song. Can you finish this one line?'

"He said, 'Oh yes, of course. How awful of me, yes, right.' He got out millions of sheets of paper. And after about fifteen minutes of ripping with his teeth at those white gloves of his, he then picked up the papers and said, 'I'll take this home and give it to you in the morning.'

"Because we got along very well, and something kind of snapped at that moment, I went over to the office door and I locked it and threw the key out the window. I said, 'Finish it, you son of a bitch! I want the one line.'

"He said, 'Come on, this isn't funny. I've got to get out of here.'

"I said, 'No.' But he called the guard at the front gate, who came over and unlocked the door.".

Joshua Logan was again to be the director. In Los Angeles, Lerner ran into Tony Thomas. Thomas recalled:

"I told him that I didn't like the film of *Camelot*, because it was my favorite musical story and I'd been in Toronto for the month before it went to Boston and then Broadway. I told him that I was greatly disappointed in the picture. He seemed to understand that. And I said that I felt it was Josh Logan's treatment of *Camelot*. He was trying to make an intimate musical out of this pageant, which should have been filmed in Wales, instead of the back lot over here at Warners. And he agreed with that. So I said, 'Now when you go up to Oregon to do *Paint Your Wagon*, at least it will be in the natural setting, and it'll be much much better.'"

Thomas said to Lerner, "I think so many of us felt that although *Camelot* didn't work exactly on stage, it should have worked exactly on film. Was it a disappointment to you too?"

Lerner replied, "Oh, a dreadful disappointment. And it should have worked on film. Again, it was deprived of its natural habitat. It should have been laid in the countryside of Wales and parts of England and parts of France. It made it such a hot-house stage piece when it was filmed, even though John Truscott did some extraordinary designing and tried to create a style for it. Nevertheless, there was no air blowing through it. There was none of the primitive quality that the outdoors would have given it. It seemed too refined. You didn't feel the primitive man struggling for some kind of articulation, and you can't do that in constructed sets. You have to be where stone is and where the earth is and where the wind is. I think that's primarily what it suffered from."

Thomas commented later, *"Paint Your Wagon* turned out to be a worse film than *Camelot*, because of the choice of artists—Lee Marvin and Clint Eastwood and Jean Seberg, none of whom was a singer. They seemed an incredible choice, to my mind, to do a musical.

"Paint Your Wagon didn't do any better than *Camelot*, I don't

think. And his loyalty to Josh Logan struck me as odd. Logan was a very strange character. I did a long interview with him when he was doing *Camelot.* It struck me that there was something odd about the relationship between Logan and Lerner, that Lerner should be so loyal to him after his having made this gargantuan mess out of *Camelot.* Why would you hire a director who has just blown $15 million making an 'intimate musical' out of *Camelot* to do *Paint Your Wagon?* I couldn't quite figure that."

Lerner, as Burton Lane noted, was friends with Robert Evans, the president of Paramount Pictures. More significantly, he was friends with the late Charles Bluhdorn, chairman of the board of Gulf and Western, which had acquired Paramount. Bluhdorn, who died in 1983, was fascinated by movie stars and show biz. He made Lerner a deal under which Alan was to produce and write five pictures for Paramount, including *Paint Your Wagon, On a Clear Day You Can See Forever,* and *Coco,* even though the stage version of the latter hadn't been completed. In any case, the film was never made.

Lerner said to Tony Thomas, "I've been very lucky because I'm doing it here at Paramount, a marvelous studio in which to work. I am in the position of being able to say that if there's anything wrong with it, it's my fault. And that's all one can ask for. What you hate is to see something dreadful that you are blamed for, that you really didn't do. All one really wants is to have some control over one's success and failure. If *Paint Your Wagon* is bad, I've nobody to blame but me. I can't say it was the fault of the studio or the actors or anybody. I was given complete free rein. And I'm grateful for that. I'm hopeful that the picture will be what I want it to be."

The making of *Paint Your Wagon* provides an instructive example of the way vast sums of money can be wasted on the decision of a single executive, in this case Bluhdorn, to the detriment of stockholders. Lerner spent $20 million on that picture, a staggering amount of money for a movie in the late 1960s.

The film version of *Paint Your Wagon* shows how far out of control Lerner could become when all responsibility was placed in his hands. Its lapses can only be attributed to him, as he was well aware, since he was its producer. The movie bears so little resemblance to the stage show, and so many of the Fritz Loewe songs, such as *Another Autumn,* have been replaced by those written with Previn, that one wonders why Lerner even kept the title.

The original has the traditional and functional two-love-story plot. One of them is about a certain Ben Rumson's daughter Jennifer and a young miner named Julio Valveras, an outcast because he is Mexican. Jennifer goes east to get an education. The second story is that of Rumson and Elizabeth, a woman he buys from a Mormon with two wives. The mining town of the story is depopulated when the gold runs out, Elizabeth runs off with another man, and Jennifer is reunited with her Julio.

The original book is not very good, for all the praise the show received at the time. Said Miles Kreuger, "I saw the original show in 1951. What was wrong with it was that it needed one more pass through, rewriting. It was structured poorly. Structure was Alan's greatest weakness as a book writer, especially when it came to originals. He was better off with *My Fair Lady* because it was based on a well-structured play. He never knew how to mete out material. There are women in the early part of Act One of *Paint Your Wagon*, with Kay Medford playing the musical hall hostess, and then there are no more women. All through Act One the men keep saying, Where are the women? And you sit there saying the same thing. At the end of Act One the stagecoach comes in and the women arrive. Then at the beginning of Act Two, there is a marvelous fusillade of dance numbers by Agnes de Mille, wonderful routines with the women, and then suddenly the women are gone again. It's a show in which you wish the women were spread out more evenly in the text."

Whatever the faults of the stage show, the movie is worse. The screen credits say the play has been "adapted by Paddy Chayefsky." Chayefsky was a by no means infallible writer, and he weakened *Paint Your Wagon*, as he weakened *The Americanization of Emily*, which for all the praise it received lacks the bite of the William Bradford Huie novel on which it was based.

The story of Jennifer and Julio Valveras is thrown out completely, and the relationship between Rumson and Elizabeth is so altered that their names might as well have been changed. All that remains of the original story is that Rumson buys her from a passing Mormon. The forefront story is that of ménage à trois involving Lee Marvin and Clint Eastwood, playing Rumson and a character known only as Pardner, and Jean Seberg as Elizabeth. She is "married" to both of them, and the two men, who are attached to each other, discreetly take turns staying away for the night while the other has sexual relations with her. The bud that appeared in *An American in Paris* and blossomed in *Camelot* advances now into decay.

Rumson and Pardner and others in the story begin tunneling under the town's gaming saloons to retrieve the gold dust that falls between the floorboards. They so undermine the town (as if a half dozen men with shovels could do this in a few weeks) that, first, a bull falls through the ground, and then the whole community goes down in collapse. This part of the story, which is the culmination of the picture, is a plagiarism from the 1966 Blake Edwards film *What Did You Do in the War, Daddy?* in which the tunneling (in that case by inept bank robbers) was used to more pointed and certainly far funnier effect. In the Edwards movie, it was a German tank, not a bull, that fell through the street, and the incident resolved the plot.

The song *I Still See Elisa* has poignancy in the original show, because it is Rumson's reverie about his dead wife. In the movie, the song has been taken from Rumson and given to Pardner—Clint Eastwood—who sings it about an imaginary girl, which renders it pointless. Anita Gordon's voice has been dubbed in for Jean Seberg, but Marvin and Eastwood do their own vocals. Marvin is awful, and not very funny in the process. Eastwood comes off best. He is quite musical and though his soft nightclub voice has a small range and grows thin when he is pushed to the top of it, he understands what a song is about. Still, his singing contains hints and inflections of jazz, for which Eastwood has a known admiration. It is inappropriate to the picture and its period. If the intent had been to cast the show with nonsinging actors, then some consistency should have been maintained, and the excellent singer Harve Presnell should never have been hired to work among them. He sets up a jarring violation of style. Cast in a small role, he gets the best song in the show, *They Call the Wind Maria,* which he delivers with such power and conviction and musicality that he diminishes everybody else in the film. It is better for a work to be entirely poor than to have moments of excellence that illuminate the mediocrity of the rest of it.

Agnes de Mille choreographed the original show. No choreographer is credited for the picture, and we may assume that there never was one or that, if there was, he or she was too embarrassed to accept a screen credit. The "dancing" under Logan's direction consists of drunken men stomping up and down in mud to barndance music. It is dreadful.

So is Lee Marvin, who drunkenly falls down in that mud. He is perpetually downing liquor in the film—and he was doing so in reality while the picture was being made. His character is a smelly, unwashed, stumbling boor whose habits allow no sympathy for a woman who could sleep with him. (The film makes it a point that Seberg's character likes to bathe.) Indeed, the score contains a song by Previn and Lerner whose lyric is perhaps more revealing than Lerner intended: *The Best Things in Life Are Dirty*.

The date of the story is specific. One of the characters says that California is about to become a state. Gold was discovered at Sutter's Mill on January 24, 1848. California's population boomed so rapidly that it soon exceeded the 60,000 required for statehood, and it became a state in 1850. So the story is set in 1849. Lerner's script, once again, is scattered with anachronisms, such as Rumson's reference to egg rolls. Rumson also says that the prostitutes might "strike for shorter hours." The time of the tale is long before the labor movement and the tactic of the strike. Someone refers to a "tourist attraction" before the concept of tourism was born. One of the characters says he is hooked on gold. The term "hooked" came into use in the jazz world in the 1950s specifically to describe heroin addiction; after that it spread and became diluted as it was applied to other addictions and obsessions. But it certainly is inappropriate to 1849.

The dialogue is filled with inner inconsistencies. Marvin, whose character is presented as loutish, uses the word "recourse" at one point. At another, referring to the prostitutes who have arrived in town, he says that the men of the town are "gettin' ready to play chamber music with those French whorns." A man of his ignorance would be incapable of so urbane a pun; it is unlikely that he would even know what chamber music is. But so out of control is Lerner's writing that he cannot resist the joke. He has forgotten that cardinal rule of writing: kill your darlings. The joke, incidentally, is not original. It is a lift from James Joyce, whose quip was better: he referred to the great whorn or the last strumpet. (Lerner's rhyming of Budapest with "ruder pest" in *You Did It* in *My Fair Lady* derives from a 1919 Larry Hart lyric, *Any Old Place with You.* Hart's three-rhyme was more accurate: "rude a pest" and Budapest.)

Lerner's francophobia (as well as his preoccupation with whores) is in full flower in the film. He seems to delight in the reference to the "bawds" in the story, the "six French tarts." He has fallen a long way from the Lise character of *An American in Paris.* If you don't get the point, it becomes inescapable in a scene in which an orchestra of Chinese musicians, assembled to welcome the whores, plays a mockery of *La Marseillaise* in a honky Oriental fashion.

The scene is in abysmal taste, and one can only wonder what French people, seeing the film, felt about hearing their national anthem thus desecrated by Alan Jay Lerner. All France is called to task for his defeats in the divorce from Micheline.

Joshua Logan's direction is hideous. The acting is in several styles and at various levels. The whole picture is played double to triple forte, everything shouted, shrill, rowdy. There are no nuances at all. Lee Marvin, a prodigious ham who could be effective under a good director, is so out of hand that one wonders whether he is merely indulging himself or mocking the script. He camps the whole picture, doing it Keystone Kops style, crooking his elbows before wading into the action, spreading his feet like a duck, mugging shamelessly. Ray Walston's Lancashire accent is unbelievably awful, and the toleration of it gives proof that neither Lerner nor Logan had much ear for these things. Again, Clint Eastwood acquits himself best. In contrast to the flint-eyed laconic stranger roles for which he is best known, he manifests a soft sensitivity that sometimes turns up in his work as a director.

There certainly is no moment of self-revelation of the kind that Maxwell Anderson said was requisite to effective drama. All that happens is that in the end Lee Marvin, fleeing advancing civilization, goes off to leave Seberg in a resolving monogamy with Eastwood, thereby (presumably) satisfying the moral expectations of the audience.

What happened? The first and obvious problem was that Lerner had taken on too many responsibilities. When he was working as a writer, his attention to the project as a whole lapsed.

In the days of the studio system in Hollywood, strict production schedules were maintained, with every day's work laid out in advance. It was known far ahead when various technicians would be needed, which actors were in which shots on which days. The planning was almost military. But there was none of that on the location of *Paint Your Wagon*. For example, two hundred horses were required for one scene. They were needed for perhaps a week. But they were on the location for approximately four months, together with their trainers and wranglers, members of the Teamsters Union and thus among the highest-paid people on the set. John Truscott, the designer who had worked on the film *Camelot*, was responsible for the costumes and look of this film, too. Reportedly he had people weaving lace handkerchiefs to be used by extras, an astonishing squandering of money on details that would never be seen on screen. While the town in which the story is set was designed to collapse near the end of the picture—an allegory to the destruction of Sodom and Gomorrah—it had to spring up again to permit reshooting from varied camera angles. The budget for sets and costumes alone was approximately $3 million, a huge figure for that time, and a pretty good one now. The picture had been planned for about two months' shooting. Instead the company was on location all that summer of 1968, staying in rented houses and rooms in Baker, Oregon, a small town about fifty miles from the main set, which was in a national park. The film's principals had to be lifted daily to the job in helicopters. The crew went into the site in buses.

Lee Marvin's drinking caused him to disappear, sometimes for days. Joshua Logan was a manic-depressive who sometimes was crippled by the low cycle of his emotions. Eventually he was prescribed lithium, which, in the later days of his life, gave him some control over the problem. But he had not begun it yet, and at the start of shooting on the picture, he was discovered asleep on a table in the saloon of the set. I think Josh knew what a mess he made of *Paint Your Wagon.* In his autobiography he conspicuously fails to mention it, and he refers to *Camelot* only once, briefly and in passing.

"It was a wild time," Karen Lerner said. "Just crazy. There was incredible waste and lack of attention to the project. It just was not well thought out, and it was done on a massive scale. And of course Alan always did love big things. He loved extravaganzas. He loved big showmanship.

"Charlie Bluhdorn had just taken over Paramount studios. Charlie had a Learjet at his disposal, and gave it to Alan and me. So we flew back and forth to Los Angeles every other weekend. In addition to this multimillion-dollar production up in the woods, Alan would leave for a day every other week to work on *Coco* with André.

"And Charlie Bluhdorn was playing moviemaker. He just loved to see the stars. He was having parties all the time. And Max Jacobson was around. To get away from all that frenzy and try to keep sane, I would ride five or six hours a day. I tried to help Alan in the beginning by pointing out that he didn't need two hundred horses and the wranglers. I said, 'I've looked at the script, I notice that you're not shooting that scene for four or five weeks.' But I gave it up after a while.

"*Camelot* was made at Warner Bros. Then Charlie Bluhdorn went to Alan and gave him a five-picture deal with Paramount to produce and write. First they did *Paint Your Wagon,* then they did *Clear Day,* and they were going to do *Coco. Coco* never happened. It was a very rich deal for Alan, except that he really shouldn't have been producing if he was continuing to write and rewrite.

"Alan tended to choose weak directors, so that he could have more artistic control. But in terms of organizing things, and logistics, he didn't do a good job. Writing came first to him. Everything else would be put on hold when he was finishing a lyric, whether it was a driver waiting in the street below or a twenty-million-dollar production.

"My father knew about Max Jacobson dispensing amphetamines. He said that it was typical of Middle European refugees to this country to give shots rather than pills, because it would build up their practices. If you give a patient a prescription, he doesn't have to see the doctor for the pills. But if you give him shots, he has to see the doctor every day. My father said, 'I think we can get him off that.' And I told him, 'I hope so. I'm worried about it.' I didn't understand then the extent to which Alan was dependent on Max Jacobson."

Was it the amphetamines that blinded Lerner to how bad this movie, including his script, was turning out to be?

In a 1978 interview with the drug magazine *High Times,* Susan Sontag said, "I use speed to write, which is the opposite of grass. Sometimes when I'm really stuck, I will take a very mild form of speed to get going again . . . It eliminates the need to eat, sleep, or pee, or talk to other people. And you can really sit twenty hours in a room and not feel lonely, or tired, or bored. It gives you terrific powers of concentration. It also makes you loquacious. So if I do any writing on speed, I try to limit it.

"First of all, I take very little at a time, and then I try to actually limit it as far as the amount of time that I'll be working on a given thing on that kind of drug. So that most of the time my mind will be clear, and I can edit down what has perhaps been too easily forthcoming. It makes you a little uncritical and a little too easily satisfied with what you're doing. But sometimes when you're stuck, it's very helpful.

"I think more writers have worked on speed than have worked on grass. Sartre, for instance, has been on speed all his life, and it really shows. Those endlessly long books are obviously written on speed—a book like *Saint Genet.* He was asked by Gallimard to write a preface to the collected works of Genet. They decided to bring it out in a series of uniform volumes, and they asked him to write a fifty-page preface. He wrote an eight-hundred-page book. It's obviously speed writing. Malraux used to write on speed. You have to be careful."

Asked why there was such a long history of writers using stimulants, Sontag replied:

"I think it's not natural for people to be alone. I think that there is something basically unnatural about writing in a room by yourself, and that it's quite natural that writers, and also painters, need something to get through all those hours and hours and hours of being by yourself, digging inside your own intestines. I think it's probably a defense against anxiety that so many writers have been involved in drugs. It's true that they have, and whole generations of writers have been alcoholics."

We should note that Sontag says she used speed only a little and cautiously. Alan Lerner used it *a lot,* with Max Jacobson delivering his shots sometimes several times a day. Lerner was assuredly getting them during the shooting of *Paint Your Wagon.* Jacobson was there, right on the set. And the kind of sprawling writing Sontag ascribes to speed users sounds very much indeed like the ungainly scripts and books Lerner was prone to produce, the few magnificent exceptions being already noted.

How else explain that the man who wrote *My Fair Lady* also wrote the movie version of *Paint Your Wagon,* which ran 166 minutes and necessitated an intermission to allow for the physical functions of the audience?

The film was released to devastating reviews. It was called "bland, directionless." The *New York Morning Telegraph* said that it "sinks inexorably like a dead tree in quicksand." Vincent Canby of *The New York Times* referred to the "rather peculiar psychological implications" of the plot, and *The Villager*'s reviewer noted the underlying homosexuality of the story. Canby said that the massed scenes of town meetings and the like "rocked with the sort of rousing, somewhat artificially hearty masculinity that marked Logan's biggest hits *South Pacific* and *Mr. Roberts.*" He said, "The Sodom and Gomorrah parallels are neither profound nor funny." Bruce Bahrenburg of the *Newark Evening News* said that a "Logan trait is to direct men as if they were in states of retarded adolescence." Pauline Kael in *The New Yorker* noted that it was "one of the three or four most expensive musical films ever made." As Lerner's budgets for Broadway shows almost always set the record for their time, the film version of *Paint Your Wagon* at $20 million topped a list of five. The other Lerner-Logan collaboration, *Came-*

lot, came second at $15 million, followed by *Star* at $14 million, *Doctor Doolittle* at $10 million, and *Sweet Charity* at $8 million.

Lerner in *The Street Where I Live* laments the passing of the old movie studios. But these big-budget musicals, two of which were Lerner and Logan projects, costing between them $35 million, were heavily responsible for that passing. Kael said they had "finally broken the back of the American film industry."

twenty-one

The pattern repeats. The society section, what newspapermen call the women's page, is interested in Karen Lerner, as they were previously interested in Nancy and Micheline. The writers are always women. The stories are meant to fulfill fantasies of the women readers. What is it like to be married to . . . ? This is before women's liberation has found its strength and stride. On February 7, 1969, the *New York Post* runs a piece by Eugenia Sheppard in her *Inside Fashion* column. She has written about at least one of the earlier Mrs. Lerners. This one is ostensibly on Karen; it is really about Alan: a boudoir view of the writer-at-work. Titled *The Very Married Lerners,* it begins with the revelation that "Alan Jay Lerner likes to write standing up." (So did Thomas Wolfe and Ernest Hemingway.) Lerner does it so he won't fall asleep.

He does it, she says, at a large antique British lap desk with two tensor lamps attached. "The lap desk is mounted on a flat table. Behind it there's a black wrought iron high chair that swivels, in case he gets tired." Such is his visibility, such is the interest in him now, that these little details have become important; at least in Sheppard's perception.

"Alan likes to write at night," Karen says. "Sometimes he writes in a small alcove off the bedroom, furnished with a long table between two comfortably upholstered banquettes." And: "He loves to work in closed places."

"Draperies," Sheppard informs us, "can be dropped across the alcove door. The tensor lamps can be turned on and Alan can write while his wife is asleep in their black wrought-iron four-poster."

Sheppard goes breathlessly on:

If there's no sign in the apartment of the mess a writer usually lives with, it's because the Lerners have just arrived from California, where they have been spending most of their time.

Mr. and Mrs. Alan Jay Lerner have been married two and a half years and they are very much married. The whole apartment, a small duplex with skylights on top of an East Side house, tells the story.

At the top of the stairs is a miniature stage that Mrs. Lerner had Tony Duquette make recently to celebrate her husband's 50th birthday. The puppets on the stage represent all his plays including a little figure of Coco Chanel at the far right. The long promised musical about the famous Paris designer will go into production in March.

The rooms are full of silver framed photographs, some of the Lerners, themselves. "This is Alan trying to get me off his lap" and "Here we are in Seattle," says Karen Lerner. The new film, Paint Your Wagon, *was made in Seattle. [Sheppard is wrong about that.] During that year the Lerner had a Learjet and commuted to their house in Beverly Hills.*

"I hate to go anywhere without my husband," says Mrs. Lerner. "The more we fly together, the more I worry when he flies alone. He was coming from California last night and I hardly closed my eyes."

Though they have a small drawing room with walls covered in a French velvet that turned out to be Chanel beige, they do most of their living in a large, sunny bedroom done in a pink and white striped Boussac cotton. The TV set is hidden in a French armoire.

"We enjoy not having a guest room," Mrs. Lerner says.

There are plenty of guest rooms in the Beverly Hills house and the Oyster Bay place that the Lerners really call home. It's at the tip of Center Island with a panorama of all Oyster Bay.

The Beverly Hills house has everything for play, like a pool and tennis court, but Lerner doesn't really like living in California. "It's neither city nor country," she says. "When I get there it's just like a resort. . . :"

Karen Lerner is fair-skinned with black hair and blue eyes. She likes shopping and her husband likes to go shopping with her. She has met Chanel only once and Chanel, in her inimitable fashion, focused exclusively on Alan. The other day she was wearing a cadet blue, side-tied dress from Irene Galitzine.

Karen Lerner always promised herself that she would never be on the opposite side of an interview. She has done so much of it herself. "I'd like to start writing again. In the meantime, I'm keeping a rather detailed journal. Maybe I can do something with that sometime."

An interesting question about Lerner arises. How well did he play piano? In 1989, Karen Lerner said, "He played in a lovely way. He wasn't a virtuoso, but he played very nicely. And he sang even better. I loved to hear him play and sing his songs or Irving Berlin's. He used to say that the song he admired most was *How Deep Is the Ocean?* because every line was a question. He would play his own work but others too. He used to love to demonstrate things like that. He'd give a little speech and say this shows this. He was very fair about other people's work. He was never proprietary. It was a strange combination of ego and generosity that Alan had."

Given that ego, his obvious musicality, and his desire to produce and direct, why did he not venture into composing, as Frank Loesser and Stephen Sondheim, both of whom were first established as lyricists, eventually did? Karen said, "I think he'd have done very well at it. But he wanted to collaborate. He had trouble getting along with all his collaborators at various times. But he wanted to be a collaborator. He didn't want to work entirely alone."

How well did Lerner actually know music? The answer comes from songwriter Maury Yeston, who at the time of Lerner's collaboration with Burton Lane was also a professor of music theory. Yeston met Lerner through Herman Levin, who had optioned a musical Yeston had written. In a short but revealing essay, published in the spring 1987 *Yale Review,* Yeston described Lerner at that meeting:

"Short, gray, ravaged. The face was ravaged. I had met Richard Rodgers the year before. Also ravaged. What was it about a life of doing Broadway shows? Was this a warning? Lerner sat, fidgeted, kept pulling at a white glove on one of his hands, taking it off, putting it on. I later learned it was there to prevent him from biting his nails and cuticles. He sat; I played and sang. Every good line registered. He would drop his head an inch and shake it back and forth, as if to say, 'Got it.' He was dapper and neat to look at, and arranged in straight lines; but the body moved in curves as if compelled from deep within, and the eyes were transported. In fact, they were the first eyes I'd ever seen truly transported by music. And then I got it. He didn't give a damn about the lyrics. For him it was all the music. The guy is a *composer* who doesn't write music but for whom the very fact of music is a kind of miracle. And when he heard it he's got to do something, and he does it with the passion and compulsion of a composer, except his stuff is words."

It was after this performance that Yeston learned of Lerner's early tutelage by Oscar Hammerstein. Alan invited Yeston to his office so that he might do the same for him. Yeston was thrilled. "Chilled," he says. "Stunned."

As he waited out the week until that next meeting, Yeston wondered what he could do for Lerner. As a teacher, he was always analyzing romantic lieder. He thought he might find some relationship of tone and text in the Lerner canon "to show him how good he was."

He made an analysis of *I Could Have Danced All Night.* The nonmusician is requested to follow Yeston's anecdote carefully, even if he doesn't understand the technical terms. You'll see why in a moment. Yeston writes: "Using Schenkerian analysis [Heinrich Schenker was an Austrian music theorist who had developed arcane techniques of music analysis then known mostly to graduate students], I could indicate how the long-range harmonic scheme of the song, through the end of the bridge, arpeggiated the tonic triad: C major, E major, G major, and finally C major. Further, the completion of the large arpeggiation at the end of the bridge is brilliantly matched by the words 'I only know.' Lerner, with his layman's ear—or so I theorized—had brilliantly perceived what the underlying musical structure was. He mirrored the musical structure with a lyric that moves Eliza Doolittle from doubt to certainty about her changed feelings toward Higgins. By the end of the large-scale arpeggiation we know, from the music as well as from the text, that the two can never again be quite the enemies they'd been. Now, how to tell him? The problem was how to avoid technical terms like *submediant* or dominant chord but still to characterize the musical form sufficiently for him to understand the marvelous subtlety of his own work."

Yeston arrived at Lerner's office. "Lerner was all kindness, wrapped in a bundle of nervous energy. His office was small—a large desk strewn with papers. On the walls some new melodies by Burton Lane, handwritten on score paper, were pinned to corkboards. . . . Lerner (I surmised) stared at the melodies until the lyrics occurred to him. I was afraid to ask how he actually did it." Yeston showed his material, and received good and gracious comment on it from Lerner. Now, Yeston decided, was the time to give Lerner his gift of analysis, hoping not to confuse him with technical talk.

"You know, I've been thinking," Yeston said, "you did an amazing thing in *I Could Have Danced All Night.* I mean, the way your lyric matches an extraordinary hidden relationship that grows out of the music's organic form."

As Lerner leaned forward, Yeston began talking of triads. "You see," he said, "each piece is in a key, and each key has a triad, and each triad has these notes, and the song does an amazing thing, going from C to E to G, like the melody—except by changing key—"

Lerner interrupted. "Well," he said, "you know Fritz is really steeped in the Viennese school of composition, and it would be stylistically typical of that school to modulate to the mediant major."

On the Sunday two days after the Eugenia Sheppard story appeared, the Academy of Dramatic Arts celebrated Lerner's twenty-five-year career. Four days later the *Daily News* columnist Suzy wrote:

They beat their way through mountains of snow to get to the Grand Ballroom of the Waldorf-Astoria to celebrate Alan Jay Lerner's silver anniversary in the theater. It was amazing how many people turned up in spite of the storm. Rex Harrison, who got up on the ballroom stage and said the high spot of his career was due to Alan (and Professor Higgins), flew all the way from Portofino for the occasion. His wife, Rachel Roberts, all in black with a white feather boa, flew in with him. Diahann Carroll sang in a white beaded dress cut down in a deep V, and so did Harve Presnell, Constance Towers, and Van Johnson and even Alan himself, who did a number from his new musical, Coco.

Al Capp was master of ceremonies. Sen. Jacob Javits spoke—and so did Alan, well and wittily. The only thing he didn't do was dance. Maybe that was because nobody asked him.

Mayor John V. Lindsay and his wife, Mary, were there smiling, etc. Mary looked soignée in a skinny black crepe dress with no back and strands of brilliants hither and yon. Mrs. Alan (Karen) Lerner, an extremely pretty brunette, wore pink silk crepe, jeweled hither and yon. The Kennedy sisters, Mrs. Stephen Smith and Mrs. Pat Kennedy Lawford, wore white-and-silver brocade and blue-and-silver brocade.

Mrs. and Mrs. George Backer invited 40 people and almost everyone showed up except the Leland Haywards, who were snowbound in the country, and the Edgar Bronfmans, who had the same trouble. At the Backer table were Mrs. Wyatt (Gloria Vanderbilt) Cooper, all in black with a Queen Elizabeth black ruff, ruffled pants and pounds of glittering necklaces, belts, rings, and bracelets, Mrs. Tom (Rusty) Guinzburg in a long paisley print with a jeweled bra, and Mrs. Sidney Gruson in white chiffon with crystal-beaded sleeves.

Then there were Mr. and Mrs. Arthur Stanton, Mary Lasker, Denise Bouche, Mr. and Mrs. Alan Pryce-Jones, Arlene Francis and Martin Gabel (who will soon be off in Barbados visiting Mrs. Williams Woodward), Dr. William Cahan, Mr. and Mrs. Stephane Groueff (she was immersed in silver sequins), Clayton Fritchey, Charles Addams, Mr. and Mrs. Irving P. Lazar (she was swimming in black ostrich feathers), Phyllis Newman, precious in pink, with her dear husband Adolph Green, Roger Edens, Betty Comden, and so on and on and on.

Mr. and Mrs. Gardner Cowles of the publishing empire sat at the Lerner table, as did the Rex Harrisons, Lee Remick and, of course, the Mayor and Mrs. Mayor.

Mrs. Backer wore a lovely white dress by Mollie Parnis (who couldn't scale the Park Ave. snowdrifts and was among the missing) and Mrs. Javits was encased in black sequins.

Alan wore a black velvet smoking jacket and a black velvet bow tie. Last night he was called a poet. That he is. Also a lyrical genius. But you knew that.

On September 4, 1968, the *New York Times* reported that *Coco*, which by now was to star Katharine Hepburn instead of Rosalind Russell, had been postponed yet again. Lerner was working on the screenplay for *On a Clear Day You Can See Forever*, which was to start shooting on December 1. The first rehearsals were set back to the summer of 1969.

Alan, meanwhile, was still thinking of Atlantis as he and André Previn continued their work.

André said, "I will tell you a story you will probably choose to disbelieve. Alan would get wild enthusiasms about things. He was determined that he knew where to find the lost treasure of Atlantis. He said, 'Listen, I have an uncle who's an oceanographer in Florida. I can get one of those two-man subs. I think we ought to go down there. I know where they buried the treasure. We'll get that sub and we'll find it.'

"And I said, 'Yes, Alan. Who's driving this thing, are you or am I?'

"He said, 'Well, we'd better get somebody.'

"I said, 'So we've gone from a two-man sub to a three- or four-man sub.'

"He said, 'You're right. We'll have to get some more.'

"'And the show?' I said.

"He said, 'Well, we can work on it on the submarine.'

"I said, 'Absolutely! What a fine idea!'

"Now I'm beginning to realize he's serious. Finally I said, 'Alan, you're a playwright, so the following scene will appeal to you. Let us say you get the submarine from the navy, which is where you'll have to get it. You and I go down under the sea, and we work on the show. You know where the treasure is, and by God you find it. We surface in Florida, and you say, 'Hello, I'm Alan Lerner, and I wrote *My Fair Lady*, and I just found the treasures of Atlantis.' They're going to lock you up for so long that we're never gonna write this thing.'

"He said, 'You don't think they'll believe me?'

"I said, 'No! Of course they're not gonna believe you!'

"He said, 'All right.' And he never mentioned it again. Now that is a really eccentric human being."

A footnote to this vignette. When I passed it along to Bud Widney, he laughed hugely and said, "Underlying it all, probably, was that Alan was looking for money for the show."

Of the show itself, André said, "*Coco* was not very good. In fact I disliked it a lot.

"It ran for a year with Kate Hepburn, and when it went over to Danielle Darrieux, who really sang it, it closed.

"What was wrong with it was, first of all, that I didn't do a very good job. I had no confidence in those days, and I had no clout, and I just went along with everything that was done in that show. I didn't have the bottle, as they say in England, to say, 'Well, wait a minute, this isn't what we were talking about.' I never asserted myself. And that's what was wrong with Michael Bennett's contribution." Bennett was the director. "Sometimes Michael would come to me and say, 'Can we gang up on Alan and ask him if we couldn't do such-and-such? And Alan had, I have to say, a stock answer: 'We didn't have to do that on *My Fair Lady.*'

"Alan got very angry at Michael Bennett because Michael wasn't in the proper awe of Alan's previous accomplishments. And Michael kept saying, 'I am, I am, but we've got to change things now.' And Alan wouldn't.

"I think what went wrong with *Coco* is that we got away from the original conception. I thought of it in terms of a very French show with *chansons*. I said to him, very early on, 'Maybe we can, say, have a five-piece orchestra in one of the stage boxes.' By the time we were through, we had turntable stages, and Cecil Beaton, and five thousand people on stage, and the whole thing was as un-French as possible. I didn't have the guts to say, 'We're getting farther and farther away from the reason we were going to do this.'

"I used to say to him, 'Talk to me like to an idiot. Tell me: What is this show about?' He'd say, 'A woman's struggle to feel that . . .'

"I'd say, 'No, no, no. Tell me how Act One ends. What happens?'

"Well, there was no story. There never was. And he wouldn't face that. Now, with perfect hindsight and a lot of experience under my belt, I would say, 'This is impossible. We haven't got a plot.' But in those days, I thought, 'What am I doing? This guy wrote *My Fair Lady* and all those other marvelous things. Leave it alone.'

"And so the show sank."

Coco opened late in 1969. John Springer said, "Whenever Alan was preparing a new show, it was the same: 'This one is going to be it, believe me.' It was always such a letdown. On the opening night of *Coco*, Alan was on cloud nine. He knew what a smash this was going to be. He had a party for a very few people, I don't imagine more than ten or twelve, at '21' in the private room. I remember I was representing Mia Farrow as well as Alan. She was married to André Previn then. There were tables for four. Mia and André and my wife June and I sat together. Alan was just euphoric. Forget *My Fair Lady*, forget *Camelot*, this was going to be the one. Alan had arranged to have three little television sets there, to get all the notices. And the notices started. And they were all bad.

"It was so embarrassing, because the first thing they panned was André Previn's score. Mia was virtually a little girl. She was very young. Alan was still trying to maintain the spirit of 'Hey, aren't we having fun!' It was the most disastrous opening night that I can ever remember. Alan's ebullience quickly evaporated after about three of the television notices. Fortunately, it wasn't a big mob of people, just a few people who were very close. My memories are indelible of André's despair, and Mia desperately trying to console him, and Alan putting on the brave front."

Coco lasted 332 performances in New York. Then a national company, still with Hepburn in the title role, was organized. The juvenile lead was Don Chastain, an actor, singer, and writer best known to the public at that point as the newscaster husband of Debbie Reynolds on Reynolds' television show. He had previously appeared on Broadway with Diahann Carroll in the Richard Rodgers musical *No Strings.* He was then the hot new actor and singer in town, on his way up. But he offended Rodgers by growing a beard for a television commercial, was fired from the show, and found he had been blackballed in New York theater by Rodgers. He never landed a major Broadway show again, and went to Hollywood. "I have never forgotten that it was Alan who brought me back to the stage," Chastain said. "Twice." Rodgers' circulation of a rumor that Chastain was "difficult" to work with—the standard smear in both Hollywood and New York by those who would destroy—would have meant little to Lerner. "Alan hated Richard Rodgers," Karen Lerner said. And in any case, Lerner was too powerful to be intimidated by him.

Lerner had auditioned Chastain in Hollywood, then had him fly to New York to do a courtesy audition for Hepburn, who had cast approval. She approved him.

"Do you remember in the movie *Dr. Strangelove* how Peter Sellers' hand would start to go up in the Nazi salute?" Chastain said. "The other hand would try to hold it down. I saw Alan actually do something similar.

"During rehearsals, Alan would stand kind of off in the wings a bit watching us. I had no idea about the amphetamines. I simply watched this man stand there, very nervous and on edge, with his hands jammed in his jacket pockets. Pretty soon, almost unconsciously, one hand would come out of his pocket, in a white cotton glove. He would stand with one hand in his armpit, the other hand going up to his mouth. Then he would begin chewing on the other hand—first the glove—as he watched us. All of this appeared to be unconscious, but it was so unusual. And also, this was Alan Jay Lerner, who wrote *My Fair Lady,* with Fritz Loewe. And I was then, as I am now, fascinated by talent. Always. It was like a struggle between the two hands. The glove would slowly come off. Then he would try to hide the hand. And then he would chew the hand. He would chew not just the nails but up into the highest knuckles. Right up to the palm, the fingers were chewed raw. They looked like hamburger. The hands were terribly scarred.

"I was a child of the sixties enough to know that speed had something to do with things *like* that. But I did not hear about Alan's visits to Dr. Feelgood until later."

And the amphetamines were beginning to strain the marriage to Karen, as they had previously strained Alan's marriage to Micheline.

· "I was married to him longer than anyone else," Karen said. "We were married for eight years. We were together for six. We separated after six years."

What was the proximate cause of the end of that marriage? Karen said, "So many things caused it. It's hard to pinpoint one. During the making of *Lolita,* a project Alan worked on with John Barry— there were many wonderful things in it, including the score—we both became interested in others.

"Things were a little bit shaky. I was extremely upset about the ongoing Max Jacobson thing. I thought, 'I'm not sure I can really handle this.' I became the heavy, saying, 'Don't go to him. Where were you last night? You weren't here, you were in Max Jacobson's office.' He'd get a shot and he'd stay there and write. Then he'd get another shot three hours later. He'd stay and scribble. I have some copies of lyrics Alan wrote some of those nights. They were just little dots, all over the place. They weren't coherent.

"You know, rats on amphetamines will eat up their own tails. He was frantic, destroying himself.

"The shots kept him awake so he could finish lyrics. Sleep was an enemy to him. He wanted to press on. He was not a person who really enjoyed relaxing. He didn't like to go to sleep. He wanted to be awake and alert all the time. Except for the harm it did him, it's a sort of neat quality.

"I remember reading a quote that Alan said he thought Nancy was the perfect wife, one hundred percent adoration and no criticism. I finally started rebelling at the idea of being one hundred percent adoring and accepting. I would say what I thought once in a while. If I had a slightly negative thought about something he was doing in *Coco,* I would speak up. Alan didn't like that. It wasn't really what he wanted from a wife. Obviously he didn't want a critic. He didn't even want someone to say what she thought. He wanted one hundred percent adoration and attention. He did like to have people agree with him.

"When he was in the process of writing something, he needed praise and he got it. From me and others. But once it was done and mounted on the stage, and I was sitting around in rehearsals, I didn't see the problem in my expressing some minor opinion. It did not go down well.

"All of that came together just before we separated in 1972, when *Lolita* was on the road, and I probably made my opinions known too much to him. It wasn't a good idea. I really should have been much more docile. That's one of the things that was starting to happen. And I didn't want to erase my own self. And I found that I had for a few years, and I didn't want to continue that way."

The next show was the 1973 stage version of *Gigi,* for which Fritz Loewe ventured out of his retirement to add several new songs. It had a budget of $800,000 and a cast that included Alfred Drake, Maria Karnilova, Agnes Moorehead, and Daniel Massey. They opened it in San Francisco, making the usual optimistic predictions for its future and saying that it needed "adjusting." Lerner said that with a West Coast opening, "There is less tension, which is both good and bad," to which Fritz added one of his dry comments: "And you don't get mugged. It's also closer to Palm Springs."

Lerner wrote in *The Street Where I Live* that *"On a Clear Day* was modestly received. *Coco* less modestly, but because of the incredible Katharine Hepburn it did well. *Gigi, comme ci comme ca. 1600 Pennsylvania Avenue,* well, you remember the Titanic."

Gigi was gone after 103 performances.

But Alan was already at work on his next project: his last collaboration with Fritz Loewe. An attorney named Joseph Tandet, who held the rights to Antoine Saint-Exupéry's charming fable *The Little Prince* had approached Alan about adapting it as a movie musical. And Alan developed a screenplay on the story. Fritz was ecstatic about the script and said he would come out of his retirement to write the score. They did much of the work in London.

"Eleven years," Lerner wrote, "slipped away in a minute and it was 'pre-*Camelot*' again. [Fritz] wrote the most beautiful score, filled with melody and bubbling with the innocence of youth."

"For three months in 1970," Karen recalled, "Fritz and Alan and I stayed at the Dorchester Hotel. I looked at the bills and said,

'Alan, I could buy a flat for what we're paying at the Dorchester.' And I went out and found one on Eaton Place, and we bought it.

"Alan and Fritz would work every day on the songs. Then they'd play them for me. I never saw Alan so happy—or Fritz either.

"We'd have dinner most evenings at the White Elephant, three blocks from the Dorchester. Then Alan would go back to work on the lyrics. Fritz and I would go gambling until two or three in the morning, while Alan worked. With their quirks of character, it was a perfect situation.

"Fritz taught me to gamble, and I won enough money to go to Paris and buy three Chanel dresses for the opening of *Coco*.

"The next time we were together was again in London. That was in 1972. Alan and I were living in the apartment I'd bought. Fritz was as usual at the Dorchester. We had a wonderful Bluthner piano. I remember them playing the songs for *The Little Prince*. Fritz or Alan would dance around the room, taking turns at the piano, playing *Closer and Closer and Closer* and *A Snake in the Grass*. It was a wonderful score."

But Alan was bitter about its disposition. He wrote, "Alas, it was never heard on the screen as [Fritz] had composed it. The director, someone called Stanley Donen, took it upon himself to change every tempo, delete musical phrases at will and distort the intention of every song, until the score was entirely unrecognizable. Unlike the theater, where the author is the final authority, in motion pictures it is the director. And if one falls into the hands of some cinematic Bigfoot, one pays the price for someone else's ineptitude. In this case the price was high, because it undoubtedly was Fritz's last score."

The picture lost money. And *The Little Prince* was indeed Fritz Loewe's last score. Lerner and Loewe would never write together again.

Enter *1600 Pennsylvania Avenue*. And exit Karen Lerner.

twenty-two

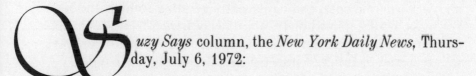

DISASTER WITH BERNSTEIN

uzy Says column, the *New York Daily News*, Thursday, July 6, 1972:

The separation of the Alan Jay Lerners now seems to be permanent, as opposed to temporary, and the London newspapers are already linking Alan with some English actress. Pretty brunette Karen Lerner is the world-famous lyricist's fifth wife. They have no children.

Three months after Karen and Alan separated, on December 4, 1972, *The New York Times* broke a story on which a team of reporters had been working for some time. The report, noting that many doctors were giving potent shots to patients with enough money to pay for them, singled out Dr. Max Jacobson as the most notorious. The story, bylined Boyce Rensberger, gave as a list of his clients Truman Capote, Cecil B. DeMille, Alan Jay Lerner, Representative Claude Pepper of Florida, Otto Preminger, Tennessee Williams—and the late John F. Kennedy. The first lady, Jacqueline Kennedy, was also named as one of the recipients of the doctor's attentions. Mrs. Kennedy tersely admitted through a spokesman that it was true. As Jacobson had accompanied Lerner to the shooting of *Paint Your Wagon*, he had also accompanied President Kennedy on the Vienna summit conference with Nikita Khruschev, a summit that was partially botched. When Jacobson was in Boston for the tryouts of *On a Clear Day You Can See Forever*, he showed Burton Lane a PT-109 tie clip, boasting, "Do you know where I got this? I worked with the Kennedys. I traveled with the Kennedys. I treated the Kennedys, Jack Kennedy, Jacqueline Kennedy. They never could have made it without me. They gave me this in gratitude."

"At all hours of the day and night," the *Times* story said, supporting what Micheline Lerner had claimed in her divorce action, "patients go to Jacobson's office at 56 E. 87th St.—sometimes to his home—to receive injections. Some go once a month, some weekly, some every day."

We will never know what effect Jacobson's ministrations had on Kennedy's judgment; we can see in *Paint Your Wagon* what effect they had on Lerner's. In followups of that first story, the *Times* noted that amphetamines chemically resemble adrenaline and noradrenaline. They increase the recipient's energy, as well as body and facial movements, and cause extreme talkativeness and nervousness. We are immediately reminded of Lerner's late-night telephone calls to Karen. And in his habit of chewing his fingers raw, we are forced to think of injected rats devouring their tails.

The *Times* cited Micheline's testimony in her divorce suit against Lerner and reported that a number of Jacobson's former patients said they "had developed a psychotic condition resembling paranoid schizophrenia."

Despite the thoroughness of the *Times* investigation, the medical profession did not take action against Jacobson for three years. Finally, on August 25, 1975, the New York State Board of Regents revoked the medical license of the German-born doctor, who was then seventy-five.

And Lerner's behavior during the writing and production of his next musical was such that one can only conclude he was still getting amphetamines, either from Jacobson or some other source.

When Alan Lerner entered Harvard, he met a sophomore—class of '39—named Leonard Bernstein. Bernstein, born August 25, 1918, in Lawrence, Massachusetts, was six days his senior. Alan continued to encounter Bernstein over the years, since they ran in the same New York society circles. Indeed it would have been difficult for anyone high in the arts in that city to have avoided Bernstein, who through both talent and ruthless ambition had attained several pinnacles of music: conductor of the New York Philharmonic and other of the world's major orchestras, "serious" composer, sometime pianist, and the composer of four Broadway shows, *On the Town, Wonderful Town, Candide,* and the hugely successful *West Side Story.* Indeed Lerner and Bernstein had written two songs for their alma mater, *Dedication* and *The Lonely Men of Harvard,* neither of which offered serious competition to Cole Porter's *Yale Bulldog Song* and *Bingo Eli Yale.* The two pieces were premiered in a Carnegie Hall performance by the Harvard University Glee Club and sailed off immediately to the land of forgotten songs.

On August 23, 1972, *Variety* reported that "Leonard Bernstein and Alan Jay Lerner may collaborate on a Broadway musical for production next season by Saint-Subber." The project's tentative title was *Opus One,* and Lerner said that the idea for it had come out of his depression over the state of the nation, particularly the Watergate break-in and the landslide reelection of Richard Nixon. He said he wanted to "write a musical about the first hundred years of the White House and other attempts to take it away from us." It would eventually bear the title *1600 Pennsylvania Avenue,* the address of the White House. The story would be told in an *Upstairs, Downstairs* fashion through the presidents and their wives from the time of George Washington to that of Theodore Roosevelt and the succession of (fictional) black servants who serve them. Structurally, the book harks back to *Love Life* and reflects Lerner's anxiety to overcome time. In her biography *Bernstein* (New York, William Morrow, 1987), Joan Peyser wrote, "On the surface the collaboration made sense. Giant figures on Broadway, Lerner and Bernstein had both been graduated from Harvard, were Jews who had spoken with compassion about the blacks, and belonged to the liberal establishment in New York. Both were passionately anti-Nixon."

Ironically, Lerner had said in a 1960 interview, "Fritz and I don't believe in musical plays with messages—particularly if the message deals with teen-age rumbles and switchblade knives. To us the best message a musical play can convey is: 'Come back and see me, often.'" The slap is obviously aimed at *West Side Story,* and here was Lerner proposing a message musical written with its composer.

Peyser says, "During this period, Lerner was married to his

seventh wife and was a patient of the New York physician who later gained notoriety for having injected many of the rich and famous with massive doses of amphetamines." She is right about the dope, of course, but wrong about the number of the wife.

On December 23, 1974, *Newsweek* got it right:

MARRIED: *Alan Jay Lerner, 56, Broadway lyricist . . . and Sandra Payne, 27, a British stage and TV actress; his sixth marriage, her first; in Port au Prince, Haiti, December 10, a day after Lerner obtained a Haitian divorce from his fifth wife, the former Karen Gundersen, who is now an NBC-TV producer.*

Sandra Payne was appearing in a play called *Forget Me Not Lane* that Alan and Karen saw in London in 1972. The gap in age between Lerner and his wives was growing wider: he was twenty-nine years older than Payne. Looked at another way, Lerner was growing older, his wives weren't.

The musical with Bernstein was off on the wrong foot from the start. Again the problem was not the score but yet another unmanageable Lerner book. Peyser describes him as he worked with Bernstein:

"Nervous, shaky, not in total control, Lerner seems to have deferred to Bernstein from the start and willingly relinquished his Lerner-and-Loewe formula for successful musicals."

Two years after the project had started, Saint-Subber checked out of it. He is reported to have said, "I loathed the show and I tried desperately to get everyone to abandon it." The producers Roger L. Stevens and Robert Whitehead stepped in, and got Frank Corsaro, who had background in both musicals and opera, to be its director. In 1986, Corsaro told Peyser:

"Stevens asked me to listen to the score. I thought it was Bernstein's most original, most interesting, best score since *West Side Story*. It was very long, very vital, and made an enormous impression on me. Then I took the book home to read.

"I couldn't believe what was there. It had no foot in any reasonable foundation. I had no doubt that there was something very wrong with it. Yet with these collaborators, how could one say no? I thought I would see what could be done for it. Bernstein was critical of a few things in the book but basically he supported it. When I came into the show, Bernstein was generally behind what was there.

"Against my better judgment I decided to go ahead. I agreed with Whitehead we would not proceed with any actual production until the book had been improved. Whitehead and I were in complete cahoots at the time. The juggling routine went on for weeks. It was only the presence of those two big names—Bernstein and Lerner—that kept the project afloat. According to Stevens, Lenny could do no wrong.

"Then there was a cruel stroke of fate. Alan had another friend, J. Paul Austin, an executive at Coca-Cola who persuaded the company to invest nine hundred thousand dollars."

On September 17, 1975, the *New York Times* carried a story under the headline: COKE BACKS LERNER-BERNSTEIN SHOW. The story noted that Coke would be the sole backer of the show. It was almost a matter of course that a Lerner musical had the highest budget of any show up to that point in theatrical history, and it was again true. The paper noted that CBS had backed the original production of *My Fair Lady* and would back the 1976 revival as well. Lerner said of John Paul Austin, "I grew up with him in Westchester. We used to play golf together." Lerner told the paper that it had in fact been Austin who persuaded him to go to Harvard instead of Princeton. Lerner had called Austin in Atlanta and then discussed the show with him over lunch in New York. The *Times* said, "A third party to early discussions was Paul Foley, head of Inter-public, and the man in charge of the Coca-Cola account and another old friend of Mr. Lerner's."

The paper notes that Robert Whitehead and Roger L. Stevens were now the producers of *1600 Pennsylvania Avenue* and had handled the negotiations. The show was scheduled to go into rehearsal at the end of October.

The reason for Corsaro's dismay is obvious: using his powerful social connections, Lerner had done an end run around Whitehead and Corsaro. He who brings in the money has the largest say in the proceedings.

"It all happened so quickly," Corsaro said. "Alan Jay went off with these Coca-Cola people, gave them a résumé, and played four or five songs for them. There is an affable, wonderful way about him and they went ahead without any further investigation. My jaw dropped. We were caught in the web. I had a long meeting with Whitehead but he chickened out. The money made the gamble possible. Against his better judgment Whitehead gave the go-ahead.

"Even if I had said no, I would have been overruled. During all of this, Bernstein was willing to do whatever he was asked—to change whatever we asked him to change. He was dashing in and out as usual—doing a million other things—but the music was never our problem. One minute Alan Jay and I would be on the same wavelength and the next minute I would be talking to a stranger." It was a phenomenon that has become more familiar in the years since then: that kind of erraticism is often encountered in those who are on drugs.

On February 23, 1976, the show opened in Philadelphia. Much of the audience left after the first act. One man demanded his money back and when he didn't get it, kicked in a pane of glass near the foyer.

Corsaro said, "Philadelphia was four or five weeks of torture. I no longer had any faith that there was any way to repair this. The score, even then, had been cut and pasted. There was a lot of frantic activity. By this time civility alone characterized relations. Midnight oil was being burned. There was a need for an arbiter to persuade Lerner either to collaborate or walk away. [Jerome] Robbins came to Philadelphia and behaved in his characteristic hateful, baleful way. [Arthur] Laurents came down and said to close it."

When Corsaro told Bernstein and Lerner that they would have to concede that the premise itself was faulty, Bernstein told him, "We're a couple of rich, old Jews. We're kind of tired. Leave it alone."

Corsaro did indeed. He left the show ten days before its opening at the Kennedy Center in Washington. The choreographer Donald McKayle quit with him. Another director, Gilbert Moses, took over in collaboration with George Faison. Both men were black. Moses began to cut the many references to racial injustice that seemed to be holding the show down.

Bernstein and Lerner were barred from rehearsals. Bernstein complained, but to no avail, according to Corsaro: "He and Lerner—those two great figures of Broadway—were forcibly kept out of the house."

During the Washington tryout period, Lerner did an interview with Tom Shales of the *Washington Post* that contains an interesting bit of name-dropping. He said, "I was at a party given for Princess Margaret and Lord Snowdon, and Princess Margaret wanted me to sing *I've Grown Accustomed to Her Face*. The conductor asked, 'What key?' and I said, 'It couldn't matter less.' Then I started, 'I've grown accustomed to her face. It [*sic*] almost makes the day begin.' And I couldn't remember one more line. We had to stop and wait until somebody brought me a copy of the lyrics."

Lerner told Shales that he couldn't sing a single song from *1600 Pennsylvania Avenue,* not because he couldn't remember them but because the songs were unusual and difficult. This comment was hardly an augury of success. It sounded as if the audience would, as an old Broadway expression puts it, walk out of the theater humming the scenery.

André Previn saw the show at this phase. He said, "I was in Washington conducting the London Symphony Orchestra. I got tickets and went. I actually couldn't believe it. If someone had said to me before, 'Leonard Bernstein and Alan Lerner are working on a show about the presidency in the bicentenary year,' I would probably have hocked my clothes to invest in it. I had never seen a show by two gigantic people like that so at a loss from moment one. It looked awful, it sounded awful. It was about *nothing.* For two and a half hours they hammered it in. When at the end of Act One, somebody spoke a line which queried the future, from behind the scrim in silhouette came the figure of Abe Lincoln walking across in the top hat and the orchestra played *The Battle Hymn of the Republic,* I gripped the seat and said, 'I'm going mad.'

"Bernstein was there in the last row, actually hitting his head against the wall. I decided it was a good night not to say, 'Hello.'

"Then I saw Alan. He knew. He said, 'It needs a lot of work.'

"And I said, 'Well, uh, er, um.'

"I have never seen so misguided a show. Those two are very big and gifted people. I didn't understand how in the time it takes to write a big show, six months minimum, that neither one of them said, 'You know what? This isn't going to happen'?"

Well before the show reached the Mark Hellinger Theater in New York, the word was out around town. The *Times* carried an ominous story on May 2, 1976, under the headline WILL LERNER'S NEW MUSICAL SING? Reporter Warren Hoge wrote that "in the months of rewriting and restructuring the beleaguered musical, the seemingly ideal union of Mr. Lerner and Mr. Bernstein has faltered, new directors have been installed, the entire structure of the show has been razed and the book has been largely overhauled."

Joan Peyser wrote:

"One curious aspect of the show was that in addition to attacking the whites the way it did, it also humiliated blacks. One scene, for example, had Thomas Jefferson exhibiting exotic foods he had discovered on his travels to his White House guests. As he shows the waffles, spaghetti, and brown Betty, the servants register wide-eyed surprise. Another scene has the blacks showing terror at a simple display of magic, but it was cut before the production got to New York. Still another had the blacks talking about the real danger of being shipped back to Africa. In compiling a list of all the reasons for the fiasco, *Time* listed as one the fact that 'the show is racist.' "

Other critics said the show was "amateurish." Some said it was "embarrassing." *Variety* called it "a bicentennial bore." Jack Kroll of *Newsweek* said that it was a "victim of myasthenia gravis conceptualis, otherwise known as a crummy idea."

It died in seven performances.

Bernstein said, "I'm shattered by the whole thing. The score was completely fragmented, not at all as I wrote it. I might do another musical, but not until the wounds heal." He never did.

Lerner went off on vacation to Bermuda with his latest wife. Having persuaded his friend John Paul Austin to invest nearly a million dollars of his company's money and then having lost it, Lerner shrugged, saying, "These things happen in the theater all the time."

One of the critics who excoriated the show was Clive Barnes of the *Post*. Barnes later wrote of two encounters that came shortly after his review appeared. Noting that the relationship of the critic to the artist "can never be completely easy," Barnes wrote:

"Just before [the show] closed, I was having a late supper in the Russian Tea Room. Across the room I spotted an old friend, Leo Sherman, and without noticing with whom he was dining, I walked over to greet him. He was with Bernstein! A quick moment of embarrassment, then Leo gestured . . . and said to Bernstein, 'You know Clive Barnes, don't you?'

"The temperature dropped low enough to freeze vodka, as Bernstein replied with a voice of cold silk: 'Unfortunately . . . yes.'

"A day or two later at a party, I espied Lerner and decided to give him a wide berth. But, smilingly, and with all the good nature of a wounded saint, he sought me out and apologized for 'giving me what must have been an extraordinarily bad evening.'

"What can you reply to either comment? Lerner's, of course, hurt the most."

twenty-three

THE LAST MUSICAL

On May 13, 1979, Robert Wahls of the *New York Post* interviewed Lerner about a tribute to Lerner and Loewe that was set for two days hence, a benefit for the Theater and Music Collection of the Museum of the City of New York. Lerner was now sixty, Fritz seventy-eight. The interview was done in Le Roy Hospital, where Lerner was resting after the removal of a cyst from his buttock.

The wives were beginning to pass into and out of Lerner's life like replacement dancers in a chorus line. His marriage to English actress Sandra Payne was brief. Now he was married to Nina Bushkin, daughter of Joey Bushkin, a jazz pianist once with the Tommy Dorsey band and the writer, in collaboration with lyricist Johnny DeVries, of a number of songs, including the early 1940s Dorsey hit (with a Frank Sinatra vocal) *Oh Look at Me Now.* Bushkin's wife, Nina's mother, inherited a considerable piece of the money from the Boston department store Filene's, and she and Bushkin lived in comfort in Santa Barbara, California, raising horses and Nina.

Nina Bushkin Lerner, Wahls wrote, made Alan comfortable, then left, commenting that Alan liked to be babied, even when he wasn't in the hospital. Lerner said, "I need lots of attention at all times. When I heard of the benefit . . . and that we were the subjects, I called Fritz in Palm Springs and said, 'I feel as though I'm dead, don't you?' He agreed. Seriously, I like attention."

Lerner, Wahls noted in his *Footlights* column, had never found another Loewe. "I've missed Fritz so much over the years," he said. "It's a joy to have him come back and walk out on the stage with him. He'll play and I'll sing a couple of songs. And I'll read my feelings about him as I wrote them in my book." He referred to *The Street Where I Live,* published a few months earlier.

Lerner told Wahls he thought Broadway was becoming run-down, but he still believed in its magic. "It is a symbol," he said. "If you can pass muster here you are accepted by the country and the world."

Two nights after this interview, on Tuesday, May 15, 1979, a group of performers gathered in the Winter Garden Theater for the tribute. It included Julie Andrews, Rex Harrison, Reid Shelton, Hermione Gingold, Alfred Drake, John Cullum, and Louis Jourdan, doing material from *Brigadoon, Paint Your Wagon, My Fair Lady, Camelot,* and *Gigi.* Excepting the additional songs they wrote for the stage version of *Gigi* and the songs for the film *The Little Prince,* it was now nineteen years since Lerner and Loewe had worked as a team. "I would be lying," Lerner said, "if I did not say I was touched and honored. But the special occasion for me is to be on stage with Fritz Loewe after all these years."

Reid Shelton, who estimated he had sung *On the Street Where You Live* 2,100 times, hinted at the tensions between Lerner and Loewe that they kept hidden from the public. Asked by a reporter for his favorite memory of the team, Shelton said, "There would be periods when they would get mad and wouldn't speak to each other. But the American musical theater always brought them back together."

Kitty Carlisle read the passage of Lerner's book *The Street Where I Live* in which he described meeting Fritz in 1942. With Fritz accompanying him on the piano, Alan sang *If Ever I Would Leave You, They Call the Wind Maria,* and *Camelot.*

The standing room audience of 1,500 included Claudette Colbert, British fashion designer Zandra Rhodes, Gloria Vanderbilt, Gordon Parks, Dick Cavett, Joshua and Nedda Logan, Gardner and Jan Cowles, Ruth Warrick, Jules Stein, and sundry socialites.

The reports of that evening leave one with a curious sense of something ended. It is as if Lerner and Loewe are already gone and are attending this gala like ghosts at their own wake. Fritz seemed happy in his retirement; Lerner kept struggling to find that one more big show, that one further hit. But the kind of show they knew how to write was passing from the scene, as surely as Italian opera and Viennese operetta before it.

Benjamin Welles said, "Alan never wanted to talk very much about Richard Rodgers. Nor did he have a very happy time with Leonard Bernstein. Bernstein was off with one of his buddies at Majorca or the Balearics or the Canaries somewhere. Alan was accustomed to working with Fritz. He really dominated Fritz. I read something the other day that Fritz dominated Alan. It was hogwash. It was the other way around. He couldn't do that with Bernstein. He never really did it with André Previn, or the other guys he tried to work with. He tried to do *Lolita* in 1971. I remember going to that in Philadelphia. It was a disaster. *Coco* was not very good. He had a very dry patch.

"The whole scene was changing. The whole mood of the country. It was Vietnam and protest and Joan Baez. Alan's bright, quick, brilliant, highly sophisticated lyricism was completely out of sync with the mood of the country. I'm glad I had it when I did, and I will not live to see it return."

If Lerner never seemed able to see how deep were the changes in the country and the culture, Fritz Loewe could. In his long taped conversation with Tony Thomas, Fritz as usual put things in accurate perspective. When Thomas asked him, "Why is it that there is so much ugly music in the world today?" Fritz said:

"I will say this. It is astounding how loud it is. It probably has to do with the fact that life nowadays is so noisy. Just think of the jet planes crashing through the sound barrier. Or the beginning of the motors of the jet. Think of the traffic, and the construction building. If you go back to the end of the century, when everyone loved chamber music very much, there were none of those noises. And you were prepared to settle down in a concert for a whole evening, just listening, by candlelight, to beautiful, quiet music. That you could not do anymore, because your nerves are now attuned to another tempo.

"When people come home, they are now so attuned to noise that in order to stimulate themselves they need more noise. So you get this new kind of music with folk singing with steel guitars that can make noise the like of which one has never heard before. You couldn't possibly talk or think in it."

"Dr. Loewe," Thomas says, because Fritz by now had an honorary

Ph.D. and liked to be thus addressed, "you have the German and the Viennese background, they used to be the great fountains of music in the world, but it seems that in this century, America has taken that . . ."

"Oh, there's no doubt about that. That is gone. Neither in Germany nor in Austria do they write musical shows anymore. That used to be their great industry. It has vanished from the earth."

"Obviously one of the great reasons why America has so much music is that so many fine artists have come from Europe to here."

"*Ja.* Also there is a great freedom of style and expression. And the Americans have great sense of harmony and rhythm. New."

"It was a matter of the right people being here at the right time."

"*Ja.* The great outputs of art travel from country to country. They don't stay forever in the same country."

"What of the future of musical comedy? Do you have any predictions?"

"I have the prediction that the musical comedy as we know it, the American musical theater, is going to pass into another era."

"A less melodious era?"

"I don't know. But obviously the popular music in America is passing through the domination of the teenager—or maybe even the Beatles have something to do with it—to something else. Now if the whole world accepts this kind of thing, it stands to reason that the other one cannot sustain their own standard, do you understand? If there is a musical show, it might have to be a combination of the new with something. Not that I say that is so—I can't imagine it—but it might be."

"Musical comedies on Broadway in recent years have been much less melodious than previous times."

"That is so. They don't any more depend on the melody of the ballad. It is the tempo and the energy and vitality that carry it through."

In an article written for the *New York Times* on the occasion of the 1980 revival of *Brigadoon,* Lerner wrote:

"The road we traveled . . . was abruptly deadened by the social rebellion of the '60s. The theater in general and theater music in particular became regarded as the Establishment and Broadway lost a whole generation of creative young artists to pop, country and Woodstock.

"Then why this growing eruption of desire for the musicals of the preceding generation? Not the musicals of the '20s and '30s but those of the post-*Oklahoma!* period. I think it is because in this computerized, dehumanized, directionless society we have created for ourselves—or allowed others to create for us—there is once again a longing for feeling, melody and a more affectionate view of humanity."

Fritz was right, Lerner wrong. The Broadway musical was well along the road to Stephen Sondheim's *Sweeney Todd*, and to *Cats*, and it would never again be as melodic as it had been when Alan and Fritz took it to its peak in *My Fair Lady*.

Fritz would never again write for the stage; and Lerner had only two shows left in him. The first was *Carmelina*, his fourth and last collaboration with Burton Lane.

"It was based on a film I did not like, called *Buona Sera, Mrs. Campbell*," Burton Lane said.

The plot was about a woman in Italy who convinces each of three former GIs that he is the father of her child. Here Lerner's theme of the woman with two men has been slightly expanded: in this story she has three. (The show lasted seventeen performances.)

"In 1979, when we were working on it," Lane said, "Alan went to a hypnotist. He wanted to stop smoking—there was a whole history of cancer in the family. The hypnotism didn't work. Then he went to an acupuncturist. He stopped with the first treatment. You get six treatments. My wife was going through a thing with asthma. I stopped smoking to help her stop. She went to all the programs, and finally she too had an acupuncture treatment and she stopped smoking, too.

"But a few months or a year later, Alan started smoking again.

"Alan had been married to an English actress, Sandra Payne. She went to England and divorced him, and Alan met Joey Bushkin's daughter Nina. We were working on the show and he said to me one day, 'Do you mind if I bring her up to hear a couple of the songs?' I said, 'Sure, bring her up.' I was stunned, because she must have been twenty or thirty years younger than Alan. I felt like saying, 'Can I carry your books home from school?'

"That marriage broke up before we even opened, before we even got to New York."

And Lerner once again had to face Roy Cohn in court, this time teamed up with Marvin Mitchelson, divorce specialist to the stars.

On the evening of April 23, 1980, Nina Bushkin dined with Mitchelson at a New York restaurant called Nirvana, where she was interviewed. "I loved him when I married him three years ago," Bushkin said. "I think at the time I thought that because of my show business background, I was going to be the one who would make the difference, who could change him." Bushkin overlooked, apparently, that Marion Bell and Nancy Olson were in show business.

She thought the age difference contributed to their problems. At this point she was twenty-nine, Lerner sixty-one, and photos from the period show him to be very gaunt, probably from the amphetamines, and at last showing his age.

"I didn't notice it all when we were alone together," Bushkin said. "Alan is very young at heart.

"But when we were with his friends it became very obvious. Some of his friends are eighty years old."

It was while he was waiting for the divorce from Bushkin that Lerner met the English actress Liz Robertson. Ben Welles said, "She was very down to earth, very loyal, much younger. It was a Pygmalion story. His fortunes were down. He'd had a lot of flops. He was emotionally insecure and wondering whether his talent had run dry. He went to England to coach a traveling provincial company doing *My Fair Lady,* and she was performing in it. Alan discovered her, and saw that he could really do something with her, and in the process fell in love with her, and vice versa."

Christine Elizabeth Robertson had few but solid theatrical credentials before Lerner met her. She grew up in Ilford, on the eastern edge of London, the daughter of a bobby who had played trombone in the British army and a mother who was a frustrated actress. Her mother gave her elocution lessons to improve her accent. She had been trained at the Finch Stage School, then worked in cabaret and performed in *Side by Side by Sondheim* in London and on a tour of Canada and in a London production of Sondheim's *A Little Night Music.* She was just two years old when Julie Andrews originated the part of Eliza Doolittle in *My Fair Lady.*

The revival had been touring when Lerner arrived to direct it for a London opening. On his second night there Lerner suggested to Robertson that they have dinner. He had been separated from Bushkin for a year. "I would have invited any leading lady out even if I had hated her," he told the woman's editor of the *Daily Mail.* "It was work. But I couldn't help thinking how terribly attractive and charming Liz was."

"I was on a diet," Robertson said. "We went to the Savoy because it was over the road but I could only eat an omelette. I was terribly boring."

Lerner said, "We talked over the number *Loverly* for a bit and then we went home for the night—separately. But each time we met, we became closer mates. I kept going away to Paris to work and coming back and taking her to dinner. That went on for three or four months."

Robertson said, "I wasn't going out with anybody at the time. When you are in a hit show, men get scared off. They think you are having a wonderful life going to champagne parties and there is no way they could entice you to go out for a Wimpy.

"Or they want to take you out purely to tell other people about it. I was, in fact, leading a very lonely existence."

"Certainly I was lonely," Lerner said. "But I don't think you can put down what happened to us to a negative base. It was all very positive.

"I had decided I had to go back to New York, I was getting phone calls, my work in Paris had folded. I wanted to stay with Liz. I wanted her to ask me to stay, but I wasn't sure she felt as much as I did."

Robertson said, "There was a special moment when I realized. When you said you were going back to New York, I suddenly knew it was much too far away. Paris hadn't been so bad. So I said, 'Oh, please don't go.' "

"And I didn't," Lerner said. "And from that moment we have been inseparable. Sometimes it does seem a strain, and difficult for people to believe that two people who have such a disparity of ages and upbringing as we have can be so compatible, but we are. But I have never known anything like this in my life. We are so totally happy that we can hardly believe it every day.

"I never really thought I could ever find this happiness. In fact, I quite despaired of ever finding it. And the fact that I did at my age is an absolute blessing."

The *New York Times* reported on August 19, 1981:

Alan Jay Lerner, lyricist and librettist of My Fair Lady, *was married last Thursday in Billingshurst, England, to Liz Robertson, whom he met when he directed her in the role of Eliza Doolittle in a recent London revival of his musical.*

Miss Robertson is appearing at the Chichester Festival in a new play, The Mitford Girls. *Mr. Lerner has just finished a screenplay of* The Merry Widow. *He is also working on a musical adaptation of Robert Sherwood's play* Idiot's Delight, *for which Charles Strouse is writing the music.*

The Unitarian ceremony was small and private. Lerner told a reporter, "I am very happy. I have never thought about the difference in our ages." He later told another reporter, "I felt perfectly at home there. It was wonderful to be married in a church. I've never felt married before."

Lerner was thirty-six years Robertson's senior. A news photo of the two of them shows a radiant and pretty girl with dark hair and rather large English teeth; Lerner, his wide mouth now rendered slightly protrusive by the gauntness of his cheeks, is wearing tinted glasses and looks every bit his age. Robertson said, "We had a quiet wedding, just twelve people, no press, on a glorious day in a little chapel in the country."

"I'm the last woman he wanted to marry," she told an interviewer a year or two later. "I'm five-eight and he's five-six. He never took out a girl taller than he, and I never went out with a man who was shorter. I also had vowed never to marry an American, nor anyone who smoked." Lerner in turn said, "I would never even date a girl who was taller than me. What did I think when I first saw Liz? I thought she was, well, frankly, tall." (There is a photo of Alan and Karen standing on the dock of the house on Center Island. Both of them are wearing summer attire and sandals. Alan and Karen are the same height. Karen is five-five.)

Robertson said that London's famed scandal press tore into them. "They really dragged us through the mire," she said. "You can't be as pure as you look, they said of me, you must have a past. I always loved Alan, but I couldn't cope with the pressure." The whispers about them included the comment that marrying Lerner was the best thing that ever happened to her career.

"We've discussed that," she said. "And we've said, well, if I couldn't sing and act, and if Alan couldn't write lyrics, we wouldn't be the kind of people we are, and we wouldn't have met.

"I need excitement. Alan has that and that is what Alan gives me. I need his continually asking my advice. 'How does this lyric sound?' I love all that."

Lerner said, "I am determined we shall never be separated. Never, never, never. I have seen what happens too often to people who are. And I'm not going to let it happen to us.

"Why be separated? These days are too precious to waste."

Liz Robertson took up residence with Lerner at his home in a quiet cul-de-sac in Chelsea, an enlarged Georgian servants' cottage carpeted in royal blue. Along its walls were all his gold records.

Lerner said that he had never liked and never led a glamorous life. Coming from a man who rented a seaplane on call to shuttle his friends out to Center Island for parties, whose house was often full of guests, who maintained homes and expensive automobiles all around the world, who socialized with movie stars and royalty and a president of the United States, who maintained his old Harvard friendships with the wealthy, who had a taste for poker games and weekend socials with cronies such as Kurt Weill, Milton Caniff, and Maxwell Anderson, who married and abandoned actresses like Barbie dolls, whose spending on furs and jewelry and cars and art and homes and boats was legendary, whose tailoring was impeccable, who paid $35 (in 1969 dollars) per haircut at Jerry Spallina's Manhattan salon, whose natural habitat was a circuit of Oyster Bay, Paris, London, New York, Los Angeles, Venice, and Antibes, the statement that he didn't like and hadn't led the glamorous life just might be said to have a certain lack of candor. Yet Lerner persisted in the attempt to portray himself as a gentle recluse, rather like Henry Higgins insisting that he is just an ordinary man: "I won't go to opening nights and show biz parties," Lerner said. He did both. "That has been the trouble in past marriages." And that is a dubious explanation of his marital failures. He said that Liz Robertson shared this attitude.

"I have to bully her to go out to work," he said. "That's why I put together this one-woman show for her at the Duke of York's. That's why I'm writing a musical for her to do in New York this October. If I didn't push her, she would just stay at home with me all day."

Shortly after her triumph in *My Fair Lady,* Robertson was asked what she had taken from the original Andrews performance of the role of Eliza Doolittle. She said, "The answer, of course, is nothing. I think of it as a new role, really, but still one of the best musical roles every written."

From the moment the show opened in London late in 1979, after touring England and Wales, it was obvious that Robertson was riding nobody's coat tails. The reviews were raves, and she was indeed a star.

"I look at myself in the mirror and wonder if it's really happened," she told William Borders of the *New York Times.* Her dressing-room mirror was adorned with telegrams and cards. "Suddenly to be a star!" she said. "Everyone notices. Lady Redgrave sent word that she was so happy to see me. Yul Brynner sent three dozen roses, with a wonderful note."

She said, "I'd like to do my own musical, create my own part, in London, and then on Broadway. After that, in the future when some other girl plays it, people will say to her, 'What do you feel that you learned about it from Liz Robertson?" She covered her face with her hand and laughed, and said, "Oh my goodness, do you think that could really happen?"

She'd get her own musical. Lerner would provide it for her. It would be his last—a musical based on Robert E. Sherwood's *Idiot's Delight*. It would not only be her Broadway debut; it would be Lerner's as a director. This time he took on the responsibilities of librettist, lyricist, and director. Again, the producer was Frederick Brisson.

About his taking on the additional responsibility of directing, Lerner told the *New York Times*, "Someone has to look down the road to see what the play should be, and I think I have that vision. Besides, [composer] Charles [Strouse] has had very good luck with lyricists directing their own shows: Martin Charnin directed *Annie*."

The Sherwood play, which won a Pulitzer Prize when it was first presented in 1936, is about a third-rate entertainer who in a hotel in the Italian Alps comes across a former showgirl with whom he once had a passionate one-night fling.

Lerner moved the locale of the show to Austria and the time to the eve of a hypothetical World War III. Its musical version, as of February, 1982, still had no title. Lerner and Strouse were referring to it as *Boulder Dam*. Lerner said, "That's what Fritz and I used to call our shows before they opened. It always felt like we were building Boulder Dam."

Dance a Little Closer was, like the Sherwood drama it was based on, essentially a message play, the kind Lerner had said in derogation of *West Side Story* that he would never write. One song contained allusions to Three Mile Island and Love Canal. Lerner said in the *Times* interview that he was "passionate" about disarmament and "violent" in his opposition to the defense buildup. He said, "I cannot believe, as a member of this human family, that that is the only solution for human existence. But I didn't do this because I wanted to write an antinuclear play, although that's part of it. It's still primarily an entertainment."

Lerner said he had written the show partly as a vehicle for Liz Robertson. At this point they had been married a year and a half. Lerner described Liz to a *Times* reporter as "my first wife." He said, "This is the first time I feel like I'm married, where I'm not looking at the door ever, and I have no secrets."

And he added this: "I find bachelorhood a bore, and very time-consuming, especially if you want to write. But I was never upset when a marriage ended. I would be now."

Strouse first met Lerner on a plane to California. He found he had forgotten his wallet and recognized Lerner in the seat in front of him. He introduced himself and, with embarrassment, explained his dilemma. He said that Alan gave him forty dollars, adding: "Alan loves this story, and has increased the amount to ninety dollars, but it was really forty dollars."

Strouse recalled another interesting detail of that first encounter. He said he took his first notice of Lerner on the plane when the latter opened a briefcase, removed a pair of white gloves, pulled them carefully onto his hands and smoothed them, then began to write. Strouse said he was mesmerized by this ritual. "I thought it was weird." (When Strouse raised this point, Lerner told the *Times* reporter that he wore the gloves to keep ink off his fingers.)

The show was set to open Wednesday, May 11, 1983, with Len Cariou as the hoofer, Liz Robertson as the former showgirl, and George Rose as Winkler, the Austrian/American diplomat. The cast also included Diane Pennington, Cheryl Howard, Alyson Reed, and Don Chastain.

"Thirteen is my lucky number," Lerner told a reporter. "This is my thirteenth show. *Brigadoon* opened on the thirteenth. There were thirteen songs in the show, thirteen letters in my name, thirteen principals in the show. We opened on the thirteenth and got all good reviews.

"From that moment on I tried to open as close to the thirteenth as possible. *My Fair Lady* opened on the fifteenth. Anything around thirteen I feel happy about." He had forgotten, apparently, the coincidence of thirteen in Micheline Muselli Pozzo di Borgo's name.

Asked if he was nervous about directing a Broadway show, Lerner said, "No—it's a relief, because I'm not sitting in the back of the theater chewing my nails, wishing to hell they'd do it the way I wrote it. The first thing a director does is take all the playwright's stage directions and cross them out.

"In *Carmelina,* for example, I just went crazy because I knew that in a week I could have turned that show around. I don't want to seem immodest about it, but I felt that."

This is at odds with Burton Lane's evaluation: "I don't know whether anything could have saved *Carmelina.*"

Lerner said, "I must tell you that everything I say excludes Moss Hart. If Moss were here now I'd hand this script to him."

The *Times* story said that "Mr. Lerner has long since resigned himself to the perennial recurrence of assertions that he has lost his knack and can't turn out a good show anymore."

Lerner said, "I went through a period right after I did *Coco*—which was a success—when I began to doubt whether what I was writing was relevant to the times in which I was writing about them. I flopped and floundered for about three years. I did try to write one topical play, *1600 Pennsylvania Avenue,* which if you were away for the weekend you would have missed. I finally realized that I'm a writer, and if I'm a writer I have to write and not worry about the public until I'm finished, and just hope for the best."

In addition to having worked for Lerner in *Coco,* Don Chastain had appeared in two Charles Strouse musicals, *Superman* and *Applause, Applause* opposite Lauren Bacall.

Chastain told me, "I got a call from Alan's people to audition for *Dance a Little Closer.* I walked into the audition, and Alan Jay, who was at that point very clean, and very relaxed—the most relaxed I'd ever seen him—looked up with a big smile and said, 'Hello, lad.' It was as if I'd seen him only the week before. Everybody believed that Alan was completely clean of drugs, and I believe it. I sang, and he was, as he always was, very appreciative. He always made me feel, as I'm sure he did a lot of people, that you were auditioning especially for him and he was especially appreciative of what you had done. At that audition, I met Liz Robertson. There was the same kind of performer's appreciation for another performer. There is a difference in auditioning for people who don't have any idea what it's like to be on that stage. Therefore I was getting from her, as I always got from Alan, that feeling of someone who had been there and knew what it took to stand out there with your ass hanging out.

"Subsequently they hired me, to stand by for Len Cariou, who was starring and who had been having some vocal problems, and to play the hotel manager.

"Now, Alan was directing the show. He was directing his wife. It's hard to know what kind of director Alan would have been for someone else's work. Because he was not a bad director. Whether he was the right director for *his* material in *that* situation starring *his wife* is another set of questions.

"I know from observation, and from my own experience, that we had certain problems that *seemed to be* generated by that factor. No matter how much Alan protested that the husband-wife relationship stayed at home, and did not affect the work, still there was no touching between the two leads. And the story was about two people who'd got it on one time and it was so earth-shattering that ten years later when they see each other it threatens both their current lives. You never got to feel that strength. Part of that problem, I think, had to do with Alan's relationship with his wife and the fact that he was so much in love, and, by all accounts of all the people around them, and by the evidence of one's own eyes, they had a deep relationship. It was obvious.

"The show ultimately became, on a personal level, less important than seeing this guy, who was one of the true geniuses of the theater—I don't care what anybody thought of him personally—in that relationship. The difference between the guy I knew on *Coco* and the man I worked with on *Dance a Little Closer* was a quantum leap. It was light years. It was a complete turnaround. I never saw him that happy, that relaxed, despite all the pressures of trying to get this goddamn show on."

This view is supported by composer Charles Strouse.

"He was deeply in love with Liz," Strouse said. "The show was a Valentine to her. I think this blinded him to other aspects of the play. He had never directed before, and it's very hard to direct your own work.

"I found him wonderful and fascinating to work with. He really tried very hard, and we became very close friends. I talked to Burton Lane about his walking away in the middle of work, but it never happened with me. I talked to Alan about all sorts of things, about love and sex and taxes. I asked him about the drugs. He denied that he'd ever used them."

Lerner learned that Don Chastain's father had been a respected boxer and that Chastain too had boxed. Chastain said, "I hated boxing, but I was good at it, because my father was a good teacher. I had boxed Golden Gloves and a few semi-pro fights around Oklahoma City, and then got out of it.

"When Alan found all this out, he started sparring with me— mock sparring, of course. We'd do it once in a while backstage, dancing around and exchanging the punches, and I had the impression that when he boxed at Harvard, he must have been pretty good. He had all the moves. He was very compact, and the once or twice I hugged him, he was very muscular, like a little wall. And this was all part of his relaxation; he was a different man than the one I'd worked for in *Coco.*"

Jonathan Tunick, who arranged and orchestrated the show, had a similar warm impression of Lerner. He said, "It was the first time I'd ever worked with him. I'd heard terrible things about him all my life. I found him a delightful man, and I became very fond of him. He was so passionately dedicated to the show.

"And it was a show in trouble. I'd see him in production meetings, intensely involved, and pulling on his fingers with the other hand, which was perhaps a substitute for eating himself alive. I loved his dedication to his artistry."

Chastain said, "But in terms of the show itself, there were problems. Some of them were solvable, some of them were inherent in the material. The real problem ultimately was that in terms of thinking about the show, and trying to make it work, the perception—Alan's, Freddy Brisson's, and all the other people, who hadn't done anything on Broadway for a while—was that if they threw enough money into the thing, if they had the most expensive sets, the most expensive costumes, the most expensive staging, that this would work, that they could buy a hit. The only time that show worked was at Michael Bennett's studio at 890 Broadway, with no sets and no costumes. The book worked, the music worked, the play worked—simply. But they laid a set on it that was an absolute disaster. They had a catwalk running from one side of the stage to the other, unsupported. There was a slanted glass wall behind the catwalk that gave you a view of David Mitchell's idea of the Alps, which could be changed from sunset to daylight to whatever through lighting. They had an actual Alp back there in perspective. It was funny. Every time somebody stepped on the catwalk, that glass wall bent and waved rhythmically. And unfortunately the slant, which nobody ever seemed to take into account, was perfect for bouncing the balcony rail lights into the eyes of the people who had paid the most money to see the show. So they were squinting through the whole show.

"We saw the set in a model, and it looked incredible. But the real thing was another matter. The floor opened and there was a skating rink. The sets were overwhelming."

Chastain's observations echo Burton Lane's objections to the sets for *On a Clear Day You Can See Forever.*

"Oddly enough," Chastain said, "some of Alan's best lyrics are in that show."

The Charles Strouse music is inventive and, for Broadway, rhythmically fresh. Lerner's exploration of the limited rhyme scheme of the English language is full of startling turns and juxtapositions. Incidentally, a song called *Mad* is an amusing compendium of contemporary annoyances, from picture books on Marilyn Monroe to TV ads for American Express and hemorrhoid medications. He couldn't resist: "I'm mad at Frenchmen. But who is not?"

Still, some of the songs might well have been written for another show. They do nothing to advance the story, seeming to hark back to the 1920s when you could stop a show anywhere and toss in a song. Harry, the lead, is a performer who is appearing at the hotel accompanied by a trio of girls. They sing a song called *Homesick* to express their yearning for the U.S.A. It is has no relationship to the story, not even an obtuse one. But the chief problem, as with most Lerner shows, is the book. The story is set on the eve of a possible World War III. Harry and Cynthia once had an act together, at which time they once—just once—made love in a drab midwestern hotel. Affecting English airs and even assuming an English history, she is now the mistress of an Austrian-American cynical diplomat named Winkler, who resembles an unintelligent Henry Kissinger. (This character replaces the munitions maker Weber of the original play.) She dumped Harry because of her social ambitions, which are expressed (during a flashback) in a song called *A Better Life.* It is a sort of reprise of *Wouldn't It Be Loverly.* But Eliza Doolittle is a pathetic waif of a figure, and her yearnings are modest and very reasonable. Eliza wants to feel as good as other people. Cynthia wants to feel better than other people. Apparently Lerner didn't understand the difference in the characters. In the original, the character named Irene is a complex phony seeking to survive; in the musical she loses whatever sympathy that necessity might generate. Thus the song makes Cynthia, as she is now known, a rather repellent creature, almost reptilian in the coldness of her hungers.

When she encounters Harry in the Austrian hotel, she affects not to know him. Meanwhile the United States has stationed air force planes in Austria, in violation of international treaty, provoking the Russians, who have massed troops on the border. It is all, it seems, a sham, a tension deliberately created to keep the great armaments industry rolling. The borders have been frozen and no one can leave Austria. Winkler meets an Italian countess who interests him more than Cynthia, and, when it is again possible to leave, he departs with her, leaving Cynthia stranded without a passport. She then admits her identity to Harry and some sort of relationship resumes, even as the planes roar overhead—on their way to, or from, the war?

As political protest, the musical is, to say the least, simplistic. So is the play on which it is based which, read now, seems stiff and contrived and populated by cardboard characters, including a too obviously nefarious munitions manufacturer. Robert E. Sherwood's denunciation of war may have had a certain amount of shock value to audiences in 1936; it won the Pulitzer Prize that year. But a bloody half century later, it seems incredibly naive, and Lerner lost whatever character interest it still had.

As drama, the Lerner book is ineffectual; it violates the Maxwell Anderson maxim: no one learns anything about him or herself from its events. No one is raised to a higher level of morality or understanding.

There is one curious line in the play. Cynthia says, of the collapse of her relationship with Winkler, "I think I lost my talent for blind adoration." This is remarkably similar to what Karen Lerner said to me about her relationship to Alan. Furthermore, Winkler sings a song saying that he likes *A Woman Who Thinks I'm Wonderful*. It has been said that the characters in a fiction writer's work are usually made out of the unresolved elements of his own personality. And anyone who thinks writers are incapable of mocking themselves and the class they come from hasn't read Evelyn Waugh.

There is no one in the play you can even like a little, not the two homosexual airline employees who want to be married, not the minister of the gospel they ask to perform the ceremony, not his harridan of a wife, not the nitwitty song-and-dance girls. Harry is a silly man affecting a cynicism of one-liners. Cynthia is essentially—not only by her actions but in her very essence—a whore. Once again, Lerner's heroine is a courtesan. And once more the courtesan is involved with two men. If these characters are a metaphor of humanity, you really can't work yourself up to care much whether the species survives.

(The script has never been published. But a manuscript reposes in the stacks at Lincoln Center Library. It is George Rose's marked copy.)

The best thing in the show was Liz Robertson. She is an original. Her voice resembles no other in theater or popular music. It is bright, penetrating, clear, a little hard, and very musical. The score is lofted by the superb idiosyncratic arrangements of Jonathan Tunick.

There has been talk of a London production of the show, but it is a poor candidate for revival. Lerner should have left it in its original time, on the eve of World War II, as a symbol of all wars. In moving it into the future, the eve of a hypothetical World War III, and writing lyrics to that effect, he made it unplayable in the era of *glasnost* and *perestroika* and the democratization of Eastern Europe. The dizzying movement of events in these countries and the Soviet Union during 1989 and 1990 render the show's premise irretrievably irrelevant. This is the problem with all satire, its dependency on events outside itself. *Dance a Little Closer* suffers the fate of most hortatory art: its relevance evaporates when the conditions it protests are changed or gone. Like *Love Life, Dance a Little Closer* is a dead musical.

Lerner's liberalism was intellectual and abstract. He grew up and lived in a world of privilege, and because of this had no understanding whatever of the common man he claimed to champion. Even *Paint Your Wagon* reveals this: the characters (particularly in the movie version) are fly-bitten lowlife, when in reality an enormous number of the people involved in the California gold rush were men of good family and high education, with doctors and attorneys disproportionately represented among them: they went there for the money, and when the gold ran out gave California a momentous thrust into the future by the intelligent investment of their profits. They set up their own banking in San Francisco, established an opera house and fine restaurants in that city when much of the rest of America was wilderness, passed remarkably advanced laws to govern their affairs, wrote the California constitution of the 1849 Monterey convention, and were the founders of that tradition of volatile social liberalism that to this day renders California politics unpredictable. But Lerner knew nothing of that; or didn't care. He looks at the common man from a great height. And that condescension is apparent in *Love Life,* too. Always he thinks that somewhere, sometime, there must have been an ideal condition of man, whether in *Camelot* or pre-industrial America or in some forgotten haunted village in Scotland. One can only imagine the hardship and disease that would have been rampant in *Brigadoon* in its "real" time. Any biography of Robert Burns makes that clear.

On opening night of *Dance a Little Closer,* the house was filled with Lerner's friends. "I never saw so much old money in a theater," one member of that audience said. "Wall-to-wall face lifts."

"It opened and closed in one night," Chastain said. "We called it *Close a Little Quicker.*"

On May 11, 1983, the Broadway career of Alan Jay Lerner was over.

twenty-four

FALLEN ANGEL

The paper trail thins out after 1980.

There are no more interviews registering the amazement of journalists that Fritz Loewe could actually turn away from his talent. It was some time after *On a Clear Day You Can See Forever* that Burton Lane came to know him. Said Lane:

"I'd met Fritz with Alan on a number of occasions. My wife and I went to Palm Springs for a weekend. We were staying at the Racquet Club when Fritz walked in. We were two composers, and in a way we were brothers-in-law—we both had worked with Alan Lerner. Fritz was very generous. He immediately said, 'You must come to my house, you must let me take you to dinner.' In that short weekend, I got to know more about him than I ever had known before. We got very friendly very quickly. He was just a darling guy.

"My wife commented on this—it was as if he took us over because he was lonely."

What Fritz told people who visited him was often contradictory, as one sees in conversations he had with Tony Thomas and Maurice Abravanel when they visited Palm Springs.

"I don't play myself anymore," Fritz told Thomas. "But the gramophone will play a little Bach, a little Mozart, very subduedly, so as not to interfere with the conversation."

"You don't listen intently to music anymore?"

"No, I do not. I grew up in music, and all the classical music I am very familiar with. I played it myself, all of it, having been a concert pianist at the age of thirteen. If I listen to the same old things that I used to play any more, it is not any more the complete enjoyment, because if you know something too well, you don't really hear it any more."

"Doesn't music play a great part in your life any more?"

"Not at all."

"That's rather strange, inasmuch as you have been so successful as a pianist and as a composer."

"Everything changes. Everything in life changes. The tree is beginning to be green in spring. It gets wonderfully lusciously green in summer and dies in the winter. It becomes bare and barren. A tree changes. Why should not a human being change?"

What he did not say was that the real reason he didn't play was that he was plagued by arthritis in his hands.

Fritz's friend of the Palm Springs years Gloria Greer, a broadcaster for KMIR-TV, the NBC affiliate in the area, noted, "He would say one thing and do totally the opposite."

Maurice Abravanel said, "I was in Palm Springs after a heart operation, so I called Fritz, who immediately invited us up. He was so warm, so nice, so flattering, saying I had been a turning point in his life, because on his first I recommended Hans Bernstein for orchestration.

"The big moment came when he said, 'You know, Maurice, I've been plagued by arthritis, I could not move my fingers, and now listen to that.' And he sat at the piano and played. He said he'd cured himself by practicing the piano, which was probably exaggerated, but it was probably a good exercise.

"He came to Santa Barbara one summer when I was director of the Music Academy of the West, founded by Bruno Walter. He took a house and he came to visit me. One day I called him. I said, 'Fritz, I have a brainstorm.' I was recording a great deal with the Utah Symphony. I made a hundred and four recordings with them, including Varèse and all the Gustav Mahler symphonies. We had quite a name on recordings in those days. I said to Fritz, 'Why don't you write a kind of concerto, a rhapsody with orchestra, on all your most popular tunes. And you practice and play the piano and we can get to the Hollywood Bowl right away and we will record it.'

"He said, 'Maurice, this is an incredible idea. I love it! Every day I will practice. I was a concert pianist before.' He had played the Liszt E-flat. It was the one concerto he really knew. And so the idea of coming to the Hollywood Bowl appealed to him. He was all excited for a couple or three weeks. This must have been in 1978. But nothing came of it."

And so Fritz had gone back to playing. He gave the same demonstration to Gloria Greer that he had to Abravanel, saying that it had cleared the arthritis from his hands. Greer said: "Music was always so important to him. He would play for hours. His hands were always beautiful. They were beautiful to the day he died. Toward the last few years, he'd get up in the middle of the night, two or three or four in the morning, and play.

"Another one of his contradictions: he always said Christmas was humbug. Yet he was very generous at Christmas.

"He supposedly didn't like children. My daughter has a little boy. When he was about two years old, I was having lunch with Fritz. My daughter came to pick me up, and brought the baby. I said, 'The moment the baby starts running or making noise, he has to leave. Fritz is going to be impatient.' I put the baby on my lap, and Fritz played with him for about forty-five minutes. The baby loved it."

Greer said he continued to exercise every day and took great pride in his physical condition. She said, "When he was wearing shorts, he'd say, 'Just feel these thighs,' and they were just like a rock. He'd had the garden built so he could walk in it."

Greer met Loewe through their mutual friend, Lillie Messinger, at whose urging, it will be remembered, Louis B. Mayer had optioned *The Day Before Spring* for $250,000, thereby giving Fritz his first big money. In a sense, Messinger was the person who changed his life.

Greer said, "I used to write a column for *Daily Variety* from here. Lillie Messinger had given me the number. I called him about certain things for the column. One day he was arriving at the Racquet Club. He got out of the car. I said, 'Hello, I'm Gloria Greer, I've talked to you on the phone.' And he came bouncing over and said, 'You're pretty!' and invited me to lunch. He never walked, he bounded. He had great enthusiasm. His eyes always twinkled. He had beautiful blue eyes. Not a handsome man, but the eyes were soft. There was a gentleness about him that a lot of people weren't aware of.

"He was very friendly with Burgess Meredith. One night we all had dinner. At that time Palm Springs High School was doing a production of *Brigadoon.* I said, 'Do you know what it would mean to those kids if you turned up at that theater?'

"Fritzy said, 'Don't be crazy.'

"Burgess and I talked to him and talked to him and we finally got him to go. We all went, and he loved it. We saw the last half of the show. Somehow the kids were aware that he was there—I suppose Burgess or I told them. Afterwards they announced that he was there. They were so thrilled.

"He didn't like to plan anything. He said, 'I don't have anybody in the world, and if I want to go somewhere I can.' Once he and Burgess decided to go to the Orient for Christmas. I think they left the next day. He'd find some buddies and say 'Let's go to Las Vegas,' and he'd charter a plane and they'd go."

"At one point, Fritz was given a doctorate of music at Redlands. He chartered a bus for all his buddies in Palm Springs. In those days he was at the Racquet Club almost every day. Edgar Eisenhower was among the people who went to Redlands with him that day on the bus.

"When I first knew him, he kept a place at the Racquet Club for his guests. He lived a grand lifestyle. He loved the luxury. He had a vicuña blanket on his bed.

"People who didn't know him well were sort of in awe of him here. They were almost frightened of him. If he didn't like you, he'd let you know it. He didn't have to be polite if he didn't want to be. For some reason, I don't know, we were friends from the day I met him. I had lunch with him probably once a week. He loved to have people come to the house.

"I first knew him shortly after *Camelot.* He had come back from Germany. He had been given the keys to the city in Berlin by Willy Brandt. He was very proud of that. He'd go places, and everybody knew who he was. Of course, as the years went by that changed. But he enjoyed the fame. He missed it, really."

His friends during the Palm Springs years included the noted designer Raymond Loewy, who lived a few doors from him, Mary

Martin, Greta Garbo, Red Skelton, and Frank Sinatra. He named the goldfish in his pond after them. Now and then Alan would come to Palm Springs to visit him.

Various women passed into and out of his life. The most constant companion was Francine Greshler, daughter of the well-known Hollywood agent Abbey Greshler, who was with him during most of the last sixteen years. He was about fifty years her senior.

Alan now made the newspapers not for flamboyant social events or for the shows he was writing. Now and then there would be a story of an abortive try at something or other, a contract to produce a series of TV specials for NBC, or a new musical he was planning, or a movie project of some kind, but none of it came to anything. Mostly he got into the newspapers now for the lawsuits filed against him.

The *New York Post* reported on December 8, 1976:

Micheline Lerner, the ex-wife of Broadway lyricist Alan J. Lerner, has been awarded a State Supreme Court judgment of $16,666.64, which she claimed the writer owed her for back alimony and child support. The judge said there was "no serious dispute that such amount is owed by the respondent." But Mrs. Lerner's lawyer said a matter of $50,000 more is still to be determined.

Lerner still had not fallen from power at that point, and the item shows him no disrespect. The tone will soon change, even in the *Times*.

From the *New York Post* November 21, 1978:

4TH EX-WIFE SUES FOR 6TH TIME

But I can't afford it! wails lyricist Alan Jay Lerner, who's been dragged into court—for the sixth time—for nonpayment of alimony by the same ex-wife. This time out, Lerner . . . is one year behind in his $4,166 monthly payments to Micheline, the fourth of his seven wives, and their son. Since Lerner's first default in 1975, says State Supreme Court Justice Felice Shea, "all payments have been made (only) under court compulsion or the threat of compulsion." Lerner keeps saying he hasn't the dough (after all, so many people need his alimony). But in a decision just handed down,

Justice Shea found the poverty plea "unsubstantiated" and rejected it "as it has been by two previous Justices." Then she applied the ol' double whammy. Micheline (represented by Raoul Lionel Felder) gets her $50,000. And due to Lerner's "deplorable payment history" he must also post a $50,000 bond to assure future payment, which will probably send Alan, 60, to seek comfort in the arms of his seventh wife, Nina, 26.

From the *Page Six* column in the *New York Post* of July 27, 1979:

MORE! MORE!

Why, it wouldn't seem right to have a week go by without somebody suing Alan Jay Lerner. The lyricist . . . is already battling the fourth of his seven wives over $50,000 in unpaid alimony. He's charged by a jeweler with owing $16,000 on a diamond necklace. And now Viking and Penguin have filed suit against him for $283,000. They claim Lerner signed with them in 1977 to do his songwriting memoirs, for which they gave him a $50,000 advance. (An additional $100,000 was due him on publication.) In 1978, Lerner's book—The Street Where I Live—*was published by W.W. Norton. Although he returned $4200 of the advance, Viking and Penguin are ever so piqued, and are seeking the rest, plus damages.*

The *New York Times*, July 28, 1979:

LERNER AND THE COURTS

Some time ago, Alan Jay Lerner . . . bought a diamond fringe necklace for some fair lady from A la Vielle Russie, a Fifth Avenue art jewelry and antique shop. Later, the jewelers filed a claim in State Supreme Court, maintaining that Mr. Lerner still owed them $19,146 for the necklace.

A default judgment was entered against Mr. Lerner on April 24, and in connection with collection of the debt the songwriter was directed to complete a court questionnaire about his finances. Now he faces a contempt-of-court citation for, according to Justice Hortense W. Gabel, he failed to reply to the questionnaire.

For that she's ordered Mr. Lerner to appear Aug. 3 to show cause why he should not be found in contempt. He already faces another contempt hearing in connection with an alimony case.

The *New York Times,* August 26, 1979:

MUSIC TO HER EARS

The dispute had come up in court so many times that everyone connected with it had grown accustomed to the pace. But yesterday there was a big difference in Alan Jay Lerner's drawn-out divorce payment case, for a judge in Manhattan ordered that the lyricist's personal property be placed in receivership with a former wife, Micheline, named as receiver.

Repeatedly over the last few years Mrs. Lerner has gone to court, maintaining that her former husband had refused to keep up with his alimony payments. This time, she was specifically seeking $12,499.98 in payments that were due last July and August. Her lawyer says that, overall, she is owed many times that amount.

As receiver, what she is most interested in are Mr. Lerner's royalties from such hits as Camelot *and* My Fair Lady, *both of which will be revived soon.*

In her order, Justice Hortense W. Gabel showed some annoyance with Lerner, pointing out that three judges had tried to get him to meet his payments. His conduct, she said, was "outrageously contumacious of the judicial process."

From the *New York Post* of April 2, 1981:

POOR ALAN

Alan Jay Lerner lost another one. Manhattan Supreme Court Justice James Leff awarded one of Lerner's ex-wives more than $47,000 in back alimony yesterday and another $7500 to her attorney Raoul Felder. Micheline Lerner, from whom Alan was divorced in 1965, still has another $176,000 in alimony arrearage claimed in other legal actions, reports our Hal Davis. Both Alan and Micheline attended yesterday's trial, Alan wearing his familiar shades but not bothering to call a single witness. Because of earlier legal disputes with dear Micheline, Alan was held in contempt of court three times and courts have ruled she can grab his royalties from such hits as My Fair Lady.

The paper did not note that Alan wore the "familiar shades" because he was blind in one eye and had impaired vision in the other.

The item makes his glasses sound like an affectation. Witness the tone of *New York Post* columnist Cindy Adams on November 5, 1981.

MICHELINE GOTALOT

Micheline Lerner, the only one of Alan Jay Lerner's seven wives to bear a child, is owed a $250,000 alimony. She was just appointed a receiver. She tied up ALL *composer Lerner's royalties from* Camelot *and* My Fair Lady. *She gets* FIRST *priority. In other words, if someone in Minsk, Pinsk, or Cincinnati even hums two bars from* Brigadoon, *some green goes to Micheline. Her lawyer, Raoul Lionel Felder, doesn't kid around.*

Aside from its malice of tone, the item is ignorant. That so short an item could contain four factual errors is an achievement of a sort. Two months before that, the *Post* itself reported that Liz Robertson had become not wife number seven but number eight. Second, Lerner had children by both Ruth Boyd and Nancy Olson. Micheline's son Michael was his fourth child, his only son. Third, Adams identifies Lerner as a composer, which he wasn't. Fourth, the Soviet Union at that time was not a member of the Berne copyright convention, and royalties were not paid to Lerner (or any other American) for performances of songs in Minsk or Pinsk or anywhere else in the U.S.S.R. Indeed, Alan once was both irked and amused by the sheer nerve of a letter from Russia asking him for the orchestrations of *My Fair Lady* for use in a pirated production.

From the *Page Six* column in the *New York Post* of July 9, 1984:

The courts have long grown accustomed to Alan Jay Lerner's face, what with seven divorces plus alimony actions and other aftermaths. Well, he's back, this time to sue his former accountant and the accountant's two partners. Alan claims they left him with an IRS bill he shouldn't have to pay. But the lyricist, whose words . . . have brought him millions, was told his court papers need a rewrite, the Post*'s Hal Davis reports. Said State Supreme Court Justice Alfred Ascione: "The allegations are mostly in narrative form, and not readily susceptible to a responsive pleading." The complaint charges accountant Israel Katz, along with Milton Pearlman and Sherman Saiger, with using Alan Jay Lerner Productions as a "conduit for various business transactions" totaling $430,000. The IRS wanted $215,000 of that sum. "It is not my income," gripes*

Lerner in his court papers. "It is their income and they should pay tax on it. I am a playwright and lyricist and not familiar with business affairs and taxes."

Let us remember that in *The Street Where I Live* in 1978, Lerner described Israel Katz as "one of the kindest and most human beings I have ever known," and "a Merlin in the metaphysical world of the Internal Revenue Service," a man who spoke English and "taxasian." Katz was the man Fritz Loewe stopped in to see in order to look at the books on the morning he and Alan were leaving for Paris to work on *Gigi.* Alan, you will recall, expressed his total faith in Israel Katz and his amusement at Fritz's paranoia.

The *New York Times,* February 20, 1986:

ALAN JAY LERNER SUED
BY U.S. FOR $1.4 MILLION

Alan Jay Lerner . . . has been sued by the Federal Government for $1.4 million in taxes and penalties.

The Justice Department said in the suit, filed Tuesday in Federal District Court in Manhattan, that Mr. Lerner, who lives in London, owes $265,000 for taxes and penalties dating to 1977, $40,000 for 1978, $127,000 for 1980 and slightly more than $1 million for 1981.

Mr. Lerner's attorney, David Grossberg, said that the Government already had a lien on Mr. Lerner's song royalties but that the amount of the Government's share was in dispute. Aside from the royalties, Mr. Grossberg said, he does not know of any property Mr. Lerner owns in this country.

Since an attorney is by definition an officer of the court, and since aside from that David Grossberg was and is a respected one, his word can be taken at face value. By now it was all gone: the massive apartment at the Waldorf, the town houses, the house at Oyster Bay, the Rolls-Royce bought with such amused élan that long-ago day with Fritz in London.

Then an ironic incident occurs. For once it is Micheline who has to pay. In June *Variety* carried this item:

Alan Jay Lerner's ex-wife must turn over $135,000 received in the lyricist's royalties to Viking Penguin and the Internal Revenue Service, according to N.Y. Federal Court Judge Charles H. Tenney.

Judge Tenney ruled Viking had first call for some $72,000, including $50,104 gained in a 1979 judgment to satisfy an advance for a book. The remainder will go to the IRS, which has claims of about $1,000,000 in back taxes against Lerner.

Both Viking and the government were found to have priority against Micheline Lerner, who claims the lyricist . . . owes her $72,000 in alimony.

The *New York Post* printed this:

UNLUCKY SEVEN

Wife-collector Alan Jay Lerner has been told by Manhattan Civil Court Judge Harold Tompkins to quit dickering around and pay his seventh wife, Nina Bushkin Lerner, the $50,000 he said he would. When the author . . . divorced her in 1981, the court told him it would cost him $600 a week in permanent alimony. But Alan was able to convince Nina that he couldn't afford that sum because so much of his loot was going to his six previous wives. Big-hearted Nina agreed to the $50,000 payoff, but when the check didn't arrive, she sued. This time she declined Alan's $28,000 counter-offer and said she wanted the amount in full. The judge agreed.

In Palm Springs, Fritz made the newspapers for his gifts in cash or assigned royalties to hospitals. He contributed substantially to the building of an indoor firing range for the Palm Springs Police Department. One of his donations was to build a children's ward to the Desert Hospital in Palm Springs, for all that he pretended a dislike of children. He told Red Skelton, "Children should hear music and sing, and not waste their time being sick."

twenty-five

FINAL
DAYS

In March of 1985 the *New York Times* reported that Lerner was planning a musical based on the 1936 movie *My Man Godfrey*, to be written in collaboration with Allan Carr, a thirty-year-old American composer who lived in England and had written two song hits with Barry Manilow. Nothing would come of it.

But the venture was indicative of his desire to enter the later age, the "new" style of musical that had come into being. So too was a brief attempt at partnership with Andrew Lloyd Webber, the composer of such successful scores as *Evita* and *Cats*.

On a weekend in early December of 1985, the Kennedy Center for the Performing Arts in Washington held a two-day celebration in honor of six Americans: dancer and choreographer Merce Cunningham, actress Irene Dunne, comedian Bob Hope, soprano Beverly Sills, and Lerner and Loewe. It was the first time the Kennedy Center honors had been given. The master of ceremonies was Walter Cronkite. The audience was full of celebrities, including Betty Comden, Adolph Green, Van Johnson, George P. Schultz, Brooke Shields, Louis Jourdan, and Kirk Douglas. Liz Robertson was one of the performers. Alan's old friend Ben Welles said, "I remember she was on the stage and doing a lot of his songs. She was very good."

Also present were all four of Alan's children, including Michael, the subject of such bitter battles with Micheline. Michael was now a reporter for *Newsweek*, stationed in Paris, partly because of his ability to speak French. (In 1989, he was in the magazine's Los Angeles bureau.)

"It's an extraordinary honor," Lerner said. "It's like being queen for the day, isn't it?"

A photo of the six honorees was published the next day in the *New York Times*. It shows them in formal dress, each wearing around his neck the gold medallion on a multicolored ribbon. The photo is disturbing. Lerner sits on Irene Dunne's right, Fritz is at her left. Fritz looks to be healthy. Alan does not: in fact he looks older than Fritz. The face is ghastly, skeletal; it has the haunted look of the terminal patient. Gloria Greer, who accompanied Fritz to Washington, confirmed the difference. "Fritz looked very well," she said. It was the last time he and Fritz would be together.

Alan and Liz Robertson were living in London, where Burton Lane visited him. "I saw him twice there," Lane said. "And he received another honor at, I think, the Players Club. I saw him there and thought he looked awful. We met a day or two later. We had lunch and we talked about another project. Suddenly he started to go bad—real bad. He was worried about his daughter by his first marriage, who had cancer. His brother Bob had died of cancer in Mexico."

Lerner's condition grew worse. He had always remained close to his children, and his daughters by Nancy Olson, Jennifer Frasier and Liza Bibb, flew to London. Alan was considering going to one of the dubious clinics of Switzerland or Germany, but his daughters prevailed upon him and in April, scarcely four months after the Kennedy Center ceremony, they brought him back to America to enter the Memorial Sloan-Kettering Center in New York to be treated for lung cancer. David Grossberg said, "He had lost weight, and he was just wasting away. His mind was alert to the very end, and he was as cheerful as you can be in those circumstances."

He was under heavy medication and sedation. One morning Jennifer arrived to find him laughing in his bed. When, during the night, he told her, the nurses had been changing shift, the new nurse asked about his condition. The nurse going off duty said he was sort of in and out of it, but otherwise doing as well as could be expected. And she added, "You know, that crazy old fart thinks he wrote *My Fair Lady.*"

André Previn's scenario had proved prescient. Without mentioning the treasure of Atlantis, merely by claiming to be the author of *My Fair Lady,* Alan had got himself branded as a loony. He— and Fritz—had passed beyond celebrity. They had become legend.

By a dark irony, Susan Olch, his daughter by his first wife, Ruth Boyd, was also in the same hospital, also undergoing treatment for cancer. They were only a few floors apart. Everyone remembers Susan Olch as a lovely woman. She was later released from the hospital and returned to California, where she died. Her husband, Dr. David Olch, shattered by her loss, died a year later of a heart attack. Her two daughters—Alan's and Ruth's granddaughters— still live in Los Angeles. Ruth remains close to them.

According to Grossberg, Alan had always been careful to keep his feelings about Micheline hidden from Michael, and he remained on good terms with all his children, as they did with each other. On the morning of Saturday, June 14, 1986, a few days after Susan's death, Liza and Jennifer, his son Michael, and Liz Robertson gathered in his hospital room. At 10:15 A.M. Alan slipped away. He was sixty-seven.

Stories circulated immediately that Alan Jay Lerner had died a pauper. David Grossberg, who is the executor of Lerner's will, said he was hardly that. "He had no buildings, no real estate, in New York State for many years before his death," Grossberg said. "He had moved to England. At one time he owned a building there, and just before the end sold that building and bought an apartment. He had a place to live, he was working, he had certain income coming from his work. Alan owed a great deal of tax to the Internal Revenue Service in the United States, which was in various states of litigation or claims and negotiations. It all sort of came to a head just about the time he died, so that the numbers the IRS were claiming became astronomical and more than he had. But Alan was living in England, and the IRS does not have jurisdiction there. Was he broke? I don't think he missed any meals. He was not a pauper or homeless."

Lerner's chief beneficiaries were Liz Robertson and his children. "There were actions brought against Alan by Micheline for monies he owed her," Grossberg said. "She has no rights with respect to the underlying works. She was entitled to receive monies because she had a priority. She no longer has that priority. The Internal

Revenue Service has certain priorities at this time." At the end of 1989, Lerner's debt to the IRS—which with interest and penalties came to much more than the $1.4 million reported at the time of his death—still had not been cleared.

Grossberg said that Israel Katz, the accountant and business adviser whom Lerner blamed for his misfortunes, had some years ago suffered a stroke that left him without the power of speech. "I would say that 'mishandled' is a fair word" for what Katz did with Lerner's affairs, Grossberg said.

"I think Alan was given poor advice many times about what to do with his copyrights and assets and investments, and as a result he made some very bad moves, which eventually led to the reduction of his income. Israel was a brilliant tax tactician. He would immediately seize upon loopholes and figure out gimmicks, many of which were good on paper but were what I would call unsound, and would not hold up necessarily against a government attack. Alan relied upon him to do many things, such as collect his income, make the deposits, pay his bills, and generally consult and decide how they would handle his finances. And I think that they were not well handled. I hate to castigate Israel alone, because I don't know to what extent Alan contributed to all of this."

Grossberg is one of those who remember Lerner with unconditional affection. He said, "Every time I got a phone call from him, it was with anticipation, because I knew there would be something well and cleverly said."

Said Benjamin Welles, "He had one of the most extraordinarily intellectually curious minds. He was one of the most brilliant conversationalists I have ever known. He could absolutely hold you."

Karen Lerner said, "What I loved about Alan was his total liveliness."

"Alan was terribly likable," John Springer said. "He wanted so much to be liked. Fritz couldn't have cared less whether anyone liked him. Alan was wildly, nervously eager to be everybody's best friend. You had to like him, because he wanted so much to be liked."

But Springer also said, "I was still handling Alan at the end, off and on, though not officially. Quite frankly, Alan owed me an enormous amount of money. He kept guiltily calling me and telling me that sooner or later he would pay me, and that Micheline was bleeding him of all the money. He owed everybody. That's no secret."

Doris Shapiro wrote, "Alan didn't like to pay his debts. . . ."

My visit with David Grossberg fell on a crystalline afternoon in early November 1989. I left his Madison Avenue office and walked a block west on Fifty-ninth Street. I waited for a light to change at Fifth Avenue, facing the southeast corner of Central Park, looking across at the trees, some already bare but many others cadmium yellow, and at the great cliff of stone that is Central Park South, rising against a flawless blue sky. I realized I was in front of A la Vieille Russie. On a whim I entered the shop and asked a question of the woman who approached me. She looked a little startled, said I should speak to her son, and summoned him from among the glass cases of jewelry. He arrived, a tall man of middle years with a certain hauteur, a polished manner, and the slightly guarded air one encounters in merchants to the very rich, probably from the conditioned habit of trying to spot phonies. I repeated my question: Had the shop ever collected the $19,146 Lerner owed for the necklace he purchased here?

No, the man said with frost in the voice. The debt had been written off to profit and loss. He said it had all been a long time ago and he didn't remember it very well, which I doubted. It had been, in fact, ten years and seven months since the default judgment had been rendered against Lerner in that suit.

The man walked me to the door, asking about this book and making it tacitly clear that he didn't want his name used. I said there was a lot of sadness in Lerner's life. He raised his eyebrows as if astonished at my naïveté, pointed to my briefcase, then said, "I have a lot more sympathy for a street kid who tries to mug you for that."

In the week after Lerner's death, the newspapers remembered the glory days, and when they mentioned the divorces at all, it was not with malice. The *Times* carried a long obituary, noting that Lerner and Loewe had "applied their intellectual sensibilities . . . toward creating a world of gorgeous fantasy."

"It was not simply their musicals that accorded a sense of style," the obit said. "It was the way they lived. With their fortunes made on their early hits, they wrote their later ones in Paris or on the Côte d'Azur. They typified a wealth and panache that was as much a part of Broadway's heyday as the entertainments on stage.

"Although the Lerner-Loewe musicals in retrospect represent a highly idealized view of life—certainly when compared with the darker approach of [Stephen] Sondheim, Harold Prince and Michael Bennett—many of them took daring leaps in adapting high culture for popular consumption."

Time magazine remarked the flamboyance of Lerner's life, then said, "His divorces were sometimes messy, and he blamed the settlements for his financial problems."

And it noted that "Mr. Lerner's theater work never thrived without Mr. Loewe. His later efforts tended to be daring, flawed, and commercially futile."

Clive Barnes recalled Lerner's gracious behavior after his review of *1600 Pennsylvania Avenue* and said, "He really was a wonderful lyricist—he had a way with a song, and could make words cling to melodies like ivy on a wall.

"As for Lerner's place in our musical theater, I compare him with two other great twentieth-century lyricists, Cole Porter and Stephen Sondheim."

Barnes concluded:

What they achieved was the particular apogee of one of the Broadway musical's most singular influences—the European operetta.

Before the Broadway musical was knocked for a loop by Elvis Presley and his Liverpudlian colleagues, the elements of Broadway were largely those of the American vernacular pop music, and the European strain that Loewe (and with him Lerner) came to exemplify . . .

They dimmed the lights on Broadway the other night, in homage to Lerner's passing. It was an appropriate gesture, for Lerner does represent, to a full extent, a Broadway that has completely vanished.

The music was popular yet sophisticated, and Lerner's plots and lyric fancies had a certain style and flair, a touch of almost patrician class, that marked them out with an off-hand ease.

Times move. Tastes change. Lerner and Loewe. We shall never see their like again. A pity. I had grown accustomed to their grace.

On July 11, 1986, not quite a month after Alan's death, various friends—Sidney Gruson, then vice chairman of the *New York Times*, Kitty Carlisle, John Cullum, Len Cariou, Richard Kiley, Herman Levin, Sidney Kingsley among them—gathered in the Shubert Theater to pay tribute. Fritz was not there; he was in Palm Springs, ill. It is an irony of Lerner's life that Fritz Loewe, seventeen years his senior, outlived him.

But not by much. In February of 1988, Fritz was taken to the

Desert Hospital, suffering chest pains and breathing trouble, according to his guardian, John Morris.

Gloria Greer said:

"The day before he died I was at the hospital. He was lying on his back and they had his hands tied to the bed. He had the oxygen tube on his nose. That made me sick. He kept saying something over and over in German. I came home and I repeated it to my mother, who speaks German. I said, 'I don't know what it means, but I think he was saying, 'I want to die.' She said, 'That's right, that's what he said.'

"There was one night nurse who was just lovely, but her daughter was getting married and she wasn't on duty. I called the hospital and the nurse was a stranger. I said, 'I'm concerned about Dr. Loewe. Could I come back over tonight?' She said, 'If you're a friend of his, I think tonight he needs a friend.' She said, 'Does he have Alzheimer's? We don't know too much about him.'

"I said, 'He forgets a lot, but I don't think he has Alzheimer's.'

"I went over. When I walked into that room, his eyes lit up like firecrackers, and the one nurse said to the other, 'Well, he certainly knows her.' I went over to the bed, and I said, 'May I hold his hand?' They untied one hand, and I sat there for two hours, holding his hand and talking to him. He couldn't talk to me. His eyes were on me like a child eight months old looking at his mother. I was a friend and I was there. I said, 'Oh, Fritz, you're going to be fine.' And I talked about his music, and I said, 'You wrote the most beautiful music in the world, but then you know that.'

"He died the next day, about noon, on Valentine's Day."

The time, precisely, was 1:51 P.M. Fritz was eighty-six.

Franz Allers, who immediately flew to Palm Springs, said, "There was a ceremony in the morning at the house, and a very wonderful one. That was supposed to have been according to his will. There was a band, and three buffets, and huge amplifiers playing our recordings." Gloria Greer and Mary Martin spoke. Red Skelton was to speak but declined because there were too many people there, a crowd of perhaps a hundred. He spoke instead at the graveside at Desert Memorial Park, saying, "He was a caring and gentle man. . . . He had seen poverty and obscurity. . . . He walked with kings and presidents. . . . He was so in love with music he forgot to find a love of his own. . . . A walk with him in his garden was like his music, a visit to heaven." The group at graveside was small, among them Skelton and his wife Lothian, Gloria Greer, Francine Greshler and her parents, and Franz Allers. Greer said,

"He was buried in a very cheap coffin, not at all the way he lived. Maybe that's the way he wanted it. I don't know."

A month later, on Monday, March 28, and with much the same cast and in the same theater as the Lerner memorial, a tribute to Fritz Loewe was held. Richard Harris, who calculated that he had played Arthur in *Camelot* 1,800 times, attended a tribute to Lerner on Sunday in Manchester, then raced four hours to London to catch the Concorde in time to rehearse for the Loewe tribute in New York. "But I'll be there," he said, "because Fritz and Alan were very good to my career, and it's out of great respect that I should be at the Shubert."

Fritz Loewe left his estate to various charities and hospitals, including the Desert Hospital and Eisenhower Hospital in Palm Springs, and to various friends, including Francine Greshler and Kitty Carlisle.

twenty-six

A LEGACY OF SONGS

A lan needn't have worried: It wasn't the chandeliers.

My Fair Lady is a remarkable piece of theatrical machinery. All the gears mesh, all the shafts turn, all the parts fit, and it moves forward with an unhesitating inevitability. It has no boring songs that make you impatient for the resumption of the dialogue; it has no boring dialogue that makes you yawn and yearn for the relief of music. And the transitions from one to the other are seamless, possibly because all the songs are either declamations or soliloquies, both of which (even in real life) have about them elements of the unreal. Fritz Loewe's musical craftsmanship was almost flawless. He had a perfect fix on himself. He was quite right in saying that he was a dramatic composer, not a songwriter.

The working habits of Lerner and Loewe were sensible. Newspaper interviewers made so much of their practices that one would conclude they were unusual. They weren't. Cole Porter worked exactly the same way: He would find a title that encapsuled the central idea for the situation, followed by music that accommodated it, followed finally by the full lyric. Generally it is best to work that way, since only a handful of composers, Bizet and Burton Lane among them, have had the curious knack of taking completed lyrics and developing them into naturalistic flowing melodies.

In Chinese and other tonal languages, the meaning of a given word may be determined by its pitch. Western languages are not considered tonal, but they are in fact a good deal more tonal than is appreciated. The meaning of a phrase may be determined by the emphasis and pitch put on its components, as we see immediately (using italics to suggest crudely the pitch of the words) in *"I* love you," "I *love* you," and "I love *you."* A sense of such nuances was commonplace among the major lyricists, such as Johnny Mercer, E. Y. Harburg, Howard Dietz, Dorothy Fields, Irving Berlin, Larry Hart, and Oscar Hammerstein II—and Lerner.

Consider the opening five notes of *I've Grown Accustomed to Her Face.* We do not know how Loewe arrived at that cell of melody, but it is probable that the two men followed their usual procedure. Lerner gave him the phrase, and he then sat at the piano noodling until Lerner said, "That's it!" Or maybe he found it on his own: though his native language was German, he had acquired a true sensitivity to the intervallic nuances of English. The phrase, which starts on the tonic, goes, in musicians' terminology, I II III V V V V II; or in the key of C, C D E G G G D. There are other ways one could set those words, but they would alter the emotional state of the character singing them. What Loewe did with them—what the partners did with them—is remarkable. The fall of a fourth, from G to D, has a tentative and puzzled quality. Higgins is amazed at this discovery that he's grown accustomed to her face. Change that melody by so much as one note and you abolish his amazement, thereby destroying the revelation that Maxwell Anderson assures us is necessary to a successful play. The whole resolution of Lerner's (as opposed to Shaw's) story is in that fall of a fourth from G to D. A falling fourth, depending on the context, has this sense of puzzlement or resigned acceptance: You would say "Oh hum" or "Ah well" as a falling fourth. The entire play hinges on that interval. It is the sound of surrender—Higgins'.

In the July 22, 1971 issue of *The Village Voice,* a writer named Donald Lazere excoriated Lerner for this resolution of the play. He wrote:

"It should be said for Lerner that he has the largesse to satirize his own vanity; Shaw's twitting of the male ego in *Pygmalion* remains the source of much of the humor in *My Fair Lady.* But while Shaw's Henry Higgins is merely indifferent to women in his egocentricity, Lerner's actively despises them. It is not Shaw but Lerner who rants, 'I'd prefer a new edition of the Spanish Inquisition than to ever let a woman in my life.' "

Such criticism confuses a writer's characters with the writer, and commits the greater critical transgression of making an assumption without information. We now know that in Higgins, and particularly in that song, Lerner was satirizing not his own vanity but Rex Harrison's: the song came directly out of that remark of Harrison's on Fifth Avenue. If Lerner speculated that Higgins be more than indifferent, that he may have a serious if hidden hostility to women, he was only confirming what many women suspect of men, not without reason. Lerner was doing only what good lyricists working in the form of the musical *must* do: taking wisps of emotion and blowing them up into larger statements.

Lazere continues, "And while Shaw the feminist has Eliza grow independent and leave Higgins for good, Lerner contrives to have her come crawling back with his slippers in hand."

In his postscript to the play, Shaw tells us what he thinks happens to Eliza afterward: She ends up owning a flower shop, marrying Freddy Eynsford-Hill, and supporting him. This is hardly independence. It is enslavement to a feckless male. And Lerner did not invent that ending for the story; he appropriated the one used in Pascal's movie version of the story, to which Shaw apparently did not object. On the contrary, after Pascal completed the picture, Shaw assigned him the rights to more of his work.

Shaw was a polemical essayist who selected the theater as the broadest possible vehicle for the venting of his opinions. We should remember that before he achieved success as a playwright, Shaw was a critic. And just as men tend to speak a third language with the accent of their second, so too they very often practice their second profession with the disciplines and attitudes of the first. Shaw graduated from criticizing music to criticizing society. That, more than the persuasive evocation of men and women and their inner lives, was the purpose of his work. But polemical art tends to fall into desuetude when the arguments it propounds are resolved and fade into the past. It is hard to feel sorry for the Joad family when you know that the migrant Okies and Arkies whom they symbolized ended up owning substantial parts of California and paying the Mexicans as little as possible. Lerner's *Dance a Little Closer* was antiquated within five years by *glasnost* and *perestroika*. Shaw's socialism seems quaint when programs advocated by radicals early in the century are conservative policy today. And his feminism is aloof, the benign indifference of a celibate who did not want a woman in his life anyway. Donald Lazere says that *Let a Woman in Your Life* is Lerner's interpolation in the play, when in real life Shaw never did let a woman in his life, excepting a wife with whom he never consummated marriage and Mrs. Patrick Campbell, with whom he carried on an extensive epicene correspondence, reminding us of the letters that passed between Tchaikovsky, who was homosexual, and Madame Von Meck. The ending of *Pygmalion* has always been unsatisfactory, and at its premiere Mrs. Patrick Campbell refused to play it as written. The play is *supposed* to be a comedy, and sets up a desire for resolution in the audience that Shaw, with a groundlings-bedamned arrogance, ignores, leaving the play on, as it were, an unresolved dominant. Mrs. Campbell fixed it, and so did Gabriel Pascal. So did Lerner, and very deftly.

It is almost impossible for an intelligent man to listen to the Higgins-Lerner diatribes against women without feeling the complete bloody fool, cringing in his seat at this telling portrait of his own habitual male arrogance. The songs are satiric, and might even be appropriated by the feminist movement as a sort of sarcastic anthem. They are brilliant, sardonic, and perfect expansions of Shaw's play.

The final scene, presenting Higgins' baffled soliloquy *I've Grown Accustomed to Her Face,* tells us not that Eliza has become dependent on him, but that he has become dependent on her. This, not the ballroom conquest, is Eliza's ultimate triumph: She has defeated Higgins. We can hardly expect Higgins to leap from his chair and cry, "Oh, Eliza! You've returned! Oh, God, darling, I've just discovered how much I need you!" Higgins does what we might expect: he hopes she hasn't overheard him, and slips back into his own characterization of himself, the role he is compelled to act. He may never tell Eliza how much he now needs her, or admit that their lives are now inextricably intertwined. It is enough that she understands it, and the slight smile of Audrey Hepburn at that point in the movie version tells us that she knows all she needs to know now about Higgins. Because of the earlier exaggeration of Higgins' misogyny, the movement of resolution when Higgins resigns himself in that falling fourth to the discovery that, damn, damn, damn, he is as human as anyone else, his revelation is all the more satisfying to us. It is in this deeper bas relief of the character that Lerner has improved on Shaw.

Noël Coward objected to calling *My Fair Lady* the perfect musical on two grounds: the use of the split infinitive in the phrase "to ever have a woman" and the mispronunciation of "Dyenesfor." There is no sound objection to the split infinitive. Still, it does seem likely that an Edwardian academic would have avoided it. Noël Coward overlooked a more serious failing that occurs in the opening when Lerner succumbs to that constant temptation of the lyricist, the exigencies of rhyming. Higgins says that anyone who speaks as Eliza does should be taken out and hung for the murder of the English tongue. The accepted past participle even today is "hanged" and a stickler like Higgins would unquestionably have used it. There are other little glitches: It is, and certainly was in the Edwardian period of the story, correct to say "I would never let a woman into my life" rather than "in." Furthermore, no Englishman would say "on the street where you live." The British say "in the street." This doesn't seem to have bothered British audiences, however, and small flaws notwithstanding, *My Fair Lady* comes as close to being a perfect fulfillment of the craft as any work in American musical theater.

Craftsmanship, however, does not explain the universality of the appeal of *My Fair Lady*.

Shaw may have intended *Pygmalion* as a dramatized polemic on two of his favorite flogging horses, class distinction and the idiocy of English orthography, but he embodied in it—whether he knew or even cared—what Joshua Logan argued was one of man's most potent and popular myths, the story of Cinderella. As Shaw was surely aware, in the latter half of the seventeenth century a girl did what Eliza Doolittle accomplished. Nell Gwynn, born in London in 1650, was, tradition holds, the daughter of a man who died in debtor's prison and a woman who ran a bawdy house. She started selling oranges in Drury Lane, where she caught the eye of Charles Hart. It is likely that Hart, a leading actor of the time and therefore a man schooled in speech, to some extent acted as her Higgins. However she accomplished it, Gwynn got rid of her street urchin accent, and became an excellent singer, as well as a dancer, and one of the most popular comediennes of the time. As a member of the King's Company, she originated a number of roles in the plays of John Dryden. Like many an actress before and since, she slept her way to the top, becoming the mistress of Charles II, whom she bore a son, named the first Baron Heddington by the king. Her gambling and lavish spending brought her to bankruptcy, but the king on his deathbed begged his friends that they not let his beloved

Nell starve, and his son and successor, James II, paid off her debts and settled on her an annuity that kept her comfortable until her death at thirty-seven. Nell Gwynn embodied the Cinderella myth, and Lerner was certainly cognizant of this historical precedent for Eliza—and of Gwynn's position as the courtesan saved by love, like Lise in *An American in Paris,* and for that matter Eliza Doolittle, though this aspect of it is muted in the Shaw play, probably in reflection of its author's asexuality.

In revisionist criticism, *My Fair Lady* and *Cinderella* may be viewed as condescending to the female, since the girl in the story is lifted from her low estate by the intercession of a male, the deus ex machina being Higgins and the prince respectively. But for centuries the myth has persisted in one form or another, as much as this may discomfit feminists. It is particularly annoying to women in the movement since the kind of success it embodies is available to one kind of girl and one kind only: the pretty ones. Nowhere does Shaw, feminist in theory or not, tell us that Eliza is ugly. We unconsciously assume early in the Lerner play that when Higgins orders that she be bathed and her dirty clothes burned, he will on viewing his sanitized protégée experience some sort of epiphany, even if he refuses to admit it, comparable to that of the hero in a hack Hollywood movie who watches as the prim intelligent librarian (or teacher or secretary) takes off her glasses and unpins her bun and shakes out her hair, and then says to her in astonishment, "But you're beautiful, Miss Mather!"

Kitty Carlisle believed, in common with other observers, that the magic moment in *My Fair Lady* is the instant when Eliza Doolittle gets "The rain in Spain stays mainly in the plain" right. She said that the audience took a deep breath and levitated. Carlisle says it happened in every production of the show she had seen, including one by teenagers in Harlem. The audience levitates because Eliza has levitated—out of the confines of her class. Cinderella returns. Horatio Alger rides again. Audiences love it.

Lazere was not the only one to consider Lerner a misogynist. Andrew Sarris, in a foreword to *The Magic Factory,* refers to "Lerner's misogynous tendencies as a dramatist."

Lazere wrote, "If Women's Lib were to compile a list of the Top Ten Male Chauvinist Pigs in America, it would have to include Oscar Hammerstein II and Alan Jay Lerner." But to subject Lerner's work to retroactive judgment by the gospel according to Women's

Lib is as inappropriate as it would be a denunciation of the precepts of Sophocles for not being in accord with those of contemporary atheism. We may find it hard to understand the anger of the Gods for the sin of hubris, but the Greeks didn't, and Sophocles and Aeschylus wrote their plays for the audiences of their era, not ours.

So many of the shows Lerner wrote, whether they were originals or stories he adapted because the material appealed to him for inner reasons perhaps even he did not understand, were about courtesans or "bad" women, such as the Rebecca Welles character he invented in the movie version of *Clear Day*. And these heroines, or antiheroines, were the social inferiors of the male protagonists of his plays.

Lerner was a product of his age, of the romanticism that was incessantly preached and portrayed in the songs and movies and stories he grew up with. Historically, the poor girl who marries a rich boy is not necessarily considered an opportunist, and the occasional conscription into the "aristocracy" of a girl from what were seen as the lower classes was vaguely viewed as a way to keep the blood from running thin. Nothing like a good healthy peasant girl to lend a little vigor to the line. But the poor boy who marries the rich girl was viewed with suspicion, if not disdain. To venture forth and save the beautiful maiden, whether tethered somewhere as a sacrifice to a minotaur or imprisoned in poverty, that's what boys were supposed to do. It is wrong to judge Lerner's work, which expresses values almost universally accepted in the 1920s, '30s, and '40s, by values of the 1990s. All his life, it would seem, Lerner was caught in a conflict between his instinctive romanticism and the cynicism about women (and religion and life generally) preached to him by his father. He wanted to believe that love transforms all; he wanted to believe that life is not finite, and that the paths of glory do not lead to an all-too-final grave.

Love Life, the show Lerner wrote with Kurt Weill, has been called a feminist play, presented to the public years ahead of its time, but it it is hard to see it as that. There is a damning line in that play, one that sounds as if his father's ghost dictated it from somewhere deep in Lerner's subconscious. Perhaps it was something he actually had heard his father say, without consciously remembering it. The character Sam Cooper says: "Women are used to hysterics. They manufacture it."

After *Love Life* had gathered dust for nearly forty years, Brent Wagner, director of the musical theater program at the University of Michigan, became fascinated by it and considered restaging it. He approached the Kurt Weill Foundation for Music in New York, where Weill's original orchestrations and various versions of the script reposed. There were also versions of the score, which had to be reconciled. In April 1987 Wagner's department presented a new production, which to many people proved that the show had many virtues. A second revival was presented at the Walnut Street Theater in Philadelphia from June 6 to 24, 1990. The book had been somewhat updated, but the show still received mixed reviews. Its fatal flaw is Lerner's premise that somewhere, sometime, life must have been Edenic, which underlies so much of his work: Camelot, a Scottish village that was made to vanish to protect it from the evils of the modern world, and bucolic America in the early nineteenth century. The suspension of disbelief is not easily offered up a writer when our underlying cultural memory is that life then was hard, the hours of work long, the causes of infection unknown, hygiene primitive, disease common, couples had eight or ten children in the hope that two or three might survive, and women died young of exhaustion and child-bearing. The show seems irrelevant, like *Dance a Little Closer.* Lerner's indignation at man's condition and the environment seems almost sophomoric in our age of horrors, when the ozone layer is being depleted, the rain forests have been substantially destroyed, we don't know where to put our garbage, petroleum spills are almost routine, the oceans are polluted, our food is full of carcinogens, and toxic wastes saturate the land and seep into the aquifer. He is like a little boy indignant to discover that there are Bad Things in the world, and *Love Life,* as protest, is pretty pale stuff. Lerner had an enormous gift of charm; he had none for articulate outrage, and he was lost when he attempted it.

According to the staff of the Kurt Weill Foundation, Lerner had corresponded at one time with Lotte Lenya, Weill's widow, about a possible revival of *Love Life.* He wanted to revise the book. But by the time Miles Kreuger worked for him, he had apparently changed his mind about it.

"I was fascinated by it," Kreuger said. "Alan had in his office, and gave me, and I still have them, various versions of the script, the earliest, the middle one, the last one. I said, 'Alan, if there is one musical that I could direct some day, one I would like to direct, it is *Love Life.'*

"He said, 'I can't ever allow *Love Life* to be revived.'

"I said, 'Why?'

"He said, 'Because I have turned into everything I satirized in that show.' That is an exact quote."

Alan Lerner's failures seem to be ascribable to his willfulness when he did not have a strong hand to restrain him. He seemed almost to know this: He was always expressing some variant on the last line of his book: "Now, if only I can remember all that Moss told me . . ."

In the end, Nancy Olson's evaluation stands up. He was a superb lyric poet, and when he was on the mark, as Charles Strouse and Burton Lane and other colleagues invariably point out, he was the best in the business. He was not a great librettist; he wasn't even a very good one. He wrote one superb book for a musical: *My Fair Lady.* And by his own account, it was produced under the critical aegis of Moss Hart, who was at least its guiding light and possibly much more. In Broadway circles, it still is mooted that that *is* Moss Hart's book. We shall never know. Lerner wrote one good original screenplay, *An American in Paris,* and one good film adaptation, *Gigi.*

But most of his books were defective, as in the cases of *Camelot* and *On a Clear Day You Can See Forever.* Some were disasters, including *1600 Pennsylvania Avenue* and *Dance a Little Closer.*

But the songs? Ah, the songs! What a legacy to leave. And the best were the songs he wrote with Fritz.

Afterword

When Richard Burton left the cast of *Camelot* to play Mark Antony opposite Elizabeth Taylor in *Caesar and Cleopatra*, the cast held a farewell party for him. Nobody said anything about his drinking—except Moss Hart. In a farewell speech, couched in cautious language, he expressed the hope that Burton would not squander a magnificent talent.

Burton embarked upon a spectacularly public affair with Taylor. In 1964 he was back in the O'Keefe Centre in Toronto, this time to play Hamlet in a version produced by Alexander Cohen. The newspapers made much of his overt cohabitation with Taylor, and the voices of moral outrage were heard—to little effect—throughout the North American continent. Burton divorced Sybil and married Taylor not once but twice. Her drinking became almost as legendary as his, and she grew fat, and they made some tawdry movies together, such as *The Sandpiper*, that reeked of their private relationship. Burton sank to making movies only for the money, and he made some bad ones.

Early in 1980, Burton returned yet again to Toronto, this time to launch a revival of *Camelot,* on a grueling schedule that would keep him on the road for a year. It was, in general, a triumph, though once in New York the curtain had to be rung down when he was physically incapable of carrying on. "Give him another drink," someone called from the audience. He was not drinking, however; his health was failing and his medication made drinking impossible. When an understudy replaced him, hundreds of members of the audience walked out, demanding the return of their money. He died four years later, in Switzerland, where he had lived for many years. He was fifty-eight years old, and he had done exactly what Moss Hart had pleaded that he not do.

Toward the end of 1989, Rex Harrison, accompanied to New York by his sixth wife, Mercia, was back on Broadway, to appear with Stewart Granger and Glynis Johns in a rusty-hinged Somerset Maugham drawing-room comedy called *The Circle.* The reviews were tinged with a respect that more resembled mercy than admiration, and a few critics wondered why, at eighty-one, and thirty-three years after his triumph on Broadway as Higgins, Harrison was bothering to go on working, especially in a featherweight play. He had been knighted earlier that year and was now officially Sir Reginald Harrison. A *New York Times* writer, Marilyn Burger, noted in a report on her interview with him: "He has been described as charming and debonair, but he has also been called a perfection- ist, an irascible, difficult, egotistical, opinionated, judgmental, short-tempered, impatient, conceited, smug, inconsiderate man."

When he was asked about his role in *My Fair Lady,* he said, "Why do you keep going back to Henry Higgins? If I'm a legend I can't say I get a glow of satisfaction out of it. . . . I'm glad I played it. I enjoyed it enormously. It came at a very good time in my life when I could do eight shows a week. . . . But I don't find that it's done anything to my life."

He left the show to enter the hospital with pancreatic cancer and died at his apartment in New York on June 1, 1990.

Kurt Weill composed only one more score after his collaboration with Alan Lerner: *Lost in the Stars,* written with Maxwell Anderson and based on Alan Paton's novel *Cry the Beloved Country.* After a severe attack of psoriasis in late February, 1950, he suffered a coronary thrombosis, and, after a period in hospital in which he seemed to be recovering, he died at the age of fifty on April 3 and was buried in the Mount Repose Cemetery in Haverstraw, near his house.

Maurice Abravanel has lived in Salt Lake City since 1947. He is widely considered the founder of the Utah Symphony, but it was formed a year earlier by Werner Janssen, whom the orchestra hated. As Abravanel put it, "After him, anybody would have been a hit." Abravanel suffered two heart attacks and retired as conductor of the orchestra in 1979. He now judges compositions, does conductor workshops, and spends the summers at Tanglewood.

"Alan and Fritz were marvelous to me," he said. "They wanted me to have a royalty on *The Day Before Spring.* I loved them."

Since Abravanel was in Berlin with Kurt Weill when Weill was one of Busoni's five students, I asked him if he thought it likely that Fritz had studied with those he said he had. "Fritz was a braggart," Abravanel said with a chuckle. "He was an artist. It's possible that he studied with Eugene d'Albert, who was not only a pianist but a great composer. It's possible that he studied with him. It's also possible that he invented it. It is also possible that he studied with Resnicek. I conducted several of Resnicek's operas. He was a craftsman of the first magnitude. But I don't know that Fritz studied with him. I did not know Fritz in Berlin."

Did Fritz really study with Busoni? Abravanel said, "This is very, very unlikely. Practically impossible." André Previn concurred, saying, "I don't know how that's chronologically possible."

Much the same view was held by Franz Allers, who is retired and lives alternately in Munich and Florida. He said, "The only time I was aware of Busoni being there was when I became a Berlin student, about 1920 or '21. Fritz was then about nineteen or twenty. He was a student at the Stern Conservatory, which was in the Kantstrasse, according to what he told me." But Busoni never taught there.

I contacted Ronald Sanders, author of the Kurt Weill biography, and asked, in view of his studies of Kurt Weill and of necessity his students, for his thoughts on the matter. He said, "I have never come across Loewe's name among the Busoni students. That doesn't prove that he wasn't one, but I never came across it in my research."

One of Fritz's friends, who didn't want to be quoted for attribution, said with a kind of amused affection, "There was a lot of fantasy in Fritz."

This compares interestingly to a remark by Henry Pleasants, the critic and music historian. He said, "I was fascinated by your efforts to check out Loewe's various bits of oral autobiography. It reminded me of my own experience with Stokowski. In both cases

I am satisfied that what we are dealing with is not a liar but a fantasist. A liar knows he's lying. A fantasist believes his fantasies."

But somewhere, somehow, Fritz had very good teachers.

"Fritz had marvelous models in Vienna," Abravanel said. "That's what gives the music its nature. There is a fine quality. It is Broadway music, but it has very deep roots, deeper Austrian and German roots than, let's say, Gershwin had Russian roots."

Tina, Fritz's former and only wife, is still alive.

In 1951 she met the admired jazz guitarist Talmadge (Tal) Farlow, from Greensboro, North Carolina. They saw each other over a period of seven years and finally were married in 1958. They moved to Sea Bright, on the New Jersey coast a few miles due south of Manhattan, and lived in an all but impenetrable privacy in a house on a tidal river, not far from the ocean. Farlow, a tall, lean, quiet man, a Gary Cooper figure with a long face and matte complexion, very American and the antithesis of Fritz Loewe, did some teaching and played occasional engagements in local clubs and schools. Part of the time he worked as a sign painter. Later on he emerged from seclusion to record or perform in concerts and jazz festivals, but he never regained the fame in the jazz profession that he once had enjoyed; yet his status among musicians verged on the legendary. Guitarists would make pilgrimages to Sea Bright just to talk to him.

One guitarist who visited the Farlows in the 1970s is Gene Bertoncini. "The house is right on the river," he said. "A little wood-frame house, very cozy, and Tal spent a lot of time watching the boats go in and out.

"Tina seemed to me a warm kind of person whose house you'd like to go to at Christmas. She was round-faced and kind of cute. If you imagined an Austrian house in the woods with a woman preparing food and putting presents under a tree, that was the impression she gave me. She epitomized Christmas. They seemed to live a very simple life, very much to themselves, and she seemed like she was very much in love with Tal."

I spoke briefly to Tina Loewe Farlow on the telephone in November 1989. She had a light Austrian accent, and her voice sounded fragile. I wanted to ask her about Fritz's early years, but some instinct told me not to do it now. I thought I should go through Tal. She told me Tal would be home later that day, and I talked to him then. Tal spoke to her on my behalf, and a few days later told me, "She doesn't want to talk about him. It's a painful subject. And she has several health problems."

I suggested that she might want to read that part of this book pertaining to her, to correct whatever errors might be in the newspaper stories about her and Fritz in that time right after the success of *Brigadoon.* Tal said she couldn't read it. She was blind.

On September 1, 1962, in a Unitarian ceremony in Los Angeles, Nancy Olson, then thirty-four, married Alan Livingston, forty-four, the president of Capitol Records, brother of lyricist Jay Livingston, and ex-husband of actress and singer Betty Hutton. Livingston has long since retired from Capitol. He and Nancy live in Beverly Hills, California. She is sixty-two now. She is very well liked and respected. My one conversation with her left me with a distinct impression that she was highly protective of Alan Lerner's memory.

In the April 18, 1977, issue of the *New York Daily News,* Liz Smith reported: "Micheline Lerner . . . has made a deal to sell her first screenplay, *Micheline Esquire,* to the French filmmaker Claude Chabrol. The movie is about Micheline's experience as a twenty-year-old trial attorney in Paris and she wants Isabelle Adjani to portray her younger self defending an American rapist. And they want Jack Nicholson for the rapist." The movie was never made. Micheline is seen from time to time at fashionable soirées and still has an arresting kind of beauty in her fifties.

Karen Gundersen Lerner resumed her career in September 1972, producing documentaries at NBC for the next seven years. In 1979, she went to ABC news to be senior producer of *20/20* for six years. In 1985 she was appointed MGM's vice president of production for the East Coast. She stayed there for two years, then resigned to become an independent film producer. Karen is dark, trim, and still pretty. There is a sense of brisk, organized efficiency about her. She lives on the East Side of New York City, a few doors east of Central Park. In March 1990 she told me, "I loved Alan more than anyone in my life."

Henderson Talbott, a Princeton, New Jersey, businessman and real estate man very much involved in the community, who married Alan's first wife Ruth in 1947, died in 1959. Ruth moved to Florida and lives now in Del Ray. She is still listed in the Social Register. Until recently she worked for a catering company called The Pampered Hostess. "But that's kaput," she told me. "I'm not rich. Besides, I don't play bridge, and I don't want to sit around with a bunch of old ladies drinking Bloody Marys. I like to work, and frankly I'm bored stiff at the moment and looking for a job." She also told me that she and Marion Bell had been very good friends over the years. "She was always a lovely person," she said.

But what had happened to Marion Bell?

In February 1990 I was visiting Miles Kreuger at the Institute of the American Musical in Los Angeles. He reminisced about his friendship with and period of working for Alan Lerner and asked if I'd spoken to Marion Bell. I told him I had been looking for her for a year, and found that she seemed to have vanished from the face of the earth. "She lives in Culver City," he said. "She teaches voice."

He gave me her telephone number and I visited her the next afternoon at her modest house about three blocks south of the MGM studio. Her father, the onetime freight agent with the Wabash Railroad, still lived with her. She is a gracious woman in her sixties, with gray hair, who teaches about ten voice students. She told me her best friend had been actress and singer Jan Clayton, who had married Alan's brother Bobby and moved to Mexico City. Bobby and Jan were now both dead of cancer. Marion Bell also had cancer, although it was being held in remission by periodic chemotherapy. She clarified many details about her time with Alan.

She said, "I saw Alan on occasion afterwards. Not very often. He knew that I had been hospitalized, and he wanted information for *On a Clear Day*. He wanted to know what it was like behind closed doors.

"I tried to earn my own living, because I was supporting a son, a wonderful son, by my second husband, Tom Charlesworth. The marriage lasted three months. I met Tom Charlesworth when we were doing *Chocolate Soldier*. He was an actor and a singer. He's dead now. I tried to work at other jobs to support my son, and my mom and dad helped. I went off on my own when my son became a teenager. He's a lawyer's word processor.

"I have my health, my son, and my father. So all is well. I try to keep my equilibrium, try not to go overboard. I try to do what I think would be appreciated by people who haven't been as fortunate as I have. I tried to be a good friend to Alan, and I'm sorry that he passed away."

She mentioned some of Alan's other wives, and then with a little chuckle said, "Maybe we should hold a convention!"

Something about Marion Bell touched me very deeply. I said, "Marion, you seem remarkably free of bitterness."

The sweetest smile came over her face. She said, "Oh, I still love Alan. I will always love Alan."

On June 7, 1987, at the Theatre Royal, Drury Lane, London, a program entitled *An Evening with Alan Jay Lerner* was presented, with a cast that included Jean-Pierre Aumont, Len Cariou, Douglas Fairbanks, Sally Ann Howes, Burton Lane, and many more. The executive producer was Alan's widow, Liz Robertson. Proceeds of the concert, and of the double compact-disc album resulting from it, went to the Alan Jay Lerner Fund for Research into Lung Cancer at the Royal Marsden Hospital.

In 1989, Robertson toured the United States in a revival of *The King and I,* opposite Rudolf Nureyev as the King of Siam. On October 23, she staged another *Evening with Alan Jay Lerner,* in the New York State Theater, with a cast that included Julie Andrews, André Previn, Len Cariou, John Cullum, Van Johnson, Hal Linden, Jane Powell, Charles Strouse, and more. Proceeds went to the Memorial Sloan-Kettering Hospital for research into lung cancer.

Lerner's elation at the time of his marriage to Robertson might sound like his usual optimism as he entered upon yet another relationship. But this time there was something different, something almost palpable in the newspaper interviews; you found yourself believing what he said about his love for her. And many of those knew him agreed with him about it. Said Alexander Cohen: "There were many women in Alan's life, and most of them were wrong. The one that I really admired most was his last wife, Elizabeth. Liz Robertson is a very up-front lady, and she really cared. She wasn't marrying Alan because she was marrying a legend." Benjamin Welles said, "Liz Robertson was probably the best of the wives for him. She gave him probably the five or six happiest years of his life. And he made her a star."

Burton Lane agreed with that assessment: "Yeah," he said, "I think that was a good marriage."

So did André Previn. He said, "She's a big winner. She's a superb lady. She's very beautiful, she's very musical. And she adored Alan. She had the most extraordinary combination of looking after him and being his romance. It was wonderful. He was very well taken care of."

Said Don Chastain: "Liz Robertson is a dynamite lady, a really super girl. Everybody in the cast of *Dance a Little Closer* was crazy about her."

Lerner made a poignant remark to Chastain. In fact, he made it several times. He said, "If only I'd met her first."

Apparently, at the end, Alan Lerner found his girl in the raincoat.

Bibliography

Alpert, Hollis. *Burton.* New York: G.P. Putnam's Sons, 1986.

Beaton, Cecil. *Self-Portrait with Friends: The Selected Diaries of Cecil Beaton, 1926–1974.* London: Weidenfeld and Nicolson, 1979.

Bragg, Melvyn. *Richard Burton: A Life.* Boston: Little, Brown, 1988.

Cottrell, John, and Fergus Cashin. *Richard Burton Very Close Up.* Englewood Cliffs, N.J.: Prentice-Hall, 1972.

Eyels, Allen. *Rex Harrison.* London: W.H. Allen, 1985.

Ferris, Paul. *Richard Burton.* London: Weidenfeld and Nicolson, 1981.

Harrison, Rex. *Rex: An Autobiography.* London: Macmillan, 1974.

Hart, Kitty Carlisle. *Kitty.* New York: Doubleday, 1988.

Higham, Charles. *Audrey: The Life of Audrey Hepburn.* New York: Macmillan, 1984.

Holloway, Stanley. *Wiv a Little Bit o'Luck: The Life Story of Stanley Holloway.* London: Leslie Frewin, 1967.

Jenkins, Graham. *Richard Burton, My Brother.* London: Michael Joseph, 1988.

Lerner, Alan Jay. *The Street Where I Live.* New York: W.W. Norton, 1978.

————. *The Musical Theater: A Celebration.* New York: McGraw-Hill, 1986.

————. *A Hymn to Him: Lyrics of Alan Jay Lerner.* Benny Green, ed. London: Pavilion Books, 1987.

Logan, Josh. *Josh: My Upside Down In and Out Life.* New York: Delacorte, 1976.

Marx, Samuel, and Jan Clayton. *Rodgers & Hart.* New York: G.P. Putnam's Sons, 1976.

Minelli, Vincente. *I Remember It Well.* New York: Doubleday, 1974.

Peyser, Joan. *Bernstein: A Biography.* New York: William Morrow, 1987.

Sanders, Robert. *The Days Grow Short: The Life and Music of Kurt Weill.* New York: Holt, Rinehart, and Winston, 1980.

Shapiro, Doris. *We Danced All Night: My Life Behind the Scenes with Alan Jay Lerner.* New York: William Morrow, 1990.

Windler, Robert. *Julie Andrews.* New York: G.P. Putnam's Sons, 1970.

Index

344

348

350